THE ATHENAEUM

*A Mirror
of Victorian Culture*

THE
ATHENAEUM

A Mirror
of Victorian Culture

———

LESLIE A. MARCHAND

1971

OCTAGON BOOKS

New York

To my Father and Mother
PIONEERS

Preface

IT HAS BEEN my aim in this volume to carve from a massive bulk of material, mainly from the magazine itself in its heyday, something like a rounded image of the *Athenaeum,* with particular attention to its fight for independent literary criticism and its reflection of the current tastes. In this I have tried to follow the example of the sturdy old Victorian periodical itself, which strove for balance above all else in its judgments of contemporaries. But even if my view is distorted by a bias of interpretation of which I am not fully aware, the evidence here assembled from the critical articles in the *Athenaeum* is sufficiently representative, I believe, to permit everyone to form his own estimate of the worth of the journal as a mirror of Victorian tastes and ideas. In any event, if I have accomplished my purpose, I have added a modest chapter to that useful group of studies of English literary periodicals which have been accumulating rapidly in the past few years.

Though my approach has been somewhat different from that of others in this field, I must acknowledge considerable indebtedness to those who have done the pioneering, especially to Walter Graham, who has plowed widely and deeply in his *English Literary Periodicals* (1930), and *Tory Crit-*

icism in the "Quarterly Review" (1921). Other studies of nineteenth century periodicals already published include: *Leigh Hunt's Examiner Examined* (1928), by Edmund Blunden; *The Story of the Spectator* (1928), by William Beach Thomas; *Benthamite Reviewing: Twelve Years of the Westminster Review, 1824-1836* (1934), by George L. Nesbitt; *Rebellious Fraser's* (1934), by Miriam M. H. Thrall; and *The Party of Humanity: the Fortnightly Review and its Contributors, 1865-74* (1939), by Edwin M. Everett. A history of the *Saturday Review* by Merle M. Bevington is now nearing completion, and it is probable that other Victorian periodicals will stand for their portraits soon.

The most immediately useful aid in writing the history of the *Athenaeum,* and the one on which I have drawn most frequently, is the *Biographical Memoir,* by Sir Charles Wentworth Dilke, prefixed to *The Papers of a Critic, Selected from the Writings of Charles Wentworth Dilke* (1875). This memoir of the editor who established the reputation of the magazine is the chief source of information concerning the *Athenaeum* in its formative years. The writer, a grandson of the Charles Dilke who edited the journal from 1830 to 1846, has given in short space a great many facts of interest about the periodical and the man who shaped its policies, but unfortunately he has been reticent at points where we would now wish for much fuller details, particularly in the account of Dilke's relations with his contemporaries. He has quoted rather sparingly, for example, from the extensive correspondence which, as editor, Dilke carried on with his contributors and friends, some of them people of considerable importance in the literary, artistic, and scientific world of the day. These letters, apparently in the hands of the biographer when he wrote the memoir, have since disappeared (at least Mr. Harry Hudson, Sir Charles Dilke's secretary at the time of the latter's death in 1911, and Miss Gertrude Tuckwell, niece and literary executrix of Sir Charles, know nothing of them).

For facts concerning the history and policy of the magazine in its early years I have consulted frequently the two-volume work compiled by John Collins Francis: *John Francis, Publisher of the Athenaeum* (1888). The elder John Francis, who entered the employ of Dilke in 1831 and who was publisher of the journal for a great many years under three generations of Dilkes, was in a position to know more of its affairs than any other man except the editor himself. This lengthy summary brought together by his son from the files of the magazine scarcely compensates for the paucity of his own memoirs. Nevertheless the volumes supply much information not elsewhere so readily available. At the time of his death in 1916, John Collins Francis was engaged in writing a supplementary volume, which, however, was never published.

The marked file of the *Athenaeum,* now in the office of the *New Statesman and Nation* in London, has been the indispensable source for the identification of reviewers, almost all anonymous. In fact, without the aid of this file, wherein the editor, from the middle of 1830 onwards, wrote in ink the names of contributors and staff writers, this book could scarcely have been written. Several volumes in the editor's file, however, have apparently been replaced in recent years and are therefore not marked, namely, the volumes for 1832, 1835-38, and 1844. While it has been no part of my intention here to give a complete bibliography of even the most important contributors to the *Athenaeum,* I am convinced that a carefully indexed list, with ample cross references, of reviews and reviewers, from 1830 to the end of the nineteenth century, would be an extremely valuable tool for scholars concerned with literary reputations, critical theory, or cultural history in the Victorian period. The frequency with which students of English and Continental literature have called on me, since I began this book, to identify the authorship of certain reviews in the *Athenaeum* sufficiently indicates the usefulness which such a bibliography made up from the marked file might have. I am holding that over, however, for another volume.

I have made free use of the unpublished Dilke Papers in the British Museum for the historical chapter of this work. Though the editorial correspondence mentioned above is not in this collection, the letters of Thomas Hood to Dilke and those between the editor and his grandson throw considerable light upon Dilke himself and his conduct of the *Athenaeum*.

Perhaps some explanation of the divisions of this volume is due the reader. The four chapters are not parts of a continuous history of the *Athenaeum*, but rather separate facets of an historical and critical study, wherein chronology is not lost sight of but is made secondary to an examination of the character of the magazine. Chapter I contains an historical summary beginning with the founding of the periodical and continuing until its demise in the twentieth century, the greater space being given to the years of Dilke's editorship. Chapter II is the story of Dilke's fight against literary puffery, set against the background of book reviewing practices in the 1830's. Chapter III, a study of the reviewers and staff writers of the *Athenaeum*, is limited almost entirely to the circle of contributors under Dilke; to go further would have complicated the task beyond the scope of this book. Chapter IV attempts to give a representative cross section of the *Athenaeum* literary criticisms by studying the review histories of some outstanding writers of Victorian England. Here it seemed impossible (or at least inadvisable) to limit the treatment chronologically, so that in this section, as in Chapter I, much is said of the attitudes and policies of the magazine before and after Dilke's regime, though the study is throughout centered upon the important years when Dilke was editor. For the shortcomings of omission, of which I am only too aware, I can plead, first, the magnitude of the material, and, second, the method and the purpose of my study: to bore for samples in the places likeliest to show the quality of the ore.

I owe the greatest debt for helpful criticism, personal interest, and kindly encouragement at every step to Professor Emery Neff of Columbia University, who has already done a notable service to students of Victorian life and literature by suggesting and directing a number of important studies in the magazines of the period. From first to last his suggestions have aided me in improving form and matter and in keeping a clear perspective. For reading the manuscript with care and making detailed criticisms I am grateful to Professors Oscar James Campbell, Hoxie Neale Fairchild, Susanne Howe Nobbe, and William York Tindall, of the Department of English, Adriaan Jacob Barnouw of the Germanic Languages Department, and Justin McCortney O'Brien of the Department of French of Columbia University. During the later stages of composition I profited considerably from the suggestions in matters of style made by Miss Helen G. Hurd, Editor of Publications, University Extension, Rutgers University.

I have most pleasant memories of the courtesies I met with everywhere in England while I was gathering material for this book. The pleasure of my work in London was increased greatly by the kindness and active help of members of the staff of the *New Statesman and Nation,* especially Mr. John Roberts and Mr. R. G. E. Willison, who gave me free access to the marked files of the *Athenaeum,* welcomed me to the friendly circle of their morning coffee and their staff luncheons, and gave me an office in which to work. I am further indebted to Mr. Kingsley Martin for introducing me to Mr. Vernon Rendall, for twenty years associated with the *Athenaeum* as sub-editor and editor, who supplied me with much first-hand information about the conduct of the magazine. My thanks are due also to Miss Gertrude Tuckwell for directing me to the Dilke Papers in the British Museum, and to the staff of the Department of Manuscripts of the Museum for permission to copy the unpublished and uncatalogued letters in that collection. I have pleasant recollections of an interview at Merton College, Oxford, with Mr. Edmund Blunden, who gave me some pertinent suggestions based on his wide knowledge of the field; and of a similar courtesy from the biographer of George Darley, Mr. C. Colleer Abbott, at University College, Durham. My final acknowledgments are reserved for those numerous authors whose books have helped me in this work, and for members of the staffs of the libraries of the British Museum, the City of New York, Columbia University, and Rutgers University.

LESLIE A. MARCHAND

Rutgers University
New Brunswick, N. J.
1 January, 1940

Contents

CHAPTER III

THE ATHENAEUM CIRCLE UNDER DILKE

CHAPTER IV

CRITICISM OF CONTEMPORARIES

THE ATHENAEUM

*A Mirror
of Victorian Culture*

"I have taken all knowledge to be my province."

Francis Bacon.

Chapter 1: A Mirror of Culture

THE LEADER in the first number of the *Athenaeum,* January 2, 1828, proclaimed rather grandly the professed aim of its founders and editors: "We shall endeavour . . . first to lay a foundation of solid and useful knowledge, and on this to erect a superstructure of as much harmony, ornament, and beauty, as our own powers and the encouraging aid of those who approve the design, will enable us to construct. If the edifice so reared be worthy of the name we have chosen for it, and, like the Athenaeum of antiquity, should become the resort of the most distinguished philosophers, historians, orators, and poets of our day,—we shall endeavour so to arrange and illustrate their several compositions, that they may themselves be proud of the records of their fame, and that their admirers may deem them worthy of preservation among the permanent memorials of their times."[1] This fanfare of pretensions and promises may seem amusing (as it did to many contemporaries) rather than impressive in the light of the accomplishments of the first two or three earnest but precarious years. But one who familiarizes himself with its long and distinguished career in the nineteenth century can-

[1] "Characteristics of the Present State of English Literature," p. 2. It is difficult to determine whether James Silk Buckingham or Henry Stebbing wrote this leader; the style and tone would point to the latter.

not but have a growing respect for the achievements of the journal in every realm that it claimed for its own.

James Silk Buckingham, who launched the *Athenaeum* at the beginning of 1828, was a traveller and journalistic adventurer with independent principles and considerable initiative but not the qualities that would make him successful in the editorship of such a journal once he had started it. With several journalistic irons in the fire already, he tried too many experiments. The *Sphynx*, "a journal of politics, literature and news," begun in 1827 as a weekly selling at a shilling, was announced in the *Athenaeum* for January 29, 1828, for twice-a-week publication at 9*d*. On February 22 the price was further reduced to 7*d*. The *Verulam*, originally a weekly devoted to science alone, was incorporated with the *Athenaeum* on May 21, 1828.[2] And at the same time there appeared the prospectus of Buckingham's new venture, the *Argus*, a London evening newspaper, which died after a few numbers. The *Oriental Herald* (monthly, 5*s*.) was his most successful journalistic enterprise, and probably the periodical that he was most capable of editing. It began in 1824 and was still flourishing when he started the *Athenaeum*.

The same unbusiness-like changeableness was evident in his conduct of the new "Literary and Critical Journal." On January 29 announcement was made that the *Athenaeum* would henceforth appear on Tuesdays instead of Saturdays. Two weeks later a pretentious editorial note proclaimed that thereafter there would be two issues a week, Tuesday and Friday, because "the reading public (which may now be said to include all who are above the condition of the merely labouring classes) is still impatient for a more rapid succession of the pleasures which they derive from this inexhaustible source."[3] The original price of 8*d*. (unstamped)

---

[2] It began on March 1, 1828.   [3] February 12, 1828, p. 120.

was reduced for a few weeks to 7*d*. On February 22, the
Athenaeum had given an assurance "to which the Editor
pledges himself most distinctly, that no further changes
shall be made, either in the modes or periods of publication."
But on April 15, it was argued with an equal show of
plausibility that the public was really more eager for the old
weekly schedule, which was then adopted, the price returning to 8*d*.

Within the limits of his own views, Buckingham had a
fearless devotion to principles of fairness, which, however,
he was prone to display somewhat ostentatiously. He was
the son of a Falmouth farmer and had spent his youth at
sea. After wandering for a number of years he established
the *Calcutta Journal* in 1818. It proved highly successful
until in 1823 its outspoken criticisms of the East India Company caused his expulsion from India and the suppression
of the paper. Some years later he was vindicated, and
allowed an annuity of 200 pounds (he had lost a considerable
fortune in the paper), the company having acknowledged
the illegality of their proceedings. A member of Parliament
from 1832 to 1837, he was a strong advocate of temperance
and social reform, and considered himself a radical in
politics.[4]

In the first number of the *Athenaeum* Buckingham
flaunted his independence, displaying his persecution in the
past as an earnest of his rigid adherence to principle, particularly to forestall the criticism of those who might suggest
that his policies would be colored by his partnership with
Henry Colburn, the puffing publisher, who owned a half
interest in the *Athenaeum*.[5]

[4] Buckingham was not a true Benthamite "Philosophical Radical," though
he made common cause with the Utilitarians on a number of questions of practical reform, including the agitation for the repeal of the Corn Laws. See
Ralph E. Turner, *James Silk Buckingham*, pp. 262-346.

[5] For a fuller account of Colburn's connection with the *Athenaeum* see
Chapter II.

And, lastly, after the severe and multiplied trials which my own principles have undergone, in the fiery furnace of Oriental despotism, after having risked my life in more than one contest with offended authorities, and seen the foundations of a fortune of at least 100,000 *l.* swept away from beneath my feet,—though a little trimming of opinion, and a slight bending to the expediency of circumstances, would have left me even more than that sum as a legacy for my children,—after this, it would be an insult to the understandings of that class, at least, to whom 'The Athenaeum' will principally address itself—to suppose they could believe for a moment that so ignoble a phantom as the fear of any author's or publisher's displeasure would make me shrink from the stern and honest performance of my duty.[6]

With all his boldness and enterprising self-assurance, however, it seems probable that Buckingham realized from the start his inability to handle a literary journal unaided. At any rate, according to the Rev. Henry Stebbing, a partnership was proposed wherein Buckingham was to furnish the capital and Stebbing and a few other literary men all the copy, without remuneration other than the possible profits from the business. But since only Stebbing and Charles Knight (printer for the Society for the Diffusion of Useful Knowledge, and later editor of the Society's *Penny Magazine*) turned up to sign the papers, Buckingham then proposed to pay for contributions at the usual rates and so encouraged the reluctant contributors to join the staff of the new journal. After the first few numbers, the choice for assistant or co-editor lay between Stebbing and Mr. James Emerson [afterwards Sir Emerson Tennent]. The latter declined and Stebbing became the working editor.[7]

[6] "Mr. Buckingham to his Readers," *Athenaeum*, Jan. 2, 1828, p. 14. Buckingham had one admirer in India, a Mr. Robert Becher, whom he had never heard of, but who in 1826 left him a legacy of 500 pounds as a token of respect for the honesty of his opinions in opposing the East India Company. Buckingham used the money to establish the *Sphynx*. (See Turner, *op. cit.,* p. 231.)

[7] See "The *Athenaeum* in 1828-30," by Henry Stebbing, *Athenaeum*, Jan.

Frederick Denison Maurice and John Sterling were in the office frequently.[8] Most of the literary articles and many of the reviews in the early numbers were written by Stebbing, Maurice, and their friends.[9]

On July 30, 1828, the *Athenaeum* combined with the *London Literary Chronicle,* and Maurice, who had been part proprietor of the *Chronicle,* became the editor, some half dozen friends joining in the purchase from Buckingham, who was by that time probably glad to be rid of it.[10] It was losing money and could not then succeed against the competition of the *Literary Gazette* and the *London Weekly Review,* with whose editors Buckingham had entered into acrimonious disputes.[11] Colburn probably had

19, 1878, pp. 88-89. If what Stebbing says is true, then Knight had either made his peace with Buckingham after a quarrel of a few months before, or had not yet fallen out with him when the *Athenaeum* started. Knight says in his *Passages of a Working Life,* II, 52-53: "My course of journalism under Mr. James Silk Buckingham [in the summer of 1827 he was engaged to write political articles and reviews for the *Sphynx,* then just started] was not agreeable. . . . Perhaps I formed too low an estimate of his knowledge and ability. . . . I cared not how wearisome were his own newspaper prolusions; but I rebelled against his unparalleled conceit. He outraged me by presuming to alter, in his own obtuse fashion, some spirited lines on the death of Canning, which Praed had sent me. I at once quitted his office . . . when he proposed an amended scale of remuneration for critiques of new books, beginning at half-a-crown and rising to a guinea, according to the length of the article."

[8] Buckingham met Maurice through his activity in the peace movement and Sterling as secretary of a political club. (See Turner, *op. cit.,* p. 237.)

[9] Stebbing wrote the first review (of Dr. Hampden's work on Butler's *Analogy*), and his article on Whately's *Rhetoric* was the leader in the second number. He confessed fifty years later that stacks of books were loaded on him for review. "Absolutely do I tremble sometimes at the recollection of the hazardous work it was, when, urged by the proprietor that the profit of advertisements depended upon it, I wrote notices of books, of the contents of which I knew little, and of the meaning less." (*Athenaeum,* Jan. 19, 1878, p. 88.) It was Buckingham's idea that every number ought to begin with a leading article or essay. Whenever paid contributors failed to send in their papers, Stebbing had to supply the deficiency.

[10] See William Jerdan, *Autobiography,* IV, 21n: "Mr. Buckingham had previously offered to sell the *Athenaeum* to me." But, he says, it and other rivals were not thriving sufficiently to make it worth his while.

[11] See *Athenaeum,* April 1, 1828, pp. 315-316; and April 8, 1828, pp. 348-

sold his interest some time before this. He was not likely to hold on to a losing venture, especially when the literary editors were reluctant to puff extravagantly the Colburn publications.[12]

The title was now changed to *The Athenaeum and London Literary Chronicle,* and on August 6, 1828, it became *The Athenaeum and Literary Chronicle.* It struggled on through the year, possibly with subsidies from the several friends (mostly Cambridge "Apostles") who contributed to the purchase. Carlyle surmised (probably rightly) that the money came mainly from Sterling,[13] who, weary of the constant drain on his purse, on November 21, 1828, wrote to R. C. Trench: "Are you inclined to buy my share in the *Athenaeum?* It will cost you, if I remember right, a little more than a hundred pounds."[14] Trench was apparently not attracted by the offer. Maurice resigned as editor in May, 1829, and was succeeded by Sterling, assisted

---

349. Buckingham was especially bitter against J. A. St. John, editor of the *London Weekly Review* and formerly sub-editor of the *Oriental Herald.* The *Review* had insinuated that Buckingham was incapable of editing a literary journal, being ignorant of contemporary literature. Moreover, according to Buckingham, the proprietors of the *Review* had attempted to dissuade him from starting the *Athenaeum,* claiming that even they could not make the *London Weekly Review* financially successful. Richardson, the founder and proprietor of the *Review,* ended the conversation by offering to bet 1,000 pounds that the *Athenaeum* would not sell 500 copies per week for the first six months. Buckingham declined, but the *Athenaeum,* he said, had sold in the first week more than four times five hundred copies. From that moment Richardson and St. John had cooled towards him and had privately hinted that the circulation of the *Athenaeum* was less than the editor claimed.

[12] It may be that Colburn had withdrawn before May 21, as seems to be implied in the wording of Buckingham's announcement of the *Argus* (with a little hopeful whistling for his other publications): "The extremely favourable reception given to Mr. Buckingham's Political and Literary *Weekly Journals* 'The Sphynx' and the 'Athenaeum,' and the desire to render available all the advantages of the complete Printing Establishment, and abundant political and literary materials and talents originally brought together for the two Journals named, and now under his sole direction and control, have led him . . ." to establish the *Argus.*

[13] Thomas Carlyle, *The Life of John Sterling,* p. 46.

[14] R. C. Trench, *Letters and Memorials,* I, 17.

by John Hamilton Reynolds, Allan Cunningham, W. D. Cooley, Charles Dance, and others. Maurice continued to help and to contribute. At the beginning of 1830 James Holmes, the printer, became a proprietor, and Sterling let his share go though he continued as editor. The *London Weekly Review,* printed by Holmes, was then amalgamated with the *Athenaeum,* which now became *The Athenaeum and Weekly Review of English and Foreign Literature, Fine Arts and Works of Embellishment.*[15] By this time the magazine was in a bad way financially. It had been offered to Alaric Watts for 80 pounds, and to Dr. Stebbing with all back stock for 100 pounds.[16] With the new year the day of publication was changed from Wednesday to Saturday.[17]

At the end of its second year the prospects of the *Athenaeum* were not very bright, but it had kept up the brave appearance of a thriving periodical and had maintained a fairly uniform character through all its vicissitudes, both in outward aspect and in general policy. There were no fundamental changes in the format or type during this period, nor, in fact, for many years following.[18] The large quarto with the three crowded columns of small type (about the equivalent of nine- or ten-point, solid, for the

[15] See *John Francis, Publisher of the Athenaeum,* compiled by John C. Francis, Vol. I. Francis (I, 32-33n.) says that the *London Weekly Review* had lost between three and four thousand pounds in less than two years. Perhaps Holmes had taken it over for its debts to him as printer and so incorporated it with the *Athenaeum* when he became a partner in the ownership of the latter journal.

[16] Francis, *op. cit.,* I, 34. Stebbing said: "The *Athenaeum* rapidly failed in circulation. It passed for a short time into the hands of Mr. Atkinson. . . . I remember his coming and offering me the proprietorship and back stock of the *Athenaeum* for just £100." (*Athenaeum,* Jan. 19, 1878, p. 89.)

[17] The Wednesday publication had begun in April, 1828, with the resumption of the once-a-week schedule. It was thought thereby to anticipate the *Literary Gazette* and other rivals appearing on Saturday.

[18] At the beginning of 1830, there was a slight change in the format, with a smaller page, narrower columns, and smaller type, "so as to make up the quantity of matter heretofore given." ("Prospectus to the New Series," Jan. 16, 1830, p. 17.)

general body, and as small as five- or six-point for quotations, editorial notes, and advertisements) is the most familiar and discouraging aspect of the *Athenaeum* to the reader of today. In fact, it is hard to believe that anyone in the late twenties and thirties of the last century could have had the hardihood to plow through such a page, or to read with avidity whatever might be said in such type. One has only to compare it, however, in type and format with other periodicals of the time to see that it was not unusual in this respect. It had much the same appearance and make-up as the *Literary Gazette,* and a clearer type and better paper than many of the popular periodicals selling for a shilling or less. Its page was not much more discouraging typographically than that of the aristocratic and expensive *Quarterly, Edinburgh,* or *Blackwood's.* The competition then was in subject matter, and the long-suffering reader had no rights that a publisher was bound to respect, so far as the ease and comfort of reading were concerned. The steam press, first used by the *Times* in November, 1814, and soon by the greater part of the publishing world, had made printing cheaper, but the appeal to the new reading public including "all who are above the condition of the merely labouring classes" still turned upon giving them as much reading matter as possible for the few pence that they could spare for such a luxury.

An editorial note in the *Athenaeum,* announcing the index to the first quarterly part, boasted that, "On a comparison of a Quarterly Part of 'The Athenaeum,' with an 'Edinburgh,' or 'Quarterly Review,' it will be found to contain at least *four times* the quantity of writing, in the same proportion of original and extracted matter, while it is little more than *double* the price . . . [the 'Athenaeum' is now] not only *the most comprehensive,* but also *the cheapest* periodical in existence."[19]

[19] March 28, 1828, p. 300.

Through this early period the *Athenaeum* was a sixteen-page paper. It sold for 8*d.,* unstamped, and 1*s.,* stamped (except for the short period of its bi-weekly appearance, when the price was reduced to 7*d.* and 10*d.* respectively).[20]

There are no wholly trustworthy figures concerning the circulation. Buckingham's editorial statement on April 8, 1828, that in the first week more than four times 500 copies had been sold, is not, under the circumstances, to be taken without some allowances.[21] In the third number announcement was made that the "whole edition of 6,250 copies of the two first Numbers of 'The Athenaeum' having been sold off, both of these Numbers are already out of Print. A Second Edition of each is, however, now in the press."[22] It seems probable, though, that the circulation declined markedly after the first two or three numbers. Maurice's son said: "The purchasers of the 'Athenaeum' [Maurice and others in July, 1828] found on taking it over that its circulation was by no means such as they had supposed it to be."[23]

The advertisements at first occupied a little more than two pages at the end of the paper, but the greater part of that space was taken by Colburn and Buckingham for their respective publications. A few other publishers shared the remainder of the columns with estates to be sold, announce-

[20] Numbers one to eighty-seven were "Printed and Published by William Lewer, 147, Strand" (later, 4, Wellingston Street, Strand). Beginning with Number eighty-eight, July 1, 1829, it was printed and published by F. C. Westley, 165, Strand, opposite Newcastle-street. This continued until Holmes became the printer at the beginning of 1830. Then it was "Printed for James Holmes, Athenaeum Office, 4, Took's Court, Chancery Lane." Westley was listed as the publisher for a few months after this.

[21] See *ante,* p. 5, n. 11.

[22] P. 349. This probably means that the total number of copies of the first two weeks was 6,250, but the slight ambiguity might have been intended to permit the reader to infer that there were that many copies of each number. How many were printed in the second edition and whether they sold are unanswered questions.

[23] *The Life of Frederick Denison Maurice,* ed. by his son, I, 97.

ments of picture sales, public lectures, circulating libraries and reading rooms. Maurice and Sterling could scarcely get advertising enough to fill a page, and on occasions it sank to two columns, and was frequently padded out with the aid of drawing masters, the Printers' Pension Society meeting, and vendors of patent medicines, who were then advertising widely.[24] Booksellers had already begun to engage in the now familiar practice of quoting in their advertisements the "opinions of the press." New and struggling periodicals often did likewise. In fact, the space taken by the latter was so great that it seems possible they exchanged these notices with other periodicals. During the latter part of 1828 and throughout 1829 Buckingham continued to advertise his *Oriental Herald* and his public lectures, and Colburn to announce his travel books and fashionable novels occasionally.

It was not the purpose of the *Athenaeum* to bid for attention by indulging in "solemn flippancy and sparkling commonplaces" but to hew to the line of principle, and especially to fight the dragon of materialism whether it were entrenched behind the *Edinburgh Review* or the *Westminster*. R. C. Trench wrote to John Kemble, September 14, 1828: "That paper, the *Athenaeum,* which, by-the-by, is entirely written by Apostles, should it obtain an extensive circulation, is calculated to do much good. It is a paper not merely of principle, but, what is almost equally important, of principles—certain fixed rules to which compositions are referred, and by which they are judged. In this it is superior, not merely to contemporary papers, but to the reviews

---

[24] One of the most frequent advertisers of this kind at the beginning of 1829 was "Rowland's Macassar Oil, of vegetable ingredients, which preserves the hair to the latest period of life." Readers were soon informed also of "Cases of Consumption of the Lungs cured by inhaling the vapour of true Barbadoes Tar." Patent medicine advertisements were not uncommon in the periodicals of the eighteenth century. See, for example, the advertising columns in the *St. James' Chronicle.*

of the highest pretension."[25]   As the statement of one
Apostle to another, both of whom were occasional contributors to the magazine and close friends of Maurice, this
may be taken to represent the view of the editors.   Trench
had written to Kemble before, on the occasion of the merg-
ing of the *Athenaeum* and the *Literary Chronicle,* that
"Maurice and that gallant band of Platonico-Wordsworth-
ian-Coleridgean-anti-Utilitarians still keep with undivided
sway at the helm."[26]

There was no noticeable change in the policy and scope of
the journal or its general appeal to readers after Buckingham gave it up, partly because its policies were directed from
the beginning mainly by "Apostles," a group of earnest
young Cambridge men who hoped to reform the world,
both in and out of the church, not by revolution or change
in institutions but by moral or spiritual regeneration.   Besides Maurice and Sterling, who were most active in the
society, the membership included R. C. Trench (later an
archbishop), Alfred Tennyson, Arthur Hallam, John Kemble (of the famous acting family), Charles Buller, R. M.
Milnes (later Lord Houghton), and several who were to become solid church of England men such as Alford, Blakesley,
G. S. Venables (parliamentary lawyer), and Spedding.   As
was to be expected, the dominant note of the *Athenaeum*
under Maurice and Sterling was one of moral earnestness.
The editors were romanticists in their views on literature and
art.   Their literary opinions were mild and liberal, except
when they were aroused by attacks on the school of Coleridge, or by what they considered Utilitarian cant.   The
tone was youthful and enthusiastic, dominated by the hope-
fulness and optimism of the reformer.   The critics insisted
on a moral message in fiction and were condescending, or
coldly polite, towards literature of "mere amusement."   Their

[25] Trench, *op. cit.,* I, 14.   [26] *Ibid.*

attitude towards religion, a subject which they referred to only as it arose in other discussions—particularly in reviews of theological works—was that of liberal churchmen leaning to evangelicalism.[27] Religious education should be liberalized—form and ritual were only superficial.[28]

A writer in the *London Magazine,* after Maurice had merged the *Literary Chronicle* with the *Athenaeum* and had become the editor of both, insinuated that the latter journal was no longer what it had been. "It has passed, he tells us, from the guidance of the acute, enterprising, matter-of-fact person who established it into the hands of a set of dreaming half-Platonic, half-Jacob Behmenite mystics, who hate all useful arts, think it vulgar to talk of free trade, pay no attention to literary novelties, and consider education a disadvantage."[29] But, the *Athenaeum* editor replies, Theodore Elbert [Sterling, who had been the butt of the *London Magazine* attack] has been a contributor since April. The author of Sketches of Contemporary Authors [Maurice] has been a prominent writer since the third number. The "practical men" then controlled it for only two weeks![30]

Partly, it may be, to demonstrate to the world that they were not devoid of practical interests, the editors gave considerable attention to the progress of the sciences and the arts. The popularization of science was one of the innovations upon which they prided themselves, though the

[27] The biographer of the Rev. Henry Stebbing in the *D. N. B.* calls him "a moderate churchman, inclining to evangelicalism." The same might be said of Maurice, Sterling, Trench, and most of the Apostles at the time.

[28] The religious liberalism of the editors did not, however, extend to agitation over the Catholic Emancipation movement.

[29] *Athenaeum,* Sept. 3, 1828, p. 716.

[30] Maurice's son and biographer, however, says: "When he assumes the editorship, his views come out more freely. He is however a good deal hampered by the necessity of giving space to some of those who had contributed during the former period of the paper, and bursts out into editorial notes of dissent." (*Life of Maurice,* I, 81.) Such a note of dissent was attached to the article called "The Wool Gatherer," Aug. 13, 1828, p. 665.

handling of scientific events, facts, and books in the *Athenaeum* at this time was superficial and almost puerile compared with the careful and authoritative reports and reviews in later times when the paper attracted the greatest scientists of the day as regular correspondents and staff writers. The elevation of the plain man as art authority and judge likewise made it unnecessary to employ a connoisseur as an art critic.

While the editors tried to display an interest in current affairs wide enough to refute the accusation that they were impractical mystics, they nevertheless made it their aim to rule politics in the narrower sense out of the reviews and articles. An editorial note in the autumn of 1828 says: "Every reader of Gibbon will perceive that the interest of the following paper, which we have received from an able Correspondent, is much more literary than political. This is our excuse for inserting it, as we have always been anxious (and of late still more so than ever)[31] to avoid any subject even remotely bearing on politics."[32]

Maurice and Sterling, however, had political views which they voiced on occasions that seemed to justify them. Maurice's son and biographer thinks they were both wrongly accused of radicalism in politics.

Mr. Carlyle in his "Life of John Sterling" has written as if the whole idea of the circle of friends at this time was simply "Radicalism," or, as he puts it, "In all things he and they were Liberals, and, as was natural at this stage, democrats contemplating root-and-branch innovation by the aid of the hustings and ballot-box." . . . Certainly they had no love for "old hide-bound Toryism," and looked forward to the passing of the Reform Bill of 1832. But a large proportion of what Mr. Carlyle here alludes to was, in fact, not at all the work of Maurice, Sterling, or any of their immediate friends, but of Mr. Silk Buckingham. . . . The assumption that the articles of Mr. Buckingham were . . . [theirs]

[31] I.e., since Maurice became editor.
[32] *Athenaeum,* Oct. 15, 1828, p. 809.

would naturally lead to the mistaken belief that Maurice and Sterling at this time belonged to the ultra-Radical camp. . . . But in fact the whole tone of the articles of both of them completely belies it.[33]

The biographer adds that "it is not a little curious to note that, during the period prior to his assuming the editorship, the editing of the paper appears . . . to have been strongly utilitarian."[34]

That Maurice and his friends were opposed to Benthamite doctrine is not difficult to demonstrate; in fact, while Buckingham was still editor, Maurice in his sketch of Sir J. Mackintosh attacked Utilitarianism.[35]   But still Carlyle was not wrong in calling them Liberals.[36]   It is well to keep in mind that there were at the time two main schools of liberalism, about one or the other of which almost all opponents of Toryism and the status quo grouped themselves. The one stemmed from the romantic humanitarianism and naturalism of an earlier period and flowered into the democratic reform movements as well as into the social views of Carlyle and Ruskin, and even the Christian Socialism which Maurice himself was later to champion.   The other sprang from the *philosophes* and the rationalists of the eighteenth century and developed into the "Philosophical Radicalism" of Bentham and Mill, and the Positivism of the mid-century.   Confusion of course arises from the fact that adherents of all creeds and parties were found in both camps, and sometimes the romantic Liberals and the so-called Radicals favored the same reforms, though for different reasons.

[33] *Life of Maurice*, I, 79-80.   [34] *Ibid.*

[35] *Athenaeum*, March 18, 1828, pp. 249-250. See also Oct. 1, 1828, pp. 777-778.

[36] Maurice early displayed radical leanings. In 1825 he acted as joint editor of the *Metropolitan Quarterly Magazine*, to which about sixteen of his undergraduate friends contributed articles. Longman's published it at first, but gave it up "at a very early stage of the proceedings on the ground that it was altogether too abusive and hostile to established authority." (*Life of Maurice*, I, 61.)

And, on the other hand, they often hated each other as much as, or more than, they hated the Tories. One has only to recall Carlyle's contempt for the "logic-choppers" among the reformers, and his flirting with the Tories at one period. Maurice belonged to the first camp, that of the romantic humanitarians, the one which was to be in the ascendancy and to have the greater influence, during at least the first half of the Victorian period, on that class which was gaining power—the middle class.

Maurice's political views appear clearly enough in his criticism of Jeffrey:

> Mr. Jeffrey appeared before the world at a time when the minds of men were all afloat. . . . In politics, the overpowering interest and frightful nearness of the French Revolution, had destroyed men's beliefs in principles, and absorbed their anxiety in the contemplation of mighty and terrible events. The aristocracy of this country, moreover, had felt or thought themselves in such imminent peril, that they had exerted all their influence over the public mind; and, by the aid of newspapers and debates, political dinners, and bloody battles, had succeeded in making speculation on the theory of government, in the highest degree unpopular and unfashionable.[37]

The *Edinburgh Review* had condoned this anti-revolutionary horror, Maurice says, "and we doubt whether it has ever contained a single article tending to enlarge or exalt men's views of the social interests of their species." There is in Jeffrey's mind, he continues, an "absence of all warm moral enthusiasm, the contempt for all plans of wide political amelioration, and the recourse for the elements of human virtue, not to any native strength or high aspirations within us, but to subtle calculations of consequences."[38]

A magazine with such high, not to say transcendental, aims as the *Athenaeum* professed could not but be apologetic

[37] *Athenaeum*, Jan. 23, 1828, p. 49.　[38] *Ibid.*

occasionally for the actual contents, which, as the editors were aware, did not always measure up to the specifications they had set before the public, whether boastful or promissory. In the very first number, they expressed the regret. that they were not able to include "all the subjects it is intended to embrace." A note "To the Readers" in the second number promised a balance of subjects "useful and agreeable," and listed thirteen categories of material to be offered:

1. Original Essays on Literature, Art, Science, Manners, and the Belles Lettres.

2. Reviews of New Books—English and Foreign; and on every subject of really popular interest.

3. Original Poetry—grave as well as gay.

4. Tales and Novelettes—Original and Translated.

5. Proceedings of Learned Societies, and Discoveries in the principal branches of scientific inquiry.

6. Short Notices of Books, not of sufficient importance to demand a long review.

7. Literary Intelligence, including announcements of Works in preparation, and those already in the Press.

8. List of Books subscribed by the Trade, and those published during the Week.

9. The Fine Arts in detail, embracing Architecture, Sculpture, Painting and Engraving.

10. The Drama—including also the Italian Opera, the French Theatre, and occasionally the Minor Performances.

11. Public Exhibitions and Miscellaneous Amusements of the Town.

12. Striking Passages of old as well as contemporary Authors.

13. Varieties, Original and Select.[39]

While an honest attempt was made to offer something in all these departments, an examination of the files for 1828 and 1829 shows a monotonous uniformity of subject matter and point of view, to which editorial protestations

[39] Jan. 9, 1828, p. 30.

could not blind the readers in that day or later. This was undoubtedly a consequence of the journal being written largely by "Apostles," the unity and ardor of whose beliefs and purposes it is difficult to overestimate. Arthur Hallam, himself one of the group, wrote to Gladstone, June 23, 1830: "The effect which he [Maurice] has produced on the minds of many at Cambridge by the single creation of that Society of the Apostles (for the spirit, though not the form, was created by him) is far greater than I can dare to calculate, and will be felt, both directly and indirectly, in the age that is upon us."[40]

In an advertisement at the end of 1828 the editors boasted that "in their original papers (of which a greater number are to be found in *The Athenaeum* than in any other Weekly Periodical), they have endeavored to secure variety in the subjects, by mixing articles of temporary with articles of permanent interest, and variety in the style by enlisting a large body of efficient contributors."[41] Nevertheless, an impartial examination will reveal that the "original papers" came mainly from men of the same mind. The popularity of the magazine was not increased by the fact that it then reflected the personalities of its editors more than at any other time.

This obstacle was perhaps insurmountable in a journal existing on such a perilous financial footing that it could not go into the market for the best literary talent but had to fill its columns from the combined mental strainings of its editors and their friends. That it was not worse and that it continued to be more than commonplace among literary journals during this time is a tribute to the mental activity and ingenuity of the editors. And the same causes, as well as a somewhat less than reverential regard for the connoisseur as a critic of art or science, operated to weaken depart-

[40] *Life of Maurice*, I, 110.   [41] Dec. 24, 1828, p. 972.

ments which, under the cloak of anonymity, could make a brave show of being authoritative.

Several distinctive features initiated in this period were to give a special character to the *Athenaeum* in later years. The habit of printing long quotations from forthcoming books as well as from other works being reviewed made the magazine interesting to a public which could not buy three-guinea books, or which did not care for the opinions of the editors. The practice of summarizing and extracting in reviews made the *Athenaeum* a forerunner of many modern literary weeklies and book review magazines. It marked a departure from the long *Edinburgh* and *Quarterly* essays which used the book under consideration only as a springboard for the reviewer's opinions.[42]

In notices of foreign books the *Athenaeum* made a worthy effort, though not as successful as that of the same periodical in the thirties and forties, to anticipate other magazines and to give a rounded picture of the literary scene abroad. As early as February 5, 1828, the editors announced their intention of "giving, from time to time, a short account of the principal publications that appear on the Continent in such an abridged manner as not to trench much on the space devoted to English literature.... But as our connection and correspondence with foreign literati will often enable us to supply the readers of 'The Athenaeum,' with notices of the most interesting works, even before they are published

[42] The *Athenaeum* was not, however, the first periodical to give a summary or digest of books for its readers. The *Journal des Scavans,* begun by Denis de Sallo, Counsellor of the Parliament of Paris, Jan. 5, 1665, "led to the beginning in England of a long line of serials devoted largely to the summarizing of books for busy or lazy readers. . . ." (See Walter Graham, *English Literary Periodicals,* pp. 22-24.) The *Athenaeum's* immediate predecessor in this style of review was the *Literary Gazette,* which began in 1817. John Banim in his *Revelations of the Dead Alive* (a satire on the follies, fashions, and manners of 1823) said that a verdict might be gained against the literary periodicals which gave one connecting page of the review to ten pages of the author, not for their praise or blame, but for their piracy. Everyone, he said, reads reviews and not books. (See Patrick J. Murrary, *The Life of John Banim,* p. 158.)

in the different capitals of Europe, we should have omitted a duty towards them" had we not taken advantage of the opportunity.[43]

In the number of April 4, 1828, appeared "French Society and Literature by a Resident of Paris," the first of a series of foreign correspondences which was to become such a distinctive feature of the *Athenaeum* in the years to come. The evidence seems to point to Stendhal as the writer of these letters.[44] He had for some years monopolized the reviewing of French books for the English press, having been a regular correspondent for the *New Monthly Magazine* and the *London Magazine*.

The interest in German literature was not so great as might have been expected from the disciples of Coleridge. The fact is that the *Athenaeum* displayed a greater inclination to be kind to the transcendental philosophy, especially when given "real English feeling" by Coleridge or Carlyle, than to the belles lettres of Germany, for the feeling that the latter was "escapist" in its tendencies was sufficiently strong to make the pre-Victorian moralists uneasy. Sterling, writing to Trench, July 24, 1829, of their friend Donne, says, he "does not intend ever to learn German. Perhaps he is right. Their works of imagination, as far as I can judge from translation, though very sweet in the mouth, are rather bitter in the belly. I am more and more convinced that Goethe rescues the individual from contending passions, not to animate it with new life, but to bury it amid the pomps and beneath the mausoleum of art."[45] Sterling feared what Germany might do to Kemble, who was travelling there.

A good deal of attention was from the first given to

[43] P. 88. There began in that number a "Literary Letter from Paris," which continued for several weeks.
[44] See Doris Gunnell, *Stendhal et l'Angleterre,* pp. 394-96. Miss Gunnell lists as probably by Stendhal: "The Society and Literature of France by a resident of Paris," March 18, April 8, 30, 1828; and "Literary Letter from Paris," April 4, 23, May 28, June 4, 1828. [45] Trench, *op. cit.,* I, 28.

Spanish literature. Intimacy between Maurice and Sterling and the refugees from the Spanish absolutist government of Ferdinand VII[46] accounts for much of the "moral enthusiasm" of the editors for the cause of the Spanish patriots, which they pleaded frequently in articles making a direct appeal for sympathy and help. Sterling, who very nearly went on the fatal Torrijos expedition to Spain in 1831, wrote some of these articles, and Maurice also put in a kind word for the refugees.[47] It is possible that a great deal of the information for such articles as "The State of Spanish Literature, from the Invasion of Napoleon"[48] was supplied by their friends among the Spanish exiles. Trench later contributed an article on Calderon which greatly pleased Sterling.[49]

Italy was given some attention also, but more for its customs, manners, art, scenery, and music than for its literature. There was one "original article," however, on "Modern Italian Novelists."[50] The attitude towards America was the customary provincial one. The era of the English traveller in America had not yet come, and the flowering of New England could not then be anticipated. A leader on "America and American Writers" summed up the matter very succinctly: "To conclude then. We do not believe America has a literature; we do not believe that it can have one till its institutions are fundamentally changed."[51] The difficulty was that in a republican country there could be no standards other than those dictated by the mob.

Contemporary opinion of the *Athenaeum* in its early years was pretty evenly divided between those who found it useful or stimulating and those who thought it merely dull.

---

[46] See Carlyle's picturesque account of the Spanish refugees in Chapters IX and X of his *Life of John Sterling.*
[47] *The Life of Maurice,* I, 85.   [48] Jan. 9, 1828, p. 26.
[49] July 30, 1828, pp. 632-633. See also Trench, *op. cit.,* I, 16-17.
[50] Sept. 24, 1828, p. 760.   [51] Oct. 14, 1829, p. 639.

Of the former, the first to greet it was a writer in the *Edinburgh Review* who paid a compliment to Buckingham while praising the Society for the Diffusion of Useful Knowledge, of which Brougham, associated with Jeffrey on the *Edinburgh*, was one of the directors.[52] The writer accused most literary journals of using the scissors too much. But "Mr. Buckingham's *Athenaeum* is of a much superior cast; and it may be hoped, will meet all the success the great merits and undeserved persecutions of its excellent conductor are well entitled to look for at the hands of Englishmen."[53]

The magazine soon gained the respect of serious thinkers, though there were not enough of these to keep it from financial difficulties. Carlyle wrote in his *Life of John Sterling:* "It was about the end of 1828 that readers of periodical literature . . . began to report the appearance, in a paper called the *Athenaeum,* of writings showing a superior brilliancy, and height of aim; one or perhaps two slight specimens of which came into my own hands, in my remote corner, about that time, and were duly recognized by me, while the authors were still far off and hidden behind deep veils."[54]

Maurice's biographer records that "although all over the country men of weighty judgment were eager in its favour, the tone adopted was, as may be judged from the specimens given, by no means such as was likely rapidly to conciliate popular favour. . . . During the months from July 30th, 1828, onwards, Francis Hare is said to have frequently remarked, 'How very interesting the articles in the "Athenaeum" have become!' Mrs. Francis Hare: 'How very stupid the "Athenaeum" is!' For the first year of its cir-

[52] It seems probable that Brougham was the author of this article. Perhaps he was returning the compliment of the *Athenaeum* which had praised the Society's publications in the early numbers.

[53] *Edinburgh Review*, XLVII (Jan., 1828) 134.

[54] P. 46.

culation the judgment of Mrs. Francis Hare was likely to afford a much better test of the probable numerical sale of the paper than that of her husband."[55]

Late in life John Stuart Mill wrote to Maurice's son that he had met both Sterling and Maurice in the London Debating Society in late 1827 or 1828. He continued: "It was during the same period that your father and Sterling wrote frequently in the 'Athenaeum,' which, under their influence and that of their friends, sent forth many valuable thoughts, and maintained an elevation of character very uncommon both then and now, in literary or any other periodicals."[56] Mill, always generous to men of different and even opposite points of view from his own, was probably perfectly sincere in his commendation. In his *Autobiography,* however, he gave a somewhat less flattering analysis: "I have always thought that there was more intellectual power wasted in Maurice than in any other of my contemporaries."[57]

The charge of dullness was a frequent one at this time, though often in the pages of rival publications it sprang from envy or malice. The *Censor,* for example, a semiweekly critical journal which lasted for only sixteen numbers, in its introductory address called the *Athenaeum* "the most dull and pedantic periodical of the day."[58] Nor is it surprising to find the rival *Literary Gazette* saying, "Mr. Buckingham's paper, notwithstanding Colburn's puffs, is *sad* stuff—heavy as unleavened bread, it cannot rise."[59]

John Wilson of *Blackwood's* had a considerable respect for Buckingham, but not much for some of his contributors.

---

[55] *Life of Maurice,* I, 97-98.   [56] *Ibid.,* p. 75.
[57] P. 107.   [58] Graham, *op. cit.,* p. 325.
[59] *The Autobiography of William Jerdan,* IV, 360n. Crofton Croker, in a private letter to William Blackwood, also accused the *Athenaeum* of dullness: "Mr. Buckingham has started another weekly review, called the 'Athenaeum,' published every Wednesday. Two numbers have appeared—the first dull beyond description, the second somewhat better, but the whole appearance promises only a lumbering concern." (Quoted in Oliphant's *Annals of a Publishing House: William Blackwood and his Sons.* I, 519.)

In Number XXXVI of the "Noctes Ambrosianae" he condescended to pay tribute to the new periodical. After expressing the hope that it would rid itself of "pert paddies," Irish journalists who would soon kill any periodical, he said: "Buckingham's politics and mine are wide as the poles asunder—but I respect the independent spirit of the man, the energy of his character, and his talents." None of the weekly periodicals, however, will ever cut out the *Literary Gazette,* "simply for one reason—Mr. Jerdan is a gentleman, and is assisted by none but gentlemen. . . ." Nevertheless, " 'Tis a pretty race. The Athenaeum is well laid in upon his flank—and there goes the Sphynx and Atlas at a spanking rate—looking within the ropes like winners; but the rider of the Ould Horse has him in hand, and letting him loose within a rod of the judges' stand, he will win the gold cup by two lengths at least—and I take him at even against the field for the Derby."[60] Again a year later Christopher North expressed the view that the *Literary Gazette* "stands, beyond dispute, at the head of its own class."[61] And this time he merely mentioned the *Athenaeum* among other weeklies.

Worthy of mention also is the slightly veiled attack by Bulwer in his novel *Paul Clifford* which appeared early in 1830. One of the characters in that novel was a Peter Mac-Grawler, a rogue and scoundrel and "editor of a magnificent periodical entitled 'The Asinaeum,' which was written to prove that whatever is popular is necessarily bad."[62] Bulwer, notoriously sensitive to criticism, had taken great offense at the slighting remarks on his popular *Pelham* in a notice of *Devereux* in the *Athenaeum* in July of the year before.[63]

[60] *Blackwood's,* May, 1828, p. 801.

[61] *Blackwood's,* April, 1829, p. 543.

[62] *Paul Clifford, The Works of Bulwer Lytton,* XXII, 21.

[63] An account of this episode may be found in an article by Vernon Rendall in *Notes and Queries,* Feb. 23, 1935, pp. 128-129. Rendall is mistaken in saying that the *Athenaeum* did not notice *Pelham* when it appeared. A review with

At the end of its second year the *Athenaeum* was only a precariously struggling literary weekly on the verge of extinction like so many others which sprang up in the late twenties and thirties, came out with brave promises, and expired after a few weeks or a few months. Its circulation was probably less than a thousand (perhaps not more than five or six hundred). It was appreciated by a few select spirits, and was carried on by the interest, enthusiasm, and financial aid of its editors. Such was the beginning of what was to be one of the most noteworthy agents for the dissemination of culture in the Victorian era.

THE REGIME OF DILKE

In the early months of 1830 it began to be apparent that some new blood had come into the management as well as the contributors' lists of the *Athenaeum*. There was more liveliness and satiric punch in some of the reviews. Increased attention was given to foreign literature, both in reviews and in correspondence from Vienna, Madrid, Naples, Rome, Florence, Munich, Berlin, and St. Petersburg, as well as Paris. Lighter familiar essays and translations of German poetry also were given some space. The general character and policy, however, remained the same.

The "Prospectus of the New Series" assured the readers that as far as the literary management was concerned, it would be "under the direction of the parties who have hitherto conducted it." At the same time, "a great accession of literary talent has been secured . . . by engaging the aid of several eminent and popular authors."[64] The literary talent referred to may have been the *London Magazine* group whom Sterling had called in to assist him when he took the editorial chair from Maurice at the end of May,

---

copious quotations and mingled praise and censure appeared on May 14, 1828, pp. 451-453.   [64] Jan. 16, 1830, p. 17.

1829,[65] though the prospectus says only that some of the best contributors to the *London Weekly Review,* with which the *Athenaeum* then combined, had been retained. Readers were assured that "all notices of new works will be unbiassed by the names or influence of publishers, by favour or enmity towards authors, or by personal feeling of any kind."

Further indications of stirrings in the editorial office may be seen in the address "To the Reader" on February 27 of this year.

... the *Athenaeum* professes to exhibit a picture of the Literature of the day, equally remote from the caricature and the fashionable portrait. ...

The departments of the Fine Arts, the Sciences, and the Drama, are all under the direction of separate individuals, distinguished by their attainments in the part allotted to them; and even in the Literary Reviews, the same classification has been carried into effect to a degree, it is supposed, hitherto unattempted.[66]

The practice of assigning books for review to experts in the various fields was indeed a departure from common practice and one which was to give distinction and prestige to the *Athenaeum* in the years that followed. That innovation alone, even if for the moment set up only as an ideal to be striven for, is perhaps enough evidence to justify the assumption that Charles Wentworth Dilke had already begun to exert some influence in the management of the

[65] The *London Magazine* had just then expired after a losing struggle following its more brilliant years under Taylor and Hessey. Others of this group besides Reynolds and Cunningham who may have joined the *Athenaeum* at this time were Thomas Hood and Charles Wentworth Dilke. For a detailed account of the *London Magazine* see R. W. King, *The Translator of Dante* [Henry Francis Cary], pp. 124-177; and Walter Jerrold, *Thomas Hood,* pp. 92-122. Jerrold lists a number of contributors to the magazine who were staff writers for the *Athenaeum* after Dilke became editor in the middle of 1830. How many of them began contributing earlier, and when, it is impossible to say. A more recent account of the *London Magazine* is given in Chap. V of Blunden's *Keats's Publisher.*   [66] Feb. 27, 1830, p. 127.

journal.[67]   Dilke's known friendship with Reynolds, Cunningham, and others of their circle makes it reasonable to suppose that he may have taken an active part in its affairs as early as the middle of 1829 when they began to assist Sterling.   Even Dilke's grandson, however, who was closer to him in his later years than anyone else, apparently did not know exactly.   He says: "From 1828 to 1832 the affairs of the *Athenaeum,* which was at the time far from a paying property, were in some confusion.   Mr. Dilke was one of several proprietors, of whom others were Mr. Holmes, the printer, Hood, Allan Cunningham, and John Hamilton Reynolds; but in 1830 Mr. Dilke's control over the paper became complete, and in 1832 he and Mr. Holmes remained the sole proprietors, Mr. Dilke owning three-fourths and Mr. Holmes one-fourth."[68]   The joint ownership possibly began early in 1830 when Sterling relinquished his share though continuing for some months as editor.   Confidence in Dilke's ability on the part of his former *London Magazine* associates undoubtedly led them soon to give him sole control of the business and editorial policies, a responsibility which he assumed with the number of June 5, 1830.

A superficial glance at the *Athenaeum* of the thirties would not reveal any radical difference in appearance from the magazine of 1828-29, but a closer scrutiny shows great though gradual changes in content and general policy.   One of the most important was that of putting the whole strength of the journal in the reviews rather than in original articles. What his predecessors had aimed at rather ineffectively Dilke carried out with a thoroughness which was surprising and impressive to his contemporaries, and which is still

[67] The profession of independence from publishers' influences also strongly suggests Dilke's hand.   See Chapter II.

[68] *Biographical Memoir* by Sir Charles Wentworth Dilke prefixed to *Papers of a Critic: Selected from the Writings of Charles Wentworth Dilke,* I, 24. Holmes continued to hold his share until 1869, when he finally sold it to Dilke's grandson.

worthy of admiration and emulation in this era of the weekly review. The complete coverage of every cultural interest of the time makes the pages of the *Athenaeum* not only an index but a summary as well of current thought and taste from 1830 to the end of the century, and after. It is the best single source of information concerning books published and their contents. William Jerdan in 1819 had boasted that the *Literary Gazette* volumes, "when they have outlived their years, [may] . . . constitute a great portion of literary history, and be indeed the annals of the republic."[69] But the *Athenaeum* under Dilke was far superior as a record of the times.

The great success and influence of the journal in subsequent years were so directly due to the shrewd management and sound honesty and good sense of Charles Wentworth Dilke that it is well before going further with the history of the magazine to consider what sort of man he was. Partly because of his retiring disposition and great modesty, Dilke's practical abilities and his influence on his contemporaries have never been given adequate treatment in any written record. He had some reputation as an antiquarian and as a critic before he came to the *Athenaeum*. After studying at Cambridge, he had entered the Navy Pay Office. His writing career began when from 1814 to 1816 he edited a continuation of Dodsley's *Old English Plays*. That work seemed to fix his interests in literary history. A number of his essays on the Elizabethan drama, on the Junius controversy, and on Pope, which he contributed to the *Athenaeum* and other periodicals in his later years, were collected by his grandson as *Papers of a Critic* (2 vols., 1875). The *Memoir* which precedes the critical papers in the first volume is now the chief source of information concerning Dilke and his work on the *Athenaeum*.

[69] *Literary Gazette,* Jan. 2, 1819, p. 1. The phrase is quoted from Isaac D'Israeli.

From 1815 to 1830, we are told, he "wrote largely in the various monthly and quarterly reviews."[70] But, his grandson says, "It is difficult to trace Mr. Dilke's numerous writings, as he never put his name to anything; never kept a copy or a note of titles, and never even told his son, or in later times, his grandson."[71] In 1822 he was writing for Taylor's *London Review* and Colburn's *New Monthly Magazine*. Charles Brown, the friend of Keats and Dilke, wrote from Italy about this time: "Galignani has republished some of Dilke's articles in his *Parisian Literary Gazette*."[72] The next year he was writing in the *London Magazine* as "Thurusa," and in 1825 he wrote much in the *Retrospective Review*. "He appears also about this time to have been editor of the *London Magazine,* in which he wrote, as did at the same time Lamb, Hood, Reynolds, Hazlitt, Poole (Paul Pry), Talfourd, Barry Cornwall, Horace Smith, Allan Cunningham, De Quincey, John Bowring, George Darley, Hartley Coleridge, and Julius Hare."[73] He apparently continued to write for the *New Monthly* at various times until at least 1829. His grandson conjectures also that he contributed to *Fraser's*.[74]

According to the grandson again, Dilke early became a Radical and continued in his radical beliefs to the end of his days.[75] In 1821 he wrote a political pamphlet under the title, "The Source and Remedy of the National Difficulties, deduced from Principles of Political Economy." It was in the form of a letter to Lord John Russell. For motto it

---

[70] *Papers of a Critic*, I, 1-2.

[71] *Ibid.*, p. 14.   [72] *Ibid.*, p. 15.

[73] *Ibid.*, p. 16. There is no further evidence than this concerning Dilke's possible editorship of the *London Magazine*, which passed into the hands of Henry Southern in Sept., 1825. From that time until its demise in 1829 it had an obscure and insignificant history, though some members of the old group still wrote for it. See *ante*, p. 25, n. 65.

[74] *Ibid.*, p. 24. Francis, *op. cit.*, I, 34, mentions also the *Westminster Review* among the periodicals to which Dilke had contributed.

[75] *Papers of a Critic*, I, 1.

bore a passage from Milton: "How to solder, how to stop a leak—that now is the deep design of a politician." Its conclusion was that the remedy of the national difficulties was the abolition of the Corn-Laws. In the preface Dilke says: "From all the works I have read on the subject, the richest nations are those where the greatest revenue is raised; as if the power of compelling men to labour twice as much at the mills of Gaza for the enjoyment of the Philistines, were the proof of anything but a tyranny or an ignorance twice as powerful."[76]

Moreover, it is evident that he was willing to stand by beliefs which were unpopular. In a letter to his son in 1840 he confessed, "I once committed myself by trying to take the tin kettle from the tail of a Socialist."[77] And in a review in the *Athenaeum,* which he probably wrote, of Lady Morgan's *Dramatic Scenes from Real Life,* there is a reminiscent note of some importance in this connection:

An ultra-liberal, before liberals, as a party, existed, her works were for many years the marked object for every creeping thing to spit its venom on. Times have changed. . . . It would, however, be absurd to deny that Lady Morgan has given great offence to honest men of all parties: the conservatives, she must herself admit, have just grounds for their dislikes; and the radicals, as they used *contemptuously* to be called, had surely no good reason for attaching themselves to her. The great battle which the latter had to fight, was against the prejudices of society. The disputes *now* respect questions on which honest men may conscientiously differ; but *then,* it was whether the one party were entitled to offer an opinion at all. Twenty years ago reformers were hunted down in society as vulgar unwashed mechanicals, and any man who desired to live quietly and pleasantly, was obliged to be silent if he entertained opinions that now pass current all England over.[78]

[76] *Ibid.,* p. 15.   [77] *Ibid.,* p. 47.
[78] July 13, 1833, p. 449. The author of the review is not indicated in the marked file. The conjecture that Dilke wrote it is based on strong internal

That Dilke was a man of staunch principles, not to say prejudices, is attested by more than one of his contemporaries. Keats, who was a close friend from 1816 to his death, found Dilke at times a little opinionated and dogmatic and called him a "Godwin-Methodist" and a man "who cannot feel he has a personal identity unless he has made up his Mind about every thing."[79]   But Keats continued to value Dilke's friendship greatly, and there is evidence enough of the latter's flexibility of mind, especially in his mellowed years, in the great number of lasting friendships he formed with people of all opinions.   Henry Chorley, long associated with him on the *Athenaeum,* wrote in later life: "No two persons could be more unlike in many matters of taste, opinion, and feeling than the editor of the 'Athenaeum,' the late honoured Charles Dilke, and myself.   But it was impossible to know and not respect him, how ever so many were his prejudices (and they were many), how ever so limited were his sympathies (and they were limited)."[80]

---

evidence (the tone is similar to that of many of his letters—and the point of view is exactly Dilke's); and on the fact that Dilke seldom marked his own contributions in the editorial file.

[79] *Letters of John Keats,* ed. H. Buxton Forman, II, 466.   This was in a letter to George and Georgiana Keats, Sept. 24, 1819.   Every student of Keats is familiar with the close and friendly relations between Dilke and the young poet.   Keats lived for a time in the Dilke house in Hampstead (Wentworth House), now the Keats Museum and library where is deposited the whole of the Dilke Keats collection.   The warm familiarity of their relationship is indicated in the playful tone of many of the letters, such as the following to Dilke in March, 1820: "You must improve your penmanship; your writing is like the speaking of a child of three years old, very understandable to its father, but to no one else.   The worst is it looks well—no that is not the worst—the worst is, it is worse than Bailey's.   Bailey's looks illegible and may perchance be read; yours looks very legible and may perchance not be read." (*Ibid.,* p. 521.)   Another witness to the illegibility of Dilke's handwriting is Elizabeth Barrett, who wrote to Mr. Boyd: "You will comprehend my surprise on receiving last night a very courteous note from the editor [of the *Athenaeum*], which I would send to you if it were legible to anybody except people used to learn reading from the pyramids." (*Letters of Elizabeth Barrett Browning,* ed. F. G. Kenyon, I, 95-96.)

[80] Henry Fothergill Chorley, *Autobiography, Memoir, and Letters,* compiled by Henry G. Hewlett, I, 104.

But his letters to his grandson (mostly yet unpublished) reveal a man of wide interests and generous enthusiasms, tolerant and keen-minded. Writing in 1864, shortly before his death, he says:

Your letters have awakened strange memories. When I was about your age I was deep in the same studies which your Essay now imposes on you. [The grandson, then at Cambridge, was assigned a topic which was to take its departure from Pope's line "For forms of government let fools contest."] I had unfortunately no previous training—no guide—few books, and only such as the reading of today suggested for tomorrow, and limited means enabled me to get hold of. I had to grope my way in the dark. Then came the business and the duties of life, and I was ever after obliged to read for the profit of the hour. . . . My essay would rather tend to show that each and every one of these forms of government may have been good in itself and under the circumstances, yet not good independent of or under other circumstances. *No form can be ever permanent—because the conditions are not permanent.* The best government, as it appears to me, is that which best represents the wishes and feelings of the governed, and by its plasticity, mobility, adaptability . . . most easily adapts itself to the varying circumstances and feelings of the people. In this respect the British Constitution has shown itself good beyond all the hopes of my early life. There then seemed no probability of escape, earlier or later, from violent revolution; yet the just will of the people peacefully triumphed. . . .[81]

In his next letter he said: "I was about your age when I read Godwin. I was groping my way, without preparatory training, without aid or help. The book [*Political Justice*] was too bad to be named, and the writer who lived by the drudging labor of writing school-books and works of that class, was obliged to publish them under another name.

[81] Dilke Papers, British Museum, Add. 43,910, Vol. V. Letter of July 14, 1864.

Yet the book made a powerful impression on me, and certainly made me a self responsible man."[82]

Dilke was widely known for his solidity of judgment, personal integrity, and devotion to truth. Dickens, who had joined him in the fight for the reform of the Literary Fund Society, wrote to the son of the editor, August 12, 1864: "I am truly concerned to hear from Forster of the death of your excellent father—even at his ripe years, and in the mournful order of nature. You know how heartily I admired and respected him, and what interest I derived from the association I was so fortunate as to have with that sound head, and staunch true heart. Never on this earth shall I fight any fight by the side of a more reliable and faithful man, though I live as long as he!"[83]

In 1829 Dilke had written to his son, "From the first hour I never taught you to believe what I did not myself believe. I have been a thousand times censured for it, but I had that confidence in truth, that I dared put my faith in it and in you."[84] Perhaps it was that love of truth which made him more catholic in his interests and less provincial than most Englishmen of his time. He travelled with his son on the Continent in 1828-29 and later left him in Florence to study. Writing to him there, Dilke added a self-revealing sermon in a postscript:

I agree with you, and love the French; but if my judgment be worth anything, the Germans are the first people in Europe, not excepting our own countrymen, who, however, are only second, if not equal, to the first. Where would you find any but a German with enthusiasm enough to walk *all over Italy,* when he could not ride, like our friend with the pipe? . . . That is the way to acquire knowledge: to make *all* sacrifices to it. But unfortunately people rarely know it is *worth* all sacrifices until they already have a good deal of knowledge.[85]

[82] *Ibid.,* letter of July 22, 1864.   [83] *Ibid.,* Add. 43,913.
[84] *Papers of a Critic,* I, 18-19.   [85] *Ibid.,* p. 23.

Moreover, he evidently practiced what he preached, for his grandson says, "He was a 'living catalogue' to his library of 12,000 volumes, and knew every book."[86] He became an eighteenth-century scholar second to none in his day. He was the first to examine carefully the Caryll-Pope letters and to discover the nature of the changes which Pope made in the letters that he published. He also entered largely into the Junius controversy. His papers in the *Athenaeum* and *Notes and Queries* and elsewhere are indispensable to all modern students in those fields. Pope's most scholarly recent biographer says: "The contributions of Dilke were chiefly concerned with the authenticity of various of Pope's correspondences, though his criticisms of biographical detail evince an incisiveness that may be the ideal and the despair of any biographer. That neither Spence nor Dilke should have written a life of Pope is a major catastrophe to this field of scholarship."[87]

But though he was a thorough and an earnest scholar, his enthusiasms were no more limited to scholarship than they were to politics.[88] His belief in progress through the advancement of knowledge stimulated his interest in science and mechanical invention and placed him in full sympathy with the main current of practical, non-sentimental, and non-transcendental, early Victorian reform. Barry Cornwall (B. W. Procter) once twitted him for his absorption in material progress: "You are sitting there in all the pride of science, railroads, your Elysian fields, chimneys, your delectable mountains, artesian wells, your castles." Procter had just sent some translations from Victor Hugo, "who will be

[86] *Ibid.*

[87] George Sherburn, *The Early Career of Alexander Pope*, p. 20.

[88] One of his enthusiasms was an admiration for Blake. His grandson says: "Mr. Dilke was a great admirer of the work of Fuseli, Haydon's friend, and of Blake, who was also the friend of both. He formed one of the best collections of Blake's drawings, and was one of the earliest admirers of his poems." (*Papers of a Critic*, I, 51.)

remembered, perhaps, when Tredgold and the 999 associates have been pounded and pulverized into fresh mag-
nesia, to supply the future bones of the mechanical geniuses
of 1939. Why do you, a man of large heart, take under
your wing (your waistcoat) the wheels, and levers, and cogs,
and spinning jennies of the time?"[89]

Dilke's editorship of the *Athenaeum,* which lasted from
the middle of 1830 until the beginning of 1846, was notable
chiefly for three accomplishments: He put the magazine on
a sound financial basis and gradually drew it out of debt,
at the same time extending its circulation and influence by
reducing the price from 8*d.* to 4*d.* He declared open war
on the system of puffery then current in literary criticism
and reviews, holding an almost tyrannical stick over his
staff, and even over contributors and foreign correspondents,
to see that they remained independent of authors and publishers. Finally, he drew about him a staff of competent
critics and correspondents who set the tone of the magazine
and established its prestige.

Dilke was unquestionably a good business manager. But
at first there were no profits, and throughout his editorship
he received no salary, having a sufficient private income
apparently to allow him to put his earnings back into the
magazine. Though the circulation began to grow as the
independent principles of Dilke's management became
noised about, some publishers who were unused to anything
but puffs in a literary review withdrew their support.

An editorial note on May 28, 1831, stated that because
of the opposition of the *Athenaeum* to "trade criticism and
paid criticism," some publishers had refused to sell it or to
advertise in it. Dilke saw that he could not save the journal
by petty economies. Some drastic measure was necessary.
On July 16 came the announcement that the price would be

[89] *Papers of a Critic,* I, 37-38. Letter of May 2, 1839.

lowered to 4*d.,* an unprecedented figure for magazines of
its class. Such a drop was viewed with alarm by some of
the other proprietors. John Hamilton Reynolds wrote when
Dilke first proposed the change:

> You astound me with your fall. It is more decided than Mil-
> ton's 'Noon to Dewy Eve' one! From 8 d. to 4 d. is but a step,
> but then it is also from the sublime to the ridiculous. Remember
> what an increase must take place to get it all home. A sale of
> 6000! Mercy on us! I certainly hoped the change would allow
> us to lower our outgoings, and consequently fatten our profits. . . .
> A midway lowering of price would better suit the public and
> ourselves. 6 d. unstamped! There is something more respectable,
> too, in the sum. Something less Tattlerish, and Mirrorish and
> Two-penny Trashish![90]

Reynolds was so excited that he wrote again the same day:

> Hood and I have been calculating this afternoon, and the re-
> sult is appalling. To lower below 6 d. would, in my opinion, be
> an unadvisable course, and such a fall would show that our
> previous state was hopeless. The difference between 6 d. and 4 d.
> would be 8 *l.* 6 s. 8 d. a week in a thousand copies. The loss
> per annum on 5000 copies would be 2,165 *l.* And you should
> remember that this very 2 d. is in reality the cream of the profit,
> for between the expenses and the 4 d. there can be the merest
> shadow of a gain. We are quite against the total change in our
> paper-constitution which you threaten.[91]

But Dilke proved himself right. There was a large audience ready for the *Athenaeum* as soon as the price was
reduced. Even Jerdan of the *Literary Gazette* was alarmed
by the competition. He confessed later in his *Autobiography* that the circulation of his journal "was considerably
affected by the 'Athenaeum' lowering its charge to half the
price, and following up that sagacious measure by the most

---

[90] *Papers of a Critic,* I, 25. Letter of Feb. 15, 1831.
[91] *Ibid.,* pp. 25-26.

diligent adoption of all business resources, so essential to successful publishing. There was no longer any laughing at the fainting competition, and my witty correspondents' squibs on the subject became rather less amusing."[92] In fact, Jerdan was so little amused at this point that when the *Athenaeum* sent a paid advertisement concerning the reduction in price, the *Literary Gazette* returned the money with the message that the proprietors would not print the advertisements of the *Athenaeum*.[93]

Dilke wrote the first day of the experiment: "You remember that at the outset we professed we should be well pleased if at starting we *doubled* our sale. We have already *trebled* it." And the next day he reported: "Our sale up to the present time has been *six times* our former sale. I begin now to have hopes that I was right, and all the world wrong, for that is about the proportion for and against the measure. A first number, of course, has novelty; but, on the other hand, I do not believe that our advertisements are yet beginning to be felt in the country."[94]

Apparently Dilke had been contemplating this change for some time but had been held back by his partners. The first editorial note announcing the reduction says that "the experiment would have been made at the beginning of this year, but that intelligent friends earnestly advised that it should be deferred until the character of the Paper was more generally known and firmly established."[95] And the

---

[92] Jerdan, *op. cit.*, IV, 360. One of the "squibs" had read:

> Mr. Dilke, Mr. Dilke,
> Though the Novice you bilke,
> Be not hasty to sing the Te Deum,
> No reader will quit
> A print that has wit,
> For your prosy and dull Athenaeum.

[93] See *Athenaeum*, Oct. 15, 1831, p. 671. See also Jerdan's condescending and not very gracious acknowledgment of the success of the rival publication in his *Autobiography* (III, 210-211).

[94] *Papers of a Critic*, I, 26.   [95] *Athenaeum*, July 16, 1831, p. 449.

following week the editor replied to certain correspondents who had cautioned him by asking a pertinent question: "If the readers of Literary Papers be so limited as they imagine, who were the thirty thousand purchasers of the early volumes of the Family Library?—who the fourteen thousand purchasers of the Lives of the Painters [by Allan Cunningham], a subject limited in its interest to the highest and most refined class of informed minds?"[96]

Reynolds, who had retired from proprietorship before the measure went into effect,[97] may soon have regretted his action, for by January 7, 1832, Dilke was able to boast that the sale had risen to a figure exceeding that of any other literary paper.[98] Twelve months later the New Year "Address" proclaimed: "Our success has been more rapid and complete than any in the history of periodical literature." Two years before, the editor said, a contemporary literary journal [*Literary Gazette*] professed that it "enjoyed by *many thousands* the greatest circulation of any purely literary paper."[99] The *Athenaeum* could now claim that distinction.

It was about this time that Dilke acquired the property (except for the quarter share owned by Mr. James Holmes, the printer, who in no way interfered with the editor's policies). Edmund Blunden has surmised from certain letters of the period (early 1833) that Charles Lamb had contributed some money to the *Athenaeum,* though he was not a "proprietor" as Reynolds and Hood were for a time.[100]

[96] July 23, 1831, p. 478.

[97] Reynolds had sold his share to Dilke on June 8, 1831, when he found that he could not prevent the drastic cut in the price, but he continued to write for the *Athenaeum* for many years.

[98] *Athenaeum*, Jan. 7, 1832, p. 1.   [99] *Athenaeum*, Jan. 5, 1833, p. 1.

[100] The evidence that Lamb had some financial interest in the *Athenaeum* is rather scanty and enigmatic; and the correspondence I have had on the subject with Blunden and with Vernon Rendall, who aided E. V. Lucas in editing the new *Letters of Lamb* (1935), fails to throw more than conjectural light on the

But, free now to develop his policies in his own way, Dilke exercised a Spartan control which established the reputation of the *Athenaeum* for fearless independence, and it continued to grow in circulation and influence.

The details of Dilke's fight against puffery will be taken up in the second chapter, but we may pause here to note the thoroughness with which he attempted to eschew even the semblance of influence by authors or publishers. He avoided all society himself and watched the members of his

problem. I can do no better than to present the evidence on both sides as given by these two students of Lamb. Blunden writes:

"I think the suggestion I made [that Lamb contributed some money to the *Athenaeum*—see Blunden's *Charles Lamb and his Contemporaries*, p. 201] arose from letter 930 in the new 'Letters of Lamb' ("No date: Early 1833"). Lamb there says that Taylor and Hessey 'made a volume at their own will, and volunteered me a third of profits, which came to £30, which came to Bilk, and never came back to me.' Elsewhere we find that Lamb called Dilke's species 'Bilkish blockheads,' and he clearly had some quarrel with Dilke's ways which is not explained. My idea is that the £30 came to Dilke in connexion with the *Athenaeum*. What else? Lamb had little to do with him otherwise. It wouldn't make him 'a proprietor,' but we see that (Letter 881 for instance) Lamb felt he had a pretty good claim on the *Athenaeum*."

Rendall contributes this to the discussion:

"I do not see that *Bilk* in Letter 930 refers to Dilke at all. 'They [Taylor and Hessey of the *London Magazine*] volunteered me a third of the profits, which came to £30. . . .' Hutchinson's edition of 'The Works of Charles Lamb,' Vol. I, gives details of the previous publication of the Essays in 'The Last Essays of Elia.' The only one which appeared in the *Athenaeum*, Jan. 12, 19, 26, and Feb. 2, 1833, is 'Barrenness of the Imaginative Faculty in the Productions of Modern Art.' As this had been printed in part in the *Reflector*, Moxon's weekly, I don't see Dilke demanding £30 for the copyright of it. (Reference is p. 703 of Hutchinson's 'Lamb.') Would 'a third of the profits' come to Dilke for this one article? (There were 15 from the *London Magazine*.) It does not seem very likely, does it? If Lamb had been a proprietor, surely Sir Charles would have mentioned that connection with the *Athenaeum* in the Preface to *Papers of a Critic*? Lamb was in favour there, but not everything of his was accepted, and Lucas thinks it doubtful in his note to letter 881, if the two items I suggested in the note were Lamb's. He was testy in his old age, and might very well talk of 'Bilkish Blockheads' when disappointed. He was certainly cross with Hood about 'A Widow,' which Hood signed with his name, including in it an indecent phrase, and this may have led to a distaste for the *Athenaeum*. But the quarrel with Dilke's ways is vague and unexplained."

staff closely to see that they were not lionized or shown special favors in quarters which might bias their judgment. His extreme measures sometimes caused temporary ill-feeling in the ranks of his contributors. Reynolds had written for permission to review a certain book. Dilke replied by asking if he was acquainted with either the author or the publisher. Reynolds, piqued, returned the book, "That you may consign it to some independent hand, according to your religious custom. I, alas! know author *and* bookseller."[101] The grandson of the editor confessed: "Mr. Dilke during the earlier years pushed his principles to the extreme only because of the bad system which had grown up in other quarters."[102] In 1840 Dilke replied to the editor of the official journal of France *(Le Moniteur Universel)* who had put his name on the free list and had asked for six English books which he needed: "You are evidently not informed of our usage in such matters. During the ten years that I have been editor of the *Athenaeum* I have never asked for a single copy of any work. Since the journal has attained its present rank copies of new works are generally sent to it —not always, and when they are not sent, and are important, they are purchased."[103] In 1842 he wrote to the Paris correspondent of the *Athenaeum:* "I cannot let a single post pass without replying to your letter. You have, it appears, been in communication with the principal publishers in Paris. Having accepted advance-sheets you are unable to condemn their works. What then is the value of your criticism? During the many years that I have had the *Athenaeum* I have never asked a favour of a publisher. Favour and independence are incompatible. It is no use under these circumstances for you to send me reviews at present."[104]

The boast of the editor in the New Year "Address" for

---

[101] *Papers of a Critic,* I, 45.
[102] *Ibid.,* p. 48.
[103] *Loc. cit.*
[104] *Ibid.,* pp. 48-49.

1833 was a mere concrete summary of accomplishments, which indicates the change in emphasis and the broadened scope of the journal after Dilke took control.

Not only have we been the first to notice important works published in Great Britain, but France, Germany, and America have yielded tribute of their best; and we this day present our readers with a literary curiosity, a new and valuable work just published in Spain.[105] It was the Athenaeum that first made known to English readers the delightful Memoirs of the Duchess of Abrantès—the pleasant papers of the Book of the Hundred and One—the travels of a German Prince[106]—Falck's Memoirs of Goethe—Dumont's Recollections of Mirabeau—Lafayette and the French Revolution—all subsequently translated and published in England. We believe, that, altogether, not less than one thousand volumes will be found to have been reviewed by us in the year 1832. The Reports of Societies, exceeding in number one hundred and fifty, have been, we believe, generally satisfactory—some indeed are exclusive, and by authority. The Biographical Memoirs of such distinguished persons as have died during the year, including Scott, Crabbe, Mackintosh, Goethe, Say, Rémusat, Spurzheim, & c., have been contributed by men of such distinguished fame and reputation in the world of letters, that it would be affectation to utter a word respecting their spirit and worth. In Art, not less than one hundred and fifty works have been critically noticed. The Theatres, the Exhibitions, and other novelties have had their proportionate attention,—and even among the Miscellanea will be found much valuable information relating to Literature, Science and Art. We do not hesitate therefore to express, not an anxious hope, but the honest conviction, that the volume for 1832, now concluded, contains a full and fair record for the period, of all that was of permanent interest to the

[105] *Memorias de la Real Academia de la Historia.* Tomo VII. Madrid. The review, the leader for the issue and for the year, was by Dr. Seoane, a Spanish physician then in exile in England. See *post,* p. 218.

[106] The reference is to the travel diary of Prince Pückler Muskau, a work which made quite a stir throughout Europe and especially in England where the vogue of gossipy literature almost equalled that of the "high life" novel, and furnished a great deal of the trade of the circulating libraries.

informed and marching mind of the age—to say nothing of the grace and ornament superadded by the many Original Papers contributed by some of our most distinguished and successful writers.[107]

The chief concern was with the amount and quality of reading material, and little attention was paid to attractiveness or typographical display. The format was not changed except that the margins were made narrower to permit more matter to be crowded into the same number of pages. The body type was still about ten-point solid, but quotations within the reviews were printed in the equivalent of eight-point instead of six-and-a-half as was the practice during the first three years. Editorial notes and footnotes remained an almost microscopic five-point.

A further increase in the amount of printed matter was promised at the end of 1835. The *Athenaeum,* the editor says, was projected by others, and when we took it, "we despoiled its aristocratic character by reducing its ample margins," and increasing the amount of material supplied as well as reducing the price. The editor's pride extended to the whole field of English periodical literature which was diffusing popular education by making culture available to the masses. He estimated that the circulation of weekly papers alone in Great Britain then exceeded half a million. "It is impossible to look at the number and character of our literary periodicals, and remember what they were, only a few years since, without 'mute wonder.' If literature have its humanizing influences—and who can doubt it?—what mighty engines, for the happiness and improvement of society, are at this moment in operation all over the world!"[108] This year, he adds, the *Athenaeum* has given

---

[107] *Athenaeum,* Jan. 5, 1833, p. 1. A similar summary of contents had appeared on Dec. 4, 1830 (p. 767), after Dilke had been editor for half a year.

[108] *Athenaeum,* Dec. 26, 1835, p. 968. It became the common pride of those interested in popular education to cite the rapid increase of periodicals as ev-

19 double numbers (18 per cent increase in reading matter). Now it is proposed to enlarge the printed sheet in depth and width, adding about 15 per cent to the contents.

Two days later Allan Cunningham wrote to Dilke: "So you enlarge the *Athenaeum*? You already give too much for the money."[109] But as the circulation and the advertising grew Dilke again proved himself right and all the rest of the world wrong; and he continued to the amazement of his friends to give more and more for 4*d.* By 1841 the double numbers in a year had increased to 26 or one every other week.[110]

A correspondent as early as 1834 had made a comparison of the typographical content of the monthly part of the *Penny Magazine,* subsidized by the Society for the Diffusion of Useful Knowledge, which sold for 6d., and the monthly offering of the *Athenaeum,* which sold for 1s. 4d., "from which it appears that, *line for line . . . we gave 959 lines for one penny,* while the Diffusion Society, in their penny prodigy, *gave but 710!*"[111]   And this took no account, the editor pointed out, of the 19 pages of advertisements (in the month) in the *Athenaeum;* moreover, the reader must consider the superiority of paper and print, and the higher quality and originality of the contents.

As Dilke gradually established the reputation of the *Athenaeum* for fairness, and as the circulation grew, the independent publishers began to flock to him and the paper soon came to be recognized as one of the best media for book advertisements. Moxon, the "Publisher of Poets," for instance, used the *Athenaeum* consistently as an advertising

---

idence of zeal for learning. Even the Tory *Blackwood's* proclaimed: "A thousand daily, thrice-a-week, twice-a-week, weekly newspapers, a hundred monthlies, fifty quarterlies, and twenty-five annuals! No mouth looks up now and is not fed." (Quoted in *The Mirror,* Dec. 26, 1829, p. 442.)

[109] *Papers of a Critic,* I, 33.

[110] See "To Correspondents," *Athenaeum,* Aug. 28, 1841, p. 679.

[111] *Athenaeum,* Feb. 15, 1834, p. 131.

medium, partly because it circulated among the class he wanted to reach, and partly because of his friendship for Dilke, whom he knew through Lamb.[112] The amount of advertising increased steadily. By the end of the decade it occupied from six to ten pages in a total of twenty-four to thirty; and by the time Dilke gave up the active editorship in 1846 the journal carried from ten to twelve pages of paid advertisements. Beginning on January 5, 1839, the advertising pages were divided, part of them preceding and part following the editorial matter. The puffing publishers, whose practices the *Athenaeum* had attacked, soon fell in line and sought space. By 1834 Bentley and Longman were buying whole columns and sometimes pages. Even Henry Colburn, whose *Literary Gazette* had refused to accept an *Athenaeum* announcement of the reduction in price in 1831, was by 1838 taking a full page on the back cover to advertise his fashionable novels, memoirs, and travel books. Other advertisements included those of periodicals,[113] learned societies, insurance companies, railway guides, shops, positions wanted (largely by retired clergymen of good classical training), and an increasing number of patent medicines.

What the circulation of the magazine actually was when Dilke took it over, and what it subsequently became, it is impossible to say with any degree of accuracy. The boast of the *Literary Gazette,* "in the plenitude of its pride" (1830) that it "enjoyed by *many thousands* the greatest circulation of any purely literary paper"[114] may not have meant a great deal when a weekly or monthly sale of 2,000 to 3,000 was

[112] See Harold G. Merriam, *Edward Moxon, Publisher of Poets*, pp. 77-78. Later the Pre-Raphaelite founders of *The Germ* advertised in the *Athenaeum*, believing it to be the best medium for reaching a select intelligent reading public.

[113] The *Athenaeum* not only carried such advertisements for other magazines, but gave itself a half page or more several times in 1830 and 1831, quoting opinions of papers all over the United Kingdom of the "fearless independence" of the *Athenaeum*. E.g., see Dec. 4, 1830, p. 767.

[114] See *Athenaeum*, Jan. 5, 1833, p. 1.

enough to carry a number of periodicals for many years. One may guess that the *Gazette* had a weekly circulation of from 7,000 to 8,000 at the time the *Athenaeum* began to be a serious competitor.[115] The *Monthly Magazine* at the height of its career had reached 5,000, and it exceeded all other magazines of its class at the beginning of the nineteenth century.[116] The *New Monthly,* one of Colburn's popular magazines, in its thriving period towards the end of the twenties sold only 2,500 copies.[117]

Most of the weekly periodicals were content with a sale which today seems incredibly small. The circulation of the *Examiner* in 1808 was 2,200, and Leigh Hunt thought that excellent.[118] Coming down nearer to the period we are discussing, we find that the weekly average of the *Spectator* in 1833 was 1,903—but the figure grew to 3,346 in 1839, 3,500 in 1840, and 3,850 in 1843. It is true that it was conducted for several years at a loss, but it was probably on a paying basis by 1840. The historian of the *Spectator* says, "The stamp returns of 1832 showed an increase of 52,950 copies in the year's circulation—or over 1,000 a week. It was second only to that of *John Bull* among the eleven weekly papers."[119]

When Jerdan boasted of the *Gazette's* circulation, he of course ignored the *Quarterly Review* and the *Edinburgh Review,* which were not "purely literary papers." But the circulations of these powerful quarterlies were not large.

[115] The *Literary Gazette* had a circulation of 3,000 not long after it was established in 1817, and it continued to grow steadily in popularity through the twenties. See A. S. Collins, *The Profession of Letters,* p. 215.

[116] Graham, *op. cit.,* p. 189.   [117] Collins, *op. cit.,* p. 212.

[118] Edmund Blunden, *Leigh Hunt and his Circle,* p. 48. Graham says (*op. cit.,* p. 314): "By 1845 the *Examiner*—then the property of Albany Fonblanque—had a circulation of 6,000 a week; and its readers were 'the intelligent and educated classes.' "

[119] William Beach Thomas, *The Story of the Spectator,* pp. 40-41. This indicates a circulation of about a thousand during the first years, since after the increase here spoken of the weekly sale was only 1,903. The paper suffered a loss of from 7,000 to 8,000 pounds the first two years, according to Thomas.

Graham says, "In ten years the *Edinburgh's* circulation had grown to 10,000 copies; by 1818 it had reached its peak of 14,000."[120]

The only definite figures we have concerning the sale of the *Athenaeum* are a little confusing. When Reynolds, excited about the proposed lowering of the price to 4*d.* in 1831, says, "Remember what an increase must take place to get it all home. A sale of 6,000! Mercy on us!" it seems obvious he thought it a little preposterous that Dilke should have believed such a figure attainable. And we know that Dilke had hoped at first only to double the sale, whereas it had increased six-fold on the second day of the experiment.[121] This would seem to indicate a circulation of 3,000 before and 18,000 after the change, and that is most probable. With 3,000 the magazine could plod along but could not make a profit for its owner; and with 18,000 it could boast in the very words of the *Literary Gazette* that it "enjoyed by *many thousands* the greatest circulation of any purely literary paper."[122]

In spite of the obstacle and the nuisance of the stamp tax, which increased the cost of each mailed copy by 4*d.,* the circulation grew steadily throughout the United Kingdom and beyond. A note carried on the masthead in 1832 indicates the means which were taken to avoid the stamp duty:

This Journal is published every Saturday Morning, and is received, by the early Coaches, at Birmingham, Manchester, Liverpool, Dublin, Glasgow, Edinburgh, and all other large Towns; but for the convenience of persons residing in remote places, or abroad, the weekly numbers are issued in Monthly Parts, stitched in a wrapper, and forwarded with the Magazines to all parts of the World."[123]

[120] Graham, *op. cit.,* p. 236.

[121] See *ante,* p. 36. In Reynolds's second letter he calculated the probable loss on 5,000 copies. Was this the actual sale or the anticipated one?

[122] See *ante,* p. 37.

[123] Copies sent to the booksellers by the coaches did not have to be stamped;

By the middle thirties it was generally accepted abroad as the outstanding British literary journal. In 1836 the masthead carried the announcement: "Continental Agent, M. Baudry, 9, rue Coq-St. Honoré, Paris." And in the same year a full-page advertisement on the back of the *Athenaeum* announced that Richard James Kennett, agent in London for American books, had "opened an agency for the supply of the *Athenaeum,* which journal he undertakes to forward regularly, by the earliest Packets, to all persons paying a yearly subscription of 1 *l.* 2*s.* 6*d.* to Messrs. Wiley, Long & Co., New York, or Messrs. Hilliard, Gray & Co., Boston. . . ."

The sale of the *Athenaeum* was undoubtedly increased abroad by the prompt attention it gave to foreign literature, art, and science. The editor made note of a significant incident in 1837:

Mr. Bentley has, we think, judged rightly that a translation of the last work of the gossiping, travelling Prince Puckler Muskau would be interesting to the public; and the sincerity of our opinion is proved by our having noticed it at some length on its first appearance in Germany. We have nothing to add to our former translations except a short passage relating to ourselves—"I found in Sfax (the Prince writes) some French newspapers. . . . I also found the English *Athenaeum,* wherein, singularly enough, I read, here in Africa, the first review, and that in *English,* of my *German* book with an *Italian* title."—Sfax is some sixty miles from Tunis. We mention this, for though the *Athenaeum,* it appears, is to be met with even in that remote corner of Africa, the place itself is not to be found in many maps. We may add this fact to the letter of the French Consul in Albania (see *Athenaeum,* 1836, p. 224), who also first read an account of the travels of his celebrated countrymen MM. Michaud and Poujoulat, in

those stitched together into monthly parts paid only the tax of a single copy. "To enable its stamped . . . edition to go by post, it was necessary that it should pass for a newspaper. Consequently the high priced issue contained a digest of commercial intelligence, with an account of the corn and money markets!" (Letter from Dr. Doran, *Athenaeum,* Jan. 5, 1878, p. 21.)

this Journal, as a flattering proof of the extending influences of English periodical literature.[124]

The "Foreign Correspondence" of the *Athenaeum,* upon which Dilke particularly prided himself, included criticism and gossip of all the European capitals and centers of art, and covered not only literary news but also (at various times, according to the specialty of the correspondent) painting, drama, opera, music festivals, exploration, and scientific developments. Sometimes the correspondence was from members of the staff sent abroad for that purpose, such as Henry Chorley (music); George Darley (art, drama), who, in his letters from Rome, Florence, and elsewhere, awakened interest in early Italian painting before Ruskin began to make discoveries there; and Mrs. Sarah Austin (German and French literature and politics). Sometimes it was from English citizens resident abroad, such as Mr. and Mrs. T. A. Trollope (Italian literature and civilization). And often it came from foreigners at home in their own countries, such as Liebig (chemistry), and Gayangos (Spanish affairs). The current interest in travel and exploration was reflected in the letters from d'Abbadie, exploring in Abyssinia and the upper waters of the Nile.

Dilke tried for a time to carry foreign correspondence from the United States, but he finally gave it up because most of the material had already been anticipated in English journals which were not bound by international copyright.[125] Dilke's attitude in general towards things American was

[124] *Athenaeum,* April 15, 1837, p. 263.

[125] Dilke wrote to Elizabeth Barrett, who had wished to secure the post of American correspondent for a friend of the editor of *Graham's Magazine:* "An American friend [probably B. B. Thatcher] who had been long in England, and often conversed with me on the subject, resolved on his return to establish such a correspondence. In all things worth knowing—all reviews of good books . . . he was anticipated, and after some months he was driven of necessity to geological surveys, centenary celebrations, progress of railroads, manufactures, etc., and thus the project was abandoned altogether." (Quoted, *Letters of Elizabeth Barrett Browning,* ed. Kenyon, I, 133-134.)

much more favorable than had been that of his predecessors
on the *Athenaeum* or than that of most other British journals. While such writers as Mrs. Frances Trollope could
sneer at "The Domestic Manners of the Americans," he was
more inclined to be prejudiced in favor of the ways of
American democracy.[126]

The close friendship which Dilke and his associates
maintained through a long period of years with eminent
Continental literary men, scientists, musicians, and artists,
helped to keep them in touch with the main currents of
civilization in all the European centers, and also furnished
the *Athenaeum* with an extraordinary array of foreign correspondents. To mention only a few, Dilke's friends abroad
included Sainte-Beuve, Janin, Heine, Quetelet, Dr. Seoane
(an exile from Spain who returned there in 1834 and took
an active part in Spanish affairs), and Edmond About. Most
of these wrote for the *Athenaeum* frequently at various
periods. Henry Chorley, music critic and Dilke's right-hand
man for many years, was an intimate friend of Mendelssohn
and Moscheles, and knew personally most of the great composers and musicians in France and Germany, visited them
abroad, and carried on a wide correspondence with them.
Mrs. Austin, a close friend of Dilke for a quarter of a century and for some time correspondent from Berlin, Munich,
Paris, and elsewhere, "brought the *Athenaeum* into pleasant
relations with Grimm in Germany, and with the leading
literary Orleanists and moderate Republicans of France,"[127]
as well as with Humboldt, De Vigny, and Cousin, the last
of whom wrote largely for the journal between 1834 and
1848.

---

[126] A review of the *New England Magazine* (Sept. 19, 1835, p. 711) begins:
"Whatever injustice the Americans may heretofore have had to complain of, it
must be admitted, that their literature has of late years been fully, and we hope
dispassionately, considered in the *Athenaeum*."

[127] *Papers of a Critic,* I, 35.

As early as September, 1833, the *Athenaeum* announced a series of articles on foreign literature of the nineteenth century from various hands, to begin the following year. The first appeared on April 19, 1834; it was an article on the literature of Spain by Don A. Galiano. There followed in the course of the next three years serial articles on American literature, by the Rev. Timothy Flint, and by N. P. Willis; on French literature, by Jules Janin; on the literature of Germany, by D. Wolff;[128] and others, including three articles on the literary scene in the Othoman Empire, by Von Hammer.

A whole chapter or an entire book could be written on the reviewing of foreign works in the *Athenaeum,* but it is impossible to say more here than that Dilke was especially assiduous in assigning such works to specialists, not only in the language in which the book was written but also in the subject with which it dealt. That he did not always succeed was only natural. The more remarkable fact is that of all British journals in the early Victorian period probably only the *Foreign Quarterly Review* and the *Westminster* competed with the *Athenaeum* in an open-minded and understanding attitude toward foreign literature, and none covered the field more thoroughly.[129]

[128] It is a curious fact that Heinrich Heine had been asked to contribute the series on German literature, but when the first article arrived it was found to be too strong a potion for *Athenaeum* readers. "We cannot consent to publish the first of the series," the editor confessed rather reluctantly in the "Weekly Gossip" column. It was an article touching religion, "full of splendid passages, but sarcastic, withering, and appalling. . . ." (*Athenaeum,* Feb. 15, 1834, p. 127.) The second paper was delayed beyond what appeared reasonable, and the editor, being "a little alarmed by the doctrines inculcated in the first," applied to Prof. Wolff to continue the series. (*Athenaeum,* Dec. 20, 1834, p. 922.) It is possible that Dilke would have liked to publish the article, but saw the impossibility of it in a journal which was in the first place committed to the policy of eschewing religious controversy and which could not afford to offend or shock its middle-class readers whose liberalism and tolerance did not extend to religious scepticism such as Heine's, however willing they may have been to welcome an honest English doubt like Tennyson's.

[129] This seems to be the conclusion arrived at by those who have made a

The typical English attitude towards foreign literature at the time is well enough illustrated in the letters which Letitia Elizabeth Landon (the well-known L. E. L., purveyor of sentimental poetry and criticism to the *Literary Gazette* and other periodicals as well as to the annuals) wrote to her friend William Jerdan from Paris in 1834. She was enthusiastic about her discoveries but a little frightened too. "I am sure a most delightful series of articles might be written on French literature. *We* know nothing of it; and it would require an immense deal of softening and adaptation to suit it to English taste."[130] After meeting Heine and Sainte-Beuve, she wrote: "We have not an idea of French literature in England. As far as I can judge, it is full of novelty, vivid conceptions, and, I must say, genius, but what we should call blasphemous and indelicate to the last degree."[131]

It was in the realm of the proprieties that most British criticism of French literature lost perspective. It is impossible to generalize with accuracy or assurance from so vast an amount of varied criticism as the *Athenaeum* presents in the field of foreign literature, but a considerable reading of it gives the impression that while Dilke's critics were not less fallible than those of other journals where the proprieties

---

study of the reputations of foreign writers, particularly French, in England in the nineteenth century. E.g., see Kenneth Ward Hooker, *The Fortunes of Victor Hugo in England*, pp. 20, 81-83. Mr. J. L. Gordon, who is making a study of English criticism of Balzac, informs me that on the whole the *Athenaeum* was less hostile in its appraisal of that much attacked writer than the majority of British literary journals. In spite of the fact that Janin, the Paris correspondent in the middle thirties, was a notorious enemy of Balzac, the reviews in the thirties and forties were less unfavorable than the general trend, but in the fifties (under Hepworth Dixon) they were more severe than the average. E.g., see a scathing review of *The Married Unmarried*, a play based on Balzac's short story, *La Grande Bretèche*, *Athenaeum*, April 1, 1854, p. 413. (This review was possibly by Abraham Heraud, who was doing the dramatic notices at the time.)

[130] Jerdan, *op. cit.*, III, 196.   [131] *Ibid.*, pp. 199-200.

were concerned,[132] they were more receptive, more understanding, and more tolerant than the average when dealing
with the social, political, or artistic ideas of foreigners.
But even this generalization breaks down unless one makes
a distinction between the criticism of Dilke's "specialists,"
who were usually conversant enough with the subjects
they wrote about to make fair judgments, and the staff reviewers of the stamp of the Rev. Hobart Caunter, Henry
Chorley, and W. Cooke Taylor, into whose not too competent hands a great many foreign works fell. The vast
bulk of foreign criticism in the *Athenaeum,* however, made
at least an attempt at fairness which was uncommon among
the majority of English literary periodicals.

In fact, so much attention did the magazine pay to foreign literature in the first years of Dilke's regime that some
well-disposed English critics gave the editor a friendly warning. In a highly commendatory article on the *Athenaeum*
occupying three columns in the *Liverpool Journal* in September, 1833, it was objected that Dilke's paper had "latterly
become too much of a foreign review." The editor of the
Journal added in a note:

We have a curious proof of this in the *Athenaeum* of the 31st
August. It contains *nine* leading reviews—of one American, three
German, two Italian, one French, and three English works. We
find that the Editor takes credit to himself for this. He says, 'If
we had not fortunately opened for ourselves an inexhaustible re-
source in foreign literature, our paper would have been a blank,
or our readers wearied with everlasting quotations from books
that must, by this time, have passed through half the circulation
libraries and reading-rooms in the kingdom.' In the present dearth
of new and good English works, there may be truth in this; but

[132] The *Athenaeum* never quoted anything from foreign literature which the
young girl might not read. A note left in the British Museum file of the
Athenaeum, apparently by someone who had been studying Dilke's articles on
Pope, says: "Dilke was a notorious sexual whitewasher."

the complaint is, that, at *all* times the Athenaeum is too diffuse in notices of foreign works.[133]

The reply of Dilke to this was that on the 31st August, "there was not a single English work entitled to a leading review *that had not been reviewed*," and that the whole space devoted to foreign literature was largely made up with extra sheets and therefore was really an addition to the magazine. "The *Athenaeum* now reflects not merely the progress and advance of literature and science in this country, but throughout the world."[134]

The editor evidently had the criticism of the *Liverpool Journal* in mind, however, when, the following week, he announced the series of papers on the "Literature of the Nineteenth Century" (to include articles on writers of all the European countries and America), and added that on such occasions an extra half sheet would be given, and that the first of the series would be Allan Cunningham's articles on "British Literature of the Last Fifty Years" (which appeared simultaneously in the *Revue des Deux Mondes*).[135]

It is perhaps fair to say that in his attention to foreign literature, as in his attempts to maintain the critical independence of the *Athenaeum* against the sinister influences of "trade criticism," Dilke was but leaning over backwards to correct a fault. His efforts to counteract the provincialism of English literary criticism antedated by many years the better known attempts of Matthew Arnold; and it is possible that Dilke's work was more effective.

The same thoroughness characterized the handling of scientific matters in the *Athenaeum*. In fact, a whole history

---

[133] Quoted in *Athenaeum*, Sept. 14, 1833, p. 622.

[134] *Ibid.*

[135] The *Athenaeum* continued throughout its history to give large space to foreign literatures, not only in reviews of new works published abroad but also in special articles. See, for example, "The Literature of Europe and America in 1869," *Athenaeum*, Dec. 25, 1869, pp. 853-866; and "Continental Literature in 1871," *Athenaeum*, Dec. 30, 1871, pp. 861-884.

of science in the Victorian era might be written from the pages of that journal alone, for it chronicled in detail the meetings of all the scientific societies, Geographical, Astronomical, Botanical, Horticultural, and Ornithological.[136] It gave the fullest reports of the Royal Society, the Royal College of Physicians, and the British Association for the Advancement of Science. Moreover, Dilke secured the outstanding scientists in each field to make the reports: Airy, Herschel, Russell, Lindley, Yarrell, Bucher, Washington, Augustus De Morgan, Sedgwick, Playfair, and Lyell. In the late thirties and forties he devoted whole numbers for two or three consecutive weeks to complete reports of the annual meetings of the British Association. In addition, all important, and many unimportant, scientific books, from Darwin's *Voyage of the Beagle* and Lyell's works on Geology to *The Origin of Species* and *The Descent of Man,* were reviewed carefully and at length in the columns of the *Athenaeum,* usually by a competent, and frequently by an outstanding, scientist. And the pages of the magazine were always open to correspondence on scientific matters and to scientific controversy.[137] Much space was given also to original articles on the more spectacular aspects of the advance of science. Many columns were filled with accounts, written by John Scott Russell,[138] of the progress of

[136] In 1836, for example, the index lists extensive reports of the meetings of the following societies: Royal Society, Royal Geographical Society, Statistical Society, Royal Asiatic Society, Royal Society of Literature, Geological Society, Institution of Civil Engineers, Society of Antiquaries, Ashmolean Society (Oxford), Meteorological Society, Zoological Society, Institute of British Architects, Astronomical Society, Oriental Translation Fund, College of Physicians, Horticultural Society, Medico-Botanical Society, Entomological Society, Linnaean Society, Society of Arts, Association of German Naturalists, Westminster Medical Society, Botanical Society, and British Association for the Advancement of Science. Most of these were reported by members of the societies concerned.

[137] For a discussion of the attitude of the *Athenaeum* at a later time towards Darwinism, see *post,* pp. 92-93.

[138] Russell was a civil engineer of considerable fame in the middle of the century. A shipbuilder on the Thames for some years, he constructed the

railways and steam transportation. A full report of the first steam crossing of the Atlantic Ocean was given prominence in several numbers.[139]

Within a short time after Dilke took control, the *Athenaeum* was much more "authoritative," in a certain sense, in its scientific departments than in its literary reviews. In its account of what was currently interesting to the scientific world, it was no more complete, perhaps, than in its survey of the belles lettres, but the recording and the interpretation of the former was much more often in the hands of specialists and outstanding men. One may judge, however, that for that very reason sometimes it was committed to the essential conservatism and distrust of daring new experiment or theory not uncommon among men whose reputations are established and who for the most part form the bulwark of the scientific societies and institutions. Dilke nevertheless had on the whole a remarkable knack for singling out men who were forward-looking as well as famous in their scientific research; so that it is not unsafe to venture the generalization that while he had active control of its policies the *Athenaeum* was more receptive to the new in science than in arts or letters.

The musical criticism of the journal can hardly be summarized in a paragraph. Henry Chorley, who wrote most of it, was a man with strong prejudices, but at the same

---

"Great Eastern," and was joint designer of the "Warrior," the first sea-going armored cruiser. (See *D. N. B.* article.)

[139] See *Athenaeum,* May 26, 1838, p. 376: "The great experiment of traversing 'the vast Atlantic' by the aid of steam has been triumphantly successful; the *Sirius* and the *Great Western* once again ride proudly in British ports. The *Sirius,* as we announced, left Cork on the 4th of April, and arrived at New York on the 23rd, St. George's Day!" See also *Athenaeum,* Jan. 5, 1839, pp. 5-8. A review by Russell of several prospectuses of steamship companies proclaims: "Steam navigation, hitherto in its infancy, is now rapidly advancing to gigantic maturity." Later in the same year (July 13, pp. 515-18) a three-page leading article by Russell discussed the status and the problems of "Steam Navigation to India." On Jan. 23, 1836, the *Athenaeum* ran an article with full page "Map of Railways in operation, in progress, and in contemplation."

time he possessed a great range of sympathies and interests. As his biographer says, he had a wide though not always a deep knowledge of music. His acute ear and retentive memory enabled him to acquire a sort of professional education from attendance at all the best London concerts and operas, and he improved his education by frequent travel on the Continent to hear music and meet musicians he could not meet in England. He visited France in 1836, 1837, 1839; and Germany in 1839, 1840, 1841. In 1834, "within a year after his connection with the 'Athenaeum,' he seems to have been entrusted with the direction of its musical department; and thenceforth the notices of opera and concert performances, together with the reviews of new music, continued to be written by him almost exclusively, down to the year 1868."[140]

During that time he passed judgment on such people as Rossini, Mendelssohn, Meyerbeer, Paganini, Liszt, Thalberg, Ernst, Malibran, Grisi, Rubini, Gounod, Jenny Lind, Chopin, whom he met in Paris, and Berlioz.[141] His *Music and Manners in France and North Germany* (1841) gave Chorley the reputation on the Continent as *the* English authority on music. And in England he had then become a "power" in musical criticism. In his later life he prided himself on his friendship with Mendelssohn, whom he met in Germany in 1839 and whom he admired above all other contemporary composers, on his fight against operatic "puffery" then com-

---

[140] Chorley, *op. cit.*, I, 284. For further discussion of Chorley's contribution to musical criticism, see Ernest Newman's introduction to the latest edition of Chorley's *Thirty Years' Musical Recollections*, London, 1926. Chorley's point of view in literary criticism will be discussed in Chapter III.

[141] See Chorley, *Autobiography*, I, 297-299. Chorley "went into raptures over Grisi, but was not quite so enthusiastic in later years as her admirers could wish." He wrote in his journal, Aug., 1839: "Grisi (in 'Norma') singing false, and certainly falling off." See also II, 86-87: In 1847 he raised a single voice of protest against the "chorus of idolatry" of Jenny Lind. This brought on him "such ignominy as belongs to the idiotic slanderer. Old and seemingly solid friendships were broken forever in that year."

mon among music journalists, and on his "discovery" of Gounod and his prophecy of the success of "Faust." In general Chorley favored the classic and French schools. He had little sympathy for the modern Germans such as Schumann and Wagner, and used his critical influence to prevent them from gaining a permanent foothold in England.[142]

Criticism of drama and opera in the *Athenaeum* was as conscientious as it was thorough. Charles Dance and George Darley were the chief dramatic critics in the thirties. Every performance was reported with an independence of judgment which was sometimes startling, not to say annoying, to many playwrights, producers, and actors. The easy-going Chorley, who also did dramatic reviewing, has recorded that Darley, on his return from abroad (1835) "took up in the 'Athenaeum' the position of dramatic reviewer—not critic to the hour—in the most truculent and uncompromising fashion conceivable."[143] Darley's severe handling of Talfourd's *Ion* (a great success when acted by Macready and Ellen Tree), when it was published by Moxon before the opening night, caused not only anger in author, producer, and actors, but also contempt for Chorley, whom Talfourd believed to be the author of the offending review.[144] The week-by-week dramatic criticism by Chorley, Abraham Heraud, and others, however, was not so caustic, though frequently not eulogistic enough to suit the managers. At one time Dilke waged war against the play-bill puffery at Drury Lane Theatre, and championed the *True Sun,* whose critic had been refused complimentary tickets because he dared to speak unfavorably of the productions of that theatre. The *Athenaeum* maintained that it would be better for periodicals to buy their tickets and so keep their independence of critical judgment.[145]

[142] *Ibid.,* II, 192-193. [143] *Ibid.,* I, 113.

[144] *Ibid.,* pp. 113-116. See also C. Colleer Abbott, *Life and Letters of George Darley,* pp. 144-45.

[145] See *Athenaeum,* Oct. 15, 1831, p. 670; Jan. 5, 1833, pp. 11-12; Feb. 2,

The art criticism of the *Athenaeum* was mainly of the kind which was in general harmony with the growing demand for popularization in all fields of knowledge and culture. To supply that demand in the realm of art, Allan Cunningham had published his *Lives of the Most Eminent British Painters, Sculptors, and Architects.* In 1831 he wrote a series of articles for the *Athenaeum* called "Living Artists," in which he took a safe and conventional view and avoided violent controversy on art theory such as Ruskin was soon to indulge in. The increasing prestige of magazines and weekly journals was opening the way for a new art criticism by journalists and amateurs rather than connoisseurs. There was an "attempt to reach a public whose taste was not definitely fixed, which was open to arguments from a variety of authorities, and which had little connection with polite society as such."[146] It is significant that the two chief art critics for the *Athenaeum* while Dilke was editor—Cunningham and Darley—were literary men primarily and self-taught amateurs in art.[147]

In art as in literary criticism the *Athenaeum* reflected the intelligent average trends of the times, but it was not the champion of any radical departures of new schools. It

---

1833, p. 76; Oct. 19, 1833, pp. 699-700. Leigh Hunt as dramatic critic (about 1805) for *The News,* edited by his brother, had kept his liberty of judgment by paying for his theatre seats. (See Edmund Blunden, *Leigh Hunt and His Circle,* pp. 42-43.)

[146] Henry Ladd, *The Victorian Morality of Art,* p. 43.

[147] For further discussion of Darley's principles as art critic, see the section on Ruskin in Chapter IV. See also Abbott, *op. cit.,* pp. 158-97. Cunningham's art criticism is taken up in some detail in Chapter III. John Hamilton Reynolds was also a reviewer of exhibitions of painting in 1830 and 1831. (See Chapter III.) Henry Chorley, man of all work, was an art critic of a grade considerably below these three. Hewlett, a friend of his later years, says: "The principal critiques upon Exhibitions of Works of Art (Royal Academy, British Institution, Water-Colour Society, etc.) that appeared in the 'Athenaeum' from 1836 to 1841, and several others of later date, were written by Chorley. So far as I have examined them they deal only with the poetical element of the subject, and make no pretension to technical connoisseurship." (Chorley, *op. cit.,* I, 138n.)

mirrored the slow but certain change which was affecting taste with the decline in this period of the tradition of the grand style and the growth of naturalism in painting and the other arts. The *Athenaeum* critics were alive to all the new movements but at no time in the vanguard of them. The increase of interest in Gothic architecture which sprang from the romantic revival of the Middle Ages had resulted in the construction of 174 new Gothic churches in England between 1818 and 1833. A critic of Ruskin says: "The magazine editors so popularized the criticism of these new monuments that one of the liveliest discussions of architectural and aesthetic principles that ever occurred in England arose over the choice of Gothic for the new Houses of Parliament."[148] In this controversy the *Athenaeum* took an active part. It gave its readers a full description of the proposed structure, with a ground plan and a perspective view engraved on steel by Mr. T. Kearnan from the adopted designs of Mr. C. Barry, the architect.[149] Francis says: "These engravings attracted great attention, as they were supplied exclusively to the *Athenaeum*. The King was so much interested that he sent to the office on the Sunday for a copy of the paper."[150]

The journal early became a depositary for miscellaneous, scholarly and antiquarian information as well as a forum for the discussion of disputed matters of literary or historical interest. Besides the papers of Dilke on Pope and Junius, there were frequent contributions by J. Payne Collier, Alexander Dyce, Sir William Ouseley, Sir Nicholas Harris Nicolas, Halliwell-Phillips, Thomas Wright, Peter Cunningham, Charles Knight, Sir Frederic Madden and T. Crofton Croker. Halliwell, Knight, and Dyce were among the first to be sceptical of Collier's emendations of Shakespeare. When the forgeries were discovered in 1852, Collier wrote letters

[148] Ladd, *op. cit.*, p. 46.
[149] May 21, 1836, pp. 358-63. [150] Francis, *op. cit.*, I, 57.

in his defense in the *Athenaeum,* and was attacked there also by Dyce and others. Dilke was on the first council of the Shakespeare Society along with Thomas Amyot, Campbell, Collier, Dyce, Halliwell, Knight, Macready, Sir Frederic Madden, Milman, and Thomas Wright.[151] To most of these the *Athenaeum* served as a forum, and many of them were regular reviewers of scholarly works for it. Later in the century practically all the outstanding scholars were occasional or frequent contributors.[152] W. J. Thoms began in the *Athenaeum* in 1846 a department called "Folk-Lore" (a term which he is said to have invented) to which correspondents were invited to contribute. Three years later, with the aid and encouragement of Dilke, Thoms started *Notes and Queries,* a journal which ever since has been a source of great assistance to scholars in all fields.[153]

Another department of considerable interest and value was started the second year of Dilke's editorship and continued throughout the journal's history, namely, "Our Weekly Gossip on Literature and Art."[154] In this column alone may be read almost a complete history of Victorian England. More valuable miscellaneous information concerning what was happening and what was being thought in the world at large as well as in the editorial offices of a literary and art journal, is packed into it than into many pages of reviews and articles. It needs only to be adequately indexed to be used to great advantage by all students of the period.

[151] See Harrison Ross Steeves, *Learned Societies and English Literary Scholarship,* pp. 98-203. The Shakespeare Society began auspiciously in 1840, but it lost influence after the debacle of Collier, who was one of its leading members. Dilke apparently took an open view on the forgeries and allowed both sides a freedom of the *Athenaeum* to discuss the matter, though Collier had been a regular reviewer of Shakespearean scholarship in the magazine.

[152] See *post,* p. 90.

[153] Dilke himself wrote a good deal for *Notes and Queries* of which he was the proprietor with Thoms (later he acquired the whole property).

[154] The first appearance of the "Weekly Gossip" was in the number of Oct. 15, 1831, p. 666.

In Dilke's regime also were initiated "Our Library Table" and "Poetry for the Million," the one giving short notices of numerous books of interest to specialists or not considered of sufficient merit to warrant a longer review, and the other giving brief space to volumes of poetry which could not be denied some value, though they were not of the high standard demanded by the critical conscience of reviewers in the main columns. Here were ranged "butterflies," like Haynes Bayly, that the *Athenaeum* critics thought it would be heartless to break on the wheel of a sterner criticism.

Though original articles were cut down to a minimum, and gave place to reviews, original poetry came to be a regular feature of the *Athenaeum* in the thirties and later, but the space given to it was seldom more than one or two columns. The great bulk of it was weak and undistinguished, to say the least, being largely written by contributors to the gift annuals. But there was also a good deal of a higher calibre from contemporary poets of at least second rank; and a number of posthumous pieces of Shelley, Keats, Coleridge, Lamb, and others saw print first in the *Athenaeum*. Much German and French poetry was first published in English translation in the journal, including some well-known pieces of Goethe, Schiller, Körner, and Hugo.

A great fund of biographical source material is to be found in the obituary notices in the *Athenaeum* in this period and later. The extent to which the writers in the *Dictionary of National Biography* have used these obituaries is indicated in the fact that the *Athenaeum* is mentioned more often perhaps than any other single source in the bibliographies at the ends of the articles.[155] No man of note

[155] "When . . . the Dictionary of National Biography was undertaken, the assistance of the *Athenaeum* was sought and given. The lists of the names whom it was proposed to include were published regularly in the journal, and readers were asked to suggest additions, correct errors, etc." ("The Athenaeum Centenary," *Nation and Athenaeum*, Jan. 14, 1928, p. 559.)

in the Victorian period died without the circumstance calling forth a biographical article written by someone competent to give an account of his life and achievements from
first-hand information. Notable examples are the articles
on Scott by his friend and countryman Allan Cunningham,
and on Lamb by Barry Cornwall.[156]

From the very beginning Dilke was careful to keep politics and religion[157] out of the *Athenaeum*, at least so far as
specific or narrower partisan discussions were concerned,
but he did not put by his beliefs for the sake of an artificial
detachment from the world of affairs. He was never merely
wishy-washy or evasive in his expression of opinion, either
in his journal or in his private correspondence with friends.[158]
So long as he was convinced of the honesty of their judgments, he gave considerable latitude to his reviewers on the
general subjects of the books they criticised, but he was consistent in avoiding the bitterness of political discussion so
common in other literary journals.

A commentary on the magazines, new and old, in the

[156] See *Athenaeum*, Oct. 6, 1832, pp. 641-653; and Jan. 3, 1835, pp. 14-15,
Jan. 24, 1835, pp. 71-73, and Feb. 7, 1835, pp. 107-110.

[157] Elizabeth Barrett wrote to H. S. Boyd, Jan. 13, 1842 (*Letters of Elizabeth
Barrett Browning,* ed. Kenyon, I, 97): "I had a letter today from Mr. Dilke, who
agrees to everything, closes with the idea about 'Christian Greek Poets' (only
begging me to keep away from theology)." Later she sent some of Boyd's
poems to the *Athenaeum:* "They are not inserted, as I anticipated. The religious
character was a sufficient objection—their character of *prayer.* Mr. Dilke begged
me once, while I was writing for him, to write the name of God and Jesus
Christ as little as I could, because those names did not accord with the secular
character of the journal!" (*Ibid.,* p. 117.)

[158] Allan Cunningham twitted Dilke on his radicalism in a letter in 1834.
(See *Papers of a Critic,* I, 31.) Dilke had many friends among the radicals,
philosophical and otherwise, a number of whom were associated with the *Athenaeum* in its early years: John Bowring, Lady Morgan, Sir Charles Morgan,
Thomas Hood. Hood wrote to the editor in 1838, apropos of Rowland Hill's
postage scheme and the use of franks by rich men: "But I'm a low-lived, un-
genteel, villainous, blackguard Radical. There is a deep stigma on the Have-nots
trying to take from the Have-somethings, but what ought to be the stigma
on the have-every-things trying to take from the Have-nothings? Chorley has
proclaimed me a 'Liberal'; I don't mind being called at once a Moderate Republican." (Walter Jerrold, *Thomas Hood: His Life and Times,* p. 392n.)

"Weekly Gossip" column in 1832 regrets that there is a
"political tone" creeping into some of the literary magazines.[159] But Dilke's friend, Lady Morgan, who handled a
great many subjects of political import in both reviews and
articles for the *Athenaeum,* spoke her mind freely on most
occasions, though she assumed, like the majority of *Athenaeum* critics, to take a higher view of questions of the
hour than that of the decidedly partisan journals. In 1839
she wrote a long paragraph in the "Weekly Gossip" on
articles in the *Quarterly* with "combustible" political feeling.
"Are we," she asks, "by accustoming ourselves to speak
daggers, to become fitted to use them in defense of selfish interests? It is certain, that within the last few years a great
change has come over the English mind; and that change is
proceeding with accelerated movement. This must be followed by corresponding changes in institutions and material
interests; and whether the breaking up of old habits and
forms of thought is the commencement of a state of decay
and drivelling, or the harbinger of a new and more healthful condition of intellect, is a question to which philosophy
and patriotism must soon turn with anxiety."[160] She concluded that these "gunpowder" articles were merely indicative of the state of "babbling bigotry" into which
discussions of political questions had fallen.

It would be possible to find examples enough of the
political sympathies of the editor reflected in many reviews
and articles of this period; more, however, in the radical
view of social problems than in any commitment on immediate political issues. A signed article by William Howitt
in 1833 "On the Present State of our Manufacturing Population; and on the General Spirit of the Age" is a very
modern-sounding, socialistic protest against the evils of cap-
italism and laissez faire. Howitt reviews the agitation against

[159] *Athenaeum,* March 3, 1832, p. 146.
[160] *Athenaeum,* June 29, 1839, p. 485.

machinery and thinks it not justified in the long view, but sees in the abuses of the factory system a strengthening of the arguments of those who would revert to hand labor. The "progress and poverty" everywhere apparent he says, may be traced to laissez faire. He anticipates Ruskin in pleading for a humanized political economy: "The maxims of political science are already too hard upon the poor, too favourable to the keen spirit of grasping avarice."[161]

While Lady Morgan and Howitt were fundamentally far enough apart in their political and social philosophies, they both leaned sufficiently towards democratic humanitarianism to gain the approval of Dilke, who gave them a pretty free rein in articles and reviews. It is a bit curious, however, that Dilke also apparently countenanced the views of W. Cooke Taylor, prolific reviewer and chief spokesman in the *Athenaeum* for that most central and most persistent view of reform in the early Victorian period—progress through moral education. Taylor was assigned to review most of the books on the condition of the laboring classes, of which a great many were published in the decade following the first Reform Bill.[162] His cautious liberalism is apparent in a review of two books of this class in 1833.

Though we do not believe with Mr. Owen, that Morality is wholly the creature of circumstances, yet we cannot hide from ourselves that there may be situations fatal to the development of the social and domestic virtues. . . .

Mr. Wade's politics are of the radical hue, and therefore we place the more value on his support of a position which, though evident in every page of history, is too often practically discredited. It is this: that the lower ranks have owed their advancement in civilization and freedom to the exertions of the classes above them, and not to members of their own community.

[161] March 16, 1833, pp. 168-169.

[162] Taylor was himself the author of a volume called *Tour in the Manufacturing Districts of Lancashire* (1842).

In fact the inferior classes in most countries have been the chief obstacle to their improvement. . . . Hence it follows, that utility prescribes a limit to the diffusion of political power among the people, and that limit is the competency of exercising the power. Both Messrs. Gaskell and Wade insist on the advantages of diffusing education; their views on the subject are sound and practical.[163]

Such opinions, uttered with frequency by Taylor and other *Athenaeum* staff writers, kept the general tone of the social criticism in that journal in harmony with the main tendencies of the time.

It followed naturally, then, that the cause of popular education was one which the *Athenaeum* could sponsor whole-heartedly. Its stoical resolve, however, not to bend to the current demand for mere "popularization" of literature and science distinguishes it from other magazines in the "cheap literature" field. Whereas the early editors had praised very highly the *Penny Magazine* as an agent of popular education, Dilke more often deplored (and not altogether because of its rivalry to the *Athenaeum*) the unfair competition of the magazines which were cheap in content as well as in price. In discussing the periodicals in 1832 the *Athenaeum* maintains that the *Saturday Magazine* (published by the Society for Promoting Christian Knowledge) is quite as dull as the *Penny Magazine,* which is an unfair rival to other ventures because its 100,000 copies spoil the sale of more worthy publications not supported by a Society.[164] Dilke's objection was not to popular education, but to the type of education or miseducation given to the new and extended reading public, not only by penny magazines

[163] *Athenaeum*, August 3, 1833, pp. 509-510. The books being reviewed were: Wade, *History of the Middle and Working Classes* and P. Gaskell, *The Manufacturing Population of England.*

[164] July 14, 1832, p. 455. See also April 28, 1832, p. 274. On the latter date there is a defense of popular literature, but the writer again regrets the monopoly of the dull *Penny Magazine.*

but by three-volume novels and memoirs selling for a guinea and distributed by the circulating libraries. Unlike the Tory *Blackwood's,* however, which protested against the folly of the cheap periodicals giving more knowledge to the lower classes than they could handle, and so creating discontent and perhaps revolution,[165] the *Athenaeum* could look with some complacence upon the spread of literature and the arts to the lowest income groups among the literate.[166]

There were two chief forces which worked for the growth of popular and cheap literature at this time. One was the desire for profit from large sales, and the other was the wish, which became almost a religion among the more earnest Victorian reformers, to educate the people for reforms and for adjustment to the progress which was about to be ushered in (by devices and in forms about which opinions might differ, but which rested always on "knowledge," either "useful" or "moral"). Tennyson struck one of the most responsive chords of the day when he wrote: "Let knowledge grow from more to more," and he was giving expression to a widespread faith when he advocated the "broadening downward" of that knowledge and the privileges based upon it.

Popular education of the kind the *Athenaeum* desired was undoubtedly furthered by agencies which were begun for quite other reasons. Cheap reprints were known, though not common, in the eighteenth century. Alexander Donaldson and John Bell were among the first to publish such reprints in a series known as *Bell's British Poets* (1777-1789). The circulating libraries which had begun before the middle

[165] See "Noctes Ambrosianae," *Blackwood's,* Nov., 1832, pp. 847-852.

[166] A paragraph in the "Weekly Gossip" announced with pride: "Many circumstances, in themselves trifling, confirm us in the gratifying belief that Literature and the Arts are spreading among us—that they are gradually pervading and refining the immense body of the middle classes. . . . Among these pleasant indications, are the wide-spreading demands for literary institutions; of our own knowledge not less than a dozen are, at this moment, projected in different cities." (*Athenaeum,* Jan. 2, 1836, p. 15.)

of the eighteenth century, were first fostered as an aid to bookselling by William Lane, founder of the famous *Minerva Press,* who thus spread the taste for Gothic novels among his fashionable clientele in country towns.[167] Richard Phillips, founder of the *Monthly Magazine,* towards the end of the eighteenth century made a small fortune selling cheap educational books.[168] In 1805 Thomas Tegg rushed through the press 50,000 copies of *The Whole Life of Nelson* in a few hours after Trafalgar and sold them at 6*d*.[169] Tegg made a fortune in cheap reprints and abridgments of popular works. (He was the original of Twigg in Hood's *Tylney Hall,* and was mentioned by Carlyle in his plea for the Copyright bill.)

By the time the *Athenaeum* began, cheap reprints were common enough, but publishers kept up the prices on new books, and the practice, made popular by Dickens and Thackeray, of printing in shilling numbers had not yet begun. Charles Knight said of the period of the early twenties: "The very notion of cheap books stank in the nostrils, not only of the ancient magnates of the East, but of the new potentates of the West. For a new work which involved the purchase of copyright, it was the established rule that the wealthy few, to whom price was not a consideration, were alone to be depended upon for the remuneration of the author and the first profit of the publisher."[170] Constable broke the spell in 1827 with his "Miscellany" in which he produced original works at the price of reprints. "His three-and-sixpenny volumes, and his grand talk of 'a million of buyers,' made the publishing world of London believe that the mighty autocrat of Edinburgh had gone 'daft.' And so the row sneered, and persevered in its old system of fourteen-shilling octavos and two-guinea quartos. The Circulating

[167] Frank A. Mumby, *Publishing and Bookselling,* pp. 233, 248.
[168] *Ibid.,* p. 252.   [169] *Ibid.,* p. 275.
[170] Charles Knight, *op. cit.,* I, 276.

Library was scarcely then an institution to be depended upon for the purchase of a large impression, even of the most popular Novels."[171]

The high aim which the *Athenaeum* set for itself was to make literature, art, and science popular without stooping to "popularize" them. That it continued to grow in prestige and circulation with such an uncompromising policy is a fact which furnishes an index to the character and mental stamina of the serious readers of the journal. What modern periodical of a similar scope would take risks with its circulation by giving up two or three numbers in succession to nothing but the reports of a scientific association meeting, as the *Athenaeum* did frequently in the thirties and forties?

Dilke and his staff early took a definite stand for "National Education," which was first seriously discussed in the thirties. A leading review in 1836, probably by W. Cooke Taylor,[172] asserted that "the system of public instruction in England is unworthy of our age and nation; that the information communicated at the majority of our public schools is deficient both in quantity and quality; that the heads of too many seminaries are 'skulls that cannot teach and will not learn'; and that the youth of France, Germany, and America enjoy opportunities" greatly superior.[173] The reviewer said that "national education is, and ought to be, a direct duty of government. . . ." The government had delegated its power to the Church, and the Church had failed. As a remedy the writer advocated the formation of a national Board of Education which would issue certificates to guarantee the efficiency of teachers.[174] A few months later the argument for national education was continued in a review of a book on "Education Reform."

[171] *Ibid.*, p. 278.
[172] The view expressed is similar to that of Taylor in other articles on education bearing his name in the marked file.
[173] *Athenaeum*, July 9, 1836, pp. 481-482.
[174] *Ibid.*

Though everyone is agreed that education is desirable, the reviewer says, what has been done so far is just nothing.[175]

The *Athenaeum* was from the beginning a warm supporter of the new University of London, and fought outspokenly for the ideals of secular, practical, and scientific studies. Sterling's articles on the universities [1828] had analyzed the deficiencies in higher education of the traditional sort in the older institutions. He had felt that his own university (Cambridge) had miserably failed to perform its proper function. Though Dilke sometimes rather boldly criticized the administration of the University of London, he followed Maurice and Sterling in defending the principles upon which it was founded, and many of its professors were occasional or regular contributors to the *Athenaeum* after he became editor.[176]

Other movements and causes in which the *Athenaeum* took an intelligent interest were the agitation for the revision of the Copyright Law, for an International Copyright, for a Penny Post, for the repeal of the Paper Taxes (the so-called "Taxes on Knowledge"), and for reform of the British Museum and the National Gallery. It was also in the van of the fight for all the non-revolutionary humanitarian reforms which were the preoccupations of serious Victorian thinkers and writers: Social legislation (a modified govern-

[175] *Athenaeum*, Feb. 18, 1837, pp. 113-114. G. M. Young says (*Victorian England: Portrait of an Age*, pp. 60-61): ". . . any attempt at educational reform had to reckon with the most intense of Victorian emotions, sectarian animosity. It must be allowed for everywhere, and a few years later it flamed up with a vehemence which consumed the most promising experiment yet projected. Immediately on his appointment [1839] Kay-Shuttleworth produced, and the Committee of Council accepted, a plan for a Training College, complete with model school and practising school. It broke down on the question of religious instruction. The dissenters would not stand the parson in a State school. The Establishment would not stand any one else."

[176] Adolphus Bernays, Professor of German, reviewed many books on the German language and literature in the early years. Later, a great many scientists connected with the University of London were staff writers for the *Athenaeum;* Augustus de Morgan, Professor of Mathematics, was a frequent reviewer in the forties and fifties.

mental interference in housing, sanitation, and working hours), prison reform, child labor control. The "Weekly Gossip" columns gave considerable space to such matters, particularly to specific measures proposed to alleviate conditions brought about by the growth of population in manufacturing centers. The *Athenaeum* in many editorial notes and reviews advocated the repeal of the Corn Laws.[177]

Although he was a consistent champion of cheap literature, Dilke carried on for a number of years the battle for justice to authors through adequate copyright protection. The Copyright Act of Queen Anne (1709), the first copyright statute ever passed in any country, had not been very effective in stopping book piracies. In 1801 the act of 1709 was altered to extend copyright from fourteen years (renewable) to the length of the author's life or twenty-eight years, whichever was the longer. The looseness of the copyright laws, however, and the immense profits to be made from literary piracy in England as well as in America, together with the increasing output of cheap reprints in the thirties, made the copyright question a burning issue for several years until the passage of the Act of 1842, which gave the copyright for the author's life plus seven years, or should the two terms not amount to forty-two years, then for forty-two years from the date of first publication.[178]

A notable series of signed articles by Thomas Hood on "Copyright and Copywrong" appeared in the *Athenaeum* in April, 1837,[179] a series which was of service to Thomas Noon Talfourd a few weeks later when he presented and defended his Law of Copyright before the House of Com-

[177] The final repeal of the Corn Laws was hailed with unmasked enthusiasm as an act which had "opened not only the markets of the earth, but, we hope, the treasures of the mind." It was "as if a great calm had fallen down upon the national heart, amid which the voice of wisdom is at length distinctly heard." (July 11, 1846, p. 710.)

[178] See Mumby, *op. cit.*, pp. 169, 228-231.

[179] April 15, 22, 29; pp. 263-265, 285-287, 304-306.

mons. In his published speech he referred in the preface to
the "pleasure and benefit I have derived from Mr. Hood's
Letters on Copyright in the *Athenaeum,* which are admirable for sense, spirit, and humour."[180]

Pleas for International Copyright were sprinkled through
the *Athenaeum* for several years before the cause was taken
up by eminent literary men such as Dickens, Carlyle, and
Macaulay.[181] The editor could speak with feeling on the
copyright question, for his journal, because of its very popularity and its originality in fields untouched by others, was
a favored prey of literary pirates. "In the *Asiatic Journal,*
for instance, we were amused and startled to find published
as an original communication, a letter from Swan River,
which letter appeared ten or twelve months ago in this
paper; and there are half-a-dozen provincial papers, whose
whole literary stock in trade is pirated from the Athenaeum."[182]

From 1830 onward Dilke and his associates wrote systematically against the stamp, advertisement, and paper
taxes on newspapers and periodicals. Literary journals were
required to pay a stamp tax of 4*d.* upon each sheet, and the
stamp upon each advertisement was 3*s.* 6*d.*[183] In addition

---

[180] See *Athenaeum,* June 3, 1837, p. 402.

[181] A good deal was said about International Copyright in the *Athenaeum*
in 1838. See, for example, April 14, p. 273, an abstract of a proposed International Copyright Bill. After Dilke's death, his grandson saw the question in a
somewhat different light. During his trip around the world he wrote to his father
from Sukkur on May 1, 1867: "International Copyright is being pressed I see.
I should have very many reasons for opposing it, but my strongest is a political
one:—the present extraordinary circulation in America of cheap reprints of
English works tends to an intimate connection of the national minds, and thence
—of the nations." (Dilke Papers, Vol. II, Add. 43,911.)

[182] *Athenaeum,* July 4, 1835, p. 515. See also *Athenaeum,* June 9, 1832,
p. 369: The editor accuses many literary papers, including the *Literary Gazette,*
of reprinting, without giving credit, articles from the *Athenaeum.*

[183] Although Dilke (after the reduction of price had enormously increased
the circulation) inserted the advertisements free of charge in the stamped edition,
the government considered the stamped and unstamped editions as two separate
publications and collected twice on the advertisement tax, 3s. 6d. for each,

there was a duty of 3*d.* per pound upon the paper. Partial freedom from the "Taxes on Knowledge" came with the Act of 1836 which reduced the advertisement duty to 1*s.* 6*d.*, the compulsory stamp to 1d., and the paper duty to 1½d. per pound. In 1849 John Francis, publisher of the *Athenaeum,* organized a committee, including a hundred members of Parliament, which worked for the complete repeal of the duties—accomplished finally in 1861.[184]

Rowland Hill's plan for a penny post was looked upon with favor from the beginning (1837).[185] In the following year (1838) the *Athenaeum* gave considerable space and praise to the scheme, especially because of its aid to literature and the spread of knowledge.[186] When the measure was finally adopted, the "Weekly Gossip" commented: "We little imagined when we first adverted to Mr. R. Hill's plan of Post Office reform, or even when we brought under consideration the results of the Parliamentary inquiry, that within twelve months the bold measures he suggested would be sanctioned and adopted by the government."[187]

Another matter of practical reform touching the interests of literature upon which the *Athenaeum* took an active editorial stand was that connected with the agitation for the reorganization of the control and management of the British Museum. The comment of the magazine on the report of the committee appointed to investigate the condition of the Museum was that more public funds should be given to such an important national institution, that more than half of the trusteeships ought to be thrown open to election, and that men of eminence in the arts and sciences as well as those

---

making a total of 7s. for every advertisement. (See a letter from Dr. Doran on the fiftieth birthday of the *Athenaeum,* Jan. 5, 1878, p. 21.)

[184] See Francis, *op. cit.,* I, 14-16.

[185] *Athenaeum,* May 6, 1837, p. 320.

[186] April 21, 1838, pp. 281-284. (Leader.)

[187] *Athenaeum,* June 8, 1839, p. 436. See also "The Athenaeum and the Penny Post," *Nation and Athenaeum,* Supplement, Jan. 21, 1928, pp. 606-608.

having some active connection with the work of the British Museum ought to be elected. "In Germany, literature is a profession, and literary men form a great and highly respected body, possessing vast influence over society, and occupying—commanding, we might say—a large share of the attention of government. . . . In France they go a step beyond; and literature not only commands the attention of government, but literary men have of late years engrossed almost the whole power of the state."[188] Whatever we may think of that, the writer concludes, we must see the advantage that money is always forthcoming in those countries for literary and scientific objects. The *Athenaeum* made a plea for an adequate general catalogue for the Museum, and urged a more systematic organization of the management.[189] The final report of the Parliamentary Committee it called "a most lame and impotent conclusion," for it took account of neither of those important needs.[190]

An account of Dilke's cooperation with Dickens and Forster in protests against the mismanagement of the Literary Fund Society has been given in his grandson's *Memoir*.[191] To this and many other matters of more general concern the *Athenaeum* devoted considerable space in the "Weekly Gossip" columns and miscellaneous notes. Such subjects as prison reform, the housing of the London poor, the reform of criminal laws, the establishment of "ragged schools," mechanics' institutions, and public parks, the condition of the Irish people, abolition of the slave trade, the discovery of photography by Daguerre, and the invention of electrotype were discussed freely and without apology in the same column with literary and art gossip. This gave the journal a universality of interest which attracted alert Victorian readers and made it a good substitute for a newspaper.

[188] April 9, 1836, p. 249.

[189] April 23, 1836, pp. 284-286.

[190] July 16, 1836, p. 507.

[191] *Papers of a Critic*, I, 43.

There are numerous evidences of the growing prestige of the *Athenaeum* throughout the period in which Dilke was editor. Its fight for independence and its attack upon the puffing publishers first aroused the attention and gained the respect of the reading public; and then the gradually increasing solidity, authority, and fairness of its reviews, established its reputation as the most trustworthy and unbiased of the literary journals. And finally, no other literary paper gave so much reliable information and authoritative criticism of the arts and sciences. In many houses, for example, the *Athenaeum,* it has been said, was habitually read solely for the sake of its musical criticism.[192] Undoubtedly many readers were likewise attracted by its covering of news of scientific interest.

One of the first ungrudging tributes to the worth of the magazine under its new editor appeared in *Fraser's* in May, 1831, where the *Athenaeum* was welcomed as "one of the most gratifying instances of combined talent and integrity, now presented by the periodical literature of England."[193]

In the autumn of 1835 Mary Russell Mitford, one of the outstanding literary ladies of the day, wrote to her friend Miss Jephson: "Do you ever see the London weekly literary journal called the 'Athenaeum'? It is the fashionable paper now, having superseded the 'Literary Gazette.' It has such a circulation that, although published at the small price of fourpence, the income derived from it by the proprietor is said to be more than 4000 *l.* per annum."[194]

Miss Mitford's young friend and admirer, Elizabeth Barrett, showed an awed respect for the journal which was

[192] See Chorley, *op. cit.,* II, 184.   [193] P. 494. See *post,* p. 164.

[194] A. G. L'Estrange, *The Life of Mary Russell Mitford,* III, 34. Miss Mitford was disposed to feel kindly towards the *Athenaeum,* for William Howitt had just written for it a glowing encomium of her *Belford Regis, or Sketch of a Country Town. (Athenaeum,* May 2, 1835, p. 334; May 16, pp. 371-372.) The estimate of the income of the proprietor is probably not accurate, since Dilke was then putting the profits back into the business. (See *Papers of a Critic,* I, 47.)

probably general at the time among literary aspirants. She wrote to H. S. Boyd on October 14, 1836, concerning the notice which one of her first published poems had attracted: "Georgie says you want to know the verdict of the 'Athenaeum.' That paper unfortunately has been lent out of the house; but my memory enables me to send you the words very correctly, I think."[195]   Again in 1844 she wrote: "For the 'Athenaeum,' I have always held it as a journal, first—in the very first rank—both in ability and integrity; and knowing Mr. Dilke is the 'Athenaeum,' I could make no mistake in my estimation of himself. I have personal reasons for gratitude to both him and his journal, and I have always felt that it was honorable to me to have them."[196]

The *Athenaeum* was accused by some of Dilke's contemporaries, as it had been in the days of Maurice, of being dull and colorless, because it did not indulge in the extravagance of praise and vituperation of those periodicals which had a special bias, such as *Fraser's, Blackwood's,* or the *Quarterly,* or merely because of its moderate tone and its avoidance of controversy in religious and political matters. Even the friendly *Fraser's* spoke contemptuously at times of the excessive moral seriousness and the lack of humor of the *Athenaeum*. In reviewing Ainsworth's *High-ways and Low-ways* the *Fraser* critic said:

The *Literary Gazette* and the *Athenaeum* have also put forth their opinions of the work. But forasmuch as the *Literary Gazette* was feeble, and the *Athenaeum* flippant on the subject, we should not have mentioned them, were it not that, as these publications must be supported by readers of some class, they cannot be wholly without influence. . . . As regards the *Athenaeum,* we may say that, though not so indiscriminate in its praise, it is often indiscreet both in praise and censure; and it not unfrequently assumes a tone of mingled authority and levity to which neither its rank nor wit entitle it. It is a sober, sensible work, and never

---

[195] *Letters*, ed. Kenyon, I, 37.   [196] *Ibid.*, p. 227.

so serious in its effects as when it attempts to be either grand or funny: on such occasions it inspires neither fear nor facetiousness, but merely that sort of feeling best expressed by the ejaculation —'Pooh!'[197]

Fraser's again accused the *Athenaeum* of dullness in discussing the latter's attitude towards the Literary Fund Club: "And with all the virtuous horror entertained by the *Athenaeum* for eating and drinking, we think that respectable rival of the *Gazette* must be duller than usual not to perceive that the club dinners must come very influentially in aid of the interests of the institution."[198]

But these were mainly the passing whims of a *Fraser* critic on a high horse writing in the customary blustering style of that magazine which attacked almost everyone. On the whole the comments in *Fraser's* indicate that it had a greater respect for the *Athenaeum* than for any other literary journal of the time. *Fraser's* praised highly the series of articles on "British Literature of the Last Fifty Years" which Allan Cunningham wrote for the *Athenaeum,* prefacing its remarks with the following: "To such of our readers as know that we rarely notice the lucubrations of other periodicals, it may seem somewhat inconsistent that the freaks of a writer in the *Athenaeum* should here form the substance of our consideration. We will explain. In the first place, the daily rising character of that publication gives importance to the opinions which its editors may think fit to promulgate, on matters connected with literature."[199]

Dilke could afford to be independent of the praise or blame of other journals, however, for he knew his audience. He had struck exactly the chord of "high seriousness" which appealed to an increasing number of intelligent readers. The general fairness of its reviews, its reliance on facts and trust in knowledge (perceived with scientific accuracy and

[197] June, 1834, p. 724.   [198] April, 1837, p. 551.   [199] Feb., 1834, p. 224.

truthfulness) to solve the problems of the individual and of society, had given the *Athenaeum* a prestige, by the time Dilke gave up the active editorship, surpassing that of even the great quarterlies. Earlier in the century a north country squire had told Tennyson's father that the *Quarterly Review* was "the next book to God's *Bible*,"[200] but after 1830 the great party journals lost much of their hold upon the public. The growth of such papers as the *Athenaeum* was both a cause and a result of the greater independence of the reading public. The new public was no longer willing to sit at the feet of arbitrary literary dictators. Carlyle said of the *Edinburgh Review* in 1849: "At present the great *Review* is considerably eclipsed, and [its] influence is quite gone."[201]

HERVEY AND DIXON

Dilke could well be proud of his accomplishment when, confident that the foundations of the journal were strong enough to support it without his constant care, he gave up the editorial chair to T. K. Hervey. On May 23, 1846, Hervey, formerly editor of *Friendship's Offering,* an Annual, who had been a regular contributor since the early years of Dilke's regime, took full control of the editorial duties, while Dilke remained in the background as proprietor and supervisor of policy.[202] John Francis, who had entered Dilke's

[200] Graham, *op. cit.*, p. 248.

[201] D. A. Wilson, *Carlyle*, IV, 121. The weekly periodicals had by that time triumphed over the quarterlies and even the monthlies. Great changes had taken place in literary journalism since Hazlitt wrote in 1822: "The Weekly Literary Journals, Gazettes, etc., they are a truly insignificant race—a sort of flimsy announcements of favoured publications—insects in letters, that are swallowed up in the larger blaze of full-orbed criticism." (Quoted in Graham, *op. cit.*, p. 314.)

[202] Dilke's success with the *Athenaeum* gave him an almost proverbial reputation for shrewdness and skill in the business management of periodicals. After he gave up the editorship of the *Athenaeum* in 1846 he was called in as "consulting physician" to put the *Daily News* on its feet. He was given absolute power in all business matters. The finances were in a precarious state. Its backers, Bradbury and Evans (Dickens's publishers) had first given the editorship to Dickens, who resigned after a few numbers, and John Forster, a close

employ in 1831 as junior clerk, had the responsibility of the business management.[203]

The policy remained very much the same under Hervey, but it was during his regime, which lasted until 1853, that the *Athenaeum* took such a lively interest in social reform movements, departing from its custom of strict neutrality in politics to urge, though only in paragraphs and short articles or editorial notes, prison reform, workmen's housing, factory legislation, the curbing of child labor, etc. Hervey and William Hepworth Dixon, who later succeeded Hervey as editor, filled the "Weekly Gossip" column in the forties with paragraphs touching these matters.

Henry Chorley perhaps felt a little chagrined that the post of editor was not given to him, for he had been Dilke's most faithful contributor for at least a dozen years, and was such a prolific writer in almost every department that many people took it for granted that he was the editor. Elizabeth Barrett, for example, before she became a contributor, wrote to H. S. Boyd (June 2, 1838): "I have seen an extract from a private letter of Mr. Chorley, editor of the *Athenaeum,* which speaks *huge* praises of my poems. If he were to say a tithe of them in print, it would be nine times above my expectation!"[204] That Dilke did not appoint Chorley as his successor may be taken as further evidence of the shrewd judgment which earned the respect of the readers of the

---

friend of both Dickens and of Dilke, became editor. The paper had been going three months when Dilke took hold. By lowering the price (June 1, 1846) from 5*d.* to 2½*d.*, he raised the circulation from 4,000 to 22,000. He continued to manage the *News* until 1849, when he left it in pretty sound condition, though the difficulty of competing with high-priced papers in news service caused Forster to resign after about a year. (See *Papers of a Critic*, I, 61-63.) Dilke also successfully launched *The Gardiner's Chronicle* which Prof. Lindley edited.

[203] See Francis, *op. cit.,* I, 10. See also *Nation and Athenaeum*, Jan. 14, 1928, p. 558.

[204] *Letters,* ed. Kenyon, I, 71. It is not surprising, then, that other writers should make the same mistake. R. W. King in his book on H. F. Cary (*The Translator of Dante*, p. 259) speaks of Chorley as "the editor of the *Athenaeum."*

Athenaeum. As much as he liked Chorley and trusted his honesty and his judgment in musical affairs, he was not unaware of the sentimental softness of the man, and also of his essential conservatism and lack of "tough-mindedness" when confronted with new ideas or problems of the day.[205] Hervey, though not the happiest choice that could have been made, was much more of Dilke's own mind in all important matters on which the *Athenaeum* wished to take a stand.

Though continuing in cordial relations with Dilke and his son, Chorley felt that Hervey showed him a lack of consideration, and that "during this gentleman's reign, an undue proportion of inferior literature was allotted to his province as a reviewer."[206] While Dilke continued to keep an eye on the *Athenaeum,* he retired more and more into his eighteenth-century studies. The result was that the magazine deteriorated, even though it had some first rate contributors and correspondents. Too much of the reviewing was given to staff members or to friends of the authors; the greater number of the important books which appeared in the forties and fifties were judged by Hervey, Chorley, and Hepworth Dixon—all third rate as critics, conservative in literary tastes, and given to panegyrical kindness when handling the works of their friends.

This was a time too when the *Athenaeum* was notorious for rather smug and pontifical judgments of authors who stepped beyond the bounds of the approved Victorian proprieties. Leigh Hunt was looked upon with suspicion be-

---

[205] Chorley, like most of the Victorian moralists, believed himself to be an advanced thinker. In his later years he wrote: "I do not remember the day of my life at which I did not earnestly believe that I was a Liberal, and feel that indignation against 'the powers that be' which time has made less violent." (Chorley, *op. cit.,* I, 34.)   But Hewlett, his literary executor and friend, drew other conclusions: "I suspect that his political opinions also were more governed by sympathy than by conviction; and that, while in virtue of the latter he was nominally a Liberal, the former stamped him, to all intents and purposes, as a Conservative." (*Ibid.,* II, 316.)   [206] Chorley, *op. cit.,* II, 2.

cause of his penchant for forbidden themes. Edmund Blunden says: "The *Athenaeum* watched Hunt with the avidity of a drill-sergeant, and was particularly concerned that at the death of Wordsworth nothing disgraceful should occur to the butt of sack."[207] This was during the time that Chorley was urging in the *Athenaeum* and elsewhere the claims of his friend Mrs. Browning to the Laureateship.[208] Hunt's book, *The Religion of the Heart*, "which *The Athenaeum* reviewed like an old lady removing a dead rat with a pair of tongs, would not seem peculiar or godless to many modern readers."[209]

Nevertheless, the reputation which Dilke had established for the magazine lived on. William Allingham wrote to Ralph Waldo Emerson, December 5, 1847:

I fear England does not on the whole receive you fitly. . . . *The Athenaeum* weekly Review, the most influential one now, I believe in England, alludes to your arrival only in a disrespectful sentence. The Editor thereof is a shrewd, prosaic, calm, harsh, sensible, 'insensible' man, who in his Review of your volume of Poems published by Chapman . . . says, after praising the language, that in 'The Problem'—the *why?* is exactly what we are at a loss to guess. Now this from one who *ex officio* is supposed to be acquainted with your writings, is rather humiliating to us all. And yet he is the best, certainly of all our weekly critics, and those who are not of his party are, nine tenths,—soft-headed, mawkish, mock-enthusiastic people.[210]

As a critical journal the *Athenaeum* declined even more under Dixon (editor from 1853 to 1869). He was a sincere

[207] Edmund Blunden, *Leigh Hunt*, p. 305.

[208] See *post*, p. 274, n. 101.

[209] Blunden, *Leigh Hunt*, p. 322. See also the amusing moral smugness in the review by Dixon of Tennyson's *Enoch Arden*, *Athenaeum*, Aug. 13, 1864, pp. 201-202. (For discussion of this review, see *post*, p. 279.)

[210] *Letters to William Allingham*, ed. H. Allingham and E. Baumer Williams, p. 41. The *Athenaeum* never was very enthusiastic about Emerson; the whole point of view of the practical reformers associated with Dilke was antithetic to Transcendentalism.

and well-meaning person, but he had neither the personality nor the character to gain the respect which Dilke had commanded.[211] It is a curious fact little to his credit that he reviewed most of his own books (at least half a dozen) in the years that he was editor.[212] Other literary papers began to arise which, though they did not eclipse the *Athenaeum*, offered strong competition. The *Saturday Review*, begun in 1855, was one of the most influential. According to H. R. Fox Bourne, "In criticism and literary culture it set an example that was much needed in 1855. 'The Athenaeum' had been in existence for twenty-seven years, and had done an immense service as an organ and censor of literature, with more than incidental reference to movements in science and art. . . . Though 'The Athenaeum' continued to be the great literary authority among newspapers, it had lost value as a safe and impartial guide before Hepworth Dixon became its editor in 1853, and Dixon's showy writing and encouragement among his contributors of the strong expression of likes and dislikes frequently grounded on noth-

---

[211] Shortly before his death, Dilke wrote to his grandson, then at Cambridge, congratulating him on his ability to make friends, and he added, ". . . of another sort of aptitude we have an example in Dixon. There is no ground of objection to his Shakespear project and conduct, but everybody seems to rejoice in the opportunity of showing a personal dislike to the man." (Dilke Papers, Add. 43,910, Vol. IV—letter of Feb. 9, 1864.) Carlyle, who had reason to be irritated at the *Athenaeum* for its critical treatment of him, never spoke but with respect of Dilke, but for Dixon he had the utmost contempt. When Miss Mulock was censured by the *Athenaeum* critic in 1860, she was comforted by Alexander Macmillan: "What does it matter what the *Athenaeum* says?" he asked. "Let them go to Jericho and fall among thieves. Words have no relation to fact or thought in such minds." Macmillan recounted that at a dinner Carlyle had been denouncing the babbling of newspapers, and Dixon said, "I should like to know everything and talk about everything." Carlyle clinched the argument later by saying: "And there's Dixon there,—he's sore distressed because his tongue is not long enough to do all the gabbling he wants to do." (Wilson, *Carlyle*, V, 390.)

[212] E.g., see his review of his *William Penn* (*Athenaeum*, Feb. 9, 1856, pp. 162-163); and of his *Personal History of Lord Bacon* (*Athenaeum*, Dec. 22, 1860, pp. 861-863.)

ing worthier or safer than personal friendships or animosities, or subservience to publishers and advertisers, caused its steady deterioration from year to year."[213]

But in circulation and profits the *Athenaeum* continued to outstrip its competitors among the weekly literary papers. In 1854 it boasted of its growing sales as indicated by the stamp returns. "As our readers know, the *Athenaeum* is not a stamped publication,—though for postal convenience a small portion of our weekly impression is issued on stamped paper. This brings us into the list prepared by the Government, without in any way indicating the extent of our circulation. . . . In these, we find that in 1851 the *Athenaeum* required 128,000 stamps; in 1852 the number rose to 140,000; and in 1853 it was 147,000."[214] The last figure would indicate a stamped circulation of nearly 3,000 a week. The total weekly sale may have been six or eight times that number.

The Right Honorable Alexander J. B. Beresford Hope, one of the founders of the *Saturday Review*, wrote later that the *Saturday* was started "with a view to make a dig into the profits of the *Athenaeum*, which clears for Dilke £5000 a year."[215] Hope "busied himself in finding out the secrets of the *Athenaeum*, which he says was edited and to a large extent written for £400 a year by Hepworth Dixon, a Quaker, the other writers being paid only at the rate of ten shillings a column."[216] But at the end of three years the sale of the *Saturday* had reached only 5,000. It forged ahead steadily for the next few years, however, and may even have surpassed the *Athenaeum* for a short while, but the latter, with the repeal of the stamp tax in 1861, lowered its price to 3*d*. (at the

---

[213] H. R. Fox Bourne, *English Newspapers, Chapters in the History of Journalism*, II, 313-314.

[214] April 8, 1854, p. 440.

[215] Henry William Law and Irene Law, *The Book of the Beresford Hopes*, p. 214.

[216] *Ibid.* Dixon was not a Quaker. Hope probably confused him with Chorley, whose family was nominally of that faith.

beginning of 1862) and again led the field of weekly periodicals in its class by a considerable margin.[217]

THE NEW ERA: THE THIRD DILKE AND NORMAN MaCCOLL

After the death of Charles Wentworth Dilke in 1864, the
property came into the hands of his son, Sir Charles Wentworth Dilke (he had accepted a baronetcy in 1862—against
the advice of his father—for his work in connection with the
Great Exhibition of 1861, of which he was one of the five
Royal Commissioners appointed by the Queen). The second Dilke took no very active interest in the conduct of the
periodical, and for the most part allowed Dixon to carry it
on as he wished, but on his death in 1869, his son, Charles
Wentworth Dilke 3rd, second baronet and apple of his
grandfather's eye, brought about a thorough reformation of
the magazine.[218] After an interval of about a year, when
Dr. John Doran,[219] a close friend of Dixon, was in charge,
Dilke put his Cambridge friend Norman MacColl in the
editor's chair, and the *Athenaeum* entered upon a new
phase of life which lasted until the end of the century.

The interest of the third Dilke in the *Athenaeum* was
something more than that of a man who has a valuable
property or profitable investment and wishes to keep it up.
To him it was a labor of love to carry on the work of the
grandfather who had trained him almost as thoroughly as

[217] The price of 3*d*. continued until Jan. 3, 1914, when it was raised to 6*d*.
According to Dr. Doran, when the *Athenaeum* reduced the price to 3*d*., "an
additional subscription list was obtained of 1,500 copies." (See *Athenaeum,*
Jan. 5, 1878, p. 21.)

[218] James Holmes, the printer, who had secured a fourth interest when Dilke
first gained control, held his share until 1869, when C. W. Dilke, III, purchased
it and became sole proprietor.

[219] Dr. Doran was a frequent contributor to the *Athenaeum* in the sixties.
An antiquarian in his interests, from 1872 until his death in 1878 he was editor
of *Notes and Queries*. The third Charles Dilke wrote to his father from Cambridge, Feb. 18, 1864: "Dr. Doran's articles are always more free from prejudice
than are his books: in the latter he thinks it his duty to moralize, which with
him means to talk cant." (Dilke Papers, Add. 43,910, Vol. IV.)

James Mill had trained his son John Stuart, but with less rigidity and more humanity and wisdom.[220] The letters which passed back and forth between grandfather and grandson while the latter was at Cambridge furnish an index to the characters of both. This correspondence (in the British Museum—unpublished) shows how meticulously and lovingly the elder Dilke directed and guided the studies of his grandson, who regarded him with a more than filial respect. It is evident that the old gentleman's mind was clear to the end and that he had not swerved from the radical leanings of his youth. Young Dilke discussed his essay reading and writing with his "Grand," as he called him, and was helped by detailed criticisms and pregnant suggestions, though he was always encouraged to form independent judgments. On July 5, 1864, he reported to his mentor: "My essay reading is going on favourably. The chief results of it upon me have been to give me a very high opinion of Godwin; and a preference for Aristotle over Plato."[221]

A disciple of Mill and an admirer of De Tocqueville, the third Dilke early became an ardent Liberal. In 1871-72 he represented the extreme radical party in England. Disraeli said that he was the most influential and powerful member of Parliament among quite young men that he had ever

[220] The second Dilke's close association with the Prince Consort and with the Conservative government made the radicalism of his son, who was a truer scion of his grandfather, sometimes embarrassing to him. His son wrote to him on the 16th December, 1867: "If I read your words rightly—you speak of my being 'too extreme.' Well, I'm a radical I know—still I have for your sake done everything I can to speak moderately. For my own part—though I should immensely like to be in Parliament, still I should feel terribly hampered there— if I went in as anything except a radical. Now I have spoken against Fenianism, in spite of my immense sympathy for it . . . radicalism is too much a thing of nature with me for me to throw it off by any effort of mine." (Dilke Papers, Add. 43,911, Vol. II.) Again, after he had obtained a seat in Parliament, he wrote: "I don't mean to let either you or Glyn frighten me into supporting the government when I think they are wrong, but I vote with them when I am at all doubtful—for instance—I voted with them against Graves on halfpenny postage which was a very tight fit for my conscience. . . ." (Dilke Papers, Add. 43,912—letter of April 18, 1869.)   [221] Dilke Papers, Add. 43,910, Vol. V.

known. If he had not been driven out of politics by a divorce scandal in 1886, it is not unlikely that he would have been Prime Minister.[222]   Though largely influenced by Mill, Dilke worked out his own political philosophy and was an independent thinker who formed his judgments from observation and experience.[223]

As early as 1864 the young Dilke, then only twenty-one, showed a live interest in the journal which his grandfather had made. In July of that year he wrote:

I have read with care the leader in this week's Athenaeum.[224] The lively opening—an instance of what Whately calls the 'introduction paradoxical'—looks like some of De Morgan's handiwork; and the general remarks upon Bentham, though the mat-

[222] In a fragment of a letter in the Dilke Papers in the British Museum (Add. 43,913) Mrs. Mark Pattison (later Lady Dilke), writing of Mrs. Grant Duff, says, " 'Dizzy,' she adds, 'predicts that Sir Charles will be premier.' " (Letter of Feb. 2, 1879.) But two days later she wrote, "Dizzy means twenty or thirty years hence. That is possible."

[223] Dilke's letters to his father and to Hepworth Dixon from various waypoints on his tour around the world in 1866-67 show that his was a mind teeming with ideas and responsive to every impression of significance to his views of political, economic and social man.   From Sydney, Australia, he sent his father a summary of some of his future literary plans, which included a work "such as that of De Tocqueville would have become had he seen Australia, and seen America now:—a kind of continuation of De Tocqueville."   He had also planned a work on "Co-operation" and on International Law, and a book on Political Economy "viewed in a modern and practical light—with stress layed on Emigration, and Facility of Communication," etc.   "I have extremely complete notes," he wrote, "towards a work on 'The History of "Radicalism" ' (treating that word *very widely*).   These I drew up in Canada, and my present tour is of some aid to me in connexion with this idea. (This is a book which I should be all my life slowly writing and improving, whereas 1 and 2 I could write and publish in a few years.)"   His last plan on the list was one which he carried out in his *Greater Britain* (1868): " 'The English World': a book on which I should be now at work did this climate allow me to work at all. In it I should propose to look to the future of countries now peopled or likely at a future time to be peopled by the English race.   I should look especially at the future of the Pacific.   At the position of the various stores of *coal* in the hands of the English race, and consequent future distribution of manufactures. I should above all consider the effect on the English race of the presence of Chinese, Irish, and German populations by its side." (Dilke Papers, Add. 43,913—letter of Jan. 4, 1867.)

[224] This was a review of Bentham's *Theory of Legislation*, July 23, 1864, pp. 103-104. Dilke was right; the review was by Augustus De Morgan, according to the marked file.

ter of them is by no means new, have been clothed with a certain amount of freshness in the telling. They are based upon Mill's article in the Westminster of '38.

I have already said all that I have to say in favour of the review, for, in my humble opinion, the account of the theory of utility given in the third column of it, while it does not pretend to philosophical completeness, is not even a clear 'popular' outline of the principle, or in any way suited for the guidance of a reader about to begin the study of Bentham's works. Again, the question at issue between the philosopher and the theologian is most inadequately summed-up. If this failure proceed from fear to speak out, the writer, even if himself an infidel, might well have shown how Austen reconciles 'Utility' with belief in a revelation and left the reader to form his own opinions as to the tenability of that author's double 'standard of reference' theory, and this without increasing the length of the paragraph. For a paper like the Athenaeum the better course would have been not to have touched at all on Bentham's method, but to have built up an article out of the consideration of the positive results arrived at by him on such questions as the following—Laws of honour, Gambling, Slavery, Sunday observance, Theatre going, Poor laws and alms giving, descent of property, marriage and divorce, State-church, all of which and many more are treated of in the volume under the title at the head of the article. On one only of these points has the writer touched—that of divorce—but he had better have left it alone than have mentioned it as he has done without extracting Bentham's plea for divorce upon consent; the most truly eloquent passage I have met with in the works of a man, who, when occasion offers, can be as eloquent as Demosthenes himself. I am not so blind a follower of Bentham as to be unable to see his faults. They are patent enough; it is his virtues and his greatness which are hidden from the general view; few of us can fail to admit the truth of Mill's remark that he was morally 'one-eyed', but I confess that I am sufficiently devoted to his principles to grieve when I see them mutilated by a friendly hand.[225]

[225] Dilke Papers, Add. 43,910, Vol. V.

The elder Dilke replied to the ardent young Cambridge student:

The criticism on the Bentham Article is excellent. You seem *to me* to prove your case. But your admissions in some degree justify the reviewer. It must ever be borne in mind that the Athenaeum is a literary newspaper. The subject is new to you, but so far as the Athenaeum is concerned is exhausted; and all that could be hoped for is 'a certain amount of freshness' in telling the ten-times told tale. I, however, am delighted with the Article, which is full of promise of a coming man by which the old journal may benefit.[226]

A short time later the grandson took an *Athenaeum* review as a starting point for a discussion of Matthew Arnold's views on education.

Matthew Arnold's essay (reviewed in last week's Athenaeum)[227] is a strange, friendless sort of waif. Up to a certain point he is in the right; that is, so long as he confines himself to demolition of existing abuses. There is no doubt but that Harrow, Eton, Rugby and Uppingham teach nothing to the ordinary boys; that they send us obstinate dunces, who may have brains, but who have long since forgotten how to use them. Shrewsbury sends up brilliant scholars who are nothing else, and Cheltenham, less brilliant men, who have this in common with Shrewsbury men—viz.—that both are for the most part drunken blackguards. To all these rules there are illustrious exceptions, Pollock from Eton, the Sidgwicks from Shrewsbury; but these men would have been what they are anywhere.

Now, to look at the opposite side of the question. Surely we cannot find a stronger argument against Matthew Arnold, than that which is to be drawn from the present state—both moral and intellectual—of France. Despotism there finds its safety in *maintaining*—nay—in *extending,* that very system which Matthew Arnold would bring among us: it is the 'Conservatoires'

[226] *Ibid.* Letter dated 28 July, [1864].
[227] See "A French Eton," *Athenaeum*, July 30, 1864, pp. 137-138. The review was by C. Cordy Jeaffreson.

and the 'Lycées' which have helped on the levelling tendencies of progress, till France has all but reached what De Tocqueville foresaw to be the worst condition of civilized man, viz.—'perfect democracy,' under monarchy; where the supreme *one* selects his instruments from among a people, all equal before the law, all having considerable school learning; but who, utterly wanting in character or soul, differ only in the extent of their superficial shrewdness.[228]

While he was still at Cambridge the third Dilke wrote a number of reviews for the *Athenaeum*. On March 15, 1866, he sent this note to Dixon from Trinity Hall:

Victor Hugo's 'Travailleurs de la Mer' has just appeared at Brussels. (I have a copy). It is all about Guernsey—a place in which I take a deep interest, and which I think I understand and know well. If you have not already sent the book to some one, or fixed on some one to review it, may I do so? It is somewhat presumptuous in me to ask to do two books at the same time, but both are pet subjects of mine. I think I could do both for next week, but Victor Hugo presses much more than Abdy.[229]

Further indication that young Dilke kept a constant interest in the paper and gave frequent advice to the editor is to be seen in several other unpublished letters to Hepworth Dixon. In one he says:

I send just a line—which pray don't answer—just to give you a hint that a book called 'Ecce Homo' is the rage here just at present. I have not read my Athenaeum carefully of late so do not know if it has been noticed:—I believe it is only just out (published by Macmillan). I have read it and think it a somewhat weak imitation of Renan without Renan's poetry—but that is but *one* opinion against a hundred.[230]

[228] Dilke Papers, *op. cit.* Letter of Aug. 6, 1864.

[229] Add. 38,794, f. 119-120. The Hugo review by Dilke appeared March 24, 1866, pp. 389-391; his review of Abdy's edition of Kent's *Commentary on International Law* came out April 7, 1866, pp. 453-454.

[230] Add. 38,794, f. 117.

From New Zealand he wrote, November 29, 1866, in a half-serious vein: "I have been, for the first time in my life, indulging in novel reading. . . . I am going to hunt up all the Athenaeum notices when I get home, and see whether I think small beer or otherwise of your staff—so bid them tremble, as I am sure they highly value my good opinion."[231]

Another letter in this group reveals the curious ego of Dixon and the decisive way in which Dilke handled the affairs of the *Athenaeum* after his father's death. Dixon apparently had wanted to publish a parting eulogy of himself when he resigned from the editorship. The new proprietor replied:

What was said when Chorley resigned was under 'Musical Gossip' and *was* musical gossip in its character. It was only an old contributor resigning on the score of infirmities. You are an editor and an editor resigning in the middle of your career—so anything said would leave the gap 'What is to come after him?' Nothing was said when my grandfather was followed by Hervey; nothing when Hervey was followed by you, and the Proprietors are of opinion that they cannot have anything said now. I hope that on thinking the matter over you will see that we could not have come to any other decision.[232]

After Norman MacColl was established as editor, however, Dilke left the policy and conduct of the *Athenaeum* almost entirely to him, being himself more and more immersed in politics, and trusting the judgment of MacColl as one of the young Cambridge men who shared his own views. He continued to keep politics and religion as such out of the editorial discussions in the magazine, though its reviews of political and historical works naturally reflected the liberal and radical leanings of its proprietor and of the new staff which MacColl gathered about him. The journal soon recovered the prestige which it had temporarily lost under

---

[231] *Ibid.*, f. 125.   [232] *Ibid.*, f. 132-133.

Hervey and Dixon, and surged ahead of all competitors to become an organ of literary criticism with unequalled influence in the late Victorian era. It was during this period that it had some of its most notable contributors and reviewers, and that it enjoyed the greatest respect of booksellers, writers, scientists, and the whole world of art and scholarship. Its reputation in the seventies and eighties for fair-minded authoritative criticism and scholarly and scientific accuracy and dependability is difficult now to realize. It is known that at least on one occasion publication of a work edited by an Oxford scholar was stopped after the appearance of the first volume because of an adverse criticism in the *Athenaeum*.[233] And it is also known to those who were acquainted with the former publisher of the magazine, Mr. John C. Francis, that at one time some of the major booksellers would not stock a book until they had seen the review in the *Athenaeum*.[234]

An increasing number of outstanding literary men of the younger generation contributed to its columns. Theodore Watts-Dunton joined the staff in 1876, and he soon became its chief reviewer of poetry and continued until the end of the century to set the tone of its literary criticism. A writer in the *Poetry Review* later in the century said: "There are middle-aged men who have learnt all they know about

[233] I am indebted to Mr. Vernon Rendall, editor of the *Athenaeum* from 1901 to 1916, for this information. According to Rendall, Robert Steele once wrote a review so severe that the publication of an edition of Roger Bacon's works was stopped.

[234] T. R. Lounsbury says: "Henry Taylor . . . wrote in 1831 to a correspondent that 'The Literary Gazette, could 'do almost anything to the sale of a book.' " (*The Life and Times of Tennyson,* p. 104.) Lounsbury adds categorically: "It is hardly necessary to observe that no literary journal was ever able to do almost anything to the sale of a book." But there is evidence that periodical criticism did affect the sale of books markedly in the nineteenth century, whatever its efficacy may be today. See, for example, the statement of Jerdan quoted in Chapter II, p. 140, n. 100, and see also Thackeray's admission that a *Times* article absolutely stopped the sale of *Henry Esmond* (*post,* p. 130, n. 78).

poetry from Mr. Watts-Dunton's delightful and profound criticisms in the *Athenaeum*."[235] Perhaps the fairest estimate, however, is that of Vernon Rendall, who says that in all his writing Watts was "a good judge of style but not a great stylist. The same criticism applies to Watts-Dunton's *Athenaeum* articles, which he himself described as 'too formless to have other than an ephemeral life.' Not lacking in good things and in generalizations of value, they are clogged with wise saws and ancient instances. They are clearsighted, and were very widely admired; but their profundity has been exaggerated."[236]

Dante Gabriel Rossetti was occasionally a contributor, and his brother William frequently wrote for the magazine after 1870. Other reviewers of note were Edmund Gosse, Andrew Lang, W. E. Henley,[237] and Richard Garnett. In the scholarly field there were frequent papers, letters, and reviews by Skeat, Furnivall, Sweet, and Trevelyan. Skeat and Furnivall reviewed each other's books in the *Athenaeum*, and contributed numerous papers on their discoveries in Anglo-Saxon and Chaucerian scholarship.

Its receptivity to new ideas and new forms in literature and the arts made the journal more forward-looking in its critical policy than it had ever been under previous editors; but at the same time it maintained a sober balance of judgment which prevented a running after temporary fashions or a blind enthusiasm for new schools. Although Watts-

[235] Quoted in Graham, *op. cit.*, p. 319.

[236] *D. N. B.* (Twentieth Century, 1912-21) article on Theodore Watts-Dunton. For further account of Watts-Dunton's connection with the *Athenaeum* see James Douglas, *Theodore Watts-Dunton: Poet, Novelist, Critic*, Chap. XIV, and Thomas Hake and Arthur Compton-Rickett, *The Life and Letters of Theodore Watts-Dunton*, Vol. I, Chap. X.

[237] Henley reviewed Meredith's *Diana of the Crossways* (*Athenaeum*, March 14, 1885, pp. 339-340) in a manner which greatly pleased the author. (See obituary of Meredith by Rendall, *Athenaeum*, May 22, 1909, p. 617.) According to the marked file, Henley also reviewed *Farina* (May 7, 1887, pp. 605-606); *Rhoda Fleming* [reprint], (July 31, 1886, pp. 137-138); *The Egoist* (Nov. 1, 1879, pp. 555-556).

Dunton, William Rossetti, and F. G. Stephens[238] gave it a decided bias towards the writers and artists of the Pre-Raphaelite school, its treatment of these was by no means entirely eulogistic.[239] The writers of the Aesthetic Movement of the nineties got a fair hearing (Walter Pater and Oscar Wilde contributed some reviews),[240] but the *Athenaeum* was not a special champion of that movement.

Voices of protest against the judgments of the *Athenaeum* in this period were not lacking. Edward Fitzgerald, who, it must be said, was rather hard to please, wrote contemptuously of the enthusiasm of Watts and others for the younger poets: "Is Mr. Rossetti a Great Poet like Browning and Morris? So the *Athenaeum* tells me. Dear me, how thick Great Poets do grow nowadays."[241] And again: "When I look at the *Athenaeum* I see there are at least four poets scarce inferior to Dante, Shakespeare, etc., Browning, Morris, D. G. Rossetti, Miss Do. They will have their day."[242] And on the other side, those severely handled in the *Athenaeum* often took as great umbrage and felt as

[238] "Mr. W. M. Rossetti writes (May, 1910), 'Frederick George Stephens was one of the seven members of the P. R. B., installed about the same time—say October, 1848—as my brother and myself. . . . In October, 1860 or 1861, he got appointed Art Critic to *The Athenaeum*, and was eventually Art Editor there. He acted thus up to the end of 1900.

'*The Athenaeum* was not declaredly an adherent of the Pre-Raphaelite School of Art; but certainly for many years, Stephens' criticisms favoured the artists of that school.' " (*Letters to William Allingham*, p. 265.)

Rendall found that Stephens wrote so badly that he dismissed him and got Roger Fry in his place.

[239] In 1850, while Hervey was editor, the *Athenaeum* had been most severe in its lecturing of the Brotherhood, calling them "the slavish imitators of artistic inefficiency." See the criticism of Rossetti's *Ecce Ancilla Domini* (April 20, 1850, p. 424), which was called crotchety, puerile, pedantic, affected and absurd, "a work evidently thrust by the artist into the eye of the spectator more with the presumption of a teacher than in the modesty of a hopeful and true aspiration after excellence."

[240] Wilde apparently wrote only one review (of Mahaffey's *Greece*), but Walter Pater was a regular contributor for a time.

[241] Quoted in Lounsbury, *op. cit.*, p. 552.

[242] Quoted in *Alfred Lord Tennyson, A Memoir*, by his son, II, 161.

wronged as did the victims of the *Quarterly* under Croker earlier in the century. Lord Houghton, whose poems were slashed by Joseph Knight, afterwards met Knight and told him he would like to kill the reviewer.[243]

At the dinner in his honor on the occasion of his retirement, Norman MacColl "contrasted the type of *Athenaeum* review with much of what has within the last few years passed for reviewing in the daily press, and argued that in the latter case the critics appeared usually to be afraid of showing their own ignorance by criticising a book, and so fell back on the safe expedient of indiscriminate praise."[244]

Another point dwelt upon by Mr. MacColl in his reminiscences was the fact that, so far from discouraging discussion of a review, he always courted it, as he believed this to be wholesome both for the reviewer and the reviewed. Mr. MacColl regretted the absence of Mr. Watts-Dunton, who for many years was mainly known to the public as a writer in the *Athenaeum*. Mr. Watts-Dunton had been regarded as the author of all the reviews of poetry which appeared in the paper, and had incurred much undeserved obloquy in consequence.[245]

While the *Athenaeum* now gave less space than in the days of the elder Dilke to science (it no longer devoted whole numbers, for example, to detailed reports of scientific meetings), it reviewed important scientific works with even greater care and competency. MacColl (in the speech referred to) mentioned that "one curious plank in the platform of the *Athenaeum* on his accession was its antipathy to Darwinism. Desiring to change the policy of the paper in this respect, Mr. MacColl engaged the services of Professor Sidgwick,[246] who (without knowing anything of the editor's motives) effected the transition with great tact, and

---

[243] I am indebted to Mr. Vernon Rendall for this information. Knight, safely ensconced behind his anonymity, could be amused at the threat, which, perhaps, was not too serious, though Houghton was undoubtedly annoyed.

[244] *Bookman* (London), March, 1901, p. 172.

[245] *Ibid.*   [246] Henry Sidgwick of Cambridge.

apparently without doing violence to anyone's susceptibilities."[247]

One of the interesting consequences of this turning to Darwinian sympathies was that the *Athenaeum* had less respect for Samuel Butler's theories of evolution than that rather crotchety writer thought they were entitled to. Butler long believed that MacColl's science reviewers (Henry Sidgwick and Ray Lankester), and also those in the literary departments, were unfair to him. In 1887 he wrote:

The *Athenaeum* attacked Erewhon savagely (Ap. 20th 1872), it sneered at *Life and Habit* (Jan. 26th 1878) which it said was "too flighty to be of much real value," yet by July 26 1879 these books had become "good reading," and it was only in the then new one that there were signs of declining power or "bad workmanship." Now (Jan. 1887) *The Athenaeum* is anxious to pretend that it was among the first to give me encouragement. . . . I may be allowed to conclude that *The Athenaeum* is not infallible.[248]

Butler added the following note to the copy which he kept of the above letter: "This is a very injudicious letter but I have no wish to pose as a monster of sound judgement. I do not think MacColl disliked or dislikes me; but he was not a pleasant person to deal with, and often gave my books to reviewers who, he perfectly well knew, would slate them of set purpose."[249]

Butler was flattered later, however, by an offer to review Grant Allen's *Charles Darwin,* though he declined on the ground that "there was too strong a personal hostility between myself and both Darwin and Grant Allen to make it possible for me to review the book without a bias against it."[250] And his feeling towards the *Athenaeum* was modi-

[247] *Bookman, op. cit.*

[248] Henry Festing Jones, *Samuel Butler: A Memoir,* II, 49.

[249] *Ibid.* The occasion of this protest was a letter by Butler on Holbein's "La Danse," to which MacColl, "on the advice of his art critic [F. G. Stephens], made objections." [250] See Jones, *op. cit.,* II, 28.

fied also by the fact that it published a number of his letters on the Darwin controversy and other matters.[251]

After MacColl became editor, the *Athenaeum* adopted a format typographically somewhat more attractive and readable. The type was changed to the equivalent of 11-point for the body and 10-point for quotations, and there was generally a more pleasing make-up, aided by wider columns and better spacing.[252] It now had to face the competition of such well-edited literary and critical periodicals as the *Saturday Review, Fortnightly, Cornhill, Macmillan's, Contemporary, Spectator,* and *Academy,* but it held its own through the century, and continued to be the most generally respected of the purely critical journals in England.

LAST YEARS

From 1901 to 1916 it was edited by Vernon Rendall, who had joined the staff as an assistant to MacColl in 1896. During that time it continued to be a literary weekly of a high caliber, and to have contributors of the first rank, but the competition was becoming keener and its preeminence was challenged by several other weeklies. When Sir Charles Dilke died in 1911, he left the property to John Collins

[251] In a letter to Miss L. I. Jones, 22 Jan. 1902, Butler said that he had recently met MacColl in the British Museum and helped him on with his coat. MacColl praised Butler's sonnet in the *Athenaeum* (Jan. 4, 1902, p. 18), but Butler was only grudgingly pleased and told his correspondent that the former editor was "a dull thing." He concluded the matter with the comment that it was probably Watts-Dunton who had written "that atrocious review" of his sonnet book in the *Athenaeum.* "He tried to cotton up to me years ago in the old *Erewhon* days, but I detested him and would have none of him." (Jones, *op. cit.,* II, 367-368.) Mr. Vernon Rendall has related to me an amusing incident indicative of Butler's attitude towards the *Athenaeum.* Shortly after Rendall became editor in 1901 Butler came into the office on some errand, and on leaving he started to back out, bowing in mock deference to the majesty of the *Athenaeum.* Rendall saw that if he took another step he would back down the stairs, and so rushed forward to save him. Butler was quite affected by this concern on the part of Rendall and apologized and became quite friendly. It was after this that he sent to Rendall the sonnet mentioned above.

[252] Except for a few slight changes in make-up the format remained the same until the beginning of the twentieth century.

Francis (publisher of the *Athenaeum* since the death of his father, John Francis, in 1882) and his cousin J. Edward Francis, the printer (nephew of John Francis). The paper continued in the Francis family for several years more.[253] From 1911 to 1916 the journal gave increasing attention to economic and political problems without abandoning its character as a literary and art journal.

From January, 1916, to March, 1919, the *Athenaeum* appeared as a 28-page monthly, but it resumed its standard form on April 4, 1919. In this interregnum it was edited by Arthur Greenwood, under whom its main feature consisted of original articles and comments on current events, politics, and social problems, the book reviews being relegated to the back pages.[254]

Another change came in 1920 when J. Middleton Murry became editor. He initiated new features, such as the "Marginalia" by "Autolycus" (A. L. Huxley). For the first time in its history it tried to lure readers by a larger type and a truly attractive appearance, but it could not recapture a reading public which had drifted to other periodicals.[255] A new feature initiated by Murry was the publication of fiction. Contributing to this department were such well-known writers as Katherine Mansfield, Anton Tchekov (in translation), Max Beerbohm, Stella Benson, J. D. Beresford, W. M. Lodge, Virginia Woolf, Stephen Hudson, Arlo Williams, and Robert Nichols. Poets contributing frequently were Thomas Hardy, Edwin Arlington Robinson, Edith Sitwell, Robert Graves, Lawrence Binyon, Conrad Aiken, T. S. Eliot, Edmund Blunden, W. H. Davies, Eden Phillpotts, Wilfred Owen, Julian Huxley, and W. W. Gibson.

[253] John Collins Francis died in 1916, and from that time until 1931 his nephew was the proprietor of the *Athenaeum* and, after the amalgamation, of the *Nation and Athenaeum*.

[254] A. W. Evans was literary editor under Greenwood.

[255] Greenwood had initiated a peculiar make-up wherein current events were given a 2-column page, and the reviews were printed on 3-column pages.

Literary and critical articles appeared from the pens of H. M. Tomlinson (literary editor, 1917-23), R. W. Chapman, T. S. Eliot, George Santayana, W. J. Lawrence, Bonamy Dobree, Logan Pearsall Smith, A. A. Milne, Katherine Mansfield, and Murry.[256]

With all this talent, however, the days of the *Athenaeum* as an individual literary journal were numbered. On February 11, 1921, it merged with the *Nation* (edited since its beginning in 1907 by H. J. Massingham), and for ten years it ran as the *Nation and Athenaeum,* edited (1923-30) by H. D. Henderson. Edmund Blunden was for a time literary editor. It was, however, no longer strictly a literary review. Like most other London weeklies, it gave the larger part of its space to current affairs, politics, and economics.

Finally, in 1931 the paper was purchased by the *New Statesman,* and it has continued as the *New Statesman and Nation, "Incorporating the Athenaeum."*[257]

[256] See Graham, *op. cit.,* pp. 319-320.

[257] From Feb. 28, 1931, to Jan. 6, 1934, the title was *The New Statesman and Nation,* [and, in smaller letters underneath] *Incorporating the Athenaeum.* Since the latter date, the last part of the title has been omitted and *The Week End Review* (incorporated with the *New Statesman and Nation* Jan. 13, 1934) substituted for it. But a reference to the old magazine was still carried in small italics at the head of the first column: "Incorporating the *New Statesman, Nation and Athenaeum, Week End Review.*"

Chapter 2: The Fight Against Puffery

AN INDEPENDENT LITERARY JOURNAL

Last, but far from least, among these journals, stands the *clarum et venerabile nomen* of the *Athenaeum*—in some respects perhaps the most notable literary achievement of the Victorian age, and one certainly not surpassed, in its kind, by any journal of our own.

[It] ... may almost be said to have been the first literary paper to have made honesty its aim.[1]

This statement by a recent commentator on Victorian civilization will scarcely seem exaggerated to one who is familiar with the literary journals of the 1830's. Of the prestige which the *Athenaeum* acquired among contemporaries, there is abundant evidence in the memoirs and letters of the period. As early as 1832, the second year of Dilke's editorship, the reputation of the magazine was sufficient to arouse general respect and sometimes wonder among those who were accustomed to nothing but partisan or "trade" criticism. A large part of that respect grew out of the vigorous and fearless campaign which Dilke carried on consistently against literary puffery, particularly that inspired by publishers who owned or controlled periodicals and used them to puff their own books. This fight was a

[1] *Early Victorian England*, ed. G. M. Young, Vol. II, Chap. IX, "The Press," by E. E. Kellett, pp. 77-78.

natural corollary of the effort of the *Athenaeum* editor to establish the reputation of the magazine as a critical review of complete independence, free from the warping influences of politics, religion, business, and so far as possible, from the bias of personal friendship or enmity.

This single aim guided Dilke's attempt to keep even a semblance of author or publisher influence from creeping into the reviews, as well as his refusal to accept gifts, of books or anything else, from authors, and his dismissal of a correspondent who sacrificed his independence of judgment by taking advance sheets from a publisher. So, too, the editor's reluctance to go into society, in order to avoid making literary acquaintances "which might either prove annoying to him, or be supposed to compromise the independence of his journal," was governed by something more than whim. It is not surprising then to find the *Athenaeum* taking an uncompromisingly stern view of flagrantly dishonest criticism which paraded itself before the public as unbiased. The circumstance would not demand so much comment were it not that criticism with an axe to grind was all but universal in literary journals.

BOOK REVIEWING IN 1830

There was no truly independent literary periodical in England in 1830. The quarterlies, with their pontifical and lordly judgments of politics and literature, did not even make a pretense of impartiality. Their long "reviews" were mere excuses for rewarding or punishing those who were with or against them in politics. Brougham, Jeffrey, Macaulay and others did their bit for the Whig cause by using a book as the starting point for an essay which had the proper political bias but which was often far removed from an actual review of the book in question. The *Edinburgh Review* made a specialty of that practice.

It is scarcely necessary to cite the famous examples of the "strafing" of political enemies in the literary field in the *Quarterly Review*. Though the savagery and scurrility of its personal attacks on Lady Morgan,[2] and on Leigh Hunt, Keats, and others of the so-called "Cockney School," had somewhat abated in the thirties when Croker and Gifford had ceased to fill its columns with vitriolic abuse,[3] high Tory principles still governed its judgment of writers whose works were far from political. The *Quarterly,* for example, generally praised the fashionable novels written by "gentlemen" and not merely by lackeys or interlopers in society.[4]

The *Westminster Review* usually looked with suspicion upon all belles lettres which could not be shown to have some "utilitarian" purpose.[5] Of course there were exceptions here as in the other quarterlies. Many excellent and politically unbiased critical articles appeared from time to time in all these journals. We have only to think of the names of occasional contributors to the *Edinburgh,* such as Carlyle, De Quincey, Hazlitt; of Lockhart's keen criticism

[2] Sydney Owenson, later Lady Morgan, had the distinction of being the first victim of the severeties of literary criticism in the *Quarterly Review* (see Vol. I, No. 1, p. 50). Gifford in the first number, possibly aided by Croker (see Lionel Stevenson, *The Wild Irish Girl: the Life of Sydney Owenson, Lady Morgan,* p. 117) wrote a scathing review of her *Ida of Athens* solely because she was known to be a writer of liberal principles. The *Quarterly* review of her *France* (1817), in which she "attributed immense merit to the French Revolution" (see Stevenson, *op. cit.,* p. 179) was so savage that Byron protested to Murray, the publisher of the magazine. Lady Morgan was later a close friend of Dilke and a trusted writer of important reviews for the *Athenaeum.*

[3] See *Athenaeum,* Aug. 18, 1832, p. 540: "The ungentle craft of criticism has grown gentle; the fire mingled with hail of the *Edinburgh Review,* which fell without remorse upon so many heads, is passed and gone, and the surly irony and searching sarcasm of the *Quarterly* is exchanged for kindlier qualities, and, on the whole, the most churlish of all critics have shown that they have something to unite them with human nature." But the "searching sarcasm" of Croker still broke out occasionally in the *Quarterly,* as in the famous review of Tennyson's poems in 1833.

[4] E.g., see *Quarterly,* Oct., 1832, pp. 165-201. For an account of the political coloring of literary criticism in the *Quarterly* see Walter Graham, *Tory Criticism in the "Quarterly Review."*

[5] See George L. Nesbitt, *Benthamite Reviewing,* pp. 96-97.

in the *Quarterly* when he was not engaged on a subject involving political prejudice; of John Stuart Mill and others in the *Westminster* when they were able to free themselves somewhat from the sterner dogmatism of the older Utilitarians. The truth remains, however, that these journals were not primarily organs of impartial literary criticism. Each had an ulterior purpose and a bias in the very principle of its foundation which almost predictably colored its judgment of books.

The monthly publications which reviewed literary works displayed the same partisan influences with even less pretense of detachment. *Blackwood's* rather gloried in its rabid Toryism. Its abuse of Leigh Hunt was indeed more severe than that of the *Quarterly*. In its early years it tore all writers of liberal sympathies to shreds. By 1830, it is true, it had grown a little milder and mellower under the editorship of John Wilson ("Christopher North"), and by 1834 it could even speak kindly of Hunt,[6] but strict impartiality could not be expected from it. Like the *Quarterly* it objected to the "fashionable novels" only when they were written by "butlers and fiddlers." But it praised *Richelieu* and *Darnley* by G. P. R. James as the work of a gentleman. And, Wilson adds, "Two or three men of birth and fashion do wield the pen, such as Lord Normanby, Mr. Lister, and Mr. Bulwer."[7]

Fraser's Magazine began in February, 1830, with a boast of independence: "We are determined to be fearless and fair."[8] Though admittedly Tory in politics, its delight in satire and cutting personalities under the leadership of William Maginn tended even more than its political bias to

[6] In the "Noctes Ambrosianae" Christopher North spoke of Hunt's *London Journal* as "the most entertaining and instructive of all the cheap periodicals." (*Blackwood's*, Aug., 1834, p. 273.)

[7] *Blackwood's*, April, 1830, p. 688. The Tory periodicals, of course, handled Bulwer more severely when he wrote on political subjects as a liberal.

[8] Feb., 1830, p. 7.

give a peculiar coloring and lack of balance to its literary opinions. The influence of Maginn's style in spicy personal attacks was so compelling that many of the young Fraserians copied him to the detriment of independent or fair criticism.[9]

The *New Monthly Magazine* was one of several journals whose critical independence was jeopardized or destroyed by the ownership or control of publishers. The *Court Journal* and the *United Service Journal* were likewise unblushingly given over to the puffing of books published by their owner, Henry Colburn. Of the purely literary journals, the one with the largest circulation and greatest influence in 1830 was the weekly *Literary Gazette,* edited by William Jerdan whose reviews showed a marked preference for the books of his publisher associates.[10]

Daily papers had no literary staffs and were for the most part easy prey to the temptation to accept "paid paragraphs" from publishers as fillers for the news columns, or as supposed unbiased "literary intelligence." These paragraphs could be collected by the publisher and sent as "opinions of the press" to the provincial papers and magazines which got most of their literary material ready made from London, sometimes from direct puff sheets, and frequently from the generally approved use of scissors and paste.[11]

[9] See Miriam M. H. Thrall, *Rebellious Fraser's.* It is possible that some of Thackeray's first papers in *Fraser's* are unidentifiable because of their being written in close imitation of the style of Maginn.

[10] Several of the weeklies, like the *Spectator,* took little account of literary criticism or book reviewing. The historian of that periodical says: "The truth is that in its early days the paper regarded all the arts as a sub-department of morals or utility; and judged the products accordingly." (William Beach Thomas, *The Story of the Spectator,* p. 212.)

[11] Except for a few short-lived literary publications which had very small circulations and slight influence, this completes the gamut of book reviewing periodicals which helped to make or mar the reputations of British authors in 1830. One might add the *Gentleman's Magazine,* antiquarian in taste and grandmotherly in tone. The *London Magazine* had just expired, and the *Examiner* under Albany Fonblanque continued to be a radical journal more interested in politics than in book reviewing. John Forster, Hunt, and others, however, did some good service to unknown writers of talent in their reviews

OBSTACLES TO INDEPENDENCE

When Dilke took control of the *Athenaeum* on June 5, 1830, he was confronted with several serious obstacles which had to be overcome before he could establish the independence of the journal. In the first place it occupied a somewhat awkwardly anomalous place in the critical field because of its peculiar history. It had still to live down the memory of a partnership (brief though it was) with the publisher Henry Colburn, the most notorious of the puffers, who had launched the journal with James Silk Buckingham. The latter undoubtedly was aware of the impression such a liaison would make upon the public, for he had included in the first number a sententious and specious defense.

The use that will, no doubt, be made of this fact, will be, that the disappointed rivals of Mr. Colburn, and the unrelenting enemies of myself . . . will . . . insinuate that the Literary independence of 'The Athenaeum' will be endangered by the union. Let them endeavor to create this impression as they may. The answer, and the antidote, are both at hand. And first, Mr. Colburn has, in the most open and explicit manner, disclaimed all exercise of authority, or interference, even in the minutest particular, as to any matter connected with the Literary management of the Work; leaving to me the sole and undivided power of doing whatever I may think just in this respect. Secondly, His pecuniary interest in the property is not greater than my own; so that, being Editor, as well as co-equal proprietor, he could not exercise such control, even if he wished it,—which, however, I

---

in the *Examiner,* which was among the first to give favorable attention to Browning and Tennyson, for example. It is perhaps significant of the general position of literary criticism at the time that periodicals which were not supported by some publisher or bookseller, or which were not organs of some sect or party, did not thrive. Jerdan in his *Autobiography* (III, 210) gives a list of these attempted literary journals: "Thus, the 'Literary Review,' the 'Literary Chronicle,' the 'Museum,' the 'Somerset House Gazette,' the 'Gazette of Fashion,' the 'New Literary Gazette,' the 'Athenaeum,' and others I have forgotten, mewed and had their day, and all but the last-mentioned sank through inanition." Jerdan attributed the success of the *Athenaeum* to the lowering of the price.

sincerely believe he does not: since with him, as with myself, the success of 'The Athenaeum' is the first object at heart; and his own stake in it is sufficiently large to prevent sinister interests from being suffered to affect this; which any interference with its independence would assuredly do.[12]

It is evident, however, that Colburn did not enter into the partnership with Buckingham with all the innocence represented by the latter. Late in 1827 Jerdan had jumped over the traces in the *Literary Gazette,* which he edited for his partner Henry Colburn, and had massacred *The O'Briens and the O'Flaherties* by Lady Morgan, then one of Colburn's favorite and best paid writers. The publisher was furious over the review, for he had paid 1,300 pounds for the novel.[13] He wrote to Jerdan on December 31, 1827:

... I think it right to apprise you that I have joined Mr. Buckingham in a new literary journal, the 'Athenaeum.' I have determined on adopting this step in consequence of the injustice done to *my authors* generally (who are on the liberal side) by the 'Literary Gazette.' I cannot any longer consent to see my best authors unfairly reviewed, and my own property injured, and often sacrificed to the politics of that paper.

At the same [time] I may state, that the step I am now taking does not seem to be likely to injure the sale of the 'L. G.' The 'Athenaeum' will be published on another day of the week; it will address persons of other politics, and, *when likely to be treated with impartiality* in the 'L. G.,' early copies shall be supplied to both publications on the same day, leaving it to chance which shall anticipate the other in its notices of them.[14]

Jerdan's account of the alliance is also illuminating at this point. He says:

[12] *Athenaeum,* Jan. 2, 1828, p. 14.   [13] See Stevenson, *op. cit.,* pp. 256-257.
[14] William Jerdan, *Autobiography,* IV, 68. Jerdan, an enthusiastic admirer of Canning, was strongly Tory in his sympathies; whereas, it appears, Colburn had no party but, like the munitions makers, encouraged all who were likely to be profitable customers.

My partner, Mr. Colburn, was so offended by my impartiality, that he purchased a large share in the 'Athenaeum,' and threw away a very considerable sum upon the support it tried to give him whilst it was equally ineffectual in its endeavors to injure his property in the 'Literary Gazette.'[15]

Not without justice, Jerdan felt that Colburn was unreasonable in his expectations. He surveyed the *Literary Gazette* reviews for 1827 to see what it was that had inflamed his partner, and he found that most of the important works of Colburn were warmly praised and largely quoted. He added innocently: "Indeed, one of its reproaches was its good nature, and being indiscriminately favourable to everybody. . . . It might be thought that such a series of panegyric should have satisfied the most exigent expectations."[16]

Undoubtedly Colburn soon regretted the step he had taken in helping to start the *Athenaeum,* even before Dilke began his anti-puffery campaign, for, considering the publisher's disappointment with the *Literary Gazette's* really fulsome praise of almost all his books, he must have been chagrined at the failure of the earnest moralists like Stebbing and Maurice, who conducted the literary departments of the *Athenaeum,* to puff his light literature. Nevertheless, this trade connection operated against the complete independence of the paper in its first two years. Colburn's advertisements (frequently filled with extracts from puffing reviews) continued to occupy a large space in the *Athenaeum* during the first half of 1828, and during that time the novels which he published almost always got the first place after the leader (then usually an original article), and they were in general very favorably reviewed. In the number of September 17, 1828, there was a leading article on the Colburn publications as a whole, not extravagantly puffing, but still serving to advertise Colburn books.

[15] *Ibid.,* pp. 20-21.　　　[16] *Ibid.,* pp. 69-70.

Even after the magazine had parted company with Colburn, its boast of strict impartiality in criticism was not yet free from suspicion. The "Apostles" had written most of the literary articles and reviews of the *Athenaeum* from the beginning. Though it is probable that they could not be corrupted by publishers' gold or threats where matters of "conscience" or "morality" were concerned (witness the occasional severe handling of Colburn's fashionable novels which they thought immoral even while he was part proprietor), like all zealots, they could see no harm in giving a boost to those who were "on the Lord's side" irrespective of literary merit. Maurice gave warmest praise to *Guesses at Truth* by Two Brothers (Julius and Augustus Hare),[17] and later puffed *The Children of Light, a Sermon,* by Julius Hare[18] (his tutor at Cambridge and one of the foremost of the Apostles) in the face of hostile criticism in almost all other periodicals. Watts-Dunton, in an *Athenaeum* anniversary article,[19] has attributed great perspicacity to the early editors in discovering new genius because Tennyson's *Timbuctoo* was highly praised in the magazine,[20] but Tennyson's affiliation with the Apostles furnishes a more plausible reason for the "discovery." At all events, the fact that the journal had come to be known as an organ of the Apostles increased the difficulties of the new editor, making it harder for Dilke to establish the prestige of the *Athenaeum* as an independent literary paper.

Another obstacle to be overcome was the friendly review, which was everywhere taken for granted and universally abetted by the anonymity of literary criticism.[21] Even the

---

[17] *Athenaeum,* Aug. 13, 1828, pp. 656-658.

[18] *Athenaeum,* Dec. 31, 1828, pp. 977-978.

[19] Jan. 1, 1898, p. 9.   [20] July 22, 1829, p. 456.

[21] It is curious that while other editors used anonymity as a convenient cloak for personal or party animosity, on the one hand, or for puffing of friends on the other, Dilke considered it a safeguard of independent reviewing. Not only were the reviews unsigned so that the author or publisher could not identify

most scrupulous writers were not above seeking a friendly puff. Browning sent a letter to W. J. Fox, editor of the *Monthly Repository,* announcing the coming publication of *Pauline.* Prof. Lounsbury says, ". . . never was there a more transparent attempt to secure, under the guise of humility, a favorable review."[22] Thackeray (though he repented it later) wrote to his friend Aytoun after the first monthly part of *Vanity Fair* had appeared, calling on him and others who had influence with the reviews to give him "a push at the present minute." He asked, "Why don't *Blackwood* give me an article?"[23] Tennyson had counted on a favorable review of his 1842 volumes by his friend Spedding, but, he wrote to Edmund Lushington: "Spedding's going to America has a little disheartened me, for some fop will get the start of him in the *Ed. Review* where he promised to put an article and I have had abuse enough."[24]

Dilke himself, with all his surveillance of reviewers and his almost ascetic denial of the luxury of praising his close associates, eventually relaxed his vigilance. Thomas Hood, Lady Morgan, and William and Mary Howitt, staff writers for the *Athenaeum,* were always well reviewed, sometimes by the editor in all probability. But then Dilke would perhaps have said that their work deserved to be praised. If he sometimes yielded to the common frailty of the friendly review, his friends knew that they would arouse his antag-

the critic and so exert influence on him, but Dilke never signed anything that he himself wrote, and he carefully refrained from putting the names of reviewers of books written by members of the *Athenaeum* staff in the marked office file. Nor were the sacred secrets of authorship of reviews permitted to go out of the office. "In 1835 we find Chorley receiving a 'wigging' from Mr. Dilke for naming to his friend, Miss Mitford, George Darley as the author of an article in the *Athenaeum.* Chorley humbly acknowledges his transgression." (*Paper. of a Critic,* I, 33.)

[22] Thomas R. Lounsbury, *The Early Literary Career of Robert Browning* p. 9.

[23] Herman Merivale and Frank T. Marzials, *The Life of W. M. Thackeray* pp. 136-137.

[24] *Alfred Lord Tennyson, A Memoir* by his son, I, 180.

onism by requesting a favorable notice; it had to be spontaneous and sincere. The extent to which he was deluged with such requests is only indicative of the generality of the practice among Victorian writers. Mrs. Gore once thought to get around him with a subtle device. She wrote (about 1835):

> You will receive in a day or two a novel of mine, called 'The Sketch Book of Fashion.' I should feel greatly obliged if you would *not notice it at all,* unless, indeed, you find that it contains something demanding reprobation. As you may imagine there is something mysterious in this Medea-like proceeding towards my offspring, I ought to add that general condemnation has rendered me somewhat ashamed of my sickly progeniture of fashionable novels, and that I have now in the press a series of stories founded on the history of Poland, which I hope will prove more worthy of attention.[25]

The writer of the Dilke *Memoir* adds, "But alas! the Polish tales were 'damned.' "[26]

But whatever Dilke may have done to minimize the evils of "private feeling" and author influence in the *Athenaeum* during his editorship, his reforms did not extend to other periodicals, nor was the Spartan tradition carried on in the *Athenaeum* itself when the management passed to others. For example, when William Hepworth Dixon (editor from 1853 to 1869) did not review his own books he passed them over to the friendly hands of his associate, Dr. John Doran, who always gave them glowing praise. And Henry Reeve (later editor of the *Edinburgh Review*), a frequent reviewer

[25] Quoted in *Papers of a Critic,* I, 34-35.

[26] *Ibid.* John Forster, acting as literary agent for Bulwer, was once annoyed by what he considered a review unfriendly to his client in the *Athenaeum.* He wrote to Bulwer, apropos of a notice of *Cheveley* by Lady Bulwer (April, 1839): "I do not say that the Athenaeum notice did not vex me . . . because, in a promise that none of the libels should appear, I had reason to expect something very different." (I am indebted to Mr. Lee Harlan for calling my attention to this attempt to influence the reviews in the *Athenaeum.*)

for the *Athenaeum* in the 1840's, wrote an article on his own translation of Guizot's *Washington* and praised the work of the translator.[27]

Of the three main distorting influences in reviewing, however—friendship or enmity between the reviewer and the reviewed; moral, political, or religious bias; and the control or influence of publishers—Dilke soon found that publishers' puffing was the most dangerous because it was the most insidious and usually masked itself as the free opinion of an unbiased critic. Personal friendship or animosity in reviews could be largely avoided by an editor who, like Dilke, was careful to assign books to critics competent in their fields and not merely to friends (or enemies) of the author. Political bias was expected from the *Quarterly* and from other partisan journals, and the reader could and did

[27] The inconsistencies of authors and their blindness to ethics where reviews of their works are concerned is doubly illustrated in a curious way in the case of George Henry Lewes, a frequent reviewer for the *Athenaeum* in the late forties and early fifties, and certainly more scrupulous than most Victorian writers in his literary practices. Writing in his "Causeries" as editor of the *Fortnightly* (June 1, 1866, p. 243) he says apropos of the different moral standards in business and in literature: "Thus the man who is eloquently indignant about the tricks of trade and commercial immorality, will in the next breath propose to you some dishonesty in Literature without a blush, without even a suspicion that he proposes anything to which an upright man could object. The man who would cut you for a wilful deception out of Literature, will cut you for your unfriendliness in not assisting him or his friend by some wilful deception in Literature." And a few years later Lewes unconsciously illustrated the principle. Speaking of a letter from John Morley to Frederic Harrison (Feb. 1, 1874), the editor of Morley's letters says (*Early Life and Letters of John Morley*, ed. F. W. Hirst, I, 295): "Then he talks of G. H. Lewes, and drubs him for wanting a new book he had published to be reviewed and praised the moment it came off the press." Lytton [R. E.], also, had sent his two volumes, *Fables in Song*, and Morley asks who is to review them. "Do you see, my dear Harrison, what an impossible thing it is for an editor to keep friends with people who write books, and at the same time keep friends with his own poor conscience? On my word, not a week passes that somebody does not barefacedly ask why we have not yet had an article on his or her book, or his or her second cousin's book." Lewes's book was *Problems of Life and Mind*, Vol. I, 1874. It was finally reviewed by Harrison, July, 1874. Lewes was very assiduous too in getting good reviews for "the little woman" (George Eliot). Lytton's book was reviewed by Robert Louis Stevenson in the *Fortnightly* in June, 1874.

make allowances for it. But the majority of readers of the *New Monthly*, the *Literary Gazette*, and the newspaper "paid paragraphs" accepted the judgments as opinions of impartial critics of literature.

The *Athenaeum* stated the matter clearly enough in the introductory paragraphs of a review of the *Memoirs of Celebrated Female Sovereigns* by Mrs. Jameson, published, and greatly puffed, by Colburn and Bentley.

We agree with the editor of the Souvenir [Alaric Watts] that periodical criticism is too much influenced by private feeling; but it is a charge to which all criticism ever has been, and ever must be subject; and against which the *Athenaeum* does not affect to have any special armour of proof: we have warm hearts in our bodies, and not flint stones; and there is no doubt we know our friends from our enemies. But what is the amount of the possible wrong judgment from this wrong bias?—out of five hundred works reviewed, we doubt if twenty, or even ten, be written either by friends or enemies. The deceptive influence, against which the public should be put on their guard, is that of book publishers;—we have no doubt, that if Mr. Watts will examine five hundred columns of reviews in the *Literary Gazette,* one half will be found filled with the praise of works published by Colburn.[28]

TRADE CRITICISM

The *Athenaeum* battle against puffery grew most directly out of its objection to what was felt to be the unethical and unfair practices of Henry Colburn and his associates in advertising the fashionable novels[29] and other sensational works that came in a steady stream from their house in New Burlington Street. It is rather difficult to date the beginning of the campaign accurately. It seemingly had its origin some time before Dilke became editor in certain attacks on Col-

[28] *Athenaeum*, Oct. 29, 1831, p. 705.
[29] Matthew Rosa, who made a special study of these novels, says: "It is hardly an exaggeration to say that nine-tenths of the fashionable novels bear the colophon of Henry Colburn." (*The Silver-Fork School*, p. vii.)

burn's undignified methods, but it flamed out into a major crusade against the system of trade criticism late in 1830 and was at its height in 1831 and 1832.

The system of publishers' puffing was not new when the *Athenaeum* was started.[30] Colburn wrote to Lady Morgan in 1816, when he was trying to persuade her to publish with him: "No other bookseller, I am certain, takes the tenth part of the pains I do in advertising, and in *other* respects I do not think any one will *in future,* cope with me, since from January next, I shall have under my sole control *two* journals."[31]

It is surprising that no book has yet been written on Colburn and his remarkable publishing career.[32] Perhaps the difficulty of getting first-hand information has been the chief obstacle, though the memoirs and letters of the period are full of references to him, as are also most of the important periodicals, for he was more of a phenomenon in the book world in the twenties and thirties than the noted but less spectacular John Murray, Constable, or Blackwood. No one seems to know when Colburn was born or anything of his origin. It is hardly necessary to credit the two statements

[30] For a brief general account of literary puffing practices in this period, see Emery Neff, *Carlyle,* pp. 127-132.

[31] Quoted in Stevenson, *op. cit.,* p. 177. Colburn made good his boast in ways which were sometimes little to the taste of "The Wild Irish Girl" despite her well-known vanity and the pleasure which she could not help feeling in the popularity her books had won her and in the generosity of the publisher. She wrote to her sister, Lady Clarke, in August, 1818: "The announcement of our arrival in London (a puff, I am sure, by Colburn) has brought down upon us a flock of friends, great and small. . . ." (Sydney, Lady Morgan, *Passages from my Autobiography,* p. 27.)

[32] The fullest account of Colburn that I have found is the chapter devoted to him in Matthew Rosa, *op. cit.,* pp. 178-206. A good deal of the information in this section comes from that chapter and from certain paragraphs in A. S. Collins, *The Profession of Letters.* Much concerning Colburn's relations with the editors of his journals is to be found in memoirs and autobiographies of those connected with them, particularly William Jerdan, Thomas Campbell, and Cyrus Redding. Of course they do not give Colburn's side of the story. Some account of Colburn's publishing career is given also in Henry Curwen, *A History of Booksellers, the Old and the New,* pp. 279-295.

quoted by Rosa, one from Samuel Carter Hall who recorded
the gossip that he was a natural son of Lord Lansdowne, the
other from William Carew Hazlitt, who had heard that
Colburn was a son of the Duke of York by one of numerous
mistresses. Rosa says, "To the gentleman who made press-
agentry a fine art, the securing of a few flattering allusions
to his own birth must have been child's play."[33]

After an apprenticeship to William Earle, a bookseller in
Albemarle Street, he got some experience in Morgan's Circulating Library in Conduit Street. With an unexplained
access of capital in 1814, he started the *New Monthly Magazine* with Frederic Shoberl (later a reader for his publishing firm, and editor of the annual, *The Forget-me-not*).
And he was already in the publishing business by that time,
for he paid £550 for Lady Morgan's novel, *O'Donnel*, in
that year. By 1816 he had become proprietor of Morgan's
Circulating Library.

The books of the most lasting fame which he published
were Evelyn's *Diary*, in 1818, and Pepys's *Diary*, in 1825. He
also published Burke's famous *Peerage and Baronetage*. It
is perhaps indicative of his knowledge of values in permanent
as well as in ephemeral literature that he saved the copyrights of these three books when he retired from active publishing and sold all his popular works to Hurst and Blackett.
Rosa says, "On his death in Bryanstone Square, August 16,
1857, seven of his copyrights realized £14,000 when sold at
auction. He had kept Warburton's *The Crescent and the
Cross*, Evelyn's *Diary*, Pepys's *Diary*, Strickland's *Lives of
the Queens*, and three forms of Burke's *Peerage and Baronetage*."[34]

When the *Athenaeum* examined Colburn's list, September 17, 1828, it found that he was publishing 65 *new* books.

[33] Rosa, *op. cit.*, p. 179.
[34] Rosa, *op. cit.*, p. 187. Rosa is mistaken in the date of Colburn's death. He
died in 1855.

Among the authors whom his high prices and advertising had attracted were Mrs. Shelley, Hazlitt, Horace Smith, Disraeli, Lister, Godwin, Normanby, Landor, Thomas Roscoe, R. P. Ward, Lady Dacre, Thomas Hood, the Banims, Bulwer, J. Fenimore Cooper, Campbell, Lady Morgan, Leigh Hunt, Hook, Lady Charlotte Bury, and George Croly. At this time the greater part of Colburn's output was "high life literature." Only four volumes were poetry. Colburn also published books by G. P. R. James, Captain Marryat, Lady Blessington, L. E. L., and many other popular writers. If we include the contributors to his several periodicals, he had by far the largest share of well-known British authors on his list.

The prices which he paid rivalled those which Murray, the most generous of publishers, paid to Byron, and they were justified by his profits. The Rev. George Croly "in offering his weird romance of *Salathiel* to Blackwood in 1827 for £500 for the first edition, asserted that by publications of the kind . . . Colburn had made some £20,000 a year for the three previous years."[35] After Hook had gained fame with his *Sayings and Doings* (for which Colburn paid £600), he could demand £1000 for his novels as a regular scale. Lady Morgan received the same amount for *France* (1817) and £2000 for her novel *Florence McCarthy* published the following year.

From 1817 forward Colburn's success as a publisher mounted at the same time that his reputation for unsavory or at least undignified methods of advertising grew into something of a byword in the trade. His enterprising and daring nature was matched by his unerring instinct for judging accurately the popular taste. He had already enjoyed some success with Lady Morgan's *O'Donnel* in 1814, and her other books, particularly *The Wild Irish Girl* (1806)

[35] Collins, *op. cit.*, p. 244.

and *Ida of Athens* (1808) had brought her considerable fame, so that he was not gambling on an untried author. Scott had praised *O'Donnel,* Miss Mitford was won over, and the novel sold two thousand copies soon after publication and became a best seller.[36] Lady Morgan refused £750 for *France,* Colburn's rather handsome offer, and even after he offered £1000, she approached Constable, who turned it down. Colburn, however, had little cause to regret his bargain, for *France* was the sensation of the season on its publication in June, 1817, and before long went into four English and two French editions.[37] He could soon afford to laugh at both the *Quarterly* reviewer who called

[36] See Stevenson, *op. cit.,* pp. 166-168.

[37] *Ibid.,* p. 222. There is considerable irony in the relations between Colburn and Lady Morgan. In the first place, he won her over from Sir Richard Phillips, her earlier publisher, a radical who might be supposed to be more sympathetic to her opinions than the man who had just started a Tory journal to bait the Jacobins in rivalry with Phillips' *Monthly Magazine.* In the second place Colburn made his first great publishing success with her *France,* which went counter to most of the principles that his journals stood for, and he puffed it in those same journals. Moreover, Lady Morgan, on her side, was delighted with Colburn's generosity, though she was a liberal—even a radical—in politics. She wrote in her diary in August, 1818: "This morning . . . comes the English post—old Colburn—no! not old at all, but young enthusiastic Colburn, in love with 'Florence McCarthy,' and a little *épris* with the author! 'Italy' by Lady Morgan! 'he is not touched but rapt,' and makes a dashing offer of two thousand pounds—to be printed in quarto like 'France'—but we are to start off immediately, and I have immediately answered him in the words of Sileno in 'Midas'—

> 'Done! strike hands—
> I take your offer,
> Further on I may fare worse!'

Morgan, of course, consenting; he is in fact charmed." (Lady Morgan, *op. cit.,* p. 16.) And then William Jerdan (see *ante,* p. 103) attacked Lady Morgan in Colburn's *Literary Gazette* and roused the publisher's ire to such a point that he took a share in a new literary paper, "on the liberal side," to protect his authors, most of whom were then (1828) on that side, from what he considered unfair treatment in his own Tory journals. Soon after, in spite of Colburn's liberality, Lady Morgan took her new book on France to Colburn's rivals, Saunders and Otley, and he turned on her with the ferocity of a jealous lover and cried down the books he had puffed for so many years. She in turn soon joined the magazine "on the liberal side," the *Athenaeum,* which he had helped to launch, and was one of the closest friends of the editor, Dilke, who was uncompromising in his fight against Colburn's puffing.

her an "audacious worm"[38] and the rivals who objected to his advertising methods.

A. S. Collins says: "But the most go-ahead of publishers for advertising was Colburn. He was a prophet of the modern spirit and his advertisements were at once the scandal and the admiration of the literary world. Around 1830 he was spending, on an average, £9000 a year on them."[39] But other publishers advertised expensively too. Wordsworth had complained that Longman advertised too much. He got £9 8s. 2d. on the first edition of his book on the Lakes and was charged £27 2s. 3d. for the advertisements. And Murray laid out even more than Longman in advertising. It was the manner rather than the fact of Colburn's advertising that aroused comment and eventually protest.

The most useful of the journals which he had boasted of having under his control was the *Literary Gazette,* which he launched on January 25, 1817, with the specific purpose of presenting a lighter and more readable sort of literary criticism than that found in the quarterlies, and naturally with the expectation that the magazine would give wide and favorable publicity to his own publications. The *Gazette* was then the only literary weekly of its kind. It may be said to be the first book review or book news periodical. Selling for a shilling, it reached a much wider audience

---

[38] *Quarterly Review,* April, 1817, p. 284. Lady Morgan was not able to laugh at the epithet; it rankled for many years. She pictured, or rather caricatured, Croker in *Florence McCarthy* as the unenviable Counsellor Conway Townshend Crawley and put into his mouth whole sentences from the review of *France.* (See Stevenson, *op. cit.,* p. 195.) And the criticism had far-flung reverbations. Disraeli drew Croker's portrait in *Coningsby* as Mr. Rigby, whose talents went to "massacring a she liberal." (*Ibid.,* p. 191.) When her husband, Sir Charles Morgan, wrote an article on "Criticism" for the *Athenaeum* nearly fifteen years later, he recalled the epithet and quoted it: "A reviewer, therefore, who sets to work in a passion and calls an author bad names, such as jacobin, atheist, 'audacious worm' and the like, may be safely suspected of having nothing of serious accusation to prefer against the book in question." (*Athenaeum,* Feb. 5, 1831, p. 89.)

[39] *The Profession of Letters,* p. 192.

than the more ponderous quarterlies. Its reviews were shorter and more gossipy, and yet they gave more information about the books reviewed than did the periodicals which used books merely as pegs on which to hang political essays. After twenty-six numbers had appeared, William Jerdan, who had bought a third interest, became sole editor. Longman and Co. bought a third control which had belonged to the publishing firm of Pinnock and Maunder.

Jerdan's publishing partners were not hesitant about encouraging good reviews of their books in the *Literary Gazette*. It is quite possible that the editor (as he often protested in his later years) was not moved by open attempts to influence his reviews in the journal, but examination of its pages shows that Colburn and Longman books were usually given the preference in space, position, and warmth of praise. The mere desire to live in peace with his partners, and the knowledge of their extreme sensitivity to any adverse criticism of their books, must have been sufficient to account for that exuberant panegyrical style so characteristic of the reviews in the Gazette. It is probable that he could not have sat in the editorial chair for twenty-five years with such exigent publishers looking over his shoulder, had it not been for his "good-nature" and the "leaning to kindness" which he admitted as guiding him in his opinions of books.

Jerdan's position must certainly have been a trying one. In his *Autobiography* he confessed that, to his chagrin and frequent embarrassment, each of the partners tried to influence him.

Even so early as the time I am now treating of, [1823] I see a letter from Mr. Orme [of the firm of Longman] alluding to an offence taken by Mr. Colburn at my review of one of his books. 'Our co-partner may be sore; but the lady deserves all she has got; and these independent articles do us a world of good'. . . .

So far so good; but some time after, I happened to write a notice of Mrs. Graham's (afterward Lady Callcott) work, which gave no less offence to Mr. Longman, and I did not visit Hampstead for two years after. Mr. Longman tried to compromise matters; and only desired that if I could not commend in certain cases where he felt a personal interest, I would abstain altogether from noticing; but even this modification I refused to accede to.[40]

A short time later Mr. Cosmo Orme complained to Jerdan of an "indiscreet article" in the *Literary Gazette,* and protested against the manner in which "S——" was treated. Orme hinted that his partners in Longman and Co. might support another literary journal which would be more discreet.[41]

The *New Monthly Magazine,* Colburn's other chief puffing journal, was not at first a literary paper, having been begun as a Tory rival of the *Monthly Magazine* conducted by Sir Richard Phillips, who had once served a jail sentence for selling Tom Paine's *Rights of Man.*[42] By 1820, however, Colburn, smelling the wind of change again with uncanny accuracy, converted the *New Monthly* to literary and general

[40] Jerdan, *op. cit.,* III, 112.

[41] *Ibid.,* IV, 75. Colburn, irritated by Jerdan's effort to be independent on one occasion, actually did support in the *Athenaeum* a rival journal. As the publisher became more avid of eulogy for his authors and more concerned at any slightest word of qualification in the panegyrics of his books, the outcries of Jerdan were sometimes pathetic, and his rationalizations amusing. See particularly, Jerdan, *op. cit.,* III, 11, 112; IV, 21-22, 22-23, 82-83. The quaint turns of his reasoning are sufficiently indicated in the following [IV, 82-84]: "In vindicating the 'Gazette' from the aspersions with which it was so insidiously assailed and misrepresented, till a pretty general belief was obtained for the falsehoods, I do not mean to say that it, or any journal of its class, can be carried on with perfect freedom, and uninfluenced by any circumstances . . . but a mere leaning to kindness, rather than severity, cannot materially delude the public taste. . . . I always found two parties who differed from any general suspicion that the 'Gazette' had coloured a trifle too highly, and these were the publishers of the works and their authors. The only exception I can remember to the former rule, was that of John Murray ridiculing me for the intense admiration I expressed for 'Anastasius.'" See also *Literary Gazette,* April 17, 1830, pp. 249-250.

[42] See Frank A. Mumby, *op. cit.,* pp. 252-253.

interests. He knew that anti-Jacobinism had burned itself
out and that the public was turning to other things. In
1821 he paid the princely sum of £500 to Thomas Campbell, one of the most popular poets of the time, to be the
nominal editor of the *New Monthly* and to contribute only
twelve articles a year, half verse, half prose. Colburn agreed
to pay extra for other contributions, and he hired Cyrus
Redding to do the routine work of editing.[43] The attempt
of the publisher to control the reviews in the *New Monthly*
met with less resistance because Campbell was too indolent
to take a firm stand. His assistant, Cyrus Redding, confessed that "Papers written by what may be styled 'trade'
writers were continually inserted in consequence, and in
1830 the practice was carried to a considerable extent."[44]

When Disraeli's novel of fashion, *Vivian Grey*, appeared
in 1826 (published by Colburn), the author puffed it in a
periodical, *The Star Chamber*, that he edited incognito.
Colburn made up a review for the *New Monthly* including
a "Key to Vivian Grey" and extracts from the *Star Chamber*, "some of feigned censure, to give critical verisimilitude."
The publisher then wrote to Redding: "I have almost acci-
dentally got this review from a high quarter, where I hope
to get others hereafter. I was compelled to undertake for
its insertion without being mangled."[45] Redding later commented in his *Recollections:* "This was all fudge, of course—
the art of wheedling an editor."[46]

Though Colburn soon became noted for his puffs, the
general outcry against him should not obscure the fact that

[43] See William Beattie, *Life and Letters of Thomas Campbell*, II, 357.
[44] Cyrus Redding, *Literary Reminiscences and Memoirs of Thomas Campbell*,
II, 234.
[45] Cyrus Redding, *Fifty Years' Recollections, Literary and Personal*, I, 322-325.
[46] *Ibid.*, p. 325. It must be said for Campbell and Jerdan, however, that at
last they could stand the Colburn interference no longer and so freed themselves,
the one by resigning and the other by buying the publishers' shares and gaining
sole control of the magazine.

he neither invented literary "log-rolling" nor monopolized the practice of it.[47] In fact, in the twenties the system was almost universally accepted as a part of business policy in publishing and periodical editorial rooms. The publisher George B. Whittaker once complained to Orme that his books were not fairly reviewed in the *Literary Gazette* and threatened to withhold his advertisements. Jerdan wrote to Orme that in the last four numbers, ten of Whittaker's publications were noticed, all but one with praise. "It is utterly impossible to produce a review which shall always be puffing: and every person of common sense must feel that individual pretensions, like those set up in our friend Whittaker's letter, must be contemned if we mean to cultivate an honest reputation with the general reader."[48] But the publishers both in and out of the business control of the magazine continued to take it for granted that a review must be an advertising puff in order to be "fair."

William Maginn, as a literary scout for Blackwood in London, wrote, June 5, 1823, "As for 'Bull' [the weekly periodical *John Bull*] I have carte blanche to do as I like. But puffs in the inner page must not exceed a quarter, or at most half, a column."[49] In view of the tone of righteous indignation taken a little later by Maginn and his associates in *Fraser's* towards the puffing trade, it is amusing to observe the following letter which he wrote to Jerdan, December 9, 1825:

[47] See Graham, *English Literary Periodicals*, p. 227: "John Dunton first made periodical criticism an adjunct to the book-selling and publishing business; he was the pioneer in comprehending and utilizing the advertising possibilites of early periodic publications to further the sale of books. Dunton frequently issued elaborate 'reviews' before the books themselves were published. His *Compleat Library* of 1692 was an advertising medium for his own wares, just as his *Athenian Mercury* had been for some months before this." See, for further details of the early development of trade criticism, R. P. McCutcheon, "John Dunton's Connection with Book Reviewing," *Studies in Philology*, XXV (July, 1928), 346-361.

[48] Jerdan, *op. cit.*, IV, 21-23. This correspondence is not dated, but it was probably about 1827.   [49] Oliphant, *op. cit.*, I, 398.

I write to you—for there is no use of talking humbug—to ask
you for a favourable critique, or a puff, or any other *thing* of the
kind—the *word* being no matter—of a forthcoming novel at
Blackwood's, "Percy Mallory," as soon as convenient. . . . Ebony
may perhaps write you about it, for he is an indefatigable letter
writer; but at all events you will oblige me by giving it a favourable and early notice in your "Gazette."[50]

Editorial space was considered a commodity, even by very
scrupulous editors, and it was not thought unethical to barter
it for one favor or another. Rintoul, owner and editor of
The Spectator, not long after its establishment in 1828 wrote
to Blackwood (September 16, 1829): "*You must contrive to
give me a lift in your October number.* It will be of great
service at this very season."[51] In return, "he reviewed *Maga,*
and noticed her whenever possible, zealously playing the
game of editorial log-rolling."[52]

Publishers, editors, and, to a large extent, authors, simply
failed to see anything dishonest in the deception of the reading public which resulted from the puffing of books in ex-
change for friendly or business favors. Colburn wrote to
Lady Morgan that the *Examiner,* the *New Times,* and *John
Bull* had not given any adverse criticism to her Italy [1819],
adding, "I am intimately acquainted with the editors, and

[50] Jerdan, *op. cit.,* III, 102. It is curious a little later to find *Fraser's* under
the editorship of Maginn accusing *Blackwood's Magazine* of puffing books published by "Ebony." Blackwood indeed wrote letters with a purpose. Charles
Knight recorded in his autobiography (*Passages of a Working Life,* I, 267):
"It was a surprise to me when I received from the dreaded Wm. Blackwood a
letter of thanks for 'your kind and early notices of my magazine.' Still more
was I surprised when he wrote 'Permit me to return you the author's and my
own best thanks for your splendid critique upon "Valerius" [Lockhart—1821].
Your opinion (which was the first given upon the work) seems to be fully
confirmed by the public voice.' Was this the style, I thought, in which it was
necessary for a publisher to administer small doses of flattery to periodical
critics, however humble, for what ought to be considered an act of justice?"
Similar tactics were employed by G. P. R. James, who thanked Henry Chorley
in a most flattering way for a good review of his works in the *Athenaeum.*
(See Chorley, *Autobiography,* I, 120-22.)

[51] Quoted in Thomas, *op. cit.,* p. 42. [52] *Ibid.*

advertising with them a great deal, keeps them in check."[53]
In 1821 he wrote, "The *Times* has acted the part of a traitor,
after getting two copies from me."[54]   In the light of this,
Dilke's resolve to accept no gifts from publishers or authors
seems less fanatical than sensible.

Quite the most astounding document revealing the extent
to which editorial opinions might be influenced is the letter
written by William Jerdan to George Canning in 1827, just
after the latter became Prime Minister. It is a fitting footnote to Jerdan's protestations of independence which fill so
many pages of his *Autobiography*.

I occupy a singular position in the literary world and may
claim the merit of some tact and discretion, if not of some talent,
in having made my journal so widely influential. The result is
that from the highest to almost the lowest class of public writers
I am of sufficient importance to possess a very considerable weight
with them. From book authors, through all gradations of the
periodical press, it is not a boast to assert that I could do much
to modify opinions, heat friends, and cool enemies. I am on terms
of personal intimacy with forty-nine out of fifty of those who
direct the leading journals of the day, and I can from time to
time oblige them all. Thus situated, I need not assure you that
I have not failed to do what I could where your interests were
involved. . . . Should you think well of what I have stated, and
find me eligible for any mark of favour which would enable me
to associate an efficient coadjutor in the *Literary Gazette,* and take
myself a somewhat higher station in society, I would without
doubt or fear of success undertake to produce very beneficial
consequences throughout the whole machinery of the press. *It
requires but cultivation.*[55]

[53] Quoted in Rosa, *op. cit.*, p. 195.

[54] *Ibid.*, pp. 195-196. Even the *Times,* however, was apparently not completely incorruptible. Bulwer wrote to Forster (April 10, 1839) concerning
Cheveley by Lady Bulwer, "We need not fear the Times. Barnes has promised
me that no notice shall be taken without my consent." (I am indebted to Mr.
Lee Harlan for calling this item to my attention.)

[55] Quoted by H. R. Fox-Bourne in the Introductory Note (pp. xxii-xxiii) to
Francis, *op. cit.*, Vol. I.

This picture of editorial ethics, and of periodical criticism pretty generally honeycombed with trade or venal personal influences must be kept before the reader who would judge either the work of Dilke on the *Athenaeum* or the comparative guilt of Colburn and his associates. Many of those who attacked Colburn before Dilke began his work in the *Athenaeum* lived in very thin glass houses. Rosa says: "Writers whose books were not published by Colburn, loved to make slighting references to his puffery. The reader could then infer that the book he was reading had been circulated purely on its merits."[56] Even Robert Montgomery, whose name later became a synonym for the over-puffed poet, had an early fling at Colburn (who was not his publisher). In *The Age Reviewed* (1827) he says, of his own book,

> Thus patronless, oh! dars't thou hope to please,
> Will Colburn puff, or Murray purchase thee?

A footnote adds: "Let but the smile of Colburn suavity, illuminate the MS. and your forthcoming prodigy will wander through all the papers in the full tide of paragraphic celebrity."[57]

And Maginn, whose hands were not then clean in the matter of puffery, added his bit to the general sport made of Colburn in a pseudo-scholarly footnote to his *Whitehall, or, The Days of George IV:* "See 'De Arte Puffandi Indirecte, vel per Head-and Sholderos,' Autore Henrico Colburn. In newspaper folio, 3591 volumes."[58]

As the outstanding practitioner of the art of the "puff indirect," Colburn was attacked on all sides, whether those who took up arms were motivated by strict honesty or by rivalry and personal prejudice. "Colburn and puffery became synonymous terms and the hand of the press agent was seen in every act he did."[59]

[56] Rosa, *op. cit.,* pp. 190-191. [57] Quoted in Rosa, *op. cit.,* p. 191.
[58] *Ibid.* [59] *Ibid.,* p. 190.

THE ATHENAEUM FIGHTS THE PUFFING SYSTEM

Although the early *Athenaeum* reviewers took every opportunity to affirm their high principles of truth, impartiality, and independence, they made no concerted effort to fight the system of publisher-controlled or influenced criticism until Dilke became editor. Their occasional thrusts at Colburn were usually aimed at the sensational or shoddy nature of the books which he published rather than at the specific corruption of literary opinions through the exertion of influence upon periodicals supposedly giving unbiased news or judgments. The step, however, was but a short one to a criticism of the methods employed by the publisher in advertising those books. And by the time the *Athenaeum* started, Colburn was fair game for any critic who made even a pretense to independence of judgment. So that in its first attacks upon New Burlington Street methods, the *Athenaeum* was but joining the general chorus.

By the middle of 1829, however, the guerrilla warfare against Colburn had extended to frequent gibes at his most notorious puffing practices.[60] In "An Hour at a Publisher's" there is a supposed conversation between Mr. Colophon [Colburn] and a lady of fashion who is an author of "high life" novels. She asks for £200 more than the £1000 agreed upon.[61] He objects that he has had many works of the same kind recently. But, she replies, they have been written by cast-off secretaries, ladies' maids, etc. Mr. Colophon then says:

Excellence of workmanship is scarcely any object. The panegyrics in the newspapers, (which some people are so malignant

[60] The influx of new blood when Sterling became editor in May, 1829, undoubtedly had something to do with the change of attitude. It is easy to see the hand of John Hamilton Reynolds in the satirical attacks on the game of puffery.

[61] The writer may have had Lady Morgan in mind, for she several times held Colburn up for a sum larger than he had offered and bargained with other publishers while the matter was pending. But the caricature is a composite one and would fit Lady Charlotte Bury and several others as well.

as to pretend that I pay for,) and the taste of the readers of
circulating libraries, level all differences of merit.

But he finally consents to pay the extra money, for her name
will be of great service.

As soon as the work is published, I will persuade my friend of
the Morning Chronicle to attack the ladies of the aristocracy, for
being so profligate as to write novels . . . and will make him add,
in a note, as a piece of secret intelligence that your ladyship is a
flagrant delinquent.[62]

Colburn's advertising methods were more specifically
held up to ridicule a few weeks later in a colloquy called
The Divan, in the manner of the "Noctes" of *Blackwood's.*
One character suggests writing a book to be called "A Trip
to Paris." Colburn would buy the title, and Maunder
(Montgomery's publisher) would put out the book with a
frontispiece of the author, a striking motto, and an appropriate dedication.

Sackville.—I shall grub with a dozen editors at the Literary
Fund Society, to-morrow; I'll engage them all to give you a lift.
Sancho.—We must also insert a knowing paragraph in the
'Morning Post', the 'Courier', the 'John Bull'; ah, Colburn is the
man for that business.
Sackville.—There is a report . . . that Colburn intends chalk-
ing the walls next season.
Blewit.—(Breathing forth fire and smoke) Puff, puff, puff.
Sackville.—I wish, sir, that the system of selling books by
machinery, as the 'Edinburgh Review' calls it, were to be discon-
tinued; I wish the public taste would rebel against it.[63]

Another clever shot at Colburn was wrapped in a Shakespearean quotation under the caption "Why authors of
anonymous fashionable novels ought to publish their names
in the 'Morning Chronicle' puffs."

[62] *Athenaeum,* July 1, 1829, p. 401.
[63] *Athenaeum,* Sept. 23, 1829, p. 599.

Bottom (publisher).—Nay, you must name his name, and half his face must be seen through the lion's neck . . . and there indeed let him tell his name, and say plainly he is Snug the Joiner.[64]

The *Athenaeum,* in this oblique firing, did not hesitate to twit Colburn and to "name his name." But the big guns of the campaign opened up in July, 1830, shortly after Dilke took control. The earliest effective shot was aimed at the first volume of *The Juvenile Library,* a new venture by Colburn and Bentley,[65] which had been ridiculously puffed in all the papers and magazines over which the publishers had any control, direct or indirect. John Hamilton Reynolds wrote an exposé of the system of puffery as a preliminary to a slashing review of the book.

No one will have the hardihood to say that the "Juvenile Library" is not become a positive nuisance in the newspapers; for it is scarcely possible to get through a single column of *Chronicle* or *Herald,* without having to suffer a Burlington Street paragraph. Nothing can be so moral and edifying as the "Juvenile Library"; nothing so pure and pleasant as its style; nothing so disinterested and generous as its object. The paragraphs, which are paid for, say all this; and some persons in London, and many credulous country readers, cannot read the same mystic hymn to the breeches-pocket day after day, without believing that things are what they are said to be.[66]

[64] *Athenaeum,* Oct. 21, 1829, p. 663.

[65] In September, 1829, Colburn took into partnership Richard Bentley, one of the brothers in his printing firm of Samuel and Richard Bentley. The partnership lasted until August, 1832, when Colburn sold the business to Bentley, retaining only his magazine holdings. The agreement was that Colburn was not to set up business within twenty miles of London, Edinburgh, or Dublin. It was the hope of Bentley to prevent Colburn from becoming a rival, but in this he was disappointed, for Colburn soon began publishing at Windsor. Bentley felt himself outwitted and accepted a sum of money to release Colburn from the agreement. The latter then opened business again in Great Marlborough Street, which became headquarters for the puffing trade. (For more details of the partnership and the quarrels of Colburn and Bentley, see Rosa, *op. cit.,* pp. 184-186.)

[66] *Athenaeum,* July 17, 1830, p. 440.

The reviewer then quoted a sample puff from the *Morning Chronicle,* and drew the obvious conclusion.

There can be little doubt that the stupidest cluster of trashy pages, the most insignificant articles, may by dint of eternal paragraph, be forced into sale. It could not otherwise happen, that Day and Martin, Rowland, Colburn and Bentley, Eady, Warren, and those after their kind, could lavish so much money in the praises of their oils, their books, their pills, and their polish, if there did not exist a class of human beings who are greedy of belief.[67] It is the duty of an independent journal to protect as far as possible the credulous, confiding, and unwary, from the wily arts of the insidious advertiser. And as we honestly think that the "Juvenile Library," judging it from the volume before us, is a hasty, pretending, ill-written work, . . . we hold it right to strike out of the path which our contemporaries have pursued, and to devote to it a candid column instead of a paid paragraph.[68]

In the same number there was a defense of Charles Lamb against an unwarranted attack in the *Literary Gazette,* which had immolated his *Album Verses* merely because, the *Athenaeum* charged, the volume was published by Moxon and not by Colburn.

If The Athenaeum were the property of the great publishers, and we were, in consequence, obliged to pour out whole columns of commendation upon all the trash they chose to publish, the public would very soon nauseate the paper, unless we did upon occasion find some innocent to slaughter for its entertainment; and here is literally a Lamb offering itself for the sacrifice. The

[67] This was already a familiar accusation of Colburn's advertising methods. He cheapened literature by putting it on a plane with commercial products which were widely advertised. The *London Magazine* (Feb., 1825, pp. 246-253) made a comparison between his publicity devices and those employed on Prince's Russia Oil, Rowland's Macassar, and Wright's Cape-Madeira. Macaulay only followed the common trend of criticism when he made a similar comparison in his attack on the much puffed Robert Montgomery. Colburn and other enterprising publishers were, however, merely adopting the advertising policies of expanding business firms, which had begun to use outdoor "chalking of the walls" and other spectacular stunts to sell new manufactured products.

[68] *Athenæum,* July 17, 1830, p. 440.

writer is an amiable, sensible man, but of 'no mark or likelihood' in the world; and his publisher, a poet himself heretofore, only just started as a bookseller, and enabled to do so by the kind and liberal patronage of another. It is then just such a work, published under such circumstances as a paper professedly independent, but essentially bookseller-bound, would rejoice in. We might be fierce and indignant or sneering and contemptuous enough to satisfy the uninitiated of our unshackled spirit, and to leaven a whole month's offensive, dull, dutiful, cringing commendation. Thank God, we are under no such necessity! . . . Mr. Lamb was never, in our judgment, a very powerful, though always a pleasant writer. . . . But . . . he is certainly not a man to write anything valueless and contemptible. . . . The Literary Gazette . . . is, it appears, only 'restrained from laughing at the present collection of absurdities, by the lamentable conviction of the blinding and engrossing nature of vanity.' Then let the Literary Gazette explain why it heretofore praised and countenanced the writer,—and itself published a portion of these verses in its own columns.[69]

Three weeks later the *Athenaeum* took up the fight again while rejoicing over the fact that Southey had raised his voice against the attack on Lamb in the *Literary Gazette.*

He comes long after us, it is true, but, to the shame of the public press, he precedes most others; and he brings with him the weight and influence of a name that must secure the judgment from the mean insinuation of being influenced by a paltry feeling of rivalry . . . unless there be more discretion both in the praise and censure of the *Literary Gazette,* not all the interest of Messrs. Longman and Co. and Colburn and Bentley, whose property it is, can uphold that paper. The public will at last understand, as well as we do, how to reconcile such severe indignation as the critic pours out on Mr. Lamb's work, with its *half dozen laudatory notices within one month* of one of the most hasty, inaccurate, and contemptible books ever published—the first number of 'The Juvenile Library.'[70]

[69] July 17, 1830, pp. 435-436. [70] Aug. 7, 1830, p. 491.

Then followed the poem by Southey, ending:
> "Dulness hath thrown *a jerdan* at thy head."[71]

From that time forward scarcely a number of the *Athenaeum* was free from straightforward allusions to the puffing trade and indictments of its chief practitioners. The
charges were scarcely new, but they had never before been
made so explicitly by an independent journal in statements
supported by concrete evidence. The disinterested character
of the magazine gave additional power to its words. Its
reputation for honesty grew when readers as well as writers
became slowly aware that a strange phenomenon had grown
up in their midst, a literary paper which served neither publishers nor party.

The *Athenaeum* reiterated the general charges against
the publishers with each new piece of evidence. First of
all, there was the direct puffing in panegyrical reviews in
periodicals owned or largely controlled by the publishers.
Dilke himself stated the case clearly in some additions which
he made to a review of *A Journal of a Heart,* by Lady
Charlotte Bury, one of Colburn and Bentley's well-paid
fashionable novelists. The publishers, he said, were not
satisfied with the praise of one of their good books. What
they wanted was "commendation for the bad book and the
costly speculation."

Now, suppose that Mr. Colburn was proprietor, in whole or
in part, of the Literary Gazette—the Court Journal—the Sunday
Times—the United Service Journal—the New Monthly Magazine;—and suppose he could, in addition, insert false and im-
pudent commendations of his volume, for a few shillings, in
other papers, where they would pass for the honest criticism of
the Editor—could he not with such means and appliances puff
the Juvenile into a sale in defiance of our scorn and ridicule?[72]

[71] Obviously a reference to the Elizabethan word "jordan," meaning chamber
pot.

[72] *Athenaeum,* Aug. 21, 1830, p. 517. According to the marked file this

Shortly after this a whole article was devoted to the *Literary Gazette.* It started with the motto: "The ox knoweth his owner, and the ass his master's crib." It called attention to the fact that

twenty-one columns of that same Literary Gazette, were taken up with extravagant commendation of books published by Messrs. Colburn and Bentley!!! and . . . that eleven columns of this extravagant commendation are bestowed on a volume of the 'National Library,' published by Colburn and Bentley, and that one *eighth of a column only* is given to a volume of the 'Family Library,' published by Mr. Murray.

This latter book was a history of India by Mr. Gleig, editor of Colburn's Library. But the book was not a Colburn and Bentley product and so was not found worthy of extracting.

Let the press of England ascertain if this statement be true, and, being satisfied of its truth, let them ask their own conscience, if it be not morally due to their readers to blazon it over the whole country.

A footnote adds:

Another extraordinary fact. In the New Monthly Magazine for August, also the property of Messrs. Colburn and Bentley . . . there are two columns of announcements of forthcoming works —and very pithy and pleasant announcements they are, enough to rejoice the hearts of country gentlemen, for certainly, all the books that have been published in the season will not equal, in stirring interest or in talent, what are to come. Now taking the announcements at 100—then by singular good fortune, it happens, that of these unequalled works, 95 will be published by Messrs. Colburn and Bentley, and only 5 have been secured by all the other publishers in the three kingdoms. Commend us to

---

review was by "D. and Picken." It is probable that Picken wrote the main part of the review and that Dilke added some general remarks on the system of puffery by which the book was ushered into sale.

the announcements in the New Monthly, but above all, to the criticisms in the Literary Gazette!!![73]

The second charge was that Colburn and Bentley inserted paid paragraphs in newspapers and brought business and personal pressure to bear upon other literary journals. Advertising was then, as always, an effective means of keeping editors in check, to use Colburn's own phrase.[74] In the review of the *Juvenile Library* the *Athenaeum* had mentioned the *Chronicle* and the *Herald* as chiefly susceptible to the paid paragraphs, but other papers were equally vulnerable. Soon after Dilke became editor a note appeared in the advertising columns stating that the magazine was in the hands of new proprietors and under a new editor, and warning the public that many of the most influential journals were the "absolute property of the great publishers." "It is equally known that paragraphs professing to be criticisms *are paid for as advertisements* in many Papers. *The Athenaeum* . . . admits *no* advertisement that is not distinctly marked as such."[75]

A few weeks later came the announcement that since the adverse review of the "Juvenile" its "parents" had withdrawn their advertising support from the *Athenaeum*. But in order that the readers of the journal might not be deprived of seeing the Colburn and Bentley advertisements, the editor quoted a few of the puffing notices of the books and magazines of those publishers from the *Morning Post*, the *Morning Chronicle*, *John Bull*, the *Age*, and the *Observer*.

We have said much on these vile paid-for criticisms; but we cannot have said enough, while any publisher shall think them worth the cost. We know the hazard we run in exposing these things, but we have set up our standard, and mean to fight the

[73] *Athenaeum*, Sept. 4, 1830, p. 556.
[74] See Rosa, *op. cit.*, p. 195.   [75] *Athenaeum*, Dec. 4, 1830, p. 767.

good fight at all hazards. We therefore publicly assert, that every one of these seeming criticisms—these professed judgments of the editor of the paper—were written by some scribe in Burlington Street, *and their insertion paid for by Messrs. Colburn and Bentley.* If we refer more frequently to these publishers than to others, it is because they are the greatest offenders in this way. . . . It surely ought to be enough for one house to have property in, and therefore influence over, the *Literary Gazette,* the *Sunday Times,* the *Court Journal,* the *New Monthly Magazine,* and the *United Service Journal,* without shaking the public faith in every other journal in the kingdom by criticisms, which, we again repeat, *were all paid for.*[76]

Sir Charles Morgan contributed an article on "Criticism" wherein he analysed and exposed the practices of the puffing publishers. The daily journals, he said, dabble in literature, and since reviewing is not considered important, it is left to party intrigue or personal malice.

Add to this that a thriving bookseller spends very many thousands per annum with the press in regular advertising, and in those puffs, remote, collateral, or direct, which, assuming the form of editorial paragraphs, are always concocted . . . by the bookseller, and paid for on somewhat higher terms than an ordinary advertisement. To suppose that this money is altogether without its effect in determining the character of newspaper criticisms on books, is to deny the most familiar workings of human nature.[77]

In reviewing Mrs. Jameson's *Memoirs of Celebrated Female Sovereigns,* the *Athenaeum* asserted that Colburn could, "for a few shillings, insert an insidious eulogy on any work in any daily paper, honourably excepting *The Times,* and, we believe, *The Herald.*"[78]

[76] *Athenaeum,* Jan. 15, 1831, p. 45.
[77] *Athenaeum,* Jan. 29, 1831, p. 73.
[78] Oct. 29, 1831, p. 705. See also *Fraser's,* April, 1830, p. 319, and *Athenaeum,* Dec. 4, 1830, p. 767, and Jan. 15, 1831, p. 45. Thackeray wrote in 1858 to Captain Atkinson [*Leisure Hour* Sept., 1883]: ". . . I know the editor

A third accusation was that the publishers deceived country readers who got their book news from the provincial papers which copied the paid paragraphs to fill space. But Colburn went even further to keep the provincial press supplied with puffs.

One of the last speculations is the *Literary Gleaner,* which contains extracts from the new works published in Burlington Street. This, we understand, is sent free to all the newspapers in the kingdom; and the fact will explain to our country readers the many little stars of intelligence which brighten the dull pages of some of our provincials.[79]

Another reiterated accusation was that Colburn and Bentley withheld copies of their books from independent reviewers until after a few "serviceable" reviews and paid paragraphs could be put in the hands of country readers and booksellers. After announcing the forthcoming publication of Grattan's *Heiress of Bruges* (published by Colburn and Bentley), the *Athenaeum* received a letter from J. Pickersgill, the managing clerk of the publishers, asking them not to print a review until *due notice* of publication had been given.

... this honest testimony to our integrity by Messrs. Colburn and Bentley deserves our best thanks. When did they ever serve a like notice on the Editor of the Literary Gazette? We ask Mr. Bentley if he interfered *to prevent* the review of the first number of the Juvenile Library from appearing in that paper previous to the publication of the work itself?[80]

---

and most of the writers [of the *Times*], and, knowing, never think of asking a favour for myself or any mortal man. They are awful and inscrutable, and a request for a notice might bring down a slasher upon you, just as I once had in the *Times* for one of my own books ('Esmond'), of which the sale was absolutely stopped by a *Times* article." (Quoted, Lewis Melville [pseud.], *William Makepeace Thackeray,* p. 286.)

[79] *Athenaeum,* Feb. 18, 1832, p. 114.

[80] *Athenaeum,* Aug. 28, 1830, p. 540.

In referring to the same incident in the following number the *Athenaeum* exposed further the working of the system.

... while a legal notice was served on this journal to withhold criticism on a forthcoming work of theirs, another forthcoming book of theirs was monstrously and extravagantly praised ... in the Literary Gazette. ... to all the world, except the initiated, the said work had seemingly ... been published some days, having been positively so announced. [But] it could not be had by any independent journal, until the criticism of the said Literary Gazette, backed by a like criticism in the Court Journal, also their property, had circulated all over the country, and the orders for the work, consequent on their commendation had been dispatched to London.[81]

When the *Heiress of Bruges* finally appeared, the reviewer summarized the matter. The *Athenaeum* had waited for the *due notice,* which did not appear, and in the meantime a commendatory criticism of five columns appeared in the *Literary Gazette.*[82]

The same tactics were applied in the puffing of Mrs. Jameson's book, which was lauded in the *Literary Gazette* and the *Court Journal* before the actual date of publication.

Now, these *criticisms* are circulated all over the country, just in time to bring up orders from 'old and young,' for the Magazine parcels on the 31st; but till it is too late for an independent, and therefore honest judgment to reach the public, not a single copy is permitted to pass from out the publishers' safe keeping: we ourselves sent last week, but could not purchase one.[83]

In September, 1832, Bentley published *Zohrab the Hostage* by Morier, author of *Hajji Baba.* The *Athenaeum* commented in the "Weekly Gossip":

[81] *Athenaeum,* Sept. 4, 1830, p. 556.
[82] *Athenaeum,* Oct. 16, 1830, p. 646.
[83] *Athenaeum,* Oct. 29, 1831, p. 705.

This work was professedly *reviewed* in the Bookseller's Gazette[84] of the *eighth* of this month, at a time when we have reason to believe, the printing was not finished—it was made the leading article, and ten columns were given, to satisfy the world of the importance of the work . . . and this serviceable paragraph has ever since been circulating all over the country—it has been impossible to take up a newspaper, without stumbling on it; we are of opinion, that not less than *one hundred pounds* has been expended in giving it currency. Now the orders from the country, for this 'interesting narrative of this delightful author,' must arrive in London by the 25th or 26th, to ensure the receipt of the work by the booksellers' monthly parcels. Will not this then be admitted as a system most ruinous to our literature, when we add, that 'Zohrab the Hostage' has not yet been seen, except by the trade critic, and that it *is not even now published!*[85]

A fifth count against the system of puffery was that it brought ruin to country booksellers who were forced by the preliminary puffing to order quantities of books which shortly after they were published became a drug on the market. A bookseller in Belfast had written:

"My failure is, in great measure, to be attributed to the extremely high prices of Colburn's new novels for my library, having in a comparatively short period, paid nearly 400 pounds, at the rate of 25s. 3d. a copy, for works that, in general, are not worth more than 7s. 6d. It is one of the most complete monopolies I at present know in any trade; and the system of letting the corps of novel-writers, who are now become the mere free-booters of the press, review and puff each other alternately, is one of the humbugs of the present day, which ought to be exposed."[86]

The *Athenaeum* added that "after the first sale consequent on the puff preliminary, the price at which they are offered to the trade in London usually varies from eightpence to one shilling the volume."[87]

[84] This was the general term used by the *Athenaeum* reviewers at the time in referring to the *Literary Gazette*.   [85] Sept. 22, 1832, p. 620.

[86] *Athenaeum*, Nov. 10, 1832, p. 734.   [87] *Ibid.*

A sixth and final charge was that the publishers deliberately attempted to fool the public by issuing books under deceptive titles, by arousing curiosity through inspired innuendoes in magazines and papers concerning authorship of anonymous books, and by suggesting that the characters of a novel were taken from real life and could be identified with certain persons in "high life."

Colburn and his press agents had an infallible way of getting his books talked about. The *Athenaeum* described the method in reviewing *The Devil's Progress,* an anonymous work which Colburn was trying to prod into sale by hinting a high-born authorship.

We believe the 'Devil's Progress' is written by Mr. T. K. Hervey: it is certainly not by the Editor of the Court Journal, although nothing can be more admirably imitative of the puff-preliminary which usually precedes Colburn's works, than the introductory Preface, professedly from the Morning Post, with its insinuations and *on dits*—its whisperings and implications, ending in a doubt as to the authorship, between the Editor of the Court Journal and his Most Gracious Majesty.[88]

Insinuations of this sort became one of Colburn's specialties in advertising his fashionable novels. After the publication of *The Exclusives,* the *Court Journal* announced: "A little work is coming out in a few days, called 'A Key to the Exclusives.' . . . We give the list as we find it, without offering any opinion as to its authenticity."[89] The following week the same journal printed a letter suggesting that Lord Chesterfield had written the novel. The editor added a jovial note intimating that he might tell who the author was if he wanted to.[90]

[88] Sept. 18, 1830, p. 584.

[89] *Court Journal,* Jan. 2, 1830, p. 13.

[90] Jan. 9, 1830, pp. 25-26. The author was Lady Charlotte Bury. It is noteworthy that even the mild Jerdan turned against this novel. It was harshly reviewed in the *Literary Gazette,* Dec. 5, 1829, p. 792. The *Westminster* and

When *The Humorist* was incorporated with the *New Monthly* under the editorship of Theodore Hook in 1837, the *Athenaeum* insinuated that Hook had lent himself to Colburn's mysteries about the editor, advertised as "one of the most distinguished writers of the day." But according to the advertisement, the new editor was to be "assisted" by Mr. Hook. We must "leave this interesting mystery, like other of Mr. Colburn's 'state secrets,' to be added to The Man in the Iron Mask." But, following the general policy of the *Athenaeum* under Dilke, the magazine was judged on its own merits. The pronouncement was that "the first number of *The New Monthly,* under the editorship of Mr. Hook, is capital, and full of 'golden promises.' "[91]

In fact, one distinguishing characteristic of the *Athenaeum* battle against puffery was its outspoken and on the whole consistent attack upon the "system," and upon individual authors or publishers only when they came in the line of fire. In an attempt to display impartiality in this regard, the reviewers frequently stretched their praise beyond what they might normally have been inclined to give when they came upon a book of tolerable merit bearing the colophon of the publishers whom they had just attacked most uncompromisingly for puffing inferior or trashy works. Nor was it uncommon for a review to begin with an accusation of the practices of the publisher in advertising a book which the reviewer then proceeded to laud for its own worth. Moreover, the *Athenaeum* did not, as did *Fraser's* and some of the other magazines which took up the fight against puffery, consistently ridicule an author who happened to be the subject of Colburn's extravagant advertising, but tried with an apparent honesty, which *Fraser's* reviewers would

---

Blackwood's had as early as 1825 exposed Colburn's use of sly insinuations concerning authorship of his anonymous books. See *Westminster,* Oct., 1825, p. 293; and *Blackwood's,* May, 1825, p. 518.

[91] *Athenaeum,* Jan. 14, 1837, pp. 26-27.

have considered merely fence-riding dullness, to see merit in at least some of the works of writers who were most notoriously puffed.

Nevertheless, *Fraser's* once reprimanded the *Athenaeum* in a rather superior way for finding nothing good in the works of Colburn and Bentley.

A weekly paper, called the *Athenaeum,* has thought proper to attack Mr. Galt very violently for this *Life of Byron*. . . .What grounds of complaint Messrs. Colburn and Bentley may have given the right worshipful worthies of this smartly-written hebdomadal, we know not; but it is evident that something of this sort must have happened, for as regularly as a book issues from the house of the booksellers in New Burlington-street, so surely is it made a subject of attack in the pages of the *Athenaeum*. This, however, . . . is a dangerous course for the adoption of the managers of this respectable periodical. . . . Heaven knows, that towards these gentlemen of New Burlington-street we have not ourselves been over sparing or merciful; but then our cruelty has not been of a sweeping character . . . as soon as they produced a wholesome publication, we proved ourselves right glad of the opportunity of uttering our laudatory opinion, and effecting the sale of the work.[92]

The plain record of reviewing in the two magazines shows, however, that the *Athenaeum* followed the policy boastingly outlined by *Fraser's* much more consistently than did the Fraserians. That its fight was not a personal one is evident from the fact that other publishers who followed in the footsteps of Colburn were just as severely handled by the *Athenaeum* critics.[93] And, having come into the

---

[92] "Galt's Life of Byron," *Fraser's,* Oct., 1830, p. 347.

[93] E.g., see the review of "The Anatomy of Society by the celebrated Mr. St. John," published by Bull (*Athenaeum*, March 12, 1831, p. 167): "Mr. St. John is a well-known . . . literary man, but in no way celebrated. . . . Mr. Bull's offences in this way are becoming too notorious to be passed over; the paid paragraph about Boaden's 'Life of Mrs. Jordan'—one of the most vile catch-penny books that ever disgraced literature—has excited general disgust; and this of 'the celebrated' Mr. St. John is little less offensive. . . . We have no quixotic

limelight for their attacks on the puffing practices of Colburn and Bentley, they made a special effort to be fair in reviewing the books of those publishers.

Andrew Picken, who had aided Dilke in the attack on puffery, found *De L'Orme* by G. P. R. James (published by Colburn and Bentley) "an able production." Though there is a suggestion of Scott in the handling of historical parts, the author may "hold his head proudly in the master's presence."

> But we must refer to the volumes themselves, which will be read with pleasure by those who, disgusted with common trash puffed to the skies through all the various channels of puffery, are still willing to enjoy a good novel.[94]

J. Fenimore Cooper had been the target of several attacks in the *Athenaeum* (sometimes with commiseration for his misfortune in being put in a bad light by the puffing of Colburn), but when *The Pilot* was reprinted as the first of Colburn and Bentley's *Standard Novels and Romances,* the reviewer said:

> This work . . . deserves . . . hearty . . . encouragement from the great body of English readers . . . it affords us much pleasure to be able to say in perfect sincerity a fair word for one of the Library schemes which has originated in Burlington Street. We are supposed by some persons to be markedly hostile to Messrs. Colburn and Bentley, and we have for some time felt annoyed that those publishers should have perseveringly withheld from us the means of showing that our antipathy was not to persons, but to unquestionably bad books.[95]

A close perusal of the *Athenaeum* reviews in the 1830's should convince a fair-minded reader that the boast of the

---

fancy for quarrelling with booksellers, but can 'screw our courage to the sticking-place' if it be necessary, to battle the whole generation."

[94] *Athenaeum,* Aug. 28, 1830, pp. 529-531.

[95] *Athenaeum,* March 12, 1831, p. 161.

editors was not an idle one. With even less than a due
allowance for human frailties in the reviewers, it is possible
to conclude that the magazine was indeed one which made
honesty its policy. With few exceptions it did condemn
bad books and praise good ones. And what is more important, when it failed, the fault could be laid to shortness
of vision and not to party or commercial bias. It was not
long before the public began to realize this, and intelligent
readers everywhere came to trust its judgment of books
more than that of any other literary journal.

Dilke's own resolve to maintain a rigid fairness trans-
cending personal prejudices communicated itself to most of
his regular reviewers. Even Henry Chorley, who had an
almost Jerdan-like "leaning to kindness" in his reviews of
lady novelists and poets, somewhat restrained his panegyric
under the eye of Dilke. Chorley indeed felt that his own
books were from policy neglected. He noted in his journal
in 1839 that the failure of his novel *The Lion* (published
by Colburn) was entire as he expected, but he was hurt
by "the wrong-headed unfairness" of a review in the *Athenaeum.*[96] Chorley noted later in an autobiographical
fragment:

> It was the rule to avoid the slightest undue favour to any of
> the staff, and even to dismiss the individual publications of con-
> tributors, oftentimes laconically, sometimes with a searching dis-
> play of errors and weak points, which in more flagrant cases
> might have been passed over.[97]

The fact that many of the *Athenaeum* group had written
books which were published by Colburn and Bentley or by
Longman,[98] might have complicated the problems of the

[96] Chorley, *op. cit.,* I, 151.   [97] *Ibid.*

[98] Besides Chorley and Lady Morgan (who was one of Colburn's favorite
authors until she broke with him in September, 1830, after she had given her
second book on France to Saunders and Otley), William and Mary Howitt,
Eyre Evans Crowe, and many other regular staff writers produced books which

Athenaeum had not Dilke insisted upon keeping the issues clear and separating the attack upon a vicious system from the reviewing of individual books and authors.

DEFLATION OF PUFFED LITERARY REPUTATIONS

The *Athenaeum* did not lag behind in deflating over-praised books and literary reputations, though here as in its fight against trade criticism it kept a better perspective and displayed a greater fairness than most other periodicals of the time. It was among the first to take the wind out of the sails of "Satan" Montgomery,[99] the conceited young poet who capitalized the current taste for piety and religious themes by writing verses, which he imagined second only to *Paradise Lost,* on grandiose topics such as *The Omnipresence of the Deity, Satan, A Universal Prayer, A Vision of Heaven,* etc. Robert Montgomery's fame today rests not at all upon the really astounding popularity of his poems in

---

bore the imprint of the puffing publishers; and many of the *Athenaeum* circle were frequent contributors to the *New Monthly.* Moreover, Hood and Cunningham were close friends of Jerdan while Dilke was engaged in exposing the notorious puffery in the *Literary Gazette,* but of course the attack was really against Colburn rather than the editor of the *Gazette.*

[99] *The Monthly Magazine* was apparently the first to raise its voice against the extravagant praise given to Montgomery. See *Athenaeum,* Oct. 8, 1828, p. 787n. In an editorial note on the back of the contents page of *Fraser's* for Feb., 1832, there was a characteristic boast in the swaggering manner of Oliver Yorke: "Our pages will show that Regina was the very first to expose the charlatanism of 'poor Montgomery.' . . . Our first notice of Montgomery was about March, 1829; and the 'Quarterlies' were pleased to adopt our tone at a much later date." But this is obviously untrue. In the first place, *Fraser's* first number came out in February, 1830, but even if the date given were correct instead of only a slip of the pen, the boast is unfounded in fact, for the first attack in the *Athenaeum* was on Oct. 8, 1828. And the latter publication had shot many sharp and effective darts before *Fraser's* entered the fight in its first number with a review of *Satan* (the *Athenaeum* review of this volume came a month before *Fraser's*). Even *Blackwood's* preceded *Fraser's* in sending a volley at Montgomery, and both were ahead of Macaulay's *Edinburgh Review* article. In an article on "Canting Poetry" in *Blackwood's* for August, 1829, p. 241, there is a jeering notice of "a young man with his milk-and-water-looking head stuck in the frontispiece of his book, looking as contented as primness and affectation will allow."

his own day,[100] but mainly upon the fact that he was the stepping stone from which Macaulay proceeded to his well-known attack on puffery in the *Edinburgh Review*.[101] But the *Athenaeum* preceded Macaulay by more than a year in deflating the reputation of Montgomery, and it continued to treat him with less than the reverence to which he thought himself entitled as his successive poems and numerous editions appeared.

It is true that when Montgomery's *magnum opus, The Omnipresence of the Deity*, was published it received a rather favorable notice in the *Athenaeum*. It should be said, however, that *Blackwood's*, the only other major critical journal which reviewed it,[102] gave qualified but rather warm praise, quoting with approval the judgment of the *Athenaeum*.[103] It must be remembered too that this review ap-

[100] When Jerdan wrote his Autobiography in 1853, he felt that Montgomery's popularity at that time justified the praise he had given him in the *Literary Gazette* years before. "When Mr. Robert Montgomery commenced his career, he was roughly handled and greatly discouraged by the critical authorities. . . . I believe I stood almost alone in vindicating for Montgomery that poetic character which has since been ratified by the public voice, and even conceded by those who used to rail at his productions. . . ." (Jerdan, *op. cit.*, IV, 310.) Jerdan says that Montgomery has vindicated himself by his many editions and cites 25 or more of the *Omnipresence*, 12 of *Satan*, 10 of the *Messiah*, 8 of *Oxford* and of *Woman*, 6 of *Luther*, etc. When his first volume appeared, Jerdan says, Montgomery was so abused that "the whole Trade took only six copies! But the 'Literary Gazette' reviews soon turned the scale, and when the third edition was called, the publisher [Maunder], in thanking me, stated that he had sold 2,000 copies over the counter in ten days—a poetical sale unequalled since the days of 'Childe Harold.'" (Jerdan, *op. cit.*, IV, 311.) He adds that the *Times* and *Blackwood's* both put in a word in Montgomery's favor. According to Jerdan's estimate, 80,000 or 90,000 volumes of Montgomery's poetry had then (1853) been sold in England, besides large sales in the United States.

[101] April, 1830, Article IX, pp. 193-210.

[102] This is true if we leave out of account the *Times* (see n. 100 above) and the Colburn publications which usually praised everything except the work of decided enemies—and Colburn had no quarrel with Samuel Maunder, the publisher of Montgomery, since he was not a potent rival. The *Literary Gazette* had said: "It is indeed a magnificent and sublime composition, and in the very highest class of English Sacred Poetry."

[103] The *Athenaeum* review had some qualifications in its praise, but it hailed Montgomery as "a young man of considerable talent and well deserving attention."

peared in February, 1828, before Dilke had any connection with the paper and when the reviews were written by Maurice, Stebbing, and others of like mind who would have a natural predisposition towards a religious poem and would treat it kindly if possible. Moreover, there was not the challenge of the excessive puffing of Montgomery to arouse antagonism in the reviewer.

The second review of Montgomery in the *Athenaeum*, that of *A Universal Prayer; Death; A Vision of Heaven; and a Vision of Hell*, was obviously by a different and a less reverent hand. A footnote apologized for the earlier praise of the poet and made some excuses for it. Unlike *Blackwood's* and *Fraser's*, however, when they set upon Montgomery, the *Athenaeum* avoided biting personalities and kept the discussion within the bounds of literary criticism. The writer said that an appropriate occasion had presented itself "for expressing the grief and indignation with which we have seen poems, simply upon the credit of a religious title, making their way from edition to edition. . . ."[104] The reviewer then turned to Montgomery.

We do not profess to conceal that the astonishing success of his last Poem 'The Omnipresence of the Deity', is one of those instances, which indicate, we think, that names have much more weight with the public than things, and that a well-chosen title may suddenly raise a very indifferent poem to a pitch of popularity which a first rate poem would have no chance of attaining. If we have carried these feelings with us to the 'Universal Prayer' . . . Mr. Montgomery has no right to complain. Before he determined upon his subject, he had no doubt counted the cost, and when he put down on the credit side three editions more than

[104] The religious subject matter undoubtedly accounted in a large measure for the popularity of Montgomery. After reading extensively in the literature and criticism of the early Victorian period, Lounsbury concluded that "there is nothing a large share of the English-speaking race enjoy more keenly than being preached to. . . . For them all other pleasures pale beside the reading of platitudes seasoned with morality and religion and garnished with the ornament of verse." (*The Life and Times of Tennyson*, p. 202.)

would otherwise be sold, as the reward of his choice, he can scarcely have thought it necessary . . . to mark down on the opposite side the murmurings of a few critics who have the rare fault of being somewhat too jealous for the honour of poetry and religion.

The 'Universal Prayer' with which the present goodly quarto opens . . . is a series of cold abstractions, not a parody upon the Church of England service, but a sort of index to it, in which that wonderful composition is exhausted of all its poetry in order to put it into verse. We must do Mr. Montgomery, however, the justice to say, that there is in this composition much less of mere trash and vapouring than in any other of his works which we have met with. The diction is, in general, natural,—a transparent medium through which the poverty of the author's mind is clearly and honestly reflected.[105]

As the number of Montgomery's editions increased, his conceit apparently grew, and the *Athenaeum* continued to take delight in ridiculing his pretensions. Numerous poetry reviews and random notes contained mocking comments on him. This "sniping" was carried on consistently until the appearance of *Satan* gave a fuller opportunity for direct attack.

Mr. Montgomery represents Lucifer as not at all a knave, and very much a fool. We have heard that he is not so black as he is painted; but the present author makes him blacker than he has ever before been delineated,—for he clothes him in a neat suit of clerical sable, and sets him to preach at the vices and follies of the world, as if he were a minister of the Gospel . . . the torrent of abuse against everything naughty here flowing from the lips of the Devil cannot possibly be equalled, unless some Millenarian teacher should happen to convert a fishwoman of the ward of Billingsgate.[106]

---

[105] *Athenaeum*, Oct. 8, 1828, pp. 786-787.

[106] *Athenaeum*, Jan. 9, 1830, p. 1. The importance which the editor assigned to the subject may be indicated by the fact that the review was the leader of the first number of the new year.

Shortly after this Macaulay's article appeared in the *Edinburgh Review* and Montgomery was thenceforth fair game for nearly all the critics in the major literary journals, with the exception of course of Jerdan of the *Literary Gazette*. The *Athenaeum*, however, accused Macaulay, who had attempted to make capital of the current outcry against literary puffery by using Montgomery as a symbol of malpractices in the trade, of being afraid to name the offending publishers and their controlled magazines.

There is in the last number of the Edinburgh Review, a very clever article on Montgomery, the author of the 'Omnipresence of the Deity,' and not the Poet of that name [James Montgomery]; and the writer of the article has said something, and to the purpose, on booksellers' puffing. To this *we* cannot object. But why has the Reviewer put the case hypothetically? why has he wrapped up his truths in the napkin of a fable? To all conversant with the system, he indeed, speaks intelligibly enough; but they . . . needed no such commentary. The thing wanting was information to those *not* conversant with it. When the Reviewer talks of a Journal the sole property of the great publishers, and of the unpaid advertisements therein inserted under the disguise and character of criticism, no author doubts for a moment the paper referred to; but those poor simple sheep, the readers, 'look up, and are not fed.' They cannot penetrate the Reviewer's fable. We regret it. There may be, and there is, something selfish in our regret. An independent paper fights up against tremendous odds;—its success must depend on the liberal support it shall receive from the public and from other independent papers.[107]

[107] *Athenaeum*, July 17, 1830, p. 435. This paragraph appeared at the beginning of the review of Lamb's *Album Verses*, before mentioned, which the *Literary Gazette* had slashed because the book came from an independent publisher. Professor Lounsbury has said of Macaulay's article on Montgomery that it "has survived not because of its merits but because it has been included in the collected edition of the author's essays. It is the popularity of these other writings which has given to it a reputation for effectiveness which it did not have at that time and never deserved at any time. Of itself it had no claim to be reprinted. It is not merely inferior to most of the other similar but now

Early in 1831, when the reputation of the *Athenaeum* for fairness and impartiality was beginning to be established, Allan Cunningham wrote to Dilke:

I send you Montgomery's new poem. He wishes for justice. But you must give him *more*. You must be *merciful*. He is now suffering under the double misery of being over and under praised. Make the *Athenaeum* the happy medium. I have ever considered him a young man of good poetic talent, who, had he been left more to himself, would have done better than he has.[108]

But the new poem, *Oxford,* was treated with little respect in the *Athenaeum* nevertheless.

It has been hinted to us by a friend, that Mr. Montgomery is suffering under the double misery of being *over* and *under* praised, and therefore it would be becoming the integrity of the *Athenaeum* to be scrupulously just towards him. . . . We have also been told that it is a dreadful thing to crush a young poet, and most sincerely do we agree with the writer; but, in truth, a man who rides triumphant on nine editions, comes not within the meaning of the words; and we think they do not apply to Mr. Montgomery, for more intelligible reasons.[109]

It is either a tribute to the comparative fairness of the *Athenaeum* in dealing with Montgomery, or an indication of the fatuous ego of the latter, that after such a general battering the poet had the temerity to send his works entire to Dilke's private house. Dilke, of course, returned them, saying, "I am sensible of your kindness, but it has ever been a rule with me since my first connexion with the *Athenaeum* to decline presents of books from authors or publishers."[110]

Even as late as 1842, when the general popularity and

---

forgotten attacks which had previously been published, it is so unfair in its criticism and so misleading in its statements as to be discreditable to its author." (*The Life and Times of Tennyson*, p. 194.)

[108] *Papers of a Critic*, I, 28.

[109] *Athenaeum*, March 12, 1831, p. 163.

[110] *Papers of a Critic*, I, 48.

success of Montgomery had somewhat overawed some critics, the *Athenaeum* continued to make sport of him. The reviewer of *Luther* begins with a few gibes at the facility with which Montgomery dashes off epics, and continues, "That poetry such as his has a certain currency in England, must be acknowledged, since it appears that 'Woman' has arrived at a fifth, 'Satan' at a tenth, and 'The Omnipresence' at a twenty-first edition. Yet it is very certain that copies cannot have been exported to China, where the importation of opium is prohibited by law."[111]

Thus the *Athenaeum* exposed the exaggerated pretensions of an overrated poet effectively and uncompromisingly without indulging in the envenomed personalities of *Blackwood's* and *Fraser's*. Moreover, the deflation of Montgomery was not an isolated incident in the review history of the magazine but was typical of its attitude towards a number of popular writers who were overpraised and overpuffed by friends as well as by publishers.

Letitia Elizabeth Landon, commonly known as L. E. L., probably enjoyed a greater popularity in the twenties and thirties than Montgomery achieved in his whole career. Although she was also favored by Jerdan, who claimed to have "discovered" her for the *Literary Gazette*,[112] most of the critics were kinder to her than they were to Montgomery. Her poetry was less pretentious and her own claims less arrogant. Though she was as systematically

---

[111] *Athenaeum*, April 2, 1842, p. 287. This review, according to the marked file, was by Marmion W. Savage, a frequent reviewer of English literature, and particularly of Shakespearean scholarship, in the forties. The fact that this is the only name of Montgomery's reviewers in the marked file, may indicate that some at least of the reviews were written by the editor himself, since he never signed his own contributions, or it may suggest Dilke's caution in keeping close the secret of the authorship of reviews of such a notorious puffer. Of course, it must be remembered that the marking began with Dilke's editorship and some volumes are not marked in the existing editorial file.

[112] Jerdan says that L. E. L. was for many years "an effective colleague" on the *Literary Gazette*. (*Autobiography*, III, 173.)

puffed by her friends as any of the literary lights of her day, she struck a note which forestalled harsh criticism and vibrated a sympathetic chord in the breasts of the vast majority of her contemporaries and of all but the most daringly independent and unemotional of the critics. She commanded sentimental themes at just the point where they were mingled with enough thought and originality to give her readers relaxed enjoyment of the former while believing themselves touched chiefly by the latter. Her themes were not grandiose but commonplace, conventional, and sufficiently pious to satisfy an orthodox clergyman.[113] In fact, she was a typical and ideal contributor to the annuals.

The *Athenaeum* record here is not so clear as in the case of Montgomery. There were curious and interesting complications in its varying attitudes towards her which can be understood properly only by a careful scrutiny of the individual bias of each reviewer.[114] But in a rapid generalization

[113] It is necessary in judging all early Victorian literature and criticism, particularly that appealing to the middle classes, to keep in mind the fact that education, both private and public, was mostly in the hands of clergymen. It is understandable then that few writers of the period, and fewer critics, even if their own training had not predisposed them to the pious note, dared to be less than cautious when writing for a widely circulated magazine. Whereas a truly popular writer, such as L. E. L. or Dickens (their contemporaries would have seen no literary sacrilege in mentioning their names together), was always too well aware, consciously or unconsciously, of the atmosphere of the period to neglect this element of universal appeal. And the general popularity of these and other writers was undoubtedly increased by their keeping the note of piety at a pitch where both Dissenters and Churchmen could peacefully intone it.

[114] For example, Henry Chorley believed that L. E. L. wrote against him as a member of the "opposition camp" at the command of Jerdan. "For years, the amount of gibing sarcasm and imputation to which I was exposed, was largely swelled by this poor woman's commanded spite." (H. F. Chorley, *Autobiography, Memoir, and Letters*, I, 108.) Nevertheless Chorley had some contact with L. E. L. despite her hostility towards him as a writer for the rival of the *Literary Gazette*. He wrote sympathetically of her in his journal: "She was incomplete, but she was worthy of being completed. . . ." He had occasion to see her once in connection with the granting of a preferment to one of her relatives, and she burst into hysterical tears. "Oh!" she cried, "you don't know the ill-natured things I have written about you!" (*Ibid.*, pp. 249-253.) Chorley wrote a kindly notice of her death in the *Athenaeum* (Jan. 5,

it may be said that the reviews under Dilke tended to show that she was a minor poet of some merit but that she had been spoiled with too much adulation and uncritical praise.

A criticism of L. E. L. characteristic of the regime of Maurice and Sterling appeared in a dialogue called *The Divan*.

> Blewit.—Miss Landon is a young woman of some talent.
>
> Sancho.—I know her books have sold very well, if that proves anything.
>
> Blewit.—That certainly proves something, Sancho. I do not know that it proves any thing in favour of their contents.[115]

The reviewer of *The Venetian Bracelet* in the next number complains that L. E. L. has been unfortunate in listening too much to the critics. "Some impertinent blockhead in the 'Westminster Review,' informed this young lady that love was a very dull and monotonous subject." She consequently tried to vary it "by describing its eccentricities and waywardness, instead of its direct simple self-devotedness."[116] But the review, a leader, is generally favorable and fatherly.

A typical review after Dilke became editor is that of her novel *Romance and Reality* at the end of 1831, wherein L. E. L. is ridiculed because of the puffing in the *Literary Gazette*,[117] which had already noticed the work to the extent of twelve columns before copies had been made available for other reviewers. In order that *Athenaeum* readers may not be cheated, the editor mockingly quotes some of the panegyrics from the *Gazette:* "The poetical productions"

1839, p. 14). But of course Chorley did not join the *Athenaeum* staff until 1834, and the earlier reviews were probably given to Caunter or W. Cooke Taylor, or (if the review was less respectful) possibly to Reynolds.

[115] *Athenaeum*, Oct. 21, 1829, p. 664.

[116] *Athenaeum*, Oct. 28, 1829, p. 669.

[117] *Athenaeum*, Dec. 3, 1831, pp. 783-784. This was at a time when the *Athenaeum* was in the midst of its campaign against the puffing publishers. It is significant that the puffers are more ridiculed than the puffed.

of Miss Landon have "extended her fame and popularity to the widest range of the| English language." ". . . she has formed a new school in our poetic literature," etc. This novel combines the merits of all the types of narrative and adds beauties of its own, and is "the most striking production since 'Waverley.'"

But the next week the *Athenaeum*, following its strict custom of never victimizing the puffed writer on account of the puffing publisher, praised the book generously in a leader, which, however, characteristically concluded that L. E. L. had powers that she had not used to the best advantage.[118]

A little later John Hamilton Reynolds made sport of her again in a fictitious letter outlining the changes in literature during the last ten years. He spoke of her as a poet "amorous and botanical" who depicted "passion smothered in lilies."[119]   And in the same year (1832) a brief review of *Heath's Book of Beauty*, one of the "Annuals" edited by L. E. L. and published by Longman and Co., ridiculed her pretended innocence of the system of puffery practiced by her publishers and friends.

Of this work we had resolved to say no more. The publication came halting after the trade criticism at a distance that was truly ridiculous; but one passage in the preface is, *under circumstances,* a jewel worth picking out and holding up to admiration.

'There are few "partial friends" now-a-days,' says the amiable writer, 'whose *previous praise or advice gives you a foretaste of the critical futurity that awaits you:* your manuscript goes from the desk to the press, and from the press to the public, *to stand or fall by a judgment which casts no shadows before.'*

Now this is unjust; we have known this lady's works quoted three months, and reviewed three weeks before publication in the *Literary Gazette:* we must think therefore that the race of 'partial

---

[118] *Athenaeum*, Dec. 10, 1831, pp. 793-795.
[119] *Athenaeum*, Jan. 7, 1832, p. 6. See also *post*, p. 178.

friends' is not extinct; and it would be strange indeed if such persons could not give a foretaste of the critical future.[120]

In most subsequent notices L. E. L. was treated with kindness, though her work was never awarded unqualified praise.[121]

Some overpraised poets who were mercilessly treated in *Fraser's* were handled with considerable gentleness in the *Athenaeum*. Two of these were Thomas Haynes Bayly and Alaric "Attila" Watts.[122] In a note in the "Weekly Gossip" in 1834 the editors apologized for a reviewer who had referred to Bayly as "the laureate of the butterflies"[123] whose name was "offensive to the ears of stern critics."[124] And the *Athenaeum* was more grieved than angered when it found the poet falling below the standard it had expected of him. "Mr. Haynes Bayly's 'Songs of Society' in this [*New Monthly*] and the *Court Magazine* for the month, are so flimsy and trifling, that we cannot help asking him, in all kindliness, whether he has *any* regard for his fame?"[125]

[120] *Athenaeum*, Dec. 1, 1832, p. 776.

[121] It is possible that Chorley wrote many of these. See *post*, p. 185.

[122] *Fraser's* ran a series of mocking poetic dialogues called "Lays of the Twaddle School." Number 1 was a "Pastoral Duett between Robert Montgomery and Thomas Haynes Bayley [*sic*]." (August, 1831, p. 52.) Number 2 was a "Lyric Lilt between L. E. L. and Lady Morgan." (Nov., 1831, pp. 433-434.) And Number 3 presented a "Classic Chant between Lord Francis Leveson Gower and Alaric Attila Watts." (June, 1832, p. 583.) The *Athenaeum* of course never took such a ribald tone even in criticising Montgomery. Number 1 is a fair example of the critical method of *Fraser's:*

> R. M. Satan saintly I sang, with meek Maw-worm mummery,
>   And old Beelzebub's bard was young Robert Montgomery.
> T. H. B. Satins and silks I sang gravely and gaily,
>   And the bard of the *boudoir* was Thomas Haynes Bayley
> R. M. To my genius and muse nothing earthly could come awry,
>   Such a devil of a poet was Robert Montgomery.
> T. H. B. With my butterflies, buttercups, butter flow'rs daily,
>   I buttered my bread—heigh, for Thomas Haynes Bayley.

[123] Bayly's most popular poem was a sentimental piece called "I'd be a Butterfly."

[124] Sept. 6, 1834, p. 659.   [125] April 4, 1835, p. 266.

Alaric Watts, editor of the *Literary Souvenir,* one of the earliest and most popular of the annuals, was a versifier who had caught the popular ear in a way that let him in for a great deal of ridicule, especially from the Fraserians. The *Athenaeum* did not join in that ridicule though it did not champion him as a poet. Watts once appealed to the fairness of the *Athenaeum* and protested against its praising *Fraser's* at the same time that it decried personalities in criticism. The editor replied that the magazine had always objected to personalities in *Fraser's* as elsewhere, but there was no denying the merit of *Fraser's.*[126]

At another time the *Athenaeum* found itself allied with Watts in a fight against puffery in the *Literary Gazette.* After boasting of its own, independence, it said, "Mr. Watts is the first who has ventured forward to beard the nuisance, and dared to put his name to the paper."[127] This did not mean, however, that Watts's poetry would be any more lauded on that account. But the magazine did not make him the subject of direct attack as in the case of Montgomery. Yet Dilke once, in rather emphatic terms, denied that Watts had ever written for the *Athenaeum.*[128]

One writer, now completely forgotten (except by collectors of literary curiosities), whose immense popularity in his own day was based on a meretricious volume of "Proverbial Philosophy" in verse-like prose, was given a cold reception from the first in the *Athenaeum.* Clement Shorter says:

The "Proverbial Philosophy" of Martin Farquhar Tupper created an excitement in literary and non-literary circles, which it is diffi-

---

[126] *Athenaeum,* Nov. 19, 1831, p. 754.

[127] Dec. 11, 1830, p. 777.

[128] A publishing firm had written to Dilke, "stating that they knew as a fact that it [a review of one of their books] was by Mr. Alaric Watts who disliked the writer of the book." Dilke replied: "It is utterly false that Mr. Alaric Watts is, or ever was, connected with the Athenaeum." This was about 1838. (See *Papers of a Critic,* I, 49.)

cult for the present generation to comprehend. It is true that when it was first published, in 1838, it was greeted by the *Athenaeum* as "a book not likely to please beyond the circle of a few minds as eccentric as the author's." In spite of this it sold in thousands and hundreds of thousands; it went through over nine hundred editions in England, and five hundred thousand copies at least were sold in America. It was translated into French, German, and many other tongues; its author was a popular hero. . . . Of "Proverbial Philosophy" itself there are few enough copies in demand today, and it is difficult for us to place ourselves in the position of those who felt its charm. What to the early Victorian Era was counted for wisdom, and piety, and even for beauty, counts to the present age for mere commonplace verbiage. Tupper's name has taken a place in our language as the contemptuous synonym for a poetaster.[129]

[129] *Victorian Literature: Sixty Years of Books and Bookmen*, pp. 27-28. See also Mumby, *op. cit.*, p. 288, for an account of Tupper and his publishers. The *Times Literary Supplement* recently (Feb. 26, 1938, p. 137) published an article called "Mr. Tupper and the Poets: a Victorian best seller." The writer says: "When he died in 1889, all the *Athenaeum* could say, in a very brief obituary notice, was that he had long outlived the great popularity he once possessed. Complete oblivion has been the fate of a book which is computed to have sold a million and a half copies in America and some quarter of a million in England. It may be noted at the same time that Tupper and his publishers are said to have made £10,000 each in England, whereas, owing to the want of American copyright . . . £80 represented his American royalties." But a letter to the *T. L. S.* (April 9, 1938, p. 252) disputes the figures of American sales. The *Athenaeum* verdict on the first edition was given in just two sentences: " 'Originally treated' indeed, as far as manner goes; the production of a benevolent enthusiast, whose motives are entitled to respect. We wish therefore that we could add, that its originality extended to the matter; or that it was a book likely to please beyond the circle of a few minds as eccentric as the author's." (April 21, 1838, p. 287.) The review of the second series spoke slightingly of Tupper's work and of the whole class of proverb books then popular. (April 8, 1843, pp. 329-330.) W. J. Rolfe (Introduction to *Shakespeare Proverbs*, collected by Mary Cowden Clark, pp. 64-66) calculated that more than a million copies had been sold. He says: "The book was generally commended by the critical journals on both sides of the Atlantic; but the London *Athenaeum* took a different view of it from the very first (1838) and was not led to change its opinion afterward. In 1867 it called the third series 'weak, twaddling and insincere.' Of its 'proverbs' it said: 'They are not short; they are not sharp; they are not clear.' On the contrary, they were declared to be 'serpentine, flabby, and obscure.' The *London Literary Gazette*, on the other hand, in a notice of the 21st edition (1855) said: 'The popularity of the *Proverbial Philosophy* is a grati-

The *Athenaeum* was at least pretty generally consistent in not being swept off its feet by the extensive popularity of a writer, nor by the extravagant or universal praise of his work in other journals.

Its activities in deflating certain much-puffed novelists were not so spectacular as were those of *Fraser's* and some other magazines which took up the cry against the "fashionables." But it was in keeping a balanced keel in the literary waters that the *Athenaeum* excelled. It was never carried away by enthusiasm for the frothy novels of the "Silver Fork School"[130] nor for the "Newgate Novels" of Bulwer and Harrison Ainsworth. It was not awed by the general popularity of G. P. R. James, Fenimore Cooper, Captain Marryat, or Mrs. Gore, but it did not attack them with the sort of spleen that attracts attention in the history of criticism. Fairness is often duller than invective, but it sounds saner after a hundred years.

ALLIES IN THE FIGHT

Although the *Athenaeum* had allies in the fight against puffery, it soon became the acknowledged leader, for in two ways its position was unique: it was the only periodical which waged war consistently against the system of trade criticism instead of against occasional glaring examples of puffery; and its rigid fairness in dealing with individual books and authors gave it a commanding prestige.

Most of the magazines which had preceded the *Athenaeum* in protesting against the tactics of Colburn and Bentley were chiefly offended by the debasement of liter-

---

fying and healthy symptom of the present taste in literature, the book being full of lessons of wisdom and piety, conveyed in a style . . . irresistibly pleasing by its earnestness and eloquence.' "

[130] A term frequently applied to the fiction picturing the intimate details of life in high society such as was written by Robert Plumer Ward, T. H. Lister, Mrs. Gore, Susan Ferrier, Bulwer, Disraeli, Lady Charlotte Bury, and others. For an account of this literary fad of the late twenties and thirties, see Rosa, *op. cit.*

ature through undignified advertising. Wilson, in *Black-wood's*, was more zealous in denouncing Colburn for encouraging broken-down roués to write memoirs of the society from which they had been cast, or for degrading the names of gentlemen by parading their private affairs in the papers for the sake of publicity, than he was in calling attention to the evils that must result from publishers owning or controlling literary journals.[131] When he did attack the system, after the *Athenaeum* campaign was well under way, the accusations were such as had already been made familiar by constant repetition in Dilke's journal. He spoke of "puffs preliminary," of paid paragraphs in the newspapers, of the system ruining the circulating libraries. This attack on puffery, however, was mainly a by-product of a diatribe against fashionable novels.

Fraser's was the only other magazine which waged consistent war against "the trade." It gave even less quarter than the *Athenaeum* to Colburn and Bentley in its hard-hitting and lively reviews and editorials. Not only did it goad Colburn for his practices, but it included in one sweeping generalization all those who were associated with him in an editorial capacity, including Campbell, Cyrus Redding, and later Bulwer, but made an exception in the case of "honest Mr. Jerdan." *Fraser's* was not afraid to name the offending publishers and the journals which they controlled. It called Colburn "Prince Paramount of Puffers and Quacks."[132]

The well-known Fraserian pungency made its articles amusing if not always convincing to an impartial reader. There was plenty of spice and sting in its anti-puffery campaign, but the very vituperative character of the attacks on the publishing house of Colburn and Bentley and on the writers whom they puffed, together with the knowledge

[131] See *Blackwood's* (*Noctes*, No. XXXVI), May, 1828, pp. 788-792.
[132] *Fraser's*, April, 1830, pp. 318-320.

that Maginn's crew of reviewers and satirists attacked everyone in much the same vein, probably made its fight less
effective than the more temperate analysis of "trade" criticism in the somewhat duller pages of the *Athenaeum*.[133]

It is characteristic that *Fraser's*, having Campbell on its
list of those who were always to be ridiculed, could see
nothing good in anything he did, and ascribed the worst
motives to his every action; whereas the *Athenaeum* frequently lauded what it found to be praiseworthy in the
New Monthly. *Fraser's*, on the other hand, apparently took
a more tolerant view of Jerdan, who was given first place
in its "Gallery of Illustrious Literary Characters." The portrait was on the whole a favorable one and Maginn went
out of his way to justify Jerdan's "leaning to kindness."

. . . if the books of Colburn and Longman obtain their due share
of notice, must it of necessity be attributed to other motives than
a fair bias in favour of partners and friends in whose choice of
works his own advice is often taken? It would be strange, indeed, if he should not sometimes express in his *Gazette* the same
favourable opinions which urged him to recommend to the publishers the purchase of a novel or poem.[134]

But in the following year the review of Bulwer's *The
Siamese Twins* gave occasion for a few gibes at Jerdan.

. . . before the book can be attacked by just and indignant criticism—Jerdan, the intimate friend of Bulwer—and bamboozled
by Bentley's visits and palaver and feeds, will puff the book, and
do both gentlemen a good turn.[135]

The constant boast of independence was a favorite theme
in *Fraser's* editorial paragraphs. In "An Apology for a
Preface to Our Fourth Volume," Oliver Yorke said:

[133] One might, for instance, compare the treatment of Bulwer Lytton by
Fraser's and by the *Athenaeum*. The former attacked him with the most biting
ridicule on all occasions; the latter warned him against the danger of Colburn's
puffing to his reputation.

[134] *Fraser's*, June, 1830, pp. 605-606.　　　[135] *Fraser's*, March, 1831, p. 204n.

We are influenced by no publisher—mixed up in no literary coteries—bound down to swear to the dictates of no club, book-selling, book-buying, or book-writing.[136]

He proposed ironically to let every contributor review his own books, "which is, we believe, the regular and ordinary practice in all the established reviews, magazines, and newspapers, at present flourishing in Great Britain."

Bulwer, for example, always reviews himself in the *New Monthly;* Croker criticises his speeches in the *John Bull;* Collier comments on his 'Theatrical Annals' in the *Morning Chronicle;* Williams considers his 'Sir Thomas Lawrence' in the *Times;* Mrs. Charles Gore explains the merits of her comedy in the *Court Journal;* Hogg's tales are critiqued by himself in *Blackwood;* Johnson's pamphlets are extolled by their author in the same periodical; Westmacott eulogizes 'Nettlewig Hall' in the *Age;* Croly descants on his 'Tales of the Great Saint Bernard' in the *Monthly;* Campbell's praises are sung by his own disinterested mouth in the *Metropolitan;* Sir James Mackintosh assures the public that his History is something quite transcendental through the *Edinburgh;* Wakley puffs the editor of the *Lancet* in the *Ballot;* Basil Hall does himself the kind office of being review-atory on his 'Travels' in the *Quarterly;* and so forth.[137]

On the whole the *Athenaeum* and *Fraser's* were on friendly terms and passed compliments back and forth occasionally, though neither would acknowledge the priority of the other in the anti-puffery fight. It is true that there were times when they entered into light combat. *Fraser's* was touchy and easily aroused, and when accused of indulging in too many personalities, it replied with characteristic fire: "Is it personality to bray asses in the mortar, to crucify puppies, break sinners on the wheel, or administer the rope-end to the posteriors of illustrious jackasses and knaves?"[138] But the *Athenaeum* came off pretty well, for it was about

---

[136] *Fraser's,* Aug., 1831, p. 2.
[137] *Ibid.,* p. 3. [138] *Fraser's,* Jan., 1833, p. 11.

the only journal that Maginn, on occasion, condescended to praise.

No other magazine in the thirties made any extensive or consistent fight against publishers' puffing, though it is true that the persistent efforts of the *Athenaeum* were commended and given circulation by a number of papers, particularly provincial ones which had little to expect or gain from book advertising.[139] In fact, the work of *Fraser's* and the *Athenaeum* combined gave such a currency to the anti-puffery fight that few periodicals could ignore it entirely and a great many took it up, at least spasmodically, as a new and popular theme in criticism.

RESULTS OF THE BATTLE

It is difficult to sum up in very definite terms the net results of the campaign, but there is evidence that the work of the *Athenaeum* was not entirely in vain and that its influence was far reaching as a consequence in fields not at first contemplated by the editors. To say that it did not destroy the puffing trade is not to admit that its efforts were futile. Such practices are so effective with gullible human nature that they have not yet ceased to be successful and profitable. But the exposure of those practices also has an effect on the reading public.

As early as the end of August, 1830, the *Athenaeum* boasted that the walls of the enemy were beginning to crumble.

. . . we know that we are independent of them [Colburn and Bentley], and that the Public are hearing this all over the country, thanks to the liberal spirit of contemporary Journals. It is not likely, therefore, that criticisms in their *own* Paper, on their *own* books, will be quite so serviceable as heretofore.[140]

---

[139] In 1831 (Feb. 12, p. 102) the *Athenaeum* recorded with pleasure that other papers were getting courage to speak out against trade criticism. It mentioned the *Albion*, the *Essex Standard*, and the *Dorset County Chronicle*.

[140] Aug. 28, 1830, p. 540. One may of course discount some of the editorial

In September of the same year the *Athenaeum* took a mischievous delight in calling attention to the premature death of the much-puffed "Juvenile Library":

By the bye, we have not seen even one little pleasant paragraph playing gentleman-usher to the *third* volume of the 'Juvenile.' How is this?—surely the only lady is out in her reckoning—we trust it will not be another miscarriage, or any monstrous birth, again 'to fright the isle from its propriety.'[141]

Both *Fraser's* and the *Athenaeum* claimed that their exposure of the puffing trade had knocked the value and deflated the sale of Colburn's fashionable novels. The hard-hitting articles and reviews in these magazines undoubtedly contributed to the decline of the fashionables, but the natural working of the laws of literary supply and demand probably had more to do with it. There is more truth in the frequent *Athenaeum* warning that "the system" would eventually bring its own ruin.

Writing of the fashionable novels in October, 1830, Andrew Picken said that they had become "as worthless and contemptible as the criticism in the Booksellers' Gazette."

. . . yet novels are written, interesting paragraphs precede them, silly people still trust, and hope; and the keepers of circulating libraries are forced to buy—but *do not to the extent they did;* there are other works as well as Lady Morgan's, lumbering the warehouses; we have heard of one bidding for the stock of novels on hand of one house, that at eightpence the volume, exceeded eight thousand pounds!![142]

---

statements during the heat of the fight when the journal was inclined to exaggerate the effectiveness of its exposure of "the system."

[141] Sept. 18, 1830, p. 584.

[142] *Athenaeum,* Oct. 9, 1830, pp. 625-626. The reviewer of Morier's *Zohrab the Hostage* in the *Quarterly* (Dec., 1832, p. 391) says: "It appears that after our eyes had been disgusted for so many years with flourishing statements of the 'unparalleled' sale of the trash we allude to, the publisher has just been detected in disposing of thirty thousand volumes of 'historical novels' and 'novels of fashionable life,' in one batch, *on condition of exportation,* at the rate of *eightpence* per volume."

By the end of the year the *Athenaeum* announced that the public and the independent publishers were turning toward it and that it got books so early from publishers as to precede the "Booksellers' Gazette."[143]

The effectiveness of the work of the *Athenaeum* was indicated in two ways rather convincingly within a year after Dilke became editor. In the number of June 4, 1831, there was a full-page advertisement giving extracts from the opinions of the press of the United Kingdom concerning the fearless independence of the *Athenaeum*. The list started with quotations from *Fraser's* and the *Metropolitan* but included mostly opinions of provincial papers. An editorial note added:

It may be as well at once to meet the suspicions of the old traders in paid paragraphs to say, that *not one word in commendation of the Athenaeum was ever paid for;* and we have not the honour of being personally known to the Editor of a single Paper in the United Kingdom.[144]

And the effectiveness of the campaign against the Colburn publications is evident in the attitude of the *Literary Gazette* towards its rival. In a note "To Correspondents" the editor of the *Athenaeum* put all the cards on the table. "The advertising page of a paper is, as is well known, open to the public."[145] The *Literary Gazette* had, "in the way of business," published the following advertisement:

The atmosphere is tainted by the corruptions of the *London Literary Gazette*—a publication which our contemporary, the *Aberdeen Magazine,* has justly designated the common sewer of the vilest bibliopolical corruption.[146]

---

[143] Dec. 11, 1830, pp. 777-778.
[144] P. 368.   [145] Oct. 15, 1831, p. 671.
[146] *Ibid.* (Quoted by the *Athenaeum* from the *Gazette* of July 30, 1831.) According to Rosa (*op. cit.,* p. 181), *Fraser's* inserted the advertisement in the *Gazette.*

The *Gazette* had been free, moreover, in announcing all sorts of literary projects such as "Sixteen Quarto Pages for Twopence." But when the *Athenaeum* sent an advertisement concerning the reduction in price to 4*d.,* the *Literary Gazette* did not print it and returned the money "with a message that the Proprietors will not insert the advertisements of the *Athenaeum!*"[147] The latter journal referred to the matter again in the following number.

While friends, known and unknown, take such interest in the success of an independent literary paper, what avails the miserable policy of the Publishing Proprietors of the *Literary Gazette* in refusing to insert our Advertisements? The truth will be known, though it be shut out even from the advertising columns of that paper . . . the old orthodox belief in all that is in print is shaken—the day for booksellers' Reviews, and for booksellers reviewing their own books, is gone; the public generally now know well enough, that the everlasting songs of praise in the *Literary Gazette* are but mystic hymns to their breeches pockets, and therefore button them the tighter; and the readers of the *Gazette* will learn this truth; though it be but the echo of public opinion that shall disturb their slumbers.[148]

Again at the beginning of 1832 an editorial leader referred to the results of the fight against puffery, which had increased the sale of the *Athenaeum* as well as its reputation for honesty.

That the establishment of this paper has done good, we are certain; the mystery of trade criticism and broad-sheet paragraphs has been utterly exposed. . . . But the exposure, though a serviceable duty to the public, has been most painful to ourselves; and we rejoice that the necessity gets less every hour.[149]

By October, 1833, the editor could boast in the "Weekly Gossip" column that the victory was already won. Com-

[147] *Ibid.*
[148] Oct. 22, 1831, p. 695.   [149] *Athenaeum,* Jan. 7, 1832, p. 1.

menting on the magazines of the month, the writer says
that the *Metropolitan's*

leading article is, we suppose, the attack on 'Publishing and Puffing,' in which the old offences of Mr. Colburn are laid bare with
no very gentle hand; this is well enough, but it is out of date—
the system was ruined by our exposure long since: it never recovered 'The National' and 'The Juvenile'; the vitality which it
occasionally manifests is a mere convulsive spasm—the death
throes.[150]

Continued assurances that the system was all but dead appeared in the *Athenaeum* until the end of the decade.

The giant which we had braced our nerves to encounter, turned
out but an 'unreal mockery,' and, like the long buried dead which
the curious have sometimes exhumed, it had apparently the form
of living strength, but crumbled into ashes on exposure.[151]

But the giant, by the *Athenaeum's* own admission, had
not yet crumbled into dust by 1837, and the magazine was
still hurling javelins at the same vital and vulnerable places
in its anatomy. The review of Disraeli's *Venetia* (published by Colburn) contained a paragraph reminiscent of
the heavy battles of 1830 and 1831.

The *Trade-wind* (for the *puffs* have of late assumed a more
constant and decided form,) has already set steadily in. The following delicate apprehension on the part of some disinterested
person, has 'glinted forth' amid the simple leaves of the *Courier*
and the *Chronicle*.[152]

A writer in the "Weekly Gossip" a little later complained
of the extent of the puffing trade once more.

Witness the advertising columns of the newspapers—witness the
disgraceful paragraphs and pretended criticisms *not* in the advertising columns. . . . A book is not now sold on its merits—but by
dint of sheer brass and blazoning in the newspapers.[153]

[150] *Athenaeum*, Oct. 5, 1833, p. 668.   [151] Jan. 5, 1833, p. 1.
[152] *Athenaeum*, May 20, 1837, p. 357.   [153] July 15, 1837, p. 522.

Whatever may have been the general effect of this persistent bombardment, Colburn himself was apparently not convinced that trade criticism was self-defeating as the foes of puffery so often argued, for he continued his unregenerate methods to the end of his publishing days. We know at least that he was still at the old game in 1843 when Thomas Hood, then nearing the end of his difficult two years as editor of the *New Monthly,* wrote to Miss H. Lawrance, author of *Historical Memoirs of the Queens of England,* who had asked to review books for the magazine:

I write in haste a few lines to put you on your guard by telling you of the arrangements for reviewing in the Magazine. I undertook to review all books except Colburn's own, with the puffing of which I of course desired to have no concern. They are *done* by the persons of the establishment—Patmore, Williams or Shoberl. If you see the Magazine you will know what wretched things these reviews are. . . . I am ashamed of them at present or should be were it not pretty well known that I have no hand in them.[154]

But that the campaign against publishers' puffing did have an influence on the ethical standards of criticism is apparent both in the reactions of the editors of the most notorious puffing journals and the pronouncements of other periodicals which took their lead, whether they acknowledged it or not, from the *Athenaeum.*

It is not unlikely that the impact of anti-puffery propaganda and the exposure to the public of the methods of publishers had something to do with the rebellion of both Campbell and Jerdan against the authority of Colburn. In a leader reviewing Volume II of the Rev. G. R. Gleig's

[154] Walter Jerrold, *Thomas Hood, His Life and Times,* pp. 369-370. See also a letter from John Blackwood, Dec. 20, 1843: "Colburn's last feat in the art of puffing a book (viz., by causing Colonel Davidson to have him up at the police court for [the return of] his manuscript, and then publishing the book within three days) has excited the admiration and envy of the whole trade." (Oliphant, *op. cit.,* II, 356.)

History of the Bible in Colburn's "National Library," the *Athenaeum* says:

> It is somewhat amusing to see, in spite of the paid paragraphs by which it is recommended to the public, that the work before us has not escaped a blow—and a hard one, too—from Messrs. Colburn and Bentley's own magazine—the *New Monthly*. In the November number, the first volume . . . was placed in invidious juxtaposition with Milman's 'History of the Jews,' and most extravagantly praised, while that talented book was as extravagantly abused;—but, behold! at the bottom of the page appears a note by the editor, and signed Thomas Campbell, disclaiming any concurrence with the sentiments expressed in the review. It was clear, therefore, that he was ashamed of the article, and that he had the honesty to say so; though, in defiance of his opinion, this fulsome panegyric was admitted into the magazine. We find that, since this *rebellion against authority,* Campbell has abandoned the *New Monthly*.[155]

Soon after this Campbell became editor of the new *Metropolitan Magazine* which started out with brave claims to independence, while it classed all other literary journals together as servitors of publishers. The *Athenaeum* struck back in an article, probably by Dilke himself, which was plain-speaking but much less abusive than one in *Fraser's* a little later.

> . . . we rejoice that not a single new periodical is announced but that it is thought necessary to favour the public with like professions. The *Athenaeum*—and we say it unhesitatingly—the *Athenaeum* has blazoned all over the kingdom the iniquities of that trade criticism by which the public have been so long cozened. But can we forget that we fought long, and at all hazards, *with the weight of Mr. Campbell's name against us?*[156]

In fact, it must be largely credited to the *Athenaeum* that by the middle of 1831 the literary atmosphere was

[155] Feb. 26, 1831, p. 129. According to the marked file this review was by the Rev. Hobart Caunter.   [156] April 16, 1831, pp. 249-250.

charged with protests against the puffing trade. It is possible that Jerdan's boast of independence would not have been so loud or so persistent had it not been for the awakening of the public to the evils of trade criticism. The *Athenaeum* once with considerable glee discovered the *Literary Gazette* stealing its thunder in a review of *The Life and Correspondence of Sir Thomas Lawrence,* by D. E. Williams.

We thought our first notice of the Life of Lawrence fierce enough in all conscience, but the *Literary Gazette* has out-heroded Herod; and while we imagined that the publisher, the editor, and the writer, all Juveniles! would have been 'thick as inkle-weavers,' they have startled us with the most intolerable wrangling. It is creditable to the *Literary Gazette,* that, in defiance of all natural affection, it has honestly slaughtered Mr. Williams; but the attack on 'book-making'—'the tricks of the trade'—'puffing'—and 'paid paragraphs' is really so like a column out of the *Athenaeum,* that we imagined we had mistaken the paper, and, feared we had been repeating ourselves.[157]

The currency which the *Athenaeum* gave to the fight against puffery was so widespread that it was taken up by writers of books on current problems as well as by other magazines and papers. Charles Babbage's *On the Economy of Machinery and Manufactures* contained a general discussion, without mentioning names, of the influence of publishers on reviewing by the control of periodicals. The *Athenaeum* commented:

It was to put an end to this system, so ably and honestly exposed by Mr. Babbage, that the *Athenaeum* was established. Such an undertaking was certain of finding a fierce and resolute opposition; it was opposed to all trading influences, and our success has been little short of a miracle.[158]

Indeed the battle against puffery had established the prestige of the *Athenaeum.* Perhaps the most tangible re-

[157] *Athenaeum,* May 28, 1831, p. 343.
[158] June 23, 1832, p. 400.

sult was that it enhanced the reputation of the magazine as the first literary journal in England run on genuinely independent principles. And that result itself may have aided, in ways which are not accurately measureable, the cause for which the *Athenaeum* fought. Recognition of the fact that a magazine could be conducted on such principles and thrive, perhaps gave a more telling blow to puffery than all the words of the controversy.

Fraser's, taking up the fight against the pretentious claims of the *Metropolitan,* gave tribute to the impression which the *Athenaeum* had made within a year after Dilke became editor. Referring to the boasting address with which the *Metropolitan* began, Oliver Yorke said:

Already has it called forth the indignant remonstrance of the *Athenaeum*—a journal which, albeit it had not the greatness, or presence of mind, to allude to our anti-humbug efforts, we feel pleasure in mentioning, as one of the most gratifying instances of combined talent and integrity, now presented by the periodical literature of England. We have watched the *Athenaeum* closely, from the commencement of its struggle with the Burlington boobies to its final triumph; and we are bound to say that it has fairly won for itself a character for candid and discriminating criticism, scarcely reconcileable with its strange omission of ourselves, when alluding to periodicals conducted on principles, over which 'publisher-influence' cannot possibly have control.[159]

Though arrogating to itself an unjustifiable share of the credit for exposing the "humbug," *Fraser's* on another occasion gave honorable mention to the *Athenaeum* while heralding, perhaps too confidently, the decline of the puffing publishers. In reviewing the "Novels of the Season" in 1831 the *Fraser* critic rejoiced that some of Colburn and Bentley's best writers were leaving them—Lister, Lady Morgan, Hook, Bulwer, Lady Charlotte Bury. Now, he con-

[159] *Fraser's,* May, 1831, p. 494.

tinued, Colburn and Bentley are losing their editors—Gleig declined to continue with the *National Library;* Campbell and Redding quit the *New Monthly;* two editors of the *Court Journal* resigned; Jerdan refused to edit the *Juvenile Library.*[160]

In the "Preface to Our Second Decade," however, *Fraser's* made what was perhaps the clearest and most realistic statement of the final results of the anti-puffery fight, and Dilke probably by that time would have held the same view of the work accomplished by the *Athenaeum:* ". . . we have, if not demolished the noble art of puffmongering (which we believe is impossible), at least let the public know its full value, and imposed some decency upon the practice."[161]

[160] *Fraser's,* Aug., 1831, pp. 10-11.   [161] *Fraser's,* Jan., 1840, p. 18.

Chapter 3 : The Athenaeum Circle Under Dilke

To FIND the common denominator of the points of view of the more than two hundred men and women who were staff writers for the *Athenaeum* in the period of Dilke's active editorship, is peculiarly difficult because of the catholicity of interests encouraged by the wide tolerance of the editor himself, and because, as we have seen, the magazine was not by its policy committed to any particular religious, political, or social-economic formula. A close examination of the contributions of individual reviewers in the *Athenaeum* circle may at first lead the reader to question the soundness of the generalizations already made concerning the policy and critical point of view of the magazine, even in any single year of its publication. It will soon be discovered that there was not one *Athenaeum* circle; there were many— and frequently they are as difficult to define as the circles made by heavy raindrops on a still pool, each running imperceptibly into others. The most that can be hoped for here is to present a general idea of who the chief *Athenaeum* staff writers, reviewers, and contributors were, what biases governed their judgments, and what important works they criticised. For the almost innumerable others whose names are to be found in the marked file, it will be possible to do little more than list and classify according to their specialties such writers as can be identified, and give a brief account of a few whose work was particularly interesting in itself or which helped to give characteristic tone to the journal. If it is impossible to impose a categorical homogeneity upon these writers, there may still be discovered a unifying pattern in all the diversity and at least some evidence to strengthen the thesis that the *Athenaeum* was the clearest and most unwarped mirror of Victorian culture among the periodical publications of the nineteenth century.

It has already been observed that Dilke tried to get specialists in every field to do critical articles and reviews. The extent of this specialization in literary as well as in art and scientific criticism and reports strikes one most forcibly on a first perusal of the marked file. From the beginning the same names are to be found from week to week under the same departments, and with singular dependability under the reviews of particular types of books. Each specialist in belles lettres, for example, had a particular corner assigned him, either of author, subject matter, form, or nationality. One reviewed nearly all the poetry of Scotland that appeared, another had a monopoly on the novels of Cooper, while a third took in all the novels with a purpose and left to a fourth novels without a purpose. It is true though that some of the chief staff reviewers jumped from genre to genre. Henry Chorley, T. K. Hervey, and Allan Cunningham, each a specialist in his own field, covered at various times poetry, fiction, drama, biography and memoirs, history, foreign literatures, music, painting, sculpture, and architecture. But this was the exception rather than the rule, and generally the staff writer, when he stepped out of his field, did the lesser routine reporting jobs and left to other and more competent specialists most of the important works.

ORIGINAL CONTRIBUTIONS

Since Dilke put the whole strength of the magazine in the reviews, small space was given to original material. Although the editor could boast of contributions from Carlyle, Thomas Hood, Leigh Hunt, Lamb, Landor, Coleridge, and some posthumous work of Shelley and Keats, none of these except Hood wrote more than trifles for the *Athenaeum*. Carlyle's only contribution was a short translation of "Faust's Curse"—which he later regretted because his name was too conspicuously displayed by Dilke.[1] Lamb, who was for a time a close friend of Dilke and considerably interested in the magazine in 1832, 1833, and 1834,[2] contributed about a dozen short poems in those years (all signed), a letter to the editor on "Munden, the Comedian,"[3] one of the *Last Essays of Elia,* "On the Total Defect of the Quality of Imagination, observable in the Works of Modern British Artists," "By the Author of Essays signed 'Elia,'"[4] and a short essay called "Thoughts on Presents of Game."[5] Posthumously some of his "Table Talk" and a few poems were published in the *Athenaeum.*[6]

Leigh Hunt's name does not appear in the editor's handwriting of the marked file, but he contributed one signed poem, "The Lover of Music to the Pianoforte," in 1832.[7] There also appeared one signed poem of Coleridge, "Water Ballad," in 1831.[8] Other slight bibliographical items of no

---

[1] See *post,* p. 322, n. 267.

[2] See *ante,* pp. 37-38, n. 100.   [3] Feb. 11, 1832, p. 96.

[4] Jan. 12, 19, 26, Feb. 2, 1833 (pp. 26-27, 42-43, 57, 73-74). This essay had been printed in part in Moxon's *Reflector.*

[5] Nov. 30, 1833, p. 817.

[6] Jan. 4, May 31, June 7, July 19, 1834 (pp. 14-15, 414-415, 433, 538). According to a penciled notation in a later hand in the marked file Lamb wrote the review of "*Sonnets.* By Edward Moxon" (April 13, 1833, p. 229). Lucas, *Life of Charles Lamb,* II, 350) says: "reviewed, almost certainly by Lamb." And a letter from Moxon says that Elia "has just written a very kind letter in the Athenaeum of my poor little book." (See Merriam, *op. cit.,* p. 49.)

[7] July 7, 1832, p. 439.   [8] Oct. 29, 1831, p. 707.

greater importance than these include a note and poem from Edward Fitzgerald[9] (signed: "Epsilon"), a short poem to "The Ettrick Shepherd" by Wordsworth,[10] several signed poems and a few "Imaginary Conversations" from Landor,[11] and a number of posthumous pieces of the great writers of the past or passing generation.

The original contributions of Thomas Hood were more numerous. Apparently his first offering was a signed poem, "The Poet's Portion,"[12] which appeared a few weeks after Dilke took control. During the next ten years he was a frequent contributor of humorous and serious verse, amusing letters,[13] and occasional reviews.[14] Reference has already been made to his series of articles on "Copyright and Copy-

[9] July 9, 1831, p. 442.   [10] Dec. 12, 1835, pp. 930-931.

[11] The "Imaginary Conversations" were all of a late date: "Alcibiades and Xenophon," Jan. 10, 1852, pp. 52-53; "Garibaldi and Bosco," Aug. 18, 1860, p. 228; "Garibaldi and the President of the Sicilian Senate," Sept. 1, 1860, pp. 289-290; "Virgil and Horace," March 9, 1861, pp. 326, 327; "Milton and Marvel," May 18, 1861, pp. 661-662; (second conversation) Aug. 16, 1862, pp. 210-212; "Macchiavelli and Guicciardini," Oct. 12, 1861, pp. 479-480. Landor also wrote a number of letters to the *Athenaeum* on various subjects from Florence.

[12] July 3, 1830, p. 409.

[13] Hood wrote a letter in purposely bad French in reply to a Frenchman's attempt at a letter in English (*Athenaeum*, Dec. 27, 1834, pp. 938-939): "Gentilhommes,—Comme je ne vis pas dans la cité mais dans la contrée, six milles depuis Londres, je n'ai pas une mode de vous envoyer le Comique Annuel, mais je vous envoy un ordre sur mon publisheur, que je vous prie accepte. Son nom est Monsieur Alfred Tête Baily, vivant à 83, Montagne à Blè. près le Changement Royale. Allez gauchement dans la rue. . . . Mon livre peut etre 'amusant' comme vous etes si bon à dire, mais il n'a pas attempté etre '*spirituel.*' Je ne suis pas un clergé-homme qui ecrit les serments. Dieu vous blesse. Je suis,

Gentilhommes,
Votre tres humble domestique,
Thomas Hood."

See also another letter in bad French, undoubtedly by Hood (Dec. 31, 1836, p. 921) expressing the wish that French writers would "prendre le trouble de speller proprement les noms de notre natifs autours et quoter leur travaux correctment."

Another interesting item from Hood's pen was his "Ode to Rae Wilson, Esquire," (*Athenaeum*, Aug. 12, 1837, pp. 585-587), a humorous reply to those who attacked his satire and ridicule of cant in religion.

[14] For an account of Hood's reviews see *post*, pp. 210-211.

wrong."[15] Hood wrote Dilke from Germany in 1836 asking if he might contribute a memoir of his friend Charles Lamb,[16] but nothing came of it because Barry Cornwall had already written his "Recollections of Charles Lamb" for the paper.[17]

Elizabeth Barrett may be regarded as another minor staff writer. Aside from occasional reviews, she sent to the *Athenaeum* between 1836 and 1843 a number of poems in her most humorless and most sentimental vein: "Man and Nature," "The Seaside Walk," "The Young Queen," "Victoria's Tears," "L. E. L.'s Last Question," "The Crowned and Wedded Queen," "Napoleon's Return," "The House of Clouds," "Lessons from the Gorse," "Three Hymns, Translated from the Greek of Gregory Nazianzen," "A Claim in an Allegory," "Sonnet, On Mr. Haydon's Portrait of Mr. Wordsworth," and "To Flush, My Dog."[18] She was immensely flattered when Dilke called on her to write a series of articles on "The Greek Christian Poets" in 1842.[19] This series was followed by another (ostensibly a review, but actually a discourse on poetry) called "The Book of the Poets."[20] The reviews credited to her in the marked file include "Poems, chiefly of early and late years, Including The Borderers, a Tragedy" by Wordsworth,[21] and "Orion:

---

[15] See *ante*, pp. 69-70.

[16] Hood wrote (in a long letter from Koblenz, Jan., 1836): "I have had a letter from Moxon applying for letters of Lamb's which he wants to publish. If you say aye to this he shall have them.—But I meant them for your use. It is too late now perhaps to write the article I proposed, but I think if you could collect for me and save all that has been written about him (C. L.) I could make a good review of it—corroborating, contradicting and giving my own view. Pray remember this in your next." (Dilke Papers, Add. 43,913.)

[17] Jan. 24, Feb. 7, 1835 (pp. 71-73, 107-110).

[18] These are all signed "E. B. B." or "Elizabeth B. Barrett" and may be found in the index. After her marriage she sent occasional poems from Italy.

[19] Feb. 26, March 5, 12, and 19, 1842 (pp. 189-190, 210-212, 229-231, 249-252).

[20] June 4, 11, 25, Aug. 6, 13, 1842 (pp. 497-499, 520-523, 558-560, 706-708, 728-729).   [21] Aug. 27, 1842, pp. 757-759.

an Epic Poem" by R. H. Horne.[22] It is possible that she reviewed also "A New Spirit of the Age" by Horne,[23] but there is no direct evidence since the 1844 volume in which the review appeared is not marked.

Other notable contributors mentioned with pride by the editor at the beginning of 1833 were: Allan Cunningham, the Ettrick Shepherd (James Hogg), T. K. Hervey, Mary Howitt, William Howitt, Richard Howitt, Mrs. Fletcher (late Miss Jewsbury), Hon. Mrs. Norton, Leitch Ritchie, the late William Roscoe, Thomas Roscoe, the Author of the "O'Hara Tales" (John Banim), the Author of "The Corn Law Rhymes" (Ebenezer Elliot), the Author of "The Hunchback" (J. Sheridan Knowles), the Author of "The Rent Day" (Douglas Jerrold), the Author of "Paul Pry" (John Poole), the Author of "The Bride's Tragedy" (Thomas L. Beddoes), the Author of "Lives of the Italian Poets" [?], the Author of "London in the Olden Time" (Miss H. Laurence),[24] the Author of "The History of the Civil Wars in Ireland" (W. Cooke Taylor), and the Author of "The Dominie's Legacy" (Andrew Picken). Although it is possible to look back from the twentieth century and say that these were all second or third rate writers (unless one adds a few writers such as Hugo whose poetry appeared in translation), it is important to remember that they were all popular and above the average of their day and such as would have been coveted by any rising periodical. Only a few of those mentioned in this group, however—Cunning-

[22] June 24, 1843, pp. 583-584.

[23] March 23, 30, 1844 (pp. 263-265, 291-292).

[24] According to the *Dictionary of Anonymous and Pseudonymous English Literature*, Miss H. Laurence was the author of *London in the Olden Time*, (1825) but if this was the Hannah Lawrance who for several years reviewed historical works for the *Athenaeum*, it is strange that the British Museum Catalogue does not list this book as hers, but only *Historical Memoirs of the Queens of England*, 2 Vols., 1838-40; and *The History of Woman, and Her Influence on Society and Literature*, Vol. I, 1843.

ham, the Howitts, Mrs. Fletcher, Hervey, Picken, and Taylor—were more than very occasional contributors.

There appeared while Dilke was editor a vast quantity[25] of mediocre or bad poetry written by habitual contributors to the annuals such as Hervey, Eleanor L. Montagu (later Mrs. Hervey), H. F. Chorley, Frances Brown, Agnes (or Elizabeth) Strickland, Maria Jane Jewsbury, Felicia Hemans, Thomas Wade, Thomas Westwood, Alicia Jane Sparrow, the Rev. Hobart Caunter, Mrs. Sigourney, Mrs. Gore, James Rice, Louisa S. Costello, and Charles Mackay. There was also a good deal of poetry of a somewhat higher order from the pens of Thomas Lovell Beddoes, John Clare, Allan Cunningham, James Hogg, Thomas Pringle, Barry Cornwall (B. W. Procter), John Hamilton Reynolds, and George Darley. Some of these latter have been "rediscovered" in recent years and have now a higher place in literary history than they were accorded in their lifetimes. This is especially true of Thomas Lovell Beddoes and George Darley.[26]

THE INNER CIRCLE

The really important writers in the *Athenaeum* circle, or circles, however, were the reviewers and departmental specialists whom Dilke gathered from widely varied backgrounds to carry on the weekly routine of the journal. The editor himself wrote very little for the magazine until after he retired from the active management in 1846. His chief identifiable contributions are editorial notes and some of the attacks on puffery in 1831 and 1832 (sometimes added to reviews by other writers). It is possible that he wrote a few notices of books which fell within the field of his

[25] Over a long period, for the *Athenaeum* never carried more than two or three poems in an issue.

[26] The two contributions of Beddoes to the *Athenaeum* were sent in by his friend Barry Cornwall, who was also a friend of Dilke and a frequent contributor of poetry and prose. See *Athenaeum*, July 7, 1832, p. 440; and May 18, 1833, p. 313. Darley wrote more than two dozen poems for the *Athenaeum*. His other contributions will be discussed later.

scholarly specialties, Elizabethan and eighteenth-century history and literature, and also of some books by Godwin, an early favorite, and by his friends Thomas Hood and Lady Morgan. But the marked file has his name in it in remarkably few places, partly because as editor he looked after the policy and the business management and left the writing to others.[27] From a dozen to twenty regular staff writers deserve special consideration, for their reviews, articles, and judgments of artistic productions shaped the policies of the *Athenaeum* and gave it the character which it maintained under the elder Dilke. Most of them were not authors of note, or even critics who had won their spurs, but literary journalists in whose ability and integrity Dilke had confidence, or specialists in the arts and sciences who might or might not be distinguished but who must be competent.

One of the leading critics in the literary and art departments during the first three or four years of Dilke's regime was John Hamilton Reynolds, who had already established a literary reputation as one of the brilliant and clever circle of the *London Magazine* in the early twenties. A parody of Wordsworth's "Peter Bell" had brought him some fame in 1819, and he had followed up that success with his *Odes*

[27] See *ante*, p. 28. Though Dilke allowed great latitude to his contributors, it seems that in his own field of the criticism of the older dramatists he exercised the greatest surveillance over reviewers. In 1838 he had a long correspondence with Charles Dance, discussing the principles of dramatic criticism, with the result that Dance, then one of the dramatic critics for the *Athenaeum*, resigned. One of the points of difference was a notice by Dance of *Every Man in His Humour*, in July of that year. Dilke cancelled the notice, and it did not appear. In his letter to Dance he defended the artistry of Ben Jonson in depicting the passions of his characters, who, in spite of their humours, were more than puppets. It is also true, he says, "that the language of the old dramatists is more coarse than jumps with the humour of our times; but while it awakes disgust it cannot waken passion. The Bible itself is 'tainted,' to use your words, with the 'unbridled expression of the time,' and it seems to me that the 'annoyance' to which you are 'subject' at a representation of the elder dramatists you cannot altogether escape from at church." (*Papers of a Critic*, I, 41-43.)

and Addresses to Great People (in collaboration with Thomas Hood, who later married Reynolds' sister and joined him and Dilke in the proprietorship of the *Athenaeum* in 1830). Many of his contemporaries thought of him as a poet of great promise and named him with Keats and Shelley as most likely to do noble service to the muse.[28]   But by 1830 the poetic fire had burned out, and Reynolds, then established as a solicitor, had come to look upon literature as a pastime and produced little except clever parodies and periodical criticism.[29]

Reynolds first appeared in the *Athenaeum* as an art critic. His approach was that of the literary man and amateur looking for the poetic and picturesque in painting, but his criticism displays keenness of perception as well as vigorous and colorful writing.   His report of the Royal Academy Exhibition in the first number edited by Dilke is typical. After praising Newton's "Shylock and Jessica," he exclaims: "How different is Turner's 'Jessica'!—A hazy old clothes-woman at the back window in Holywell-street, would show a delicate and soft-eyed Venus, compared with this daub of a drab, libelling Shakespeare out of a foggy window of King's yellow."[30]

The *Athenaeum* critics had no great awe of the academicians.   Reynolds spoke of Sir Thomas Lawrence's portraits at the British Institution as "interesting" and "disappointing."   In all his portraits "it will be perceived, that, how-

[28] For an account of the literary career of Reynolds, see the Introduction to *John Hamilton Reynolds: Poetry and Prose,* London, 1928, ed. by George L. Marsh. In this introduction, however, Marsh has not given much attention to Reynolds's contributions to the *Athenaeum,* nor has he mentioned the fact that Reynolds wrote art as well as literary criticism.

[29] One of the first ventures of Reynolds into criticism was a defense of Keats against the famous attack in the *Quarterly.* This was first sent to an Exeter newspaper in 1818 and was reprinted by Hunt in the *Examiner.* Reynolds also attracted considerable attention by his informal essays in the *London Magazine* (1821-24) under the pseudonym of Edward Herbert.

[30] June 5, 1830, p. 347. For a discussion of criticisms of Turner in the *Athenaeum* see *post,* pp. 346-348.

ever they may possess a certain animation—a life, which other painters would do well to aim at attaining, his expression never goes beyond mere vitality. Depth of character, profoundness of thought, are qualities never to be detected in any work of his."[31]   In his final report on the Royal Academy Exhibition for that year Reynolds said: "It is a positive disgrace to the Academy and the country, that with a professed zeal for the glory . . . of Art, its present dingy and dirty warehouse should be endured a day longer."[32]

In the following year Reynolds and Dilke together reviewed the Royal Academy showing. The strictures on patronage and on the Academy itself suggest the hand of Dilke rather than Reynolds. "We are satisfied," the critic says, "that no country in the world could produce such a collection of works, equal in number and excellence, the result of one year's labour of native artists." But what of all this talk of want of patronage?

The truth is, there is too much patronage . . . it is the only apology for one-half the academicians having found admission there. The Academy is a corporate and a chartered body—it grubs on in the dark—it toad-eats the aristocracy. Who are the men invited to their annual festival? Men eminent in literature—men of informed minds, the associates of the academicians in private life, the glory and boast of England?—No; but my Lord A and B; and other nonentities. This is the interchange between corporate art and patronage. There must be more life got into the Academy; as we said once before, we must rattle its old bones about.[33]

Patronage, the writer says, should be from the many enlightened lovers of art, and not from a few. Mechanics Institutes, he adds, tend to spread the knowledge of art, to raise and

[31] May 29, 1830, p. 331. This was before the marking began in the editor's file, but Reynolds undoubtedly wrote the reports of the exhibitions before as well as after June 5.
[32] June 12, 1830, p. 364.   [33] May 14, 1831, p. 315.

dignify it, and "to do more for it than all the patronage of all the crowned heads and the aristocracies of Europe."[34]

The literary criticism of Reynolds in the *Athenaeum* was not extensive, though he wrote a number of leading reviews between 1830 and 1834,[35] but it displays more than average good sense, good humor, and nimbleness of mind. He does not take the Pharisaical tone so common in the literary criticism of the time, especially in dealing with fiction or poetry which had no definite moral or didactic purpose. He could even praise dispassionately the artistry of one of Colburn and Bentley's fashionable novels, adding, however, that one might wish, "without being accused of squeamishness or canting," that the author had "put forth the same zeal, the same energy and pathos, in all his other scenes, that he evidently throws into his pen, when he treats of some luxurious vice or dangerous sorrow."[36]

Reynolds entered wholeheartedly into Dilke's fight against publishers' puffing, though, as we have seen, he was on one occasion exasperated by the editor's extremist views of the pernicious effects of acquaintanceship between reviewer and author or publisher.[37]   It was Reynolds who made the attack on "The Juvenile Library," the ridicule of which was one of the most effective blows of the *Athenaeum* against puffery.

Reynolds wrote with feeling of the farewell benefit performance given by Edmund Kean before his departure for "the Land of Guess and Dollar." In a reminiscent paragraph he recalled Kean's first night as Shylock, when he played

---

[34] *Ibid.*

[35] It is probable that Reynolds continued to write for the *Athenaeum* during the years 1835 to 1838, but because of the missing volumes in the marked file it is impossible to say with certainty. In 1838 he retired from London and did little writing during the rest of his life. When the marking is resumed in 1839 his name does not appear.

[36] June 19, 1830, pp. 374-376. (Review of *The Oxonians; a Glance at Society*. By the Author of 'The Roué'.)   [37] See *ante*, p. 39.

to an empty house, and his great success with *Richard III*.[38] When Kean died three years later Reynolds wrote an eloquent obituary.[39]

Other important contributions of Reynolds were reviews of Galt's *Life of Lord Byron,* which met with his strong disapproval because Galt "has not the mind to enter into and allow for the capricious wanderings and fine prejudices of the poet";[40] of *Conversations of James Northcote, R. A.,* by William Hazlitt (Hazlitt's mind, he said, had soured, but still he was great);[41] and of the *Letters and Journals of Lord Byron,* by Thomas Moore. The last work he found much superior to that of Galt. It was a difficult task to edit "a private correspondence so daring, reckless and personal, as that which rushed from the pen of Lord Byron. The noble poet was a poet in all things, and mighty in all things." Reynolds granted that Moore had done well for the most part, but that having no great affection for Lady Byron, he had left a few things in the published correspondence which should "scarcely have been preserved to gratify the sour palate of posterity." He concluded: "The perusal of the work has impressed us with a higher idea of Lord Byron's genius than even his poetry gave us."[42]

Reynolds did most of the reviews of Hood's "Comic Annuals" and other books, when Dilke himself didn't write them. Since Hood was an amusing fellow who was above criticism, the reviewer's task was only to present him attractively to the public or allow him to speak for himself in copious extracts and reproductions of his drawings.

Early in 1832 appeared what was apparently intended for the beginning of a series of "Edward Herbert" letters such as Reynolds had written for the *London Magazine.*

[38] July 24, 1830, p. 461.
[39] May 18, 1833, pp. 313-315.   [40] Sept. 4, 1830, pp. 552-555.
[41] Oct. 2, 1830, pp. 611-612; and Oct. 23, 1830, pp. 660-662.
[42] Jan. 1, 1831, pp. 1-6.

His comments on the literary changes in the decade preceding are intelligent and cleverly phrased. He takes some bold strokes at the fashionable novels and says of the popular poetess of the day:

L. E. L., a young lady of letters, has been for some years amorous and botanical; but she clearly proves the truth of what one of her rose-predecessors has said, that 'not even Love can live on flowers!'—Passion smothered in lilies, is passion smothered to all intents and purposes: I wish we could have a leek and onion poet by way of a change. L. E. L. may be very amiable, but she looks upon all her readers as Children in the Wood, and hastens as quickly as possible, tenderly to 'cover them with *leaves!*'[43]

For the rest, the review bibliography of Reynolds is made up of novels, memoirs, and miscellanies on sport, whist, and modern wines. Of course, much of his work is that of an informal essayist rather than a penetrating critic, but it helped to give a lighter and more balanced quality to the *Athenaeum* following the unrelieved seriousness of Maurice and Sterling.

Allan Cunningham was another of the *London Magazine* group who joined the *Athenaeum* staff when Dilke took over the paper. A Scottish poet turned literary journalist, he was proud of the literature of his native land and particularly of Robert Burns whose simplicity and honesty he admired but whose natural vigor he could not quite transfer to his own poetry. After studying sculpture with Chantrey he cultivated an acquaintance with all the arts and made himself a competent though hardly a keen critic. At the beginning of Dilke's regime he shared the Fine Arts columns with Reynolds and did most of the important poetry reviews, especially of the older writers. His first criticism was of "The Tam o'Shanter Group," a sculpture

[43] *Athenaeum,* Jan. 7, 1832, p. 6.

exhibit by Mr. Thom. The good-natured manner of the critic is immediately apparent:

These statues, we happen to know, have given little pleasure to some academy-bred artists—they consider them beneath the dignity of true sculpture. . . . We love them because they raise mirthful emotions—because they are lively images of living life; —we love to turn from the heroism of Percy, to the humour of Falstaff—from the saints of Raphael to the sinners of Hogarth . . . the land groans with mediocrity in marble, and we are glad to see an original genius arise who works in his own spirit.[44]

Shortly after Dilke became editor Cunningham, then engaged in the production of his extensive and popular *Lives of the Most Eminent British Painters, Sculptors, and Architects* (1829-33), began a series of articles for the *Athenaeum* on "The Living Artists" which he continued at intervals for a period of two years. The first sketch, that of Pickersgill, opened with a discourse on Lawrence, who "was indeed a glorious flatterer—he gave elegance to the coarse, and beauty to the unlovely; . . . he was seldom a poet in art, save when he got some unlovesome lady of wealth or rank before him, and then he lavished his charms, and completed on canvas what was left unfinished in nature." But Cunningham preferred "vigour to elegance, and accuracy of colour to the most flattering hues." Pickersgill, he believed, was a man of distinguished talents, who because of his lack of the "splended spirit of flattery" had been unhappy in his subjects. Cunningham's view of patronage differed from that of Reynolds and Dilke: "We wish him 'high dames and mighty earls,' instead of such small deer; for painting, let us preach and lecture as we will, can only be effectually patronized by the wealthy and the noble."[45]

The other articles in the series (there were 17 in all) gave flattering attention to most of the accepted masters

[44] June 19, 1830, p. 379.   [45] July 10, 1830, pp. 425-426.

among British painters, and also to some, like Stothard and
John Martin, who had not been taken into the Academy.
The praise of Turner, however, was patronizing and qualified: "In landscape, and landscape only, lies this artist's
strength. The Lord deliver us from his human nature! . . .
We marvel often too at the wild extravagance of his colouring, and ask, through what medium he looks on the hues
of nature."[46] On the whole though, Cunningham's panegyric was unstinted and his criticism was not likely to
give offense to the artists nor to the educated middle class
readers who were seeking guidance in the appreciation of
art. That it was kindly rather than discriminating, superficial rather than based on any definite aesthetic principles
was no hindrance to its popularity. At least the general
tolerance of Cunningham's artistic creed made room for
everything that was not startlingly new in technique or too
great a departure from the current demand for pictures
which told stories or taught moral lessons.

Cunningham's literary criticism was likewise not profound, but genial and broadly tolerant, with a leaning towards the simple and natural, the warmly human, as
opposed to the artificial, the grandiose, or the sophisticated.
Minor poets of "real fire" fared pretty well in his hands,
though of course he had the touchstone of Burns to keep
him from overpraise. "The triumph of Burns is the triumph of natural powers," he said in reviewing the edition
of Burns in "The Aldine Poets" series.[47] All poets of enthusiasm and feeling aroused his sympathy. "It is with no

[46] April 23, 1831, p. 266.

[47] *Athenaeum*, July 17, 1830, p. 433. Cunningham's own *Life and Works of
Robert Burns* was given a great deal of space in the *Athenaeum* when it appeared in 1834. Since none of these reviews is marked in the editorial file, it is
possible that Cunningham did them himself. Dilke could justify such a pro-
cedure on the ground that the reviews were mainly extracts and commentaries
on the life of Burns, and no one was better fitted to handle that subject than
Cunningham.

little pleasure that we see edition following edition of the works of Thomson. It is a proof to us that religion and poetry are still of the well-beloved things of the earth."[48]

Among contemporary poets he admired most the "bold and manly" ones like James Hogg, "a bard of God's own making,"[49] who ought to be taken in by the Royal Society of Literature—none being more worthy than Coleridge, and even of this there might be some doubt, he added.[50] Any young writer who produced "true and genuine poetry" was sure of kindly treatment from Cunningham. Such was William Kennedy (sometime a reviewer of poetry for the *Athenaeum*): ". . . though he has . . . indulged in a little more woe than we really like, and exhibited some sensibilities in which we cannot share, he has, nevertheless, amply justified our high opinion of his talents."[51]

Cunningham's contributions to the literary departments included, besides the rather rambling and commonplace "Biographical and Critical History of the Literature of the Last Fifty Years," several articles on Scott, for whom he had a fervent rather than critical respect, and many reviews of miscellaneous biographical and historical works, particularly Scotch, and of some popular fiction. Though there was nothing distinguished in his criticism of either art or literature, he was as near to the moderately liberal, intelligent, average romantic view of the early thirties as Dilke might have found to please the readers of the *Athenaeum* in that period. His contributions dwindled and ceased in 1840, two years before his death; by that time his scholarly son Peter had taken a place in the *Athenaeum* circle.

The most prolific general reviewer of books—poetry, fiction, memoirs, drama, and almost everything else—for the

---

[48] Aug. 7, 1830, p. 481.   [49] Nov. 6, 1830, p. 691.
[50] See "The Songs of James Hogg" [second notice], Jan. 15, 1831, pp. 36-38.
[51] Oct. 16, 1830, p. 645.

Athenaeum for a period of more than thirty years was Henry Fothergill Chorley. After reading a number of his reviews one cannot but see some justice in the slightly malicious picture given by Harriet Martineau:

The most complete specimen of the literary adventurer of our time whom I knew was one who avowed his position and efforts with a most respectable frankness. Mr. Chorley, who early went to town, to throw himself upon it, and see what he could make of it, was still about the same business as long as I knew him. He had a really kind heart, and helpful hands to needy brethren, and a small sort of generosity which was perfectly genuine, I am confident. But his best qualities were neutralized by those which belonged to his unfortunate position,—conceit and tuft-hunting, and morbid dread of unusual opinions, and an unscrupulous hostility to new knowledge . . . the difference between one kind of adventurer and another is, I believe, simply this;—that the one has something to say which presses for utterance, and is uttered at length without a view to future fortunes; while the other has a sort of general inclination toward literature, without any specific need of utterance, and a very definite desire for the honours and rewards of the literary career. Mr. Henry F. Chorley is, at least, an average specimen of the latter class; and perhaps something more.[52]

Perhaps the "something more" was the scrupulous Quaker honesty which at best prevented him from allowing personal animosity or envy to color his critical judgments, and at worst gave a sentimental softness to his reviews of mediocre writers who did not offend any fundamental tenet of his creed, religious, social, or artistic.

Chorley had early been brought into the more liberal literary and artistic circles of Liverpool, where he was reared,

[52] *Harriet Martineau's Autobiography,* pp. 317-318. The "new knowledge" which it grieved Miss Martineau most that Chorley would not accept was that connected with Mesmerism which she was championing in the forties, and which the *Athenaeum* attacked (the articles were probably by Dilke, but Chorley got the blame for them—see *Papers of a Critic,* I, 53).

by Mrs. William Rathbone, a sympathizer with liberal thought of the sort that, among dissenters, grew out of the French Revolution. Such men as William Roscoe and Robert Owen came to her house. Chorley had a natural talent for music, but because in his environment it was impossible to develop it, his artistic impulses broke out in other directions—painting, poetry, and (later) fiction and criticism. He was a red-haired boy, sensitive and shy, but also buoyantly enthusiastic and ambitious, and the disparity between his high aims and his limited achievements sometimes caused a tendency to self-assertion and impatience which he struggled against.[53]

Chorley was introduced to the *Athenaeum* by the elder Miss Jewsbury (afterwards Mrs. Fletcher), who was an early contributor to the magazine. At her suggestion, Dilke wrote to Chorley for an account of the ceremony that was to inaugurate the new railway between Liverpool and Manchester (September, 1830). Feeling unable to do the subject justice from a scientific point of view, Chorley wrote Dilke offering to serve him with "lighter contributions of prose or verse," or musical papers. Several lyrics and one or two musical criticisms were inserted in the following year. His earliest criticism was an account of a Musical Festival in Dublin, "when Paganini was compelled to mount on the case of the grand pianoforte, and exhibit his gaunt face."[54]

Towards the close of 1833 he applied to Dilke for a staff position, offering to begin at £80 a year. Dilke offered him £50 for six months to do rewriting and other drudgery, and Chorley accepted "with pleasure and without hesitation." He left Liverpool on the last day of 1833 in a stagecoach.

[53] For other references to Chorley as a critic, see *ante*, pp. 54-56; 146, n. 114; and *post*, p. 275, n. 104. The information concerning Chorley's life comes mostly from his posthumous *Autobiography*, edited by H. G. Hewlett.

[54] Chorley, *Autobiography*, I, 91.

The literary coteries around the *Athenaeum* office treated him as an interloper, but Dilke early formed a good opinion of his ability. In the first year, besides his routine labor, he was given for review books by Moore, Landor, Southey, Crabbe, Mrs. Hemans, William and Mary Howitt, and Mrs. Jameson, and the obituary notice of Coleridge fell to his hands.[55] He also in this year (1834) reviewed *The Revolutionary Epick* by Benjamin Disraeli[56] and did some criticism of musical performances, operas, concerts, and festivals, and of some of the principal exhibitions of pictures and drawings.[57]

Dilke hired him for the second six months at £65 and put even more drudgery upon him. His work was seldom finished before 10:00 P.M., but he found time to write verse for the *Athenaeum* and the annuals, and a book called *A Seaport Town*. He wrote to his friend Mrs. Rathbone on April 15, 1834: "My connection with the 'Athenaeum' continues all I could possibly wish *in every respect*. Had I sought all the world over, I could not have found a situation more to my mind."[58]

The first appearance of Chorley's name in the marked file is on April 26, 1834. Under "Music: King's Theatre" he wrote the second paragraph beginning, "We have barely space to do more than notice the admirable performance of 'Don Giovanni,' on Thursday evening, given for the benefit of Zuchelli. Grisi, as Donna Anna, sung and acted herself back into our first opinion of her."[59] By 1836-37 his name

---

[55] None of these is credited to Chorley in the marked file, where his name appears only a few times in 1834 in connection with musical criticism. Perhaps Dilke considered his contributions as only a part of the office routine, or perhaps they were not marked because they were not paid for by the line as were other reviews.

[56] See *Athenaeum*, March 29, 1834, p. 236, and June 21, 1834, pp. 468-469.

[57] John Ella was then still the principal music critic and Allan Cunningham was doing most of the important art criticism.

[58] Chorley, *op. cit.*, I, 98-99.   [59] April 26, 1834, p. 315.

was so intimately connected with the *Athenaeum* that he was frequently embarrassed by having to bear the opprobrium of certain literary groups whose members believed him to have been the author of harsher reviews than Chorley ever wrote.   This was particularly true after the episode already mentioned of the review of Talfourd's *Ion*.[60] One disgruntled writer sent him a newspaper cutting which spoke of "the Chorleys and chawbacons of literature."   Another abusive letter began: "You *Worm*!!!"[61]

About 1835 Chorley was introduced by N. P. Willis to the literary salon of Lady Blessington, and his head was somewhat turned by her attentions.   Certainly he was uncommonly gentle in reviewing her books and annuals.   She took an active interest in his concerns, "inviting him habitually to her dinners and *soirées,* enlisting him as a contributor to the Annuals of which she was editress, and giving the weight of her personal recommendation to the publishers with whom he wished to negotiate.   The homage which was all that he had to offer in return, was loyally rendered, as many a generous review and flattering verse may attest."[62] In fact, Chorley had a particular fondness (or weakness) for literary ladies and became something of a specialist in reviewing books by women writers, which he usually praised with a generous hand guided by a forlorn bachelor's chivalry toward "the sex."   Almost every flattering review in the *Athenaeum* of Lady Blessington, Miss Mitford, Mrs. He-

[60] See *ante*, p. 56.

[61] Chorley, *op. cit.*, I, 117.

[62] *Ibid.*, p. 183. Dilke's grandson says: "Lady Blessington, it is to be feared, was one who both 'encouraged' and 'spoilt' Chorley. But he was never much spoilt after all. Mr. Dilke wrote to him, that he might go to Lady Blessington's, 'because she is Lady Blessington,' but nowhere else, and Chorley replied that he agreed that 'of all tuft-hunters, literary tuft-hunters are the worst.' This was during a short absence of Mr. Dilke from town in which Mr. Cooke-Taylor was acting as editor, with Chorley, and N. P. Willis, the American poet, better known as 'Namby Pamby Willis,' for his 'subs.' " (*Papers of a Critic*, I, 31.)

mans, Elizabeth Barrett, Geraldine Jewsbury, and many others may be traced to the pen of Chorley.[63]

Chorley was a favorite of Miss Mitford,[64] who introduced him to John Kenyon, the family of Charles Kemble, George Darley, Justice Talfourd, Browning, and later Mrs. Browning.[65] George Darley had at first held aloof from Chorley until Miss Mitford persuaded him of his mistake. He wrote then: "Forgive me when I confess that, most ignorantly and unjustly thinking you altogether devoted to the popular literature of the day, and that little sympathy could, therefore, exist between us, I have let pass opportunities for cultivating your acquaintance."[66] Chorley's other literary acquaintance and friends included, early and late, most of the notable men of the day in literature and the arts. He was intimate and cordial with Browning, Thackeray, G. P. R. James, and especially Charles Dickens, who, in his last years, had a great esteem for Chorley.[67]

From 1836 to 1843 he was a frequent foreign correspondent for the *Athenaeum,* particularly on matters connected with music,[68] but he also sent notes on exhibitions, and literary gossip, from Paris, Berlin, Dresden, Munich, Bonn,

[63] Recognition of Chorley's abilities as a "ladies' critic" came in 1850 when he was appointed to succeed Mrs. Loudon as editor of the *Lady's Companion,* a post which he held for about a year.

[64] Miss Mitford described Chorley as "clever, crotchety, and kind"; from the early thirties they were "cordial friends and correspondents." "Later, however, she was very hurt at his unfavourable criticism of her last book *Atherton,* his almost fanatical frankness not having allowed him to show a more kindly tact towards his old friend." (Marjorie Astin, *Mary Russell Mitford, Her Circle and Her Books,* p. 97.) The unfavorable criticism, however, did not appear in the *Athenaeum* where *Atherton, and Other Tales* was reviewed very favorably by Geraldine Jewsbury (April 15, 1854, p. 463).

[65] For a more detailed account of the relations between Chorley and Mrs. Browning, see *post,* p. 191, n. 83. See also *Letters of Elizabeth Barrett Browning,* ed. Kenyon, 1897, I, 191-192, 229-235. Chorley had corresponded with Miss Barrett as early as 1844, when she carried on what was almost a flirtation with the critic of the *Athenaeum* who had praised her poems so highly and whom she then regarded with some awe.

[66] Chorley, *op. cit.,* I, 207.   [67] See *post,* pp. 307-308, n. 211.

[68] See *ante,* pp. 54-56, for an account of Chorley as music critic.

Cologne, and various towns in Italy. He was abroad for several months almost every year during this time. In Paris he met Paul de Kock[69] and Alfred de Vigny, with whom in 1839 he went to see the famous actress Rachel in Voltaire's *Tancrède*. Chorley had met Louis Napoleon at Lady Blessington's and saw a good deal of him. Later he was invited to translate a book written by Louis in prison following the failure of his coup d'état, but he refused the task, not wanting to become involved in politics.[70]

His art notes were routine and undistinguished except by his prejudices. In reviewing the Royal Academy Exhibition in 1840, he echoed the current popular criticism: "Splendour of colour, once Mr. Turner's chief excellence, is the rock upon which his fame will be wrecked." He admired M. Biard's "The Slave Trade" but felt constrained to add that though vigorous it had a disagreeable subject: "Though we have our Newgate literature, we are still, happily, in Art, far from that state which, in the search after strong effects, permits the seeker to riot among all that is physically and morally monstrous, hideous, and distorted." He turned with relief to Eastlake's "The Salutation of the Aged Friar," "the spirit of which . . . steals into the mind like a hymn of thanksgiving after the riot of a demon's sabbath."[71]

Perhaps Chorley has taken too much credit to himself for "discoveries" of writers whose books in the ordinary routine fell to his lot as a reviewer, and could not but be recognized for something superior to the mediocre works which he was accustomed to giving some kindly notice. He boasted that he had been one of the few to detect "the print of a man's foot in the sand" when Browning's *Pauline* was

---

[69] Paul de Kock gave Chorley a copy of his novel "Gustave" from which he [Chorley] tore out a picture which he said not even Byron would have printed. (Chorley, *op. cit.*, I, 264.)   [70] Chorley, *op. cit.*, I, 269-275.

[71] *Athenaeum*, May 16, 1840, pp. 400-402.

reviewed (with extracts) in the *Monthly Repository*, but he failed to see the extraordinary worth of *Men and Women*.[72] He said later too that he had proclaimed the advent of a great poetess after reading Miss Barrett's "Romaunt of Margret" in the *New Monthly*, but so did he also of many a sentimental poet whose volumes he reviewed in the *Athenaeum*. He prided himself on being the first English reviewer to call attention to the *Twice-told Tales* of Hawthorne,[73] but the glory is also Dilke's, for the *Athenaeum* generally anticipated other English periodicals in notices of American and Continental books.

It is rather curious that Chorley should have prided himself on his discovery of American literary figures when he had really very little understanding of or sympathy with American ways. The few "transatlantic birds" he met intimately made no permanent impresson on him though he may have been interested in them temporarily. Miss Sedgwick, who visited England in 1839, he pronounced "decidedly the pleasantest American woman I have ever seen, with more of a turn for humour, and less American sectarianism. The twang, to be sure, there is in plenty." But he was shocked at her publication of some intimate letters concerning people she had met. "I fear the next cage of Transatlantic birds will not run much chance of being very liberally dinnered and soiréed here."[74] N. P. Willis (hardly a representative American literary man, but more of a dandy) attracted Chorley for a time. "And agreeable I found Mr. Willis," Chorley says, "and kindly in his way, though flimsy in his acquirements and flashy in his manners—a thorough literary getter-on, but a better-natured one than many I have since known."[75] His meeting with Hawthorne in later years was something of a disappointment. He was

---

[72] For discussion of this review see *post*, p. 292.
[73] Chorley, *op. cit.*, II, 4.
[74] Chorley, *op. cit.*, I, 279-281.   [75] *Ibid.*, pp. 170-171.

surprised at the tone of Hawthorne's English journals: "It is hard to conceive the existence of so much pettiness in a man so great and real."[76] The mild and fatherly tone of his review of *Twice-told Tales* is most characteristic of Chorley: "We have already so often expressed our pleasure in his gem-like tales . . . that none, we apprehend, will mistake for covert censure the recommendation we must now give him on the appearance of this second volume— to beware of monotony . . . we conceive our author to be a retired and timid man, who only plays on his two strings because he lacks courage or energy to master a third."[77]

For a number of years, particularly in the forties, Chorley was a regular reviewer of French fiction. This fact accounts in part for the moderate and cautiously favorable view of French writers which made the *Athenaeum* in this period seem less rabid than many contemporary English literary journals in dealing with such writers as George Sand and Balzac. He was constrained to admire the "intimate truth and vivacity" of George Sand's *Consuelo*. Her "persuasive eloquence" reconciles the reader to improbabilities in the story. Of course, "to preach the noble moral, that the highest art cannot be reached without the highest virtue, is a labour Madame Dudevant can never completely nor consistently accomplish, her mind having lost its purity and balance. Nevertheless, enough of what is true and noble is set forth in 'Consuelo' to engage all those who are philosophically interested in the subject; while as a romance, it is full of contrast, adventure, and interest."[78] Like Elizabeth Barrett, Jane Carlyle, and George Eliot, he was won over almost in spite of himself. On another occasion he wrote: "It is impossible to read the French lady's narratives and

[76] *Ibid.*, II, 246-248.

[77] Aug. 23, 1845, pp. 830-831. The *Twice-told Tales* was noticed along with Willis's *Dashes at Life with a Free Pencil*. Chorley predicted for some of Willis's poems "a place among the 'Poems of the Heart.' "

[78] Aug. 26, 1843, pp. 766-768.

speculations, even when they are the most revolting (the epithet is not too strong for certain among them), without being painfully impressed by their sincerity."[79]

Chorley was enthusiastic about Victor Hugo,[80] but rather apologetic in praising the work of some others less demonstrably moral in their romancing. Scribe, Dumas and Eugène Sue were generally dismissed with condescension, except when their moral tone was found to be too pernicious. It is amusing to find Chorley, who prided himself on being a liberal, so perturbed by the social morality of *The Wandering Jew,* which dangerously pictured a lady of rank treating a working girl as a sister. "There is serious hazard, or gratuitous folly, as may be, in propounding examples impossible to be generally imitated." He was unwilling to dwell further on "so mischievous an example of power perverted."[81]

Chorley's review of Balzac's *Cousin Pons* showed that he cared little for the new French realism, though he could not but feel the power of the novelist. He confessed that "having by chance once taken up his hateful story of 'Cousine Bette' there was no laying it down." He found in it the same "minuteness and power" which had held him so fast in *Eugénie Grandet* and *Un Grand Homme de Province.*

[79] *Athenaeum,* March 22, 1845, p. 289. (Quoted from a review of *The Countess Faustina,* by Ida Countess Hahn-Hahn.)

[80] For an account of the *Athenaeum* criticism of Hugo, see Hooker, *op. cit.* Chorley translated several of Hugo's poems for the *Athenaeum* and reviewed *Les Misérables.*

[81] *Athenaeum,* Nov. 1, 1845, pp. 1049-1050. In 1836 Chorley wrote to Dilke from Paris: "My first introduction has been to Eugène Sue, a fierce, black-faced fellow, who looked ready and willing to eat me up." (*Papers of a Critic,* I, 43.) But Chorley was equally unfavorably impressed with Jules Janin, who, nevertheless, was employed by Dilke to write a series of articles on French literature (1837-1838). Again sent to Paris on *Athenaeum* business in 1837, Chorley wrote: "I saw Janin yesterday. He is wilder and dirtier than ever. His dressing-gown full of holes, and his braces very immodestly absent. He piques himself on the mildness and sobriety of his article, written, he says, à *l'Anglaise,* and on the extreme moderation of his criticisms. Said I, 'Par example, sur Paul de Kock!' " (*Ibid.,* p. 44).

"Here is a newer tale, little less hateful: but so full of vigour as to assure us that M. de Balzac is not yet 'written out.'" He objected to the mercenary and callous selfishness of the characters, to the expression of cynicism: ". . . this Balzac library seems to us, as a sign of the times, infinitely more discouraging than the ravings of Sue's benevolence or the evangelical Pantheism of George Sand."[82]   Chorley's obituary notice of Balzac, however, perhaps because of his soft-hearted desire to say only good about the dead, developed into a paean of praise which displayed an honest admiration of literary genius and a temporary suspension of disgust at the "hateful story." He gave special mention to "'Le Père Goriot,' 'La Femme de Trente Ans' (that most exquisite picture of Beauty in the afternoon of her charms and triumphs—still charming, still triumphant!), 'Eugénie Grandet,' and 'Un Grand Homme de Province à Paris,' as indications of the richness of the vein, when once . . . it was opened. Greater power has rarely been put forth in fiction than the above works display. It is true that we have in them too much of the anatomy of bad passions and false morals, (the fault of the author or of the society depicted by him?) but withal such a clearness of vision— such a direct attack on our sympathies or antipathies—such a mastery over the craft of story-telling, as enthral us with a fascination the like of which is rarely evoked on this side of the Channel."[83]

[82] *Athenaeum*, July 31, 1847, p. 809.

[83] *Athenaeum*, Aug. 24, 1850, p. 897. Elizabeth Barrett was several times wroth at Chorley for censuring Balzac and George Sand. On April 5, 1846, she wrote to Browning complaining of the unfairness of an article in the *Athenaeum* which judged summarily and morally Balzac and French literature. (*The Letters of Robert Browning and Elizabeth Barrett Barrett*, II, 35.) On April 27 of the same year she wrote: "I have glanced over the paper in the *Athenaeum* and am of an increased certainty that Mr. Chorley is the writer. It is his *way* from beginning to end—and that is the way, observe, in which little critics get to tread on the heels of great writers who are too great to kick backwards." (*Ibid.,* p. 102.) This time she objected to strictures on the morality and greatness of George Sand.

On the whole Chorley was more at home with the common English virtues and solid Victorian moralities such as he found in Dickens, the Brownings, and many of the innocuous lesser writers of the sentimental humanitarian school. A perusal of the marked file between 1840 and 1866, (in the latter year he ceased to write other than musical gossip, and retired from the paper in 1868) indicates what a wide variety of history-making Victorian literature came under his judgment in those years. In addition to books already mentioned he reviewed: Tennyson's *Poems* (1842), Browning's *Dramatic Romances and Lyrics* and *Men and Women,* Hawthorne's *Mosses from an Old Manse* and *The Scarlet Letter,* Dickens's *Christmas Carol, Martin Chuzzlewit, David Copperfield* (shared with Hervey), *Bleak House* (also shared with Hervey), and *Our Mutual Friend,* Macaulay's *Lays of Ancient Rome,* Thackeray's minor sketches, *Pendennis,* and the first part of *Vanity Fair,* Disraeli's *Sybil* and *Tancred, Jane Eyre* and *Wuthering Heights* by the Brontës, *Aurora Leigh* and *Poems before Congress*[84] by Mrs. Browning, Longfellow's *Evangeline,* Mrs. Gaskell's *Mary Barton* and *Cranford,* the *Autobiography* of Leigh Hunt, Mrs. Stowe's *Uncle Tom's Cabin,* Ruskin's *Modern Painters* (Vols. III and IV) and *Stones of Venice* (Vol. II), Holmes's *Professor at the Breakfast Table, Poems* by Clough, *The Defense of Guenevere* by Morris, several early novels of Trollope, Cooper's *Ned Myers* and *Ravensnest,* and Melville's *Mardi, White Jacket,* and *The White Whale* [*Moby Dick*].[85]

The list of obituaries written by Chorley is equally impressive: Thomas Hood, George Darley, Mary Lamb, Heinrich Heine, Captain Marryat, Frederick Chopin, Miss Edge-

---

[84] Chorley's severe handling of this book almost lost him the friendship of the Brownings. See Chorley, *op. cit.,* II, 105. Apparently Chorley reviewed Elizabeth Barrett's *Poems* (1844). (See *Letters of E. B. Browning,* I, 207.)
[85] Several of these reviews are discussed in Chapter IV.

worth, Johann Strauss, Miss Mitford, Samuel Rogers, Alfred
de Musset, Alfred de Vigny, Mrs. Browning, Hawthorne,
Thackeray, Mrs. Gaskell, N. P. Willis, Eugène Scribe,
Dickens.[86]

With due recognition and allowance for his crotchets
and prejudices (which were often only the prejudices of the
cultured Victorian society for whom he was a spokesman
and interpreter), one must grant that Chorley did have a
sensitive response to the best genius of his day, and occasionally was not blind to some erratic talents. As was the case
with a great many critics of the Victorian era (perhaps this
is true of the critics of any period), his honesty could more
easily transcend personal considerations, and even fly in the
face of friendship itself, than flout the current social ideals
or *mores* which required certain reticences, moral justifica-
tions, or reflections of popular moods in the judgment of
literature as in its creation. Chorley was undoubtedly not
the best or most penetrating of the critics in the *Athenaeum*
circle, but perhaps he mirrored more truly the average opinions of the majority of the readers of the journal during the
first three or four decades than did almost any other critic
associated with the periodical in the same period.

Another prolific reviewer of important general works
for the *Athenaeum* during the whole of Dilke's editorship
was W. Cooke Taylor, a literary journalist who by sheer
bulk production of books, magazine articles, and reviews,
made himself a specialist in the several fields of his interests
—especially in ancient literature and history, American literature, Irish affairs, National Education, the condition of
the working classes, and philosophy and religion. His self-
assurance as well as his outspoken (though really mild)

[86] Some of these obituary notices are single paragraphs in the "Weekly
Gossip," and others run to two or more pages.

liberalism aroused ire in various quarters. Lockhart wrote of him in 1849:

Old Louis Philippe is in a rage about a history of his house by one Dr. Cook [*sic*] Taylor, a Whig protégé, who died the other day just after appointment to a Professorship in one of these new Irish Colleges. He was cleverish—but a wild, unconscientious, ignorant, scrambling Paddy, and his line forsooth is to defend Égalité throughout or nearly so, but give Louis Philippe bones and body to the Devil, as the most consistent of scoundrels, unredeemed by a single honest quality from his cradle to Claremont. "Mr. Smith" [Louis Philippe] is angry enough, and talks of prosecuting Bentley! What a descent—but Guizot will be sure to stop him.[87]

Taylor's contributions to the *Athenaeum* went through a wide gamut from a review of *The Animal Kingdom* arranged by Baron Cuvier to Macaulay's *History of England*.[88] Throughout he revealed himself to be a Broad Church liberal with Whiggish views of political and social reform and romantic views of literature. He leaned further towards the practical "progress through science" view, however, than towards the romantic idealism of the more sentimental humanitarians. Certainly Lockhart wronged him in saying that he defended "Egalité" throughout. In reviewing the Parliamentary report on the "Hand-Loom Weavers," he observed: "Incidentally, in his notice of the Mechanics' Institute, Mr. Fletcher reveals that the best check against Socialism, as against any other systematic nonsense, is the diffusion of knowledge and the cultivation of intelligence." The evidence presented showed, he said, "that the advance of manufactures and the progress of the factory system have tended to improve, and not to debase the morals of the people." The need for reform legislation remained never-

[87] Andrew Lang, *The Life and Letters of John Gibson Lockhart*, II, 327-328.
[88] The sound Whig views of Macaulay pleased Taylor. See *Athenaeum*, Dec. 9, 1848, pp. 1229-1231; second notice, Dec. 16, 1848, pp. 1260-1262; third notice, Dec. 23, 1848, pp. 1295-1296.

theless: ". . . this Report fully confirms what we have more than once endeavoured to impress upon our readers,—namely, that the rapid progress of machinery and manufactures in modern times is a new element of society, and cannot, therefore, be regulated by antiquated laws and forms."[89]

In a number of articles on National Education and on the education of the middle classes[90] Taylor defended the practical studies and the sciences as opposed to an exclusive occupation with the classics, although he himself had had a classical training. In an article, "Hints for the History of Roman Literature," he supported the thesis that "The literature of Rome possessed as little claim to originality as its constitution. . . . The characteristics of the literature of all Augustan ages are nearly the same: the virtues are elegance, symmetry, and a refinement almost emasculate; the vices are weakness, fastidiousness, the sacrifice of energy to polish, and of strength to beauty, the restraint imposed on native vigour, and the almost total absence of originality."[91] The influence on imitators had always been pernicious, he added.

A fair share of the vast number of books on geography and travels which issued from the presses in the thirties was given to Taylor to review, so that he came to consider himself an authority on India and the Orient. "Mill's History of British India," he said, "is one of those rare works destined to immortality. . . . At the same time, it must be borne in mind that Mr. Mill was a zealous apostle of the Utilitarian philosophy. . . . This partizanship aggravated the influence of those disadvantages under which the historian laboured; he was ignorant of the Oriental languages, and he had never visited India."[92]

[89] May 30, 1840, pp. 427-429.
[90] See *ante*, pp. 67-68.   [91] July 23, 1831, p. 473.
[92] April 4, 1840, pp. 272-273. (*The History of British India*. By James Mill,

Taylor's reviews of philosophical and religious works
show him to have been a most typical man of the Victorian
enlightenment—he could reconcile science and "true religion," the practical concerns of "progress" and the "religion
of the heart." He spoke out with vigor against a book
called *Popular Geology subversive of Divine Revelation,* by
the Rev. H. Cole:

Some passages in Professor Sedgwick's commencement sermon,[93]
which we noticed at the time as a rare example of sound philosophy united with sound theology, do not coincide, it appears,
with Mr. Cole's interpretation of the first chapter of Genesis;
and this he deems sufficient ground for heaping on the heads of
geologists in general, and the professor in particular, all the
abusive epithets accumulated by the *odium theologicum* of past
ages. Ignorant of geology, manifestly unable to appreciate the
scope of Sedgwick's reasoning, unacquainted with the letter of
the Old Testament or the spirit of the New, Mr. Cole assumes a
more than papal infallibility, and pronounces his anathemas with
a complacency that would be fearful if it were not ludicrous. . . .
Indeed, we should hardly have noticed his ravings at all, were
it not that such intolerance is seriously injuring the cause of true
religion.[94]

He had high praise for Cousin's *Introduction to the History of Philosophy* because "his philosophical speculations
are not matters of learned curiosity and elegant entertainment—they are pre-eminently practical, and tend to promote

Esq. With Notes and Continuation, by H. H. Wilson, M. A., F. R. S. Vols. I
and II.)

[93] Adam Sedgwick, Professor of Geology at Cambridge, was made Prebendary
at Norwich in 1834 and was popular as a preacher. "A reformer in politics, he
was not without prejudices against some changes. The same was also true in
science. Though so eminently a pioneer, new ideas met sometimes with a hesitat-
ing reception. He was rather slowly convinced of the former great extension of
glaciers advocated in this country by Louis Agassiz and William Buckland, never
quite accepted Lyell's uniformitarian teaching, and was always strongly opposed
to Darwin's hypothesis as to the origin of species." (*D. N. B.* article by the Rev.
Prof. Bonney, F. R. S.)   [94] Oct. 11, 1834, pp. 740-741.

both social and individual happiness."[95] Likewise the post-humous work of Benjamin Constant, *Du Polythéisme Romain, considéré dans ses rapports avec la Philosophie Grecque et la Religion Chrétienne,* he found worthy of admiration for the impartiality and completeness of its demonstration of the necessity of religion and the superiority of Christianity.[96] But Taylor found the master philosophical work in a treatise by the Rev. T. Chalmers, *On the Power, Wisdom, and Goodness of God, as manifested in the Adaptation of External Nature to the Moral and Intellectual Constitution of Man:* "Since the days of Bishop Butler, no single work has appeared displaying more profound phi-losophy, clearer and more cogent reasoning, or a larger share of the pure 'religion of the heart,' than this treatise by Dr. Chalmers. It displays in every page the powers of a master mind, united to the tenderness of generous affections."[97]

Mill's *System of Logic* was favorably noticed by Taylor,[98] but Hume fared rather badly in his hands. In his review of *The Life and Correspondence of David Hume,* by J. H. Burton, he tore down Hume's scepticism by arguments sup-posedly scientific (miracles are only deviations from the known laws of nature, etc.) and pronounced categorically that "Hume's authority in mental and moral science has been irretrievably overthrown."[99]

Taylor's part in the *Athenaeum* plea for National Educa-tion and for factory legislation has been discussed else-where.[100] From 1833 on he was doing many important reviews in the fields already mentioned and in several

[95] March 16, 1833, pp. 165-166.
[96] May 18, 1833, pp. 306-308.   [97] June 22, 1833, pp. 396-397.
[98] Dec. 16, 1843, pp. 1101-1102. For a discussion of this and other reviews of Mill's books in the *Athenaeum* see *post,* p. 360. It was on the advice of Taylor that J. W. Parker undertook the publication of Mill's *Logic.* (See Bain, *J. S. Mill,* p. 66n.)
[99] March 14, 1846, pp. 261-263.   [100] See *ante,* pp. 67 ff.

others. His view of history is aptly summed up in his notice of Sismondi's *History of the Fall of the Roman Empire:* "Sismondi regards History as a collection of experiments in the social sciences. . . . History, studied aright, teaches no lesson so strongly as the duty of indulgence and mutual toleration . . . instead of seeking to gratify our vanity, by pointing out the defects in past political systems, he is more anxious to pourtray their merits, to discover something that we should admire, rather than something that we should hate or despise."[101]

A fair share of American works fell into Taylor's hands; in fact, he came to look upon America with a patronizing fondness. "We feel interested," he said in reviewing Bancroft's *History of the United States,* "sincerely, fondly interested—in the history of America's progress, for it is the history of our own triumphs."[102] In considering American poetry, he noted with pleasure that "the poetry of America is fast rising into eminence, and several of her bards may take their place when they please among the poets of Britain."[103] At another time he confessed that "Mr. Longfellow is an especial favourite of ours."[104] And he found it "very creditable to the character of American literature, that, notwithstanding its narrow limits, it should contain so many examples of intellect devoted to the service of religion, and no instance of genius prostituted to gild vice or ornament immorality."[105]

Less representative of the average level of *Athenaeum* critics but no less an integral part of the circle of independent spirits which Dilke gathered about him were Sir Charles and Lady Morgan. From 1825 to the end of her life (1859) Lady Morgan was one of Dilke's most intimate friends. In

[101] July 12, 1834, p. 513.
[102] Aug. 23, 1834, p. 617.
[104] Dec. 10, 1831, p. 796.
[103] Nov. 26, 1831, p. 767.
[105] Dec. 17, 1831, p. 812.

the years when the *Athenaeum* was fighting puffery, the editor avoided going into society to escape the annoyance of literary acquaintances who might compromise the independence of his journal, and he saw his friends only at his own house "and at Lady Morgan's, when he was sure of his fellow guests."[106]   It is probable that Dilke had more in common, intellectually, with the Morgans than with many of his trusted staff writers. His liberalism (or radicalism), like that of the Morgans, sprang more directly from eighteenth-century rationalism than from romantic idealism. Whatever may have been their reserve in the pages of the *Athenaeum,* they possessed a considerable grain of scepticism in religion[107] and shared a faith in democratic institutions which made them feel that they walked on a common ground.

At any rate the contributions of Sir Charles Morgan, and later of his wife, "The Wild Irish Girl," enlivened the pages of the *Athenaeum* at a time when much of its criticism was rather solemn commonplace. Sir Charles began with two original papers on "Criticism" in 1831.[108]   His dislike for Kantian idealism and for the romanticism based upon it comes out in his review of Buchez's *Introduction à la Science de l'Histoire, ou Science du Développement de l'Humanité.* In that book, he says, "the philosophy of Bacon is eked out with the mysticism of Kant, and with the political theories of Robert Owen and the Saint-Simo-

---

[106] *Papers of a Critic, op. cit.,* I, 32. Lady Morgan recorded in her *Memoirs* several delightful evenings at Dilke's home: "a charming dinner made for me at Mr. Dilke's"; "danced a reel with the *grave editor.*"

[107] John Stuart Mill wrote in his *Autobiography,* p. 32: "The world would be astonished if it knew how great a proportion of its brightest ornaments—of those most distinguished even in popular estimation for wisdom and virtue—are complete sceptics in religion; many of them refraining from avowal, less from personal considerations, than from a conscientious, though now in my opinion a most mistaken apprehension, lest by speaking out what would tend to weaken existing beliefs, and by consequence (as they suppose) existing restraints, they should do harm instead of good."

[108] See *ante,* p. 114, n. 38, and p. 130. See also *post,* pp. 240-241.

nians." The book reveals "the intellectual calibre and political tendencies of that portion of *'la jeunesse de France,'* which arrogates to itself the praise of leading the vanguard of civilization." The young people of France were too long shut out from political power, Morgan says, and throwing themselves into literature and science, they decided that anything more than forty years old must be bad. Then at the opportune moment one of the most ardent of the group introduced the philosophy of Kant "and found in the vagueness of its language and doctrines an appropriate field for the display of that rhetoric which speaks only to the passions. . . . The *absolu* and the infinite, accordingly, took immediate possession of every brain; and the students, instead of reading and experimenting, shut themselves up in the dark, to hold a closer communion with their own reveries, and to receive divine revelations from that metaphysical nonentity, their *'moi.'* . . . The result has been,—in letters, the absurd excesses of Romanticism—in philosophy, a revival of the refuted errors of the seventeenth century— and in ethics, the theory of universal pecuniary equality, of the independence of the sexes, and an infallible despotism over thought." But, he concludes, we may hope for a more balanced view from the French, who are, after all, a rational people. Still "there is ground for fearing that . . . John Bull may take a fancy to decorate himself in the cast clothes of his neighbour's intellectual wardrobe."[109]

Thomas Hood wrote to Dilke in the late twenties: "I suspect the Tories grudge the *New Monthly* very much to a Liberal editor [Thomas Campbell] who can allow such latitude as our friend Sir Charles Morgan requires now and then."[110] It may seem at first glance a little bold also for Dilke to give such latitude in the *Athenaeum* to writers who flew so directly in the face of a triumphant romanticism.

[109] July 27, 1833, pp. 489-490.
[110] Quoted in Stevenson, *op. cit.,* p. 254.

But a large share of the readers of the magazine, the intelligent middle class, had a sufficient distrust of mysticism, particularly from foreign sources, and a dislike of "impractical" and somewhat licentious French romanticism, to welcome the balanced pragmatic criticism of the Morgans so long as their rationalism steered clear of materialism and paid lip service to "progress."

Mysticism was indeed the *bête noire* which Morgan attacked on every occasion. In a review of a French work on Francis Bacon his point of view is clearly set forth. Every branch of science submitted to Bacon's method has been renovated, he says. "In one department alone (the philosophy of the mind), has the Baconian system been less rigorously applied, and it is precisely in that department that error and mysticism have preserved, unshaken, their stronghold and domination. . . . Locke, so far as he went, was eminently successful in disseminating the pure and steady light of incontrovertible truth." But now in this boasted age of intellect an effort is being made, "to revive the dreams and reveries of Plato, and to replunge mankind into all the darkness and debility of that mystical philosophy." A footnote quotes from Thomas Jefferson's *Correspondence:* "Plato is one of the race of genuine sophists. His foggy mind is for ever presenting the semblance of objects, which, half-seen through a mist, can be defined neither in form nor dimensions, etc."[111]

Sir Charles Morgan was a humanitarian rationalist, but his political faith, though it embraced democratic reforms, included little sympathy for equalitarian idealisms such as Saint-Simonianism; in fact, the Saint-Simonians were damned with the other mystics. In an original paper, "The Times We Live In," he says:

In spite of all the amendment in public opinion, (and in some respects, this amendment is confessedly great) the habit of slavish

[111] March 15, 1834, pp. 199-201.

dependence on authority is as strong as ever. . . . What a pretty specimen of the march of Gallic intellect is the politico-statistico-moralo-religious theory of the St.-Simonians. . . .

Judging from the products of the press, the vaunted progress of the mind is rather hollow, he finds:

If any doubt be entertained of the equivocal progress of mind in England, let the doubter take up the first newspaper that comes to hand, and peruse the advertising columns of those literary midwives, the publishers. The bulk of modern publications is made up of every variety of new-invented sectarian theology, the darkest views of the divine dispensations, and of the future destinies of the human species in the world to come. . . . Next to this mass of imbecile credulity, or barefaced roguery, come volumes upon volumes of grammars, textbooks, and elementary treatises, on all that is commonplace. . . . Then follow reprints of old authors, cuttings up and fritterings of natural science . . . and a few works of effete imagination.[112]

The works of Jeremy Bentham, he concludes, are the only pretense to original thinking that we have. The learned societies are "the headquarters of conceit, pretension, and *ennui*," where one may be edified by "a concordat between Cuvier and the first chapter of Genesis."[113] Until his death in 1843 Sir Charles Morgan was a frequent reviewer of medical and other scientific works in the *Athenaeum,* and in addition was an occasional contributor to the general literary departments.

In quantity, though not in clarity and vigor, Lady Morgan's reviews exceeded those of her husband. Her specialties were books in Italian and French, particularly those dealing with political and social institutions and the history of ideas and manners, but she also reviewed a large number

[112] Aug. 10, 1833, pp. 530-531.

[113] *Ibid.* Cuvier was much in favor in the Geological Society because he supported the "Catastrophic" theory which most English geologists clung to tenaciously in opposition to the "Uniformitarian" theory of Lyell and Scrope. See John W. Judd, *The Coming of Evolution,* Chap. IV.

of books in English—belles lettres, books on Ireland, and discussions of what Carlyle called "The Condition-of-England question."

Henry Chorley, who didn't share Dilke's fondness for Lady Morgan, has nevertheless left an excellent portrait of her:

> One of the most peculiar and original literary characters whom I have ever known, was Sydney Lady Morgan, a composition of natural genius, acquired accomplishments, audacity that flew at the highest game, shrewd thought, and research at once intelligent and superficial; personal coquetries and affectations, balanced by sincere and strenuous family affections; extreme liberality of opinions, religious and political; extremely narrow literary sympathies, united with a delight in all the most tinsel pleasures and indulgences of the most inane aristocratic society; a genial love for Art, limited by the most inconceivable prejudices of ignorance! in brief, a compound of the most startling contradictions.[114]

Chorley observed that both Lady and Sir Charles Morgan were fearless and bold in their scepticism, but they were proof against new impressions, and (what provoked Chorley) they couldn't endure German literature or music.[115]

Chorley could not resist the charms of a woman writer, however, and he paid Lady Morgan a perhaps too handsome compliment in considering the prefatory address to a new edition of her famous early novel, *The Wild Irish Girl:* "We need not tell the world what manner of thing this was sure to be,—like all Lady Morgan's writings, a genuine Irish Melody, parcel sad, parcel gay. . . . Lady Morgan's

[114] Chorley, *op. cit.,* I, 230. For some account of the literary career of Lady Morgan, see *ante,* p. 112, n. 37, 38.

[115] What annoyed Chorley even more perhaps was that Lady Morgan cordially hated Lady Blessington and would not leave her alone. "I have never heard venom, irony, and the implacable and caricatured statement of past mistakes heaped *Pelion-wise* on *Ossa,* even by woman on woman, so mercilessly, as by Lady Morgan in regard to Lady Blessington." (Chorley, *op. cit.,* I, 242-243.)

knowledge of the world has not utterly effaced 'the freshness of morning' from her style,—because it is still 'of or
belonging to' her feelings. Her pen cannot be put to paper,
it would seem, without the act exciting a certain conscious
enjoyment, and evoking a crowd of allusions, illustrations
and imaginings which at once remove her from the catalogue of the *blasés,* and such as go on making bricks when
the supply of straw is come to an end."[116]

The first appearance of Lady Morgan's name in the
marked file is in 1833 at the end of a review of *Iddio e
L'Uomo: Salterio.* Di Gabriele Rossetti [the father of
Dante Gabriel Rossetti]. The reviewer expresses warm
praise for Rossetti and the Italian exiles. Literature in Italy,
she says, suffers from the "degraded and helpless condition
of the Italian press."[117] Because of her own books on Italy
and on France she felt competent to speak with a great
deal of assurance of all matters connected with those countries. In addition Dilke trusted to her judgment a great
many important books dealing with social and political history. She devoted more than three pages of a "leader" in
1839 to a review of *Reports of Lectures delivered at the
Chapel in South Street, Finsbury,* by W. J. Fox, the liberal
Unitarian preacher. The generalizations at the beginning
are characteristic of her style. She makes a distinction between the "tuition of Words" and the "teaching of Things."
The latter has the more constant force and must in the end
have more influence, she says, than verbal tuition which tries
to perpetuate itself by resisting adaptation. "The stronger
therefore the disposition of things towards change, the more
obstinately unbending is usually the direction given to verbal
tuition," and so it loses its real power. The changes in
things have been so rapid in England, she says, that there

---

[116] *Athenaeum,* Aug. 1, 1846, p. 782.
[117] Aug. 17, 1833, pp. 553-554.

is now great disparity between external opinions and underlying opinions.[118]

These lectures are important, she maintains, because they give expression to a wide-spreading undercurrent of opinion and indicate the discrepancy between the wisdom of institutions and that of things. They are significant, she adds, as corresponding to the "thoughts passing in the minds of a large and active portion of the people." Fox's first seven lectures considered the national morality, manifested in various social classes. In his view, she says, morality is not a duty, but whatever conduces to human happiness. We cannot shut our eyes to the fact that "the demand for more popular morals is the growing demand, and . . . it must . . . drive the clergy out of the cold and formal conventionalities." She gives some space to a discussion of "The Morality of the Press": "The press, however, is, after all, the mere mirror of society." And finally she takes exception to Fox's universal preference for moral over physical power—sometimes, as in the French Revolution, only physical force will prevail against existing prejudices.[119]

Lady Morgan again and again expressed her faith in democratic institutions, mainly in reviews of works on politics and history. Of Alexis de Tocqueville's *Democracy in America* (Part II, Vols. III and IV, translated by Henry Reeve) she said: "The popularity of this work in England is rather a striking phenomenon. Of all the nations of Europe, the English are most suspicious of general reasonings. Facts and figures 'without note or comment,' (and often without guarantee) are their delight." As a matter of fact, she concludes, this is a "heavy book" which has been "more praised than read." It owes part of its popularity in

---

[118] *Athenaeum*, Feb. 2, 1839, pp. 83-86.

[119] *Ibid*. The general utilitarian foundation of her moral and social philosophy made Lady Morgan anathema to all the romantics who in one way or another were seeking an *Absolute*.

England to the belief that it is a censure on American Democracy and that it has "made out a case against the boasted impeccability of the constitution of the United States." But the praise it has received, she says, exceeds the merit of the work, which looks down at the problem from too great a height of speculation. It doesn't "penetrate the feelings, and comprehend the prejudices and the workings of character in others," a necessity in philosophy as well as in drama. De Tocqueville is led into further error by his "habitual abuse of abstract language." His theory of the "tyrant majority" is full of holes as applied to American institutions. It is not true, she protests, that nations, more than individuals, "systematically and perseveringly act wrong." "Order, in the long run, reigns over disorder; and if popular authority sometimes plays the fool, the folly forms the exception, and not the rule."[120]

The same gusto and independence is apparent in all of Lady Morgan's contributions to the *Athenaeum,* which included reviews of Carlyle's *French Revolution,*[121] *Chartism,* and *Past and Present,* Michelet's *Histoire de France* (Vols. III and IV), the *Poor Law Commissioners' Reports,* and the *Tour of the Manufacturing Districts of Lancashire,* by W. Cooke Taylor.

The criticism which George Darley contributed to the *Athenaeum* between 1834 and his death in 1846 has been so excellently discussed by his biographer, C. Colleer Abbott,[122] that it seems unnecessary to open the subject here again in detail, but no picture of the *Athenaeum* circle would be complete without some account of the unique

[120] *Athenaeum,* May 16, 1840, pp. 391-393. Sir Charles Dilke, grandson of the editor, and a more penetrating thinker than Lady Morgan, took a different view of de Tocqueville. See *ante,* p. 84, n. 223, and p. 87.

[121] Although the volume for 1837 is not marked in the editorial file, this review is almost certainly by Lady Morgan. See *post,* p. 328, n. 290.

[122] *The Life and Letters of George Darley.*

personality and style of this poet-critic. Darley was probably introduced by some of his *London Magazine* friends (he had contributed essays to the latter publication in 1822-23 under the name of "Peter Patricius Pickle-herring"). B. W. Procter, with whom Darley was intimate, was a regular contributor to the *Athenaeum* and may well have suggested his name to the editor. At any rate, early in 1834 Darley's foreign correspondence began to add piquancy to the pages of the journal. He wrote first from Rome, notes on buildings, galleries, paintings, and frescoes, but not with guide-book conventionality of judgment or phrasing. "They are the reconsiderations of a student of Sir Joshua's *Discourses* whose taste is often at variance with his authority."[123] Later he sent similar lively and often iconoclastic letters from Florence, Munich, Paris, Dresden, and Berlin.

When Darley returned to England in 1835 he became a regular, though not prolific, critic and reviewer for the *Athenaeum*. He dealt mainly with plays (Chorley says he had the "position of dramatic reviewer—not critic of the hour"),[124] editions of the classics, and books on art. His criticism was outspoken and spicy, and he took little care to avoid offense even to his closest friends. He once wrote sharply of some statement of Allan Cunningham on Sir Joshua Reynolds and was rather surprised that Mrs. Cunningham should have cut him on the street.[125] His dramatic criticism was particularly uncompromising, and on several occasions it caused trouble for himself, the *Athenaeum*, and

[123] *Ibid.*, p. 105.   [124] See *ante*, p. 56.
[125] See Abbott, *op. cit.*, pp. 138-141. Cunningham himself came off somewhat more admirably in this affair than Darley, in spite of the fact that he was "extremely *touchy* on the merits of his compositions." A writer in the *Scottish American Journal*, Sept. 7, 1871, says: "Mr. Cunningham was somewhat whimsical in his tastes, and rash in his judgments. He could not bear to hear any of his productions criticised, even by his most intimate friends, and considered professional criticism the most contemptible and worthless of occupations." (Rev. David Hogg, *The Life of Allan Cunningham*, p. 11.)

his friends.[126]   His fiercely honest reviews are a refreshing
contrast to a great deal that was merely commonplace or
wishy-washy in the *Athenaeum* criticism which tried to be
judicious and only succeeded in finding that "much could
be said on both sides."   One is inclined to forgive some of
the almost quixotic seriousness of Darley in the service of
the highest standards of art, in gratefulness for the tonic
candor of his judgments of some contemporaries.   Miss Mitford wrote in a rather shocked tone: "He calls Miss Barrett
mediocre. He cannot think so."[127]   And he counseled Milnes to "take a course of intellectual tonics against this
Wordsworthian rabies."[128]   Rather bracing too, in the heavy
atmosphere of literature and criticism of moral purpose, is
Darley's frank adherence to poetry of imagination rather
than sentiment.   To his "dear friend and faithful adviser,"
Allan Cunningham, who had criticised the want of humanities in Darley's "Nepenthe," he wrote: "The truth is I am
sick of them—so much has been said about the human affections and home feelings and sympathies of the heart, etc.,
not only by Lord Byron and Wordsworth and Mrs. Hemans,
but by every young man and woman that can square a few
lines into the form of poetry.   I hate those humanities, not
only as a surfeit, but because they have brought down, to
my mind, the tone of our poetic genius."[129]

It is ironic that Chorley, whom Miss Mitford almost
forced Darley to meet in 1836,[130] should have left the most
glowing and perhaps the fairest tribute to this rare and tal-
ented poet-critic:

[126] See *ante*, p. 56. R. W. King (*The Translator of Dante, op. cit.*, p. 259)
says of Darley: "For himself he invents a number of pseudonyms mostly in
allusion to his severity as a critic, which, though it does not seem to have troubled
Taylor in the *London Magazine* days, was the despair of Chorley, the editor [*sic*]
of the *Athenaeum*."

[127] Abbott, *op. cit.*, p. 148.   [128] *Ibid.*, p. 143.

[129] *Ibid.*, p. 123.   [130] *Ibid.*, p. 155.

As a critic, it would be difficult to rate him too highly. Though his manner might be too uncompromising, and his language made perhaps too poignant by characteristic allusions, distinctions, and similes to suit those who shrink from the more severe aspect of truth—though his periods were at times 'freaked' with eccentricities of phrase which in most other persons would have been conceit—his fine and liberal organization, which made him sensitive to Poetry, Painting, and Music, and to their connexion—his exact and industriously gathered knowledge—above all, his resolution to uphold the loftiest standard and recommend the noblest aims—gave to his essays a vitality and an authority which will be long felt. Intolerant of pretension, disdainful of mercenary ambition, and indignant at sluggishness or conceit,—he will be often referred to, by the sincere and generous spirits of literature and art, as one whose love of truth was equalled by his perfect preparation for every task that he undertook.[131]

Darley had little to do with the products of the current literary mill. Some of his most interesting reviews are those occasioned by new editions of older writers such as his papers on Butler, Prior, and Johnson in 1836.[132] He had a liking for Butler whom he compared to Hogarth;[133] Prior he thought only the perfection of genteel rhyming wits, whose "rural imagery seems all taken from fans and fire-screens . . . their passion walks upon high-heeled pumps—their rhythm, with a neat click-clack, upon pattens."[134] In spite of his recognition of Johnson's mediocrity of ideas and clumsy rhetoric, he had real fondness for the man and his wit:

In wisdom, he was but a simular Solomon; in philosophy, we doubt if he could have drawn such remote consequences as

[131] *Athenaeum,* Nov. 28, 1846, p. 1218. (Obituary notice.)

[132] See Abbott, *op. cit.,* pp. 155-157. Abbott had assistance from Miss Evelyn Darley in identifying the reviews which appeared in volumes not marked in the existing editorial file.

[133] *Athenaeum,* July 23, 1836, pp. 514-517. (Review of *Hudibras.* With notes by Dr. Nash.)

[134] *Athenaeum,* Aug. 6, 1836, p. 549.

Hume, or brought multifarious erudition to such a burning focus upon proper points as Gibbon; his Dictionary subsists like a Papacy, a venerable pile of absurdities and errors; his eloquence is a vice of language:—but his wit, quick, cleaving, and poignant, full of imagination, learned allusion, humour, and savage jocularity, was admirable and tremendous. He spoke earthquake, and spat forth central fire. . . . Perhaps little else is requisite to prove wit his forte, than the circumstance of its flowing from him in such free and simple language; while his wisdom however extempore, came like frozen water, in a rattle of disjointed fragments, from a fountain. . . . No country, save England, could have produced a Johnson, a Hogarth, or a Cobbett.[135]

Darley's work as a critic of Art will be discussed in some detail in Chapter IV. His last review for the *Athenaeum* was that of the second volume of *Modern Painters,* written when he was a dying man.[136] The *Athenaeum* lost one of its most gifted, though most eccentric critics in the last year of Dilke's editorship.

OTHER STAFF REVIEWERS

Of the other staff reviewers of general works and belles lettres, only a few deserve special mention either for the extent or the quality of their work. Thomas Hood's reviews were not numerous, but they were always lively and full of the graces and humor of his inimitable style. Whatever he touched seemed to blossom out into the flower of wit with less effort than was required for others to bring forth a lumbering humor. Whether he reviewed *The Gardens and Menagerie of the Zoological Society*[137] or *Vegetable Cookery,*[138] the subject sparkled and the puns rolled forth with an irresistible spontaneity. *"The Maid-Servant's Friend.* By

---

[135] *Athenaeum,* April 9, 1836, pp. 251-252. (*Boswell's Johnson,* 10 vols. Murray.)

[136] *Athenaeum,* July 25, 1846, pp. 765-767. For a discussion of this and other reviews of Ruskin in the *Athenaeum,* see *post,* pp. 348 ff.

[137] June 25, 1831, p. 403.　　　　[138] Jan. 12, 1833, p. 20.

a Lady brought up at the Foundling Hospital" was a serious treatise that delighted him:

The housekeeper who peruses the above title, and then reads the work itself, will meet with an agreeable surprise. Every master and mistress in the United Kingdom knows what a maid-servant's friend is—sometimes he is a brother, sometimes a cousin (often a cousin), and sometimes a father, who really wears well and carries his age amazingly. He comes down the area—in at a window—or through a door left ajar. Sometimes a maid servant, like a hare, has many friends—the master of the house, after washing his hands in the back kitchen, feels behind the door for a jack-towel, and lays hold of a friend's nose—friends are shy; sometimes the footman breaks a friend's shins while plunging into the coal-cellar for a shovel of nubblys.[139]

Perhaps the best of Hood's work that appeared in the *Athenaeum,* however, was contained in the copious extracts from his *Comic Annual* and *Hood's Own,* which were sometimes given several pages in successive issues. The only books notable in themselves which he reviewed were John Sterling's novel *Arthur Coningsby*[140] and Dickens's *Master Humphrey's Clock* and *Barnaby Rudge.*[141]

It is a little difficult to account for the apparent confidence of Dilke in the critical judgments of T. K. Hervey, a very minor poet and undistinguished critic who began writing for the *Athenaeum* in 1831 and continued with a singular prolific regularity until the middle fifties. In the forties he was rivalled in quantity only by Chorley and Hepworth Dixon. While he was editor (1846-53) he took the choicest books to review (sometimes, as we have seen, to the chagrin of Chorley, who was a little envious)[142] and pro-

---

[139] Jan. 4, 1834, pp. 11-12. This paragraph was reprinted in Edmund Blunden's article in the *Athenaeum Centenary Supplement, Nation and Athenaeum,* Jan. 21, 1928, p. 602.   [140] Jan. 26, 1833, pp. 50-51.

[141] For Hood's view of Dickens, see *post,* pp. 302 ff.

[142] See *ante,* p. 78.

nounced rather commonplace or philistine judgments on such books as *Pippa Passes, Dombey and Son,* Tennyson's *Ode on the Death of the Duke of Wellington, Pendennis, Nicholas Nickleby, David Copperfield* (first notice), and *The Newcomes.*[143] Hervey's chief claim to fame before he came to the *Athenaeum* was the publication in the *Literary Souvenir* in 1825 of a poem called "The Convict Ship" and the editing of the annual *Friendship's Offering* for 1826 and 1827. Much of the current production of poetry, good and bad, fell to his hands for review in the *Athenaeum* as did also innumerable memoirs, French works and translations from the French, books of travel, and (unaccountably) some of the art criticism, especially sculpture gallery reports. He interested himself considerably in social problems, and it is possible that it was here that he had most in common with Dilke.[144] To say the most for him, he was a competent, but not an original or inspiring, literary journalist.

Even stranger is the connection of the Rev. John Hobart Caunter with the *Athenaeum* in the first three or four years of Dilke's regime. A conventional clergyman of the Church of England, a writer of sermons, theological works, popular histories, and pious verses for the annuals, he had little to recommend him except a facile pen. His reviews of theological works were the acme of clerical complacency.[145] Perhaps it is the measure of the extremity of Dilke's tolerance that some of Caunter's effusions in this field were not edited or rejected. Having been in India in his early youth, Caunter also specialized in books of Eastern travel and geography. He even constituted himself an authority

[143] The judgments of Hervey on several of these books are discussed in Chapter IV.   [144] See *ante,* pp. 77-78.

[145] See, for example, his review of G. R. Gleig's *History of the Bible,* Oct. 30, 1830, pp. 676-677; and of *Modern Methodism Unmasked,* Aug. 28, 1830, pp. 536-537.

on poetry, drama, and music, and reviewed many French memoirs and novels.

The catholicity of Dilke's sympathies is again evidenced by his intimacy with the Quaker couple, William and Mary Howitt, who wrote occasionally for the *Athenaeum* from 1834 to about 1845. William Howitt's *Popular History of Priestcraft in all Ages and Nations* (1833) made him known to the active liberals of his day and Dilke welcomed his papers on social and industrial problems[146] as well as his "Byronian Rambles"[147] and country topics. Mary Howitt's tales for children and her translations of the novels of Fredrika Bremer and the fairy stories of Hans Christian Andersen made her the ideal reviewer of Scandinavian works and children's books. She was also a literary correspondent from Germany during the residence of the Howitts there in the early forties.[148]

Two disparate characters who helped to add to the variety of the *Athenaeum* circle in the early forties were Henry Reeve and Augustus De Morgan. The former, foreign editor of *The Times* from 1840 to 1855 and then editor of the *Edinburgh Review* until 1895,[149] probably made his connection with Dilke through Henry Chorley, with whom he kept house from 1838 until his marriage in 1841. Reeve was more interested in politics than in literature.[150] He was

[146] See *ante*, p. 62. *Howitt's Journal* was an entertaining and instructive periodical of liberal leanings which had a considerable popularity in the late forties.

[147] See *Athenaeum*, Aug. 23, 30, Sept. 6, 1834 (pp. 627-628, 640-643, 657-659).

[148] For more details of this interesting couple, see Mary Howitt's *Autobiography*, ed. by her Daughter, Margaret Howitt.

[149] Graham says (*op. cit.*, p. 237): "It is probable that his long connection with the *Review* changed the character of the periodical somewhat, and made it less important as a medium of literary criticism."

[150] Reeve was only a very moderate liberal who managed to satisfy Delane of the *Times*, which represented the views of the clubs and salons of London. But

closely connected with French journalists and men of affairs, being an intimate friend of M. Guizot, the French
ambassador. For the *Athenaeum* he reviewed various French
works, notably Guizot's *Washington* in Reeve's own translation.[151] De Morgan, Professor of Mathematics at University College, London, contributed reviews of mathematical
works, and later of many books on philosophy and political
science.[152] His "Budget of Paradoxes" appeared first as a
series of papers in the *Athenaeum*.[153]

John Abraham Heraud, poet and dramatist of epic ambitions and trials, began writing for the *Athenaeum* in 1843
and continued with great regularity until his retirement in
1868, doing most of the drama reviews during that time,
and until 1854 a great variety of general literature. He had
established a reputation in the thirties (perhaps following
up the success of the notorious "Satan" Montgomery) with
two Miltonic epics, *The Descent into Hell* (1830) and *The
Judgment of the Flood* (1834) and thereafter took himself
seriously as a "worshiper of the vast, the remote, and the
terrible." He had written for the *Quarterly Review* and
had assisted in editing *Fraser's* from 1830 to 1833. He had
a large circle of acquaintances with literary men, being
familiar with Coleridge, Southey, Wordsworth, and Lockhart, and intimate with the Carlyles. Though Carlyle
thought him "the cheerfullest, best natured little creature

---

eventually he "began to show independence in his views. Delane, finding these
views unpleasing to the clubs, took pen in hand, told Reeve to be careful, and
finally compelled his resignation." (Young, *Early Victorian England*, II, 22.)

[151] Sept. 19, 1840, pp. 726-727.

[152] See *ante*, pp. 84-86, and *post*, pp. 363-365.

[153] *Athenaeum*, 1863, 1864, 1865, 1866. The "Budget" discusses logical and
mathematical fallacies with wit and keenness of logic. De Morgan revealed himself to be a free thinker in reviews of religious and philosophical works. In
1866 he resigned his professorship at University College, London, because he
regarded the refusal of the council to elect James Martineau to the chair of mental philosophy and logic as a piece of religious intolerance.

extant,"[154] he was sometimes bored by him and was probably not greatly flattered that Heraud, a student of German, considered himself a disciple and imitated his master's Germanic style.[155]

Besides doing a great many reviews of books of travels and explorations (with which minor journalists were always laden), Heraud judged numerous volumes of poetry, some German works, and a good deal of the literature and history of the United States. The most notable books that came to him were: *Introductory Lectures, on Modern History* by Thomas Arnold, *Ballads and Other Poems* by Whittier, Carlyle's *Moral Phenomena of Germany* and *Cromwell's Letters and Speeches*, *The Cricket on the Hearth* by Dickens, *Biographical History of Philosophy* by G. H. Lewes, *Poems* (1846) by Longfellow, Hazlitt's translation of Guizot's *History of Civilization*, *Poems* (1847) by Emerson, the *Autobiography* of Goethe, Melville's *Omoo*, Medwin's *Life of Shelley*, Milnes' *Life of Keats*, *Poems* (1851) by Meredith, and *Poems* (1854) by Arnold.

CRITICS OF FOREIGN LITERATURE

Of the reviewers specializing in foreign literatures, one of the most interesting and least known was John Rutter Chorley, older brother of Henry Chorley, the music critic. Henry said that John "was more gifted than genial—gifted in right of a probity, which no provocation could undermine and no temptation shake; in right of a versatility, combined with accuracy of knowledge, which I have never known surpassed in any human being."[156]   He drew with "force and exactness," and he became adept at calligraphy.   He

[154] Wilson, *Carlyle*, II, 245.

[155] For an account of Heraud's work on *Fraser's Magazine* and his imitation of Carlyle, see Thrall, *Rebellious Fraser's*, pp. 88-93. Those less patient than Carlyle made sport of Heraud's Cockney accent. John Stuart Mill said: "I forgive him freely for interpreting the Universe, now when I find he cannot pronounce the h's." (Wilson, *op. cit.*, II, 246.)

[156] Chorley, *op. cit.*, II, 257.

mastered the violoncello and played the bassoon in later life. In languages he was no less than a prodigy. At the school of the Royal Institution in Liverpool he was made for punishment to recite the "Æneid" and the master gave in after he had repeated from memory all the first book and was starting on the second. By his own effort he acquired an accurate knowledge of French, German, Spanish and Italian—he picked up German from young Germans in commercial houses in Liverpool. Though he was one of the first translators of Béranger's lyrics, his brother Henry thought he was inclined to exaggerate things German and the German character to the disparagement of the French. Later he became a specialist in Spanish drama, and bequeathed invaluable sets of Spanish plays with his own annotations to the British Museum. When a title page was missing, his skill in calligraphy made it possible for him to supply it. The Academy of Letters of Madrid printed at its own expense his catalogue of the plays of Lope de Vega, with codices, in Spanish, as the most complete extant. And in all his life he spent only three months in Spain, and then on business which gave him little time for study.

Henry Chorley, in the short memoir which is the only biography of this remarkable scholar, said: "To such earnest men of letters as Professor Ticknor,[157] of Boston, Don Pascual de Gayangos, of Spain, [and] our great historian of the French Revolution and the Life of Cromwell, his time, his

---

[157] Ticknor's preface to his *History of Spanish Literature* (third edition) acknowledges his indebtedness to John Chorley with whom he corresponded frequently and whose extensive library he consulted. Ticknor wrote to his wife, July 31, 1857: "I dined *tête-à-tête* with Chorley . . . and I had a very interesting talk with him till nearly midnight. He is a shy, reserved man, being quite retired with an invalid sister, to whom he seems to devote himself; but he is one of the persons in whose acquaintance I have had most pleasure in London. He is a first-rate Spanish scholar; evidently better than Ford [Richard, author of a "Handbook of Spain"], or anybody else hereabout." (*Life, Letters, and Journals of George Ticknor*, II, 385.)

heart, his labour were always open and to be disposed of at their service." And he added rather pathetically:

But well-a-day for the smaller fry of literature, unless, perchance, they belonged to Spain or to Germany! Till within a very few years of his death, I was somewhat misjudged by him, as one who had chosen my life for purposes of mere amusement. That my life had been turned aside from its natural current— that whereas he should have been a great and ruling power in the world of letters, I might have become a fair musical composer (my ideas, for better for worse, having always first occurred to me in that form), never, during a long portion of our two lives, seemed to occur to him. I never had word or sign from him to testify that anything I have published gave him pleasure.[158]

John Chorley was for many years a most intimate friend of Carlyle, who wrote in 1867: "I often urged him to write a book on Spanish literature—some good book, worthy of himself and of his wide and exact knowledge, but he would never consent to try. He could have written like few men on many subjects, but he had proudly pitched his ideal very high. I know no man in these flimsy days, nor shall ever again know one, so well read, so widely and accurately informed, and so completely at home, not only in all fields of worthy literature and scholarship, but in matters practical, technical, naval, mechanical, & c., as well."[159]   Chorley's devotion to Carlyle was shown by his painstakingly sifting and copying the manuscripts of the latter's unfinished history of the Commonwealth (published many years later as *Historical Sketches,* edited by Alexander Carlyle), and by his leaving on his death in 1867 a bequest of £2000 to his old friend of Chelsea.

John Chorley's earliest contribution to the *Athenaeum* indicated in the marked file was a review of three translations of *Faust*[160] in 1834. He did not write regularly, how-

[158] Chorley, *op. cit.,* II, 280-281.
[159] *Ibid.,* pp. 284-285.   [160] July 5, 1834, pp. 501-502.

ever, until after 1840, when his name begins to appear (he was never as prolific as his brother) in connection with German works. In 1843 he reviewed some Italian literature, such as Manzoni's *History of the Pillar of Infamy*,[161] and a few French books. After 1845 he specialized more and more in Spanish literature, and from 1846 to 1854 he was the principal reviewer of German, Italian, and Spanish publications.

Two other specialists in Spanish literature, history, and scholarship helped to make the *Athenaeum* of the thirties and forties the most complete and the most accurate of all the British literary journals of the time in the interpretation of Spain to England. One was the Spanish exile, Dr. Mateo Seoane, a regular reviewer of Spanish and general literature from the middle of 1830 until he returned to Spain in 1834, after which he sent some foreign correspondence from Madrid. The other was Don Pascual de Gayangos, Spanish scholar and orientalist, who wrote regularly for the *Athenaeum* in the late thirties and early forties. He was correspondent from Madrid in 1840-41 and reviewed many English and Spanish books before he was selected in 1843 to occupy the chair of Arabic language at the University of Madrid.[162]

Dilke was equally fortunate in securing competent re-

[161] April 1, 1843, pp. 304-305.

[162] Both Seoane and Gayangos attained eminence in Spain after returning there. Seoane distinguished himself for work in the cholera epidemic, and became an adviser to the minister of Public Instruction after presenting a plan to the government for the reorganization of the teaching of medicine. Gayangos was proficient in English as well as his native language and resided in England a great part of his life. He was the author of an authoritative *History of the Mohammedan Dynasties of Spain*, derived from Arabic texts and written in English. He was elected a member of the Academy of History of Spain and late in life became Minister of Public Education and Senator. During his residence in England the British Museum put under his direction the cataloguing of its Spanish manuscripts and documents. He found time also to translate Ticknor's *History of Spanish Literature* into Spanish and French.

viewing of German literature. Probably his most reliable reviewer in this department besides John Chorley was Mrs. Sarah Austin, long a cordial friend of the editor, and foreign correspondent from Germany and France.[163] With her numerous translations she helped to introduce to Englishmen some of the best minds in Germany such as Ranke and Niebuhr, and she did a like service for the readers of the *Athenaeum* in her interpretation of current literary productions of Germany and France. Her connection with the journal began in 1834 and lasted, intermittently, for many years. Few English women had a more thorough understanding of continental literature, and her reviews were authoritative if not brilliant. Having translated the report on *The State of Public Instruction in Prussia* (1834) addressed to Count Montalivet, Minister of Public Instruction, she pleaded ardently the cause of national education. In the preface of her translation she said: "Society is no longer a calm current, but a tossing sea; reverence for tradition, for authority, is gone. In such a state of things who can deny the absolute necessity of national education?"[164] This is a point of view which she continued to support in reviews and correspondence, lending her aid to Dilke's propaganda for national education in England. One of her last publications consisted of two letters addressed to the *Athenaeum* on girls' schools and the training of working women. Other specialists in German literature on the *Athenaeum* staff were Adolphus Bernays, Professor of German at King's College, London, Mrs. Wm. Busk, translator of German works for *Blackwood's*,[165] and Joseph Gostick, another translator, who

---

[163] Concerning her part in introducing foreign literary men to Dilke, see *ante*, p. 48. Her husband, John Austin, the famous jurist, was a close friend of Bentham and the Mills and one of the original "Utilitarians."

[164] Quoted in *D. N. B.* article on Sarah Austin. See also Janet Ross, *Three Generations of English Women.*

[165] See *Blackwood's*, April, 1832, p. 693. Christopher North boasts that "Maga" was the first to do justice to German literature, having given translations

reviewed German literature and philosophy in 1845 and following years.

The reviewers of French literature for the *Athenaeum* were more numerous, and, in the handling of belles lettres at least, less competent than the specialists in the other foreign literatures. Perhaps the fact that every educated man supposedly knew French made the reviewing of books from across the Channel seem less of a task for an expert, but at any rate the major portion of the poetry and fiction of France fell into such hands as those of Henry Chorley, W. Cooke Taylor, Henry Reeve, Louisa Stuart Costello, Lady Morgan, Eyre Evans Crowe (sometime Paris correspondent for the *Morning Chronicle* and later for the *Athenaeum*), T. K. Hervey, and other literary journalists and men of all work. Much the same may be said of the reviews of American books, which were generally assigned rather haphazardly on the basis of the interests rather than the particular knowledge of the reviewer.

It is perhaps stretching a point to speak of many of the foreign correspondents of the *Athenaeum* as staff members or as a part of the "circle" at all, for some, like T. Adolphus Trollope in Italy, were Englishmen residing abroad and having no direct contact with the *Athenaeum* group in London, and some were foreign literary men or scientists who seldom if ever set foot in England, such as Sainte-Beuve, Victor Cousin, Quetelet, Liebig, and B. B. Thatcher (who sent letters to the *Athenaeum* from Boston and New York). Aside from the special articles he wrote on French literature, Jules Janin was not a staff reviewer for the magazine (unless, of

---

of many of the finest things "by Lockhart, De Quincey, Gillies, Blair, Mrs. Smythe, Mrs. Busk, and other ladies and gentlemen of genius and erudition, who in general improved upon their originals, often changing geese into swans, and barn door fowls into birds of Paradise."

course, he wrote reviews in the years which are not represented in the marked file). Philarète Chasles, on the other hand, was a frequent reviewer at the same time that he was Paris correspondent, sending over to London reviews of new books as they were published. He wrote the notice of George Sand's *Lelia* in 1833[166] and continued to be a staff writer on French works for several years. Correspondence on literary matters often came temporarily from staff members travelling on the continent, or taking a short holiday in Paris or other centers. Hervey sent a few letters from Paris in 1840, and of course Chorley, Darley, Mrs. Austin, and other "regulars" were frequently travelling in Germany, France, and Italy, and sending gossipy letters on literary affairs as well as music and art.

DEPARTMENTAL SPECIALISTS AND OTHER STAFF WRITERS

It is possible here only to name a few of the staff members who conducted the specialized departments of the magazine. When Dilke took control in June, 1830, musical performances were regularly reported by J. Augustus Wade, Irish composer and sometime conductor of operas in London, and Bell (possibly Robert, editor of the *Atlas* and later of an edition of the English poets) did the dramatic reviewing. Travel and exploration generally fell to a certain Smith. Wade and James Rice (already mentioned) occasionally shared the dramatic and art criticism with Bell who also did reviewing of general literature. In fact, it is apparent that at first, though Dilke was trying to carry out his policy of specialization, many of his staff writers had to turn their hands to various tasks. Even Smith and Parke, who were responsible for miscellaneous science notes and reviews, did a good deal of general utility writing, Smith going from "Goethe, Schiller, and Madame de Staël" to the "Scorpion Spider," and Parke jumping from "Agriculture in Egypt"

---

[166] *Athenaeum,* Sept. 28, 1833, pp. 646-647.

to "Steam Engines" and "Water Color Drawings." Lyell's *Principles of Geology,* however, was given to another science reviewer, Gillespie,[167] whose name appears frequently during the first two years of Dilke's management.[168]

Other staff writers of 1830 and 1831 are W. D. Cooley, geographer (travel and exploration), Frederick Mackenzie, water color painter and topographical draughtsman ("Art in the Provinces," etc.), Neville Butler Challoner (new musical publications), Richard Duppa, artist-journalist, whose specialties included botany, art, and politics, John Ella, violinist and director of concerts, who was music critic from late in 1831 until Chorley succeeded him in 1834, Charles Dance, dramatic critic, Sedgwick[169] (scientific and medical works), Bucher (Royal Geographical Society and other scientific society reports), Hannah Laurence (history and antiquarian studies), James Augustus St. John (books relating to Egypt and the Near East and also some French works), Sir William Ouseley, antiquarian and orientalist, Burnett the engraver, Walter Arnold (poetry, German literature), J. White [Rev. James of Bonchurch?] (historical and classical works), Prof. John Lindley, botanist, William Yarrell, zoologist. Less frequently appeared the names of Captain Chamier, nautical novelist and naval historian, Jacob, Atkinson, Gray (possibly the naturalist Samuel Frederick), Martin, Drakin, Walker, Graves, Davidson, and a dozen or more others difficult to identify either by name or profession. A little later a few somewhat more familiar

[167] I have been unable to identify Gillespie with any assurance. It may have been Thomas Gillespie, later professor of humanity at St. Andrews and a contributor to *Blackwood's.*

[168] See *Athenaeum,* Sept. 25, 1830, pp. 595-597; second notice, Oct. 9, 1830, pp. 628-629; the second volume was reviewed by S. Smith, Dec. 6, 1834, pp. 881-882. (Perhaps this was William "Strata" Smith, "the father of English geology.")

[169] It is possible that the "Sedgwick" written in some places in the marked file is Adam Sedgwick, Professor of Geology at Cambridge. Though Dilke's grandson named him as a contributor in 1849, there is no conclusive evidence that he began writing for the *Athenaeum* as early as 1831.

names are recorded: C. Cowden Clarke, Dr. John Bowring, Sir William Fairbairn (engineer), John Washington, secretary of the Royal Geographical Society, Sir Nicholas Harris Nicolas (scholar and antiquarian), John Constable, R. A., and even Washington Irving (a small item sent in by his nephew). In 1833 and 1834 Dilke's right hand man for scientific news and reviews was Perceval Barton Lord, whose name appears with regularity under a great variety of science notes.[170]

A few popular authors of the day, whose names have now faded considerably, wrote for the magazine frequently in the thirties: Maria Jane Jewsbury (later Mrs. Fletcher), Andrew Picken, Leitch Ritchie, Barry Cornwall (B. W. Procter), Agnes Strickland (author of the extremely popular *Lives of the Queens of England*), Thomas Roscoe (son of the better known William Roscoe), Douglas Jerrold, and Louisa Stuart Costello. Some of much less note in their own day, but who still have a claim to remembrance outside the pages of the *Athenaeum,* are James Rice, a minor poet of the Keats-Reynolds circle,[171] Frank Fladgate, a friend of Reynolds and once a promising literary aspirant,[172] William Kennedy, another whose bright poetic star faded out very soon, and William Pitt Scargill, whose familiar essays on literary and other subjects gave some extra spice to the *Athenaeum* in 1833 and 1834.[173]

[170] Lord studied botany and physiology at Edinburgh. After finishing his work there in 1832, he came to London and contributed valuable medical reviews to the *Athenaeum,* especially two on consumption (March 15 and 22, 1834) which were copied by medical journals on the Continent and in America. In 1834 he was appointed assistant surgeon to the East India Company and went to Bombay, from which place he sent foreign correspondence to the *Athenaeum.*

[171] Rice is mentioned frequently in the biographies of Keats and Reynolds. Dilke called him "the best, and in his quaint way one of the wittiest and wisest men I ever knew." (*John Hamilton Reynolds: Poetry and Prose,* Introduction, pp. 21-22.)

[172] Fladgate is also mentioned in the biographies of Keats and Reynolds.

[173] See *post,* p. 300. A writer in *Fraser's* (May 18, 1835, p. 608) said Scargill "must be at least something very like a man of genius."

To give here all of the almost innumerable names in the marked file would be a rather fruitless task inasmuch as many of them are not to be found in the *Dictionary of National Biography* or other common biographical sources and are extremely difficult to identify, especially in the case of common surnames such as Smith and White—and usually only the surnames were written in the file. Some not already mentioned, however, who joined the staff before Dilke retired may be given passing attention, if only to indicate how many specialists Dilke had drawn to the paper. Among these were: Anthony d'Abbadie, African explorer and linguist who sent letters to the *Athenaeum* from Abyssinia in 1839, 1840, and 1841, Thompson (general science), Graham (poetry, anthologies, etc.), Dillon (correspondent from Paris in 1839 and 1840), Frederick Metcalfe (antiquities, travels in the East, letters from Munich and Vienna in 1841), James W. Wild (architecture, correspondence from Egypt in 1842 and 1843), Charles Richard Weld (Statistical Society), Marmion W. Savage[174] (informal essays, English literature, Shakespeare), Joseph Bonomi[175] (letters from Egypt and the Near East, sculpture), Gordon (perhaps Lady Duff Gordon, daughter of Mrs. Austin), who wrote some reviews of French history, W. H. Leeds (architecture), Sir John Herschel (science—mostly signed letters on astronomy and other matters), Robert Hunt (chemistry), Robert Fortune (correspondence from the Orient), Edwin Lankester (science, biology), Mrs. Anna Jameson, Wreford (letters from Milan, Naples, and elsewhere), Mrs. Percy Sinnett (German works), G. B. Airy (Astronomer Royal), Sir Henry Cole [whose pen name was Felix Summerly] (architecture), Prof. Richard Owen, naturalist, conservator of the Hun-

[174] Savage, an Irish novelist and journalist, succeeded Forster as editor of the *Examiner* in 1856. His first wife was a niece of Lady Morgan, who may have introduced him to Dilke.

[175] Both Bonomi and Wild accompanied the German Egyptologist, Dr. Carl Richard Lepsius to Egypt in 1842 on the expedition sent by the king of Prussia.

terian Museum, and later recipient of many honors from the scientific world, Samuel Solly, anatomist and surgeon (science gossip from Paris), C. L. Eastlake (Fine Arts), Lovell Reeve, conchologist (zoology), R. H. Schomburgk (science, exploration), Captain Meadows Taylor (letters from India), Thomas Medwin (correspondence from Germany), and possibly John Forster.[176]

THE CIRCLE AFTER DILKE

After T. K. Hervey became editor (1846) the *Athenaeum* circle gradually changed, new names appearing constantly in the file, and many of the old ones dropping out. Departmental specialists still did much of the reporting of the sciences and the arts, but some of the most notable acquisitions to the staff were in the field of general literature, belles lettres, social science and political economy. A partial enumeration may again suggest the variety and extent of this ever-changing circle. Reviewers of general literature included (in the period from 1846 to 1869): Hepworth Dixon, the most extensive reviewer of all general literary works in the fifties and sixties (with the possible exception of Chorley), George Henry Lewes, Newmarsh (economics, including Mill's *Principles of Political Economy*),[177] Henry Morley, W. M. Rossetti, Christina Rossetti, George Joseph Gustave Masson (historical works, French history and literature), Madame de Peyronnet (French books and Paris correspondence), D. Owen Maddyn, Geraldine Jewsbury, Mrs. Gaskell, Thomas Wright (literary studies), Halliwell-Phillips (Shakespearean studies), Dante Gabriel Rossetti, John Oxenford, who succeeded John Chorley as the chief reviewer of

---

[176] Charles Kent, in his *D. N. B.* article on John Forster, says: "In 1833 Forster was writing busily on the 'True Sun,' the 'Courier,' the 'Athenaeum,' and the 'Examiner.'" But Forster's name does not appear in the marked file at any time, and no mention is made of the connection with the *Athenaeum* in its obituary notice in 1876 (Feb. 5, p. 201).

[177] See *post*, p. 363.

226 THE ATHENAEUM

German works, William Allingham, W. Blanchard Jerrold,
James Hannay, Ferdinand Freiligrath (German works),
Gerald Massey, Hyde Clarke (Oxford scholar), J. Cordy
Jeaffreson, W. Carew Hazlitt, Robert Buchanan, Emanuel
Deutsch (German and French works), Campbell Clarke
(who replaced Chorley in reviews of music and drama for a
while before Grüneisen became music critic), David Mas-
son,[178] Joseph Knight (who took Heraud's place as dramatic
critic in 1868), Edmund Gosse, J. Westland Marston, Au-
gustus De Morgan (already mentioned), Julia Kavanagh
(French literature and history), J. Payne Collier, and Dr.
John Doran.

In more limited fields were: T. Hudson Turner (state
papers and historical studies), Sir Lyon Playfair (chemistry), Sir Charles Lyell (Royal Society reports), Thomas
Watts (later Keeper of Printed Books at the British Museum), Percy Bayle St. John and Horace St. John (foreign
correspondence from Egypt and Abyssinia), George Walter
Thornbury (Fine Arts—several reviews of Ruskin),[179]
George Scharf, secretary and later director of the National
Portrait Gallery, J. R. Leifchild (science—reviewer of Darwin's *Origin of Species*),[180] F. G. Stephens (art critic from
1861 to 1901), W. R. Shedden-Ralston (Russian scholar of
the British Museum), Charles Beke (Abyssinian explorer—
letters from Abyssinia and the Near East), Walter Skeat,
and F. J. Furnivall.

[178] It is a little difficult to distinguish the contributions of George Joseph Gustave Masson from those of David Masson, since only the surname is marked in
the file, and since both wrote reviews of history and French works. It is probable,
however, that the latter began about 1844. (See David Masson, *Memories of
London in the 'Forties*, p. 214.)

[179] See *post*, pp. 354 ff. The names of several of these reviewers will be encountered again in Chapter IV, and some of them have already been mentioned
in Chapter I dealing with the general history of the magazine.

[180] See *Athenaeum*, Nov. 19, 1859, pp. 659-60. See also *ante*, p. 92. J. R.
Leifchild was the son of John Leifchild, independent minister in London and for
a while joint editor of *The Evangelist*.

Enough has been said already (in Chapter I), about the *Athenaeum* critics after 1870. In the fifty years that followed that date the circle of reviewers and staff writers widened vastly, and the changing points of view of the literary, artistic, and scientific criticism in the magazine, sketched slightly in the first chapter, might make the subject of an interesting but a separate volume.

The *Athenaeum* circle in the days of the elder Dilke was not a small group of "young intellectuals," eager for revolution in the world of letters, art, science, or politics, welcoming innovators and iconoclasts and daring experimenters; neither was it mainly a group of critics and creative writers who had made, or who were to make, literary history. It was rather a large conglomerate average body of men and women of honest judgment but varied personalities and points of view, who for the most part had some claim to competence in the fields about which they wrote, and who reflected almost every intelligent current opinion. The only points of view not represented in the *Athenaeum* were those of extreme Tory and conservative groups. To what degree the *Athenaeum* criticism of contemporary literature expressed individual views and to what extent it was a mirror of the dominant literary and social ideals of the time will be the next matter for consideration.

Chapter 4: Criticism of Contemporaries

CRITICISM AS SELF-REVELATION

THERE IS no better index to the character of a literary periodical than its view of new genius and rising contemporaries. The honest critic may, as Anatole France maintained, be writing of himself in relation to Molière, Shakespeare, or Racine, when he speaks of the literature of the past; but when he writes of his contemporaries there is even less likelihood of his judgment being shaped by any "standards" more real or more objective than individual temperament and the intellectual atmosphere of the period and group to which he belongs. The evidence of the preceding chapters should be sufficient to show that the *Athenaeum* reviewers were on the whole, in relation to the general critical practice of the time, exceedingly honest critics. It remains to be seen, then, what they revealed of themselves and of the early Victorian scene.

It is customary to think of Victorian criticism as smug, fatuous, and often ridiculously wrong in its judgments. It is not uncommon for critics and scholars of our own day to accept it for an axiom that our ancestors did not recognize genius when they saw it. Professor Lounsbury, who made an extensive study of the criticism of the period of the thirties and forties in tracing the literary reputations of Tennyson and Browning, came to a melancholy conclusion:

The chief impression produced upon me by them [critical articles] taken as a whole is the general worthlessness of most contemporary criticism. Especially is this true of works of the imagination. When it comes to the description of matters of fact, superior knowledge may point out errors of detail, but where taste and culture are the leading factors, we never have much more than an expression of the reviewer's likes and dislikes.[1]

Nor was this a passing mood; for Professor Lounsbury it became a settled conviction:

Any survey taken of the critical literature of any period almost inevitably leads to a depreciatory estimate of its character. Every generation has always the fullest confidence in its own judgment. It is perfectly convinced that the decisions it has reached about the merits of the authors of the past supersede all that have gone before, and will be recognized as binding by those who follow after. . . . Were we to draw general conclusions from the specific data furnished by the literary organs of that time [the 1830's], we should be forced to take the ground that contemporary criticism, at least of works of the imagination, was the most untrustworthy and valueless occupation to which the human mind can devote itself. . . . But the critics of that day professed that they were looking earnestly for successors to the great writers of the previous period. Yet they were unable to discover the rise of any new poetical luminaries above the horizon. The trouble with them was that they could not recognize them after they were risen. . . . And it made no difference apparently from what quarter the criticism came. The wisest and greatest of men were often as much subject to aberration in their views, were as much struck by judicial blindness as the obscurest and least esteemed.[2]

That such generalization is dangerous should be evident to anyone who is familiar with the history of criticism; and

[1] Thomas R. Lounsbury, *The Life and Times of Tennyson,* (quoted in Introduction by Wilbur L. Cross) p. xii.   [2] *Ibid.,* pp. 124-126.

that it is far from fair to the critical valuations of contemporaries in the pages of the *Athenaeum* is a thesis easy to demonstrate. If fatuity of judgment characterized many of the Victorian appraisals of contemporaries, were the same critics less fatuous in their estimates of writers of the eighteenth century? And haven't we forgotten to give credit to some of the critics of contemporaries in the past whose judgments we now consider our own? Will our criticism of writers of the past be as outmoded a hundred years from now as our judgments of our own contemporaries? This last question we can ask in jest, but somehow it never gives us humility.

The reader who expects here, however, either an unqualified defense of Victorian criticism or an indictment of its shortcomings and blindnesses will be disappointed. The following account of what the *Athenaeum* critics thought of contemporaries now enrolled among the great literary names of the nineteenth century is meant rather as a key to the beliefs and attitudes of a particularly cultivated, alive, and generally fair-minded middle class. It should have more than a passing interest for anyone wishing to look into the Victorian mind. Here one may see Victorianism trying to be open-minded, uplifting, and fair, unbiased by politics, religion, or special creed. The prejudices of the journal are not, in the main, party prejudices, but human prejudices, affected by the whole intellectual atmosphere of the period.

At the start it is well to remember that the *Athenaeum* was less homogeneous than some of its contemporaries. As has been seen, its reviewers were widely diverse in their fundamental beliefs, from the radical Dilke to the generally conservative Henry Chorley; from the jovial and sometimes irreverent Thomas Hood to the pious and orthodox Reverend Hobart Caunter; from the logical-minded Sir Charles Morgan to the sentimental Miss Strickland or Miss Barrett.

It is foolish to pretend that because religion and politics as such were ruled out of the reviews its columns were free from the bias which particular creeds or philosophies lend inevitably to the opinions and judgments of those who possess them. Moreover, once convinced of the general honesty and integrity of his reviewers, Dilke gave them a much freer hand than would be likely, for example, in the one-tuned pages of *Fraser's,* dominated by the clever and caustic Dr. Maginn.

Having professedly no official axe to grind, the reviewers, nevertheless, ground to a varying sharpness the axes which they themselves sometimes unconsciously provided. And a curious paradox emerges soon from the study, namely, that though the *Athenaeum* was, from the beginning and through the century, mainly in the control of men with radical leanings, its policy was generally considered conservative. But the reasons are not far to seek. Political radicalism and literary conservatism often go together. Dilke himself, though open-minded on most matters, delved deeper and deeper into eighteenth-century scholarship and left the fate of contemporaries in the hands of such literary journalists as Chorley, W. Cooke Taylor, and T. K. Hervey. The lowering of the price to fourpence gave the *Athenaeum* the largest circulation of any literary periodical. Because it appeared every week and covered a vast field, it was inevitable that much of the increasing output of contemporary poetry and fiction should fall into incompetent hands, in spite of Dilke's zeal in trying to find specialists for every department.

But to say that its literary judgments of contemporaries were the result of mere personal whim, prejudice, or stupidity, is to misread, or not to read at all, the literary and social background of the time. In fact, the opinions of the *Athenaeum* reviewers reflect, it will bear repeating, with a fascinating accuracy the current intelligent, though not frequently the most advanced, views on almost every subject they touch. But before taking up the *Athenaeum* valuations of individuals, let us examine briefly the state of critical theory in the 1830's and then see how it is mirrored in general articles and reviews in that literary journal.

A NEW ROMANTIC CRITICISM

By 1830 Romantic criticism was mainly triumphant in England. The influence of Wordsworth, and more particularly of Coleridge, Hazlitt, Lamb, De Quincey, and Leigh Hunt, as well as many less original though no less popular critics in the periodicals, had wrought a change in the literary atmosphere in which the younger writers and critics moved and formed their tastes and judgments. Some of the older critics, and indeed some of the younger whose minds had been nourished on little more than the traditional public school pseudo-classicism, retained a nostalgic longing for "classical" virtues of "correctness," "dignity," and the "Grand Style." But they were in a minority, and all but the few intransigents of this group compromised with the period by praising the classical virtues of the writers they admired, though these writers belonged unquestionably to the Romantic camp.

It is significant that Macaulay, though his temperament and legalistic training predisposed him to admire the "good sense" attitude of the eighteenth century, could devote several pages of his review of Moore's *Life of Byron,* in the *Edinburgh Review* for June, 1831, to a defense of the romantic poets against the false doctrine of "correctness" as it was interpreted in the age of Pope. "If by correctness be meant the conforming to rules which have their foundation in truth, and in the principles of human nature, then correctness is only another name for excellence.[3] On this ground the critical defense of the romantics was easy. "In the sense in

³ Vol. LIII, p. 553.

which we are now using the word correctness, we think that Sir Walter Scott, Mr. Wordsworth, Mr. Coleridge, are far more correct poets than those who are commonly extolled as the models of correctness,—Pope, for example, and Addison."[4]

Even the Tory critics in the *Quarterly*, in *Blackwood's*, and later in *Fraser's* could be ardent defenders of freedom in art and literature, when the demand for freedom did not encroach upon the political field. John Wilson (the "Christopher North" of *Blackwood's*), who, like other writers for the established reviews, could be dictatorial and dogmatic enough in pronouncing judgment upon writers, had an almost childlike enthusiasm for many of the romantics and was generous with "appreciative"[5] criticism of breakers of the rules, both ancient and modern. His defense of Spenser against the criticism of Dryden and others is a document of Romanticism as significant in its way as Wordsworth's *Preface*. Dryden, he said, had not "by nature any sense of the beautiful, the pathetic, or the sublime. He is the only powerful poet of whom it can be said that he never drew a tear—never awakened one thought that lay too deep for tears. Of the shadowy world of idealities and abstractions, he has nowhere shown one glimpse of knowledge; and even on his own ground, how far inferior was he to Spenser!"[6]

While the literary philosophy of Victorian Romanticism was inherently grounded in the speculations of Coleridge (and of course in the German philosophy from which he—

---

[4] *Ibid.*, p. 554.
[5] Chateaubriand had helped to popularize the idea of criticism as appreciation rather than mere judgment of a work of art or literature. He urged his contemporaries "d'abandonner la petite et facile critique des défauts, pour la grande et difficile critique des beautés." (*Mélanges Littéraires, Œuvres Complètes.* VI, 530.) Victorian critics frequently searched painstakingly for the "beauties" in a poem which in general they were forced to condemn because its ideas were weak, unmoral, or wrong.
[6] *Blackwood's*, Sept., 1834, pp. 423-424.

and many Victorians as well—more or less directly drew),
it could be said that he was only the unconscious prophet
of it, for he rightly belonged to the earlier romantic group
who found their chief good in "individual intensity of insight and feeling."[7] Some of his disciples, particularly Frederick Denison Maurice, stated the theory of the new romantic
criticism in a manner more congenial to the serious intelligent middle class who read the *Athenaeum.*

In the third number Maurice began a series of "Sketches
of Contemporary Authors." In No. XII he gave his views
of Lord Byron, but with characteristic seriousness entered
first into a general discourse on the function of poetry:

The mind of a poet of the highest order is the most perfect
mind that can belong to man. There is no intellectual power, and
no state of feeling, which may not be the instrument of poetry,
and in proportion as reason, reflection, or sympathy is wanting, in
the same degree is the poet restricted in his mastery over the resources of his art. The poet is the great interpreter of nature's
mysteries, not by narrowing them into the grasp of the understanding, but by connecting each of them with the feeling which
changes doubt to faith. . . . He sympathizes with all phenomena
by his intuition of all principles; and his mind is a mirror which
catches and images the whole scheme and working of the world.
He comprehends all feelings, though he only cherishes the best.[8]

A great poet may be of any class, he granted, but—

He cannot be a scorner, or selfish, or luxurious and sensual. He
cannot be a self-worshiper, for he only breathes by sympathy,
and is its organ; he cannot be untrue, for it is his high calling to
interpret those universal truths which exist on earth only in the
forms of his creation.[9]

<hr />

[7] The phrase is used by Raymond M. Alden to describe the distinguishing
characteristics of the early romantics. (Introduction to *Critical Essays of the Early
Nineteenth Century*, p. xii.)

[8] *Athenaeum*, April 8, [this is an error in printing; the correct date is April
11] 1828, p. 351. The philosophical basis for this very typical statement of
romantic theory, is, of course, to be found in Schelling.

[9] *Ibid.*

There was nothing new in the view of the poet as a seer, a prophet; it was common enough among the romantic poets, especially Wordsworth and Shelley, and in English critical theory it goes back at least to Sidney's *An Apology for Poetry*. But an examination of the implications of Maurice's particular statement of the doctrine may lead to a better understanding of the most potent governing principles of the greater part of serious Victorian criticism of literature.

Perhaps the sharpest line of demarcation between the earlier Romantic movement (during the first three decades of the nineteenth century) and Victorian Romanticism is to be found in the active desire and attempt of the latter to apply its intuitional knowledge to social rather than individual uses. The poet, the seer, then becomes the prophet of "progress," on every plane, because his mind has contact with eternal truth. This was the highest function of all literature, to find in the deep well of creative imagination, which was fed from the purest sources of nature, the water of life for a spiritual-social regeneration, the belief in which was a common denominator of the Victorian mind.

As a typical Victorian, Carlyle was "intuitively" right in scorning Coleridge for shutting himself in his garden and concerning himself with abstract speculations on "imagination" and "fancy," "objective" and "subjective." The early ridicule of Keats and the unconventional life and supposed atheism of Shelley are not sufficient to account for the general neglect of those romantic poets in the early Victorian period. While they could admire the intensity of feeling in these writers, the most typical Victorians recoiled a little at their apparent self-absorption and their failure to make an "interpretation of life" a chief poetic concern. Carlyle spoke in a letter to Browning (March 8, 1853) of Shelley's universe "all vacant azure, hung with a few frosty mournful if beautiful stars."[10] And he had an equal contempt for Keats

[10] Quoted in H. V. Routh, *Towards the Twentieth Century*, p. 123. In the

whom he called "a miserable creature, hungering after
sweets which he can't get. . . ."[11]

One modern critic has called the period from 1820 to
1850 the "Period of Hope."[12]   The inspiration for it came
partly from the humanitarianism of French individualists
and revolutionaries and partly from the German philosophers
who had seemed to offer rational proof for what the romantics wanted to believe. The new romantic could no longer
bathe selfishly in the well of truth; he must use its waters
for the general healing. Not only must the poet "look in
his heart and write"; he must find there the "interpretation
of nature's mysteries," "the feeling which changes doubt to
faith," "the whole scheme and working of the world."
When he cannot find it he is uneasy, self-accusing, or self-   ·
persuasive.

The pious language of much early Victorian literature
frequently blinds us to the fact that religious heresy was
generally much less shocking to the Victorian mind than
heresy against this belief in the validity of "dreaming true"
and in the possibility of adjusting the vision to actual life.
Shelley found "the peace of self-fulfilment . . . in cultivating
Beauty as a cosmic force."[13]   But Tennyson was ill at ease
in his "Palace of Art" until he could let his neighbors in.
H. V. Routh says:

. . . what most impresses the student of this period is the show
of confidence, even the insistence with which the writers asserted
each his own adjustment, and his claim to have won to truth; the
more ardent and imaginative spirits wrote as if they were sure of
themselves, however much irritated by the uncongenial atmosphere around them. They were at one with life. Not, of course,

---

view of most serious Victorian reformers Shelley's interest in social problems was
apparently too ethereal to free him from the accusation of living in an ivory
tower.   [11] Wilson, *Carlyle*, IV, 15.
    [12] See H. V. Routh, *Money, Morals and Manners as Revealed in Modern
Literature*.
    [13] Routh, *Towards the Twentieth Century*, p. 4.

with the actual circumstances in which they lived, nor with the opinions to which they had to listen, nor generally with the government to which they had to conform, nor even with the landscape they wished to enjoy. But with something which these and such like things could promise to become. . . . So one does not think of adjustment to circumstances—to appearances—but to the fuller, more perfect development which can be glimpsed beyond.[14]

What the Victorians believed in most strongly, according to Routh, was the fellowship of the human spirit. "So they tried to reserve an area on which their religious and philosophical differences might be forgotten in the claims of humanity and spiritual kinship."[15] There was always some tolerance for those who were earnest in their desire to spread the new enlightenment, even though they may have been misguided as to method or lacking in skill of expression.

This belief in the spiritual-social value of literature had a marked effect on the periodical criticism of the period. It accounts for the general tone of "high seriousness" in the reviews of books which had any claim to be classed as belles lettres; and even in part for the dictatorial note of authority in the writers for the quarterlies who saw themselves as the guardians of the gates of literature against the barbaric hordes of triflers who could not "see true" and who considered literature only a pastime. It explains the special significance which the reviewers attached to such words as "Genius," "Great Poet" (frequently distinguished from a merely "True Poet"—and both from a man with only talent). It explains also the fatherly, condescending kindness to *true poets* who have shown that they can at moments catch glimpses of the real Promethean fire, but who must still be pigeon-holed in the second or third category of literature. It accounts too for that custom, so common with the *Athenaeum* critics and so annoying to authors, of begin-

[14] *Ibid.*, p. 7.   [15] *Ibid.*, p. 12.

ning with general praise of the intentions and purport of the book and ending with an analysis of its shortcomings from the standpoint of an ideal concept of what such literature should be; and for the alternate method of showing how far it falls short of an ideal genre, and then giving it a qualified approval in a lower category.[16] The reviewer always had to keep before his reader the fact that he knew what great literature was, and that when he praised anything less he was not really lowering his standards.

A natural corollary of the belief in the high purpose of literature was the complaint, so often repeated, that the great bulk of poetry was hastily written with the intent only to amuse or to titillate the fancy rather than stir the imagination. Sometimes this eager desire for a literature of transcendent meaning led to a preference for what to later readers sounds like rhetorical bombast, such as Henry Taylor's *Philip van Artevelde*,[17] over *mere* lyrical poetry of exquisite music like Tennyson's poems of 1830 or 1832.

THE ATHENAEUM CREED

The early *Athenaeum* reviewers reflected almost perfectly the current romantic views of literature. The very first article, in Volume I, No. 1, on "Characteristics of the Present State of English Literature" sounded the war cry of lofty purpose with which the magazine started. There is a great welter of worthless reading matter produced under the impetus of increased wealth and an extended reading public, the writer says. But we must keep our standards high and recognize good books. We now erect this bul-

[16] George Darley wrote to Bryan Waller Procter in 1840: ". . . see what *my* great friend, the editor of *The Athenaeum* has done for me.—A *whole* column of criticism, the censurer cutting the throat of the encomiast all through it!" (See Ramsay Colles, Introduction to *Complete Poetical Works of George Darley*, p. xxix.)

[17] Published in 1834, *Philip van Artevelde* gave Taylor a reputation, both in the popular mind and in the esteem of the most exacting critics, far above that of any other new poet of the decade.

wark against the "influx of second barbarism" to oppose "the torrent of dissipation, frivolity, and corrupt taste, which seems to threaten the extinction of all intellectual greatness or refinement amongst us, and which leaves to other nations, more especially to our great continental rivals, France and Germany, the glory of advancing rapidly in the career of useful and ennobling productions."[18] The writer adds tolerantly that he is "far from despising works of fiction, which embrace some of the loftiest productions of human intellect, or under-rating the value of pleasurable and entertaining compositions."[19]

Though the strictly "moral" tone of the reviews changed somewhat under Dilke, Maurice yet spoke the unconscious minds of many of the later reviewers in the first of his "Sketches of Contemporary Authors": "The same capacities exist at all times among men; but there certainly never has been a state of society which would permit the development of those capacities in anything like the perfection which they are destined to arrive at hereafter." The germs of moral advancement he added, are in the greatest writers of every country. We may learn something too from the more popular and less wise and pregnant writers, but the best is that which "assists the workings of the spirit of truth within us."[20]

Stebbing, with sweeping generalizations, tried to show the relation of periodical literature to the "whole scheme and working of the world." He divided "works of imagination" into two classes: "loftier species of poetry" and poetry of a lower class and lighter works of fiction. "Of the former, we have at present in England not a single true specimen." Periodical literature, he said, may be of value for several minor reasons and because it encourages the pursuit of science and intellectual improvement. But it is

[18] *Athenaeum,* Jan. 2, 1828, p. 2.
[19] *Ibid.*   [20] *Athenaeum,* Jan. 16, 1828, p. 33.

not likely to "afford encouragement to any of the higher exercises of the imagination." In Germany it is different—periodicals address a more serious audience. They are more inclined to delight in "freer workings of the imagination."[21]

The frequent contrasting of the actual state of literature with what it ought to be, which is so common in all the criticism of the thirties, is exemplified in the *Athenaeum* in articles "On Female Authorship," on the "State of the Literary Market in England," "On Youthful Authorship," on "Fashion in Literature," and the like. An editorial note in the "Weekly Gossip" in 1832 bemoaned the fact that British literature "from the dignity of its state and the elegant and vigorous simplicity of its language, has descended to the tittle-tattle of well-bred conversation: for the fine imagination and purified passion of true genius, we have the frivolous gossip of the drawing-room and the tell-tale scandal of the private chamber."[22] Much of the criticism of the low state of current literature was of course leveled against the popular "fashionable novel" and its cousin the "memoir" of "high life." But the *Athenaeum* placed its hope in the "greater refinement of the middle ranks of society."[23]

Sir Charles Morgan, an eighteenth-century rationalist in most of his views, could mould his expression in the *Athenaeum* to reflect the general feeling of its readers. Writing "Of Certainty in Taste," he stated boldly at first that the senses are the basis of all taste, but admitted that the results of sensitive impressions are different when made by the same object on several individuals. "On the other hand, there are, confessedly, certain points on which most sane men agree," and this agreement, he added, forms the basis for aesthetic rules. "But rules, after all, are only the means to an end. . . . In all, therefore, that is not merely mechanical,

[21] *Athenaeum*, April 1, 1828, pp. 305-307.
[22] Jan. 14, 1832, p. 34.
[23] May 7, 1828, p. 432. (Last article by Stebbing on "Periodical Literature.")

rules are conventional chains, and genius is right in neg-
lecting them. Still to violate a rule without obtaining a
redeeming excellence, is bad taste—to obtain new beauties,
no matter how, is good taste." Public opinion must in the
end be the judge, but "when the more transcendent order
of ideas and sensations comes in question, there is no crite-
rion but feeling."[24]

There was much in that article which might have accorded equally well with eighteenth-century rational "good
sense" and with romanticism supported by Hegelian logic.
The appeal which German idealism had for the Victorian
romantics was that it could take the sting out of even rationalism and make it possible for all men of good feeling to
unite under a common banner of advancement which was
itself a sufficient goal. The common enemy was no longer
reason or science, but materialism. Seen in this light, many
of the apparent inconsistencies of early Victorian criticism
are understandable.

Readers of the *Athenaeum* might, for instance, have
perused with equal relish two articles which appeared within
a year of each other in the middle thirties. Though they
were undoubtedly from different hands, almost any of the
most frequent contributors could have written either or both.
One, an article on "Poetry and Prose," begins with the
familiar lament "Poetry is at a discount in the present day;
it is in consequence of the great quantity of *knowingness*
that prevails: we are familiar with everything, therefore we
reverence nothing."[25] At first this suggests the fear of Keats
and some of the other early romantics that scientific analysis
of the spectrum would spoil the beauty of the rainbow, but
the article ends on a somewhat different note.

Inquiry has its eyes open, and its heart closed,—poetry closes
its eyes and opens its heart. . . . Inquiry is suspicious, captious,

[24] Nov. 2, 1834, pp. 804-807.   [25] Oct. 31, 1835, p. 817.

and ever on the look-out for faults and imperfections; poetry is confiding, gentle, seeking for beauties, making beauty still more beautiful, and like charity, covering a multitude of sins. . . . People now-a-days do not see the *use* of poetry, and there is a general opinion got abroad, that nothing is valuable that is not useful.[26]

The bugaboo was of course Utilitarianism, which was usually associated with a thorough-going materialism and so despised. The general opinion seems to be, the writer continued, that usefulness concerns the well-being of the body. "A thorough-paced Utilitarian has little regard for any of the senses except the grosser ones of feeling and taste."[27]

The other article was a review of Chateaubriand's "Essay on English Literature." It tore the French romantic to shreds for various reasons, but especially because his doctrine of "imagination, unbridled by experience, and tyrannizing over reason, is the pregnant cause of error—of false taste, false politics, false religion, and false literature. The truth is, that this deification of the imagination, at the expense of reason, is the trick of those who are too idle to reason, and are ambitious beyond their legitimate means of distinction. The doctrine is the alpha and the omega of charlatanism, and its sole purpose to lead the world by the nose."[28]

This might have sounded to many of the less philosophical like blasphemous heresy against that belief in the creative power of the imagination which was the very foundation of Victorian as of earlier romanticism, but fortunately the majority of alert readers knew what the critics of the *Athenaeum* circle meant by "reason." Philosophers from Beattie to Hegel had been busy proving that imagination could be bridled by experience, by reason, and still its

[26] *Ibid.*
[27] *Ibid.*   [28] July 16, 1836, p. 497.

ultimate authority would rest in "the internal sense." Intuition and reason were happily no longer contradictory, and the *Athenaeum* critics only proved themselves the more intelligent Victorians when they gave space for arguments sometimes against restrictions upon the imagination of an older rationalism deriving its authority from the rules of the eighteenth century, and sometimes in defense of reason, which is only the right employment of the creative mind in the tasks of improvement and progress. At least until these principles came to the test later in the nineteenth century, no inconsistency was seen to be inherent in them.

Nor, in the minds of contemporaries, were there inconsistencies in the practice of bemoaning on the one hand the low state of literature, and praising on the other the mediocre talent which then presented itself. It was not uncommon to hold up the giants of the past as examples of greatness to be emulated by those who must avoid following the rules laid down by these masters. The minds of the critics looked to the future when the creative imagination, aided by reason and all modern "improvements" in science and philosophic thinking, would produce a great literature which would have a vital moral-social influence on the lives of contemporaries, but they could picture it only in forms long established. The great literature of the past had been in epic and dramatic forms; therefore the critics were constantly on the lookout for a new epic or a new dramatic poem which they could proclaim as the full embodiment of the "New Spirit." And much of the less than mediocre talent was striving to write great epic poems or dramas. But the reviewers compared these with the work of Homer or Milton and were saddened.

The leader of July 16, 1828, "On the Decline of Epic Poetry" (possibly by Maurice or Stebbing) declared that the Epic is usually the greatest touchstone of the literature of any age. It is surprising then that in an age of refinement "when literature is more a popular pursuit than in any other age, this noblest species of poetry should be left neglected, or, at least, without a successful votary." Epic poetry was originally a sacred medium of moral instruction, the writer said. "Of late years, poetry has lost its moral value and influence, and has accordingly degenerated into its lighter species . . . and it is not till the muse again acquires her old religious influence that . . . [Tragedy and Epic] will be restored to their former glories."[29]

Though Dilke's reviewers were just as eager as the early editors to welcome a great epic, they were generally more willing to look for sparks of the true fire in the current religious and sentimental poetry. The Reverend Hobart Caunter, in reviewing "The Undying One; and Other Poems" by the Hon. Mrs. Norton, had much praise for this "delightful volume . . . after all, genius, or whatever else we may call it, all, indeed, that is truly and intellectually great, rests on the affections and the heart—deep thinking is consequent on deep feeling."[30]   And Maria Jane Jewsbury, perhaps because she was given so much bad poetry to review, thought up an adequate reason for praising it.   In reviewing "Omnipotence, a Poem" by Richard Jarman, she proclaimed that "Imaginative literature, even when second-rate, has a use, and a *national* use;—it helps to stave off barbarism."[31]

This is quite characteristic of the *Athenaeum* reviewers during the poetic interregnum of the thirties. While awaiting the great epic or dramatic poem, the nature of which each had in his mind's eye (and which many of them, e.g., T. K. Hervey and Abraham Heraud, tried to write), they could not neglect such small deer of the sentimental

---

[29] P. 591.
[30] *Athenaeum*, June 19, 1830, p. 371.
[31] *Athenaeum*, April 30, 1831, p. 280.

school as L. E. L. and Mrs. Hemans to whom they were allied by natural ties of sympathy too close to be readily admitted.

It may be concluded that the *Athenaeum* circle was generally on the side of romanticism tempered by reason and guided by the intellect. The voices of all the most competent critics of that group which built up the prestige of the *Athenaeum* in the thirties—Allan Cunningham, John Hamilton Reynolds, George Darley, William Pitt Scargill, Dilke himself, and many others—were raised in defense of a free spirit in literature, directed not by rules or arbitrary judgments but by the simple power of the mind in which all believed they were not afraid to trust. Knowing this general point of view and bearing in mind some of the reasons for it which were absorbed unconsciously from the literary atmosphere, we may approach with a better understanding the *Athenaeum* view of the most important contemporary writers of the early years of its existence.

THE OLDER GENERATION

Who were the writers of the older generation most usually regarded as great or of the first rank among contemporaries during the early years of the *Athenaeum*? One might name twenty or thirty who had grown accustomed to the highest encomiums in critical journals, but less than a half or a third of these are remembered by any but literary historians today; while several others, now in the unquestioned literary canon, were either derided or little known in their own day. Lounsbury, who made a close study of the periodical criticism of the period, listed as "Surviving Reputations of the Georgian Era": Keats, Shelley, Byron, Coleridge, Wordsworth, and Scott; and of the second rank, Crabbe, Campbell, Hunt, Landor, Moore, Rogers, and Southey.[32] But this is not the whole story;

[32] *The Life and Times of Tennyson*, pp. 128-129. Though Keats and Shelley

many critics of the time would have added Joanna Baillie, Miss Mitford and a dozen more of similar caliber. By bringing in prose, one might mention Lamb, Hazlitt, and perhaps Godwin, but these were not usually spoken of in the same breath with those already listed; and, indeed, it is only their later reputation which inclines us to pick their names from a group of at least a dozen who were most often mentioned with respect in the criticism of the thirties. It is significant, however, that no prose writer of the older generation had a hold on the critics equal to that of the poets with the possible exception of Scott, and he was not infrequently more highly praised as a poet than as a novelist.

The romantic conception of the poet as a prophet of the "New Age" sufficiently explains this partiality for the writers whose most important work had been done before 1820, in the first full sweep of the "creative imagination" working upon romantic principles. Of these, Wordsworth, Byron, and Scott were the names to conjure with, not always, however, with the same intent or emphasis. To take each in turn and consider the critical evaluation of his work by the *Athenaeum* will perhaps be more illuminating for our purpose than any further attempt to generalize concerning the average critical opinion of the time.

It is to be expected of course that the magazine while in the control of the Apostles would not be sparing in the praise of Wordsworth as well as Coleridge, the latter the theorist and the former the outstanding practitioner of the romantic principles which inspired the writers and critics of the "Period of Hope." In the second of his "Sketches of Contemporary Authors" Maurice showed his preferences while criticising Jeffrey and the *Edinburgh Review*. Jeffrey's

---

were little known and less regarded during this period, their influence on some of the younger poets such as Tennyson and Browning justifies their being included as contemporaries of the early Victorians; and that Byron was still a potent contemporary spirit in the thirties is everywhere evident.

"disgraceful obstinacy in depreciating Wordsworth, and exaggerating the merits of various men of undeniable elegance of mind, but of no creative power whatsoever, is lamentable proof of wilfulness and prejudice. He has given us no tolerable estimate of the merits of any living poet, except perhaps Mr. Moore, whom his mind is exactly calculated to appreciate."[33] All men, Maurice says, who have attempted to widen our intellectual and moral domain he has treated with contempt—Lessing, Goethe, Coleridge, Wordsworth, Godwin. Toward the end of the same year (1828) an *Athenaeum* reviewer vehemently stated his indignant dissent "from a charge brought against Wordsworth by a powerful writer on sacred poetry, in the present Number of 'Blackwood,' of being indifferent to religion because his religion has not very frequently taken the form of theology."[34]

Under Dilke the same admiration for Wordsworth continued to be a settled conviction of *Athenaeum* critics, though they sometimes had less concern for his philosophy than for his poetry. The name of Wordsworth is most often the touchstone by which the critic measures the shortcomings of current poetic effort. If the reviewer wants to put a poet such as Robert Montgomery in his place, he shows how ridiculously short he comes of Milton; but if he wants

[33] *Athenaeum*, Jan. 23, 1828, p. 49. The reference is of course to Jeffrey's famous "This will never do" review of *The Excursion*, (*Edinburgh Review*, Nov., 1814). By the beginning of the fourth decade of the century Wordsworth was referred to with more respect in the *Edinburgh* and in most of the magazines, even those which did not speak of him enthusiastically or subscribe to his theories of poetry.

[34] Dec. 3, 1828, p. 917. Here is early evidence of the stand which the *Athenaeum* made even while it was in the hands of theologians (albeit Broad Church liberals) for a non-dogmatic, non-theological religion of humanism based on intuition and reason harmonized and made one by transcendental philosophy. That this was the guiding principle of the strong middle current of intelligent Victorian criticism is sometimes lost sight of in the clouded verbiage of piety which persisted as a habit from an earlier religious orthodoxy, the aims of which were not so different from those of the "Period of Hope" as to prevent their adherents from cooperating in many common causes, particularly those who cared less for philosophical foundations than for practical results.

to encourage a "true poet," such as R. C. Trench, he can keep his eye on reasonable heights and say that though the poet may not reach the lofty regions of Wordsworth's genius, yet there is something Wordsworthian in some of his lines.[35]

Although Dilke's reviewers had less of a feeling of religious awe in Wordsworth's presence, they continued to regard him as so far above their younger contemporaries as to be almost beyond criticism. Maria Jane Jewsbury admitted that *clever* people would not admire Wordsworth; he would be appreciated most by those who have a "due share of poetic sensibility." She herself had grown up with a love for his poetry, but she would "be very sorry to join in the fulsome adulation that has by some been poured forth in its praise; it may haunt us like a passion—be to us a dream worth ten thousand realities, and yet we may demur to making it a religion."[36]

Allan Cunningham, in his series of papers on the "Biographical and Critical History of the Literature of the Last Fifty Years" which appeared in the *Athenaeum* in the last months of 1833, reiterated the average opinion. Though he gave less space to Wordsworth than to Burns, Rogers, Scott, Southey, Hogg, and Byron, he classed him with Burns (Cunningham's favorite) as a leader in the movement away from artificial restrictions and back to nature.

Wordsworth is the poet of nature and man—not of humble life, as some have said—but of noble emotions, lofty feelings, and whatever tends to exalt man and elevate him on the table land of honour, morality, and religion. His style is worthy of his topics— simple, unaffected, and vigorous: he occasionally becomes too minute in his delineations, and some of the subjects which he

[35] See a review of "Sabbation; Honor Neale; and other Poems" by R. C. Trench, *Athenaeum*, March 31, 1838, p. 230.

[36] *Athenaeum*, June 25, 1831, pp. 404-405.

treats of, are too homely for inspiration. His poetry is making its way, as true feeling and impassioned thought ever will.[37]

The reviewer of "Yarrow Revisited" in 1835 was just about to welcome a volume by "another true poet, James Montgomery" when Wordsworth's book arrived. He was not then in a mood to criticise "poetry so pregnant with wisdom, and so elevated with thought as Wordsworth's. . . . But ere we allow this golden book to speak for itself, we cannot but express our sincere pleasure in the undiminished powers of the writer. . . . He is as lofty and as noble in his contemplation as ever."[38]

Even after the publication of Tennyson's 1842 volumes, Wordsworth was still the unaltered idol of the *Athenaeum,* if we are to judge from a review by Elizabeth Barrett of "Poems, chiefly of early and late years, including The Borderers, a Tragedy." She made the customary comparison between Wordsworth and Byron to the disparagement of the latter, though she could pity "Poor Byron (true miserable genius, soul-blind great poet!)." His poems "discovered not a heart, but the wound of a heart; not humanity, but disease; not life, but a crisis."

. . . it was not in the projection of a passionate emotion, that William Wordsworth committed himself to nature, but in full resolution and determinate purpose. Byron was a poet through pain. Wordsworth is a feeling man, because he is a thoughtful man. . . . Wordsworth's eye is his soul. He does not see that which he does not intellectually discern.[39]

He is a religious poet, and "he is scarcely least so when he is not writing directly upon the subject of religion."[40] He has triumphed in spite of the "ribald cry of that 'vox populi' which has, in the criticism of poems, so little the character

[37] Oct. 26, 1833, p. 718.
[38] *Athenaeum,* April 18, 1835, pp. 293-294.
[39] *Athenaeum,* Aug. 27, 1842, p. 757.
[40] *Ibid.* Cf. *ante,* p. 247, n. 34.

of divinity." Nature justified him she said, without the aid
of the *Edinburgh Review*. But Miss Barrett was not blind
to the poet's faults.

'Hero-worshippers,' as we are, and sitting for all the critical
pretence . . . —at the feet of Mr. Wordsworth,—recognizing him,
as we do, as poet-hero of a movement essential to the better being
of poetry, as poet-prophet of utterances greater than those who
first listened could comprehend, and of influences most vital and
expansive—we are yet honest to confess that certain things in the
'Lyrical Ballads' which most provoked the ignorant innocent
hootings of the mob, do not seem to us all heroic.[41]

Not the best of Wordsworth's poetry may be found in this
volume, she admitted, but it is worthy of its forerunners,
"the hand trembling not a jot for years or weariness."
Finally, the reviewer would drop a tear for the series of
sonnets in favor of capital punishment.[42] The fervor with
which the early Victorian world clung to its fidelity to the
seer-poet, of which Wordsworth was the symbol and the
earthly embodiment, is indicated in the praise which Elizabeth Barrett heaped upon the aging prophet in spite of
what her sharp critical sense told her of his loss of power
and his desertion of the humanitarian causes which were
dear to her.

The important thing to her, however, was that "Mr.
Wordsworth's life does present a high moral to his generation."

It is advantageous for us all, whether poets or poetasters, or
talkers about either, to know what a true poet is . . . so as to raise
the popular idea of these things, and either strengthen or put
down the individual aspiration.[43]

If the praise of Wordsworth was all but universal in the
pages of the *Athenaeum,* the same cannot be said of Byron.

[41] *Ibid.,* p. 758.
[42] *Ibid.*   [43] *Ibid.,* p. 759.

Almost all of the eminent Victorians began with an admiration for Byron which they later turned from, some with fierceness of moral accusation and others with pity and regret. The *Athenaeum* reflected almost every attitude common among critics at the time, even the most narrow sectarian moral view, though in general it was less likely to hit the extremes of condemnation, condescension, or idolizing which were the current notes of Byronic criticism. Here the individual temperament of the critic came into play much more freely than elsewhere, for the name of Byron had greatly varied associations in different minds, some of them almost too complicated to sift out. Nevertheless, perusal of the *Athenaeum* may help one to get a panoramic view of Byron's reputation in the thirties and early forties.

Whatever the opinion may have been of Byron, the interest in him was universal. Whether constrained to praise or blame, the reviewer knew that his subject had news value. The *Athenaeum* announced in its first number that it was fortunate in being able to gratify its readers by giving extracts from Leigh Hunt's forthcoming work on *Lord Byron and Some of his Contemporaries.* The magazine favored its readers in like manner on or before the appearance of Moore's *Letters and Journals of Lord Byron,* and it gave large space also to the flood of memoirs and reminiscences which followed in great profusion for several years after, as well as to Murray's edition of Byron's life and works.

The reviewer of the first work praised Hunt's revelation of a new side of Byron:

The greater number of the readers of Byron seem to consider him as indeed a little capricious and misanthropic, yet, on the whole, a very agreeable, romantic, and magnanimous personage.

Nevertheless,

His poems, with all their power, exhibit indubitable signs of selfishness, waywardness, and affectation. Among the states of feeling which he describes with so much intensity, we doubt whether any great proportion were really painted from his own feelings.

The conclusion of the writer was that the works of Byron may be "a warning to every mind, the mightiest or the meanest, that there are failings and vices which will even break the sceptre and scatter to the winds the omnipotence of genius."[44]

The typical moral judgment of Byron was most completely exhibited by Maurice in his article in the "Contemporary Authors" series:

No one, probably, will be inclined to maintain, that Lord Byron's poetry produces a good moral effect, except those who are anxious to spread the disbelief of the goodness of God, and to bring about the promiscuous intercourse of the sexes.[45]

If one were honest with himself, and asked what he got from Byron, would he not confess that "he had been imbibing discontent, disgust, satiety, and learning to look upon life as a dreary dulness, relieved only by betaking ourselves to the wildest excesses and fiercest intensity of evil impulse?"[46]

We entirely omit the question of the direct irreligion and indecency of his writings. . . . For ourselves, we lament the Anti-Christian and impure tendencies of his mind, not so much for any positive evil they can do,—this, we suspect, being much overrated,—as because they are evidences of the degradation of a powerful mind, and of the pollution of much and strong good feeling. . . .

We wish not to deny that Lord Byron was a poet, and a great one. There are moods of the mind which he has delineated with remarkable fidelity. . . . The sceptre of his power is, indeed, girt with the wings of an angel, but it is also wreathed with earth-

---

[44] *Athenaeum*, Jan. 23, 1828, p. 55.

[45] *Athenaeum*, April 8 [*sic*—error in printing—actually April 11], 1828, p. 351.   [46] *Ibid.*

born serpents; and, while we admire we must sigh, and shudder while we bow.[47]

And yet Maurice could rise to the defense of Byron when his right to a place among the poets of Westminster Abbey was being debated. In a leader on "Lord Byron's Monument" he made an eloquent plea for the healthful catharsis of Byron's writings—a plea which clearly foreshadowed Tennyson's defense of "honest doubt." Milton, he said, reached "the state of a mind at rest, and harmonized, not from perceiving so little that it cannot understand the grounds of scepticism, but from knowing so much that it comprehends how they are satisfied. . . . That Byron's mind never worked its way into clearness in like manner, is no evidence that the state of feeling which is expressed in 'Cain' did not correspond with that through which every man of genius . . . passes before his character is consummated."[48]

Consider the distinction, he continued, between the scepticism encouraged by "Cain" and that produced by reading Hume's "Essays." One could exist in the state inspired by Hume indefinitely with tranquillity, whereas one couldn't exist comfortably for an hour in the state of mind induced by "Cain." The reason is that the whole of Hume's scepticism lay out of himself. "Wordsworth and Coleridge belong to the coming ages . . . but Byron is ours; for our own sakes, if not for his, let us show that we are not ashamed of the influence he has exerted over us."[49]

From this time forward the criticism of Byron in the *Athenaeum* is mainly defensive, sometimes of his reputation

[47] *Ibid.*, p. 352.

[48] *Athenaeum*, Oct. 1, 1828, p. 767. (There was also a leader on the same subject in the previous number, Sept. 24, pp. 751-752.) The influence of Maurice and others of the "Apostles" in the shaping of Tennyson's mind, particularly on matters connected with religion and philosophy has been discussed in various studies of the latter—especially in Harold Nicolson's *Tennyson* and in a Master's thesis (unpublished, but in typescript in the New York Public Library) by Jessie Folsom Rice (University of Chicago, 1913).   [49] *Ibid.*, p. 768.

as a man, and sometimes as a poet, but also frequently it is the self-justification of the critic, the rationalization of one who feels that he must somehow fit the universal appeal of the Byronic mood into the pattern of the current optimism.

In another leader, a second notice of the first volume of Moore's *Letters and Journals of Lord Byron,* the reviewer states the belief that the effect of its publication will be "to raise Lord Byron in the esteem, or, at least, liking of those who are now most inclined to condemn him, and still more decidedly to lower him in the opinion of his vulgar idolators."[50]   In spite of his faults as a poseur, "it is impossible to contemplate, without sympathy, the misfortunes of his position and circumstances, the occasional flashes of wisdom, and the constancy and warmth of some of his affections."[51] Again, a review running through two numbers praises the *Conversations on Religion with Lord Byron and Others* by the late James Kennedy, M.D., whose contention was that Byron "was not a dull, deliberate and reasoning sceptic, but one whose faith had been staggered by the contradictions between the professions and the conduct of religious people."[52]

Reynolds perhaps touched the height of the *Athenaeum* praise of Byron in reviewing Moore's second volume when he referred to the "sublime drama of Manfred."[53]   Allan Cunningham expressed the more nearly average and representative view of the *Athenaeum* critics.   He deprecated Byron's "sentiments dark and terrible," but admired the "calm dissection of the human heart" and the "language audaciously powerful and fluent."

The cynical, sneering, and sarcastic spirit of our times—the doubting of everything, and believing in nothing—found a poet

[50] *Athenaeum,* Jan. 30, 1830, pp. 49-52.
[51] *Ibid.*
[52] *Athenaeum,* June 26, 1830, pp. 390-391.   (See also June 19, pp. 369-371.)
[53] *Athenaeum,* Dec. 25, 1830, pp. 801-804.

in George Gordon Lord Byron. . . . Yet, with all the repulsiveness of his men, and the melo-dramatic sort of characters of his women, he invests them with such life—paints their thoughts so truly, and their actions with such wondrous force of light and shade, as render them welcome, with all their sins against virtue and decorum . . . and while we cannot find an echo in our own hearts for a third of the fearful things he utters, we follow him still. His radical defect is a want of sympathy with universal nature. . . . We read his noblest strains with an uneasy heart and a troubled brow.[54]

This note was echoed again and again through the pages of the *Athenaeum.* The only notable variation is the occasional plea for Byron as a champion of liberty and the people's rights, as in the Quaker poet William Howitt's account of the funeral at Newstead where Byron was reverenced by the radicals, chiefly of the working class. "The religious world had a high prejudice against him for his manifold sins of speech, opinion, and life: they of course were not there."[55]

The reputation of Scott stood, in the main, apart from if not above the missiles of critics in the "Period of Hope." Of course, the more earnest moralists of the time, including the *Athenaeum* circle under Maurice and Sterling, may have felt at times a fear that the love of Scott would lead the unthinking away from the contemplation of the "elevated thoughts" of Wordsworth and Coleridge, and they always resented praise of the Scottish poet (or novelist) which disparaged in comparison the work of any "True Poet" or writer who was also a prophet. One charge brought against

[54] Allan Cunningham, "Biographical and Critical History of the Literature of the Last Fifty Years," *Athenaeum*, Nov. 16, 1833, p. 771.

[55] "A Byronian Rample," *Athenaeum*, Aug. 23, 1834, pp. 627-628. The *Athenaeum* again took up the fight editorially against the religious bigotry of the ecclesiastical authorities who were responsible for the exclusion of Byron's bust from Westminster Abbey. (See paragraphs in "Our Weekly Gossip," Sept. 8, 1838, p. 659, and June 22, 1844, p. 576.)

Lockhart as editor of the *Quarterly* was that he belittled the rivals of Scott in the field of the historical novel. In the review of *Nigel,* before Lockhart took the editorship, the critic had dared to comment on the sameness of Scott's plots and characters, but that was changed under the son-in-law critic, the *Athenaeum* charged. Now Scott suffers from overpraise or illogical praise in the *Quarterly* which "draws a charmed circle round the father-in-law of its Editor. . . ."[56] Of course the blame rested with Lockhart, and the critic hastened to praise Scott for his proper virtues. We soon discover that the sore point was that Lockhart had belittled Horace Smith in comparison with Scott in a review of *Brambletye House.*[57]

This carping note was mainly abandoned, however, under Dilke when Allan Cunningham again voiced the general sentiment: "Scott is a poet truly national and heroic." He is comparable to Homer in his songs of battle and action such as the "Pibroch." "This song is characteristic of all Scott's poetry—action, action, action, is its fault as well as its excellence."[58]   Scott and Byron were two names often spoken together by anyone wishing to praise poets who appealed to the hearts of the people, but the critics who pounced upon Byron let Scott escape.[59]

It is something of a tribute to the genial humanity and broad sympathies of Scott that he could be praised alike by

[56] See "Letters of Crito: Critical Qualifications of Mr. Lockhart, as Editor of the Quarterly Review," No. 1, *Athenaeum,* Jan. 16, 1828, pp. 41-42; No. 11, Jan. 23, 1828, p. 59; No. III, Feb. 5, 1828, pp. 91-93.

[57] Horace Smith had contributed a parody of Scott to the *Rejected Addresses* (1812) in which he collaborated with his brother James. In the late twenties he was considered a writer of great promise, but in the thirties he dwindled into a contributor to the annuals.

[58] Allan Cunningham, "Biographical and Critical History of the Literature of the Last Fifty Years," *Athenaeum,* Oct. 26, 1833, pp. 717-718. After the death of Scott, Cunningham had ranked him "above all novelists who ever wrote, with the exception of Cervantes." (*Athenaeum,* Oct. 6, 1832, p. 653.)

[59] See, for example, the series of controversial articles which ran in the *Athenaeum* from March 23, to June 8, 1844, under the heading of "Modern Poets."

all parties, but it is also an indication of the general eager-
ness to enroll everyone who was not actually resistant in
the common cause of moral progress. Both George Eliot and
Ruskin were allowed by very pious parents to read *Waverley*
as well as the *Bible* in their childhood.[60]

When we come to the other poets listed by Lounsbury
as of the first rank among the surviving reputations of the
older generation—Keats, Shelley, Coleridge—it becomes apparent that the classification was made with reference to a
much later judgment. Certainly most critics of the thirties
would have thought it utterly ridiculous to value Shelley
and Keats above Crabbe, Campbell, Moore, Rogers, and
Southey.

According to Lounsbury, concurrent with the movement
against Byron, which began about 1830, was the propaganda
for Wordsworth and Shelley (though the former would
have been shocked to hear his name linked to Shelley's).
This movement began to be strong at Cambridge during
Tennyson's residence there (1828-31). Hallam and other
admirers of Shelley had caused "Adonais" to be reprinted
at Cambridge in 1829 in an edition of 500 copies (the first
printing since the Pisa edition of 1828). And then to the
worship of Shelley in this small coterie was added that of
the much less known Keats.

Shelley had been known, and continued for many years
to be known outside of this circle, more for his atheistical
and extreme social views than for his poetry. "Queen Mab"
had been most frequently reprinted. In December, 1829,
Hallam, Milnes, and Thomas Sunderland went to Oxford
to represent Cambridge in a debate on the question: "Resolved, that Shelley is superior to Byron as a poet." The
Cambridge men took the affirmative, and they were shocked
to find that no one at Oxford knew anything about Shelley.

[60] Ruskin was also permitted to read Byron.

The students in the Oxford Union had the vague notion that the debate was to be about Shenstone. The members of the Union finally concurred in the decision that Byron was the greater, for, if Shelley had been a great poet, they would all have read him, whereas, in fact, many of them didn't even know his name.[61]

From 1830 to 1840 Shelley's reputation rose rapidly. Magazine editors sought his unpublished writings. Critical attention increased in volume and warmth. Regret was usually expressed for incidents of his life and for his views, but there was a disposition among the critics to forget and forgive in view of his poetic genius. His collected works were first published in 1839. "Queen Mab" was omitted, but was speedily replaced in a second edition, because of the demand made for it by Shelley's admirers. Keats was scarcely mentioned in the thirties, and frequently his name was misspelled and spoken with contempt.[62]

It was the pride of the *Athenaeum* editors in later years that the periodical was among the first to champion both of these neglected poets. Several special reasons, aside from the general inclination of the magazine to favor writers of the "Romantic School," may help to account for the particular attention given to Shelley and Keats in the *Athenaeum* at a time when few voices were lauding them. It was to be expected that the Cambridge Apostles group would honor them along with Wordsworth and Coleridge and all others who drew their inspiration from the inner springs of feeling. They did not share the distrust which many of the more earnest Victorians had of the intense self-absorption and detachment from real life inherent in Shelley's aesthetic idealism as well as in the "art for art's sake" tendencies of Keats. Deep feeling, they believed, was

[61] For a fuller account of this debate see F. M. Brookfield, *The Cambridge Apostles*, pp. 128-130. See also Lounsbury, *op. cit.*, pp. 154-157.
[62] See Lounsbury, *op. cit.*, pp. 159-161.

a good in itself through which contact might be made after all with a cosmic intelligence sufficient for the guidance of affairs larger than mere individual self-satisfaction.[63] Moreover, the personal friendship of Dilke, John Hamilton Reynolds, and others of the *Athenaeum* circle with Keats, and the common cause which the reviewers made against the ruthless unfairness of party criticism such as that of the *Quarterly* and *Blackwood's* in attacking the poets of the so-called "Cockney School," undoubtedly contributed to the favorable notices of those unfortunate poets.

Maurice's eighth sketch of contemporary authors was an extremely panegyrical defense of the character and poetry of Shelley. On broad religious grounds, not narrow sectarian ones, he maintained, Shelley was not an atheist. He may have rebelled against "a degrading and polluted idea of God," but he did trust in "the concentration and essence of good."

He uniformly referred, for the reason and the truth of things, to invisible principles within us or without, of which natural appearances are merely the clothing and the shadow; and they who would attempt, by an abuse of language, to give the notion that he ought to be classed with the empirical metaphysicians, or the mere mechanical philosophers, might as well tie the breathing body to the dead carcase. . . .

We do not say that he wrote better poetry than Coleridge or Wordsworth; but that more habitually than they, or indeed than any one else we can remember, he thought and felt poetically. He cannot be conceived as performing the most ordinary action,

---

[63] Routh has stated very well the results of the attempt to carry the "Romantic Quest" into the Victorian world. German philosophers had promised not only the discovery of self but also a truer contact with cosmic intelligence. What their disciples found in their hearts was disappointing. "Many, like Werther . . . found . . . the bitterness of thwarted love and wounded vanity. So the philosophy of the romantic movement created the wish rather than the means towards revelation, and its influence was to continue all through the century more as a baffled quest or an obligation than as a clue to certainty." (*Towards the Twentieth Century*, p. 22.)

and not investing it with a wild gracefulness, or imaginative splendour. . . .

The great moral peculiarity of his writings is, his constant inculcation of man's capacity for a higher condition than the present. . . .

The instruments by which Shelley advanced these high moral objects, were a magnificent imagination, a fairy-like fancy, a powerful intellect, a delicacy and range of perfection, which were scarcely ever equalled, and a faculty of expression, which, we have no hesitation in saying, has been in our day quite unrivalled. In this last quality, we would include both richness of diction, and the talent for composing melodious and significant verse. . . . So that, excepting Milton, there is nothing in the language at all comparable to the mingled strength and sweetness, the involved and changeful harmony, of his metre.[64]

The review of the Cambridge edition of *Adonais* gave another opportunity for heralding "the gradual and steady rise of Shelley's fame." Nevertheless it was still necessary to clear away the misconceptions concerning his character and opinions. "We deny, in the first place, that his growing popularity arises from his opinions; and we maintain, secondly, that his opinions are not likely to do harm." If we take religion to be "the faith . . . in the invisible, as the life and support of the visible . . . this faith appears to us to have existed in the mind of Shelley as strongly as in that of any saint or philosopher that ever existed." His religious opinions have done less harm than those of infidels such as "the flippant, sensual, and conceited Gibbon," Hume, and Voltaire. Moreover, the reviewer concluded, all the infidels of England dislike Shelley. Therefore it is clear that "his fame must be based on something other than his religious scepticism."[65]

[64] *Athenaeum*, March 7, 1828, pp. 193-194.
[65] *Athenaeum*, Sept. 2, 1829, pp. 544-545.

The reviewers under Dilke were usually more concerned with Shelley as a poet than as a philosopher or romantic prophet, but they also felt constrained to answer the charges brought against him most frequently of immorality, irreligion, or obscurity. The publication of his "The Wandering Jew" in *Fraser's* in July, 1831, gave Maria Jane Jewsbury an excuse for writing a critique of Shelley for the *Athenaeum*. It was time, she said, to draw a line "between his metaphysical subtleties and moral mistakes, and the remaining mass of his true, pure, beautiful poetry." Though deprecating some of his beliefs, the writer praised him above Byron, who was more popular because his poetry was more "palpable and impassioned."

With the exception of Coleridge, the English language has not such a consummate master of harmony—nor, with the same exception and the addition of Wordsworth, a poet possessing such an exquisite knowledge of external nature, from its grander aspects amongst seas and mountains, to its fine and silent pencilling amongst moss and flowers.[66]

If he had lived a little longer he would have come through "the burning desert of Infidelity" and then his name could have been inscribed amongst poets as "full of wisdom and perfect in beauty."

From July, 1832, until April, 1833, the *Athenaeum* was supplied with original Shelley material by Captain Medwin: first, with Medwin's *Memoir of Shelley* (before its publication in book form), and second, with unpublished "Shelley Papers," mostly prose fragments written in Italy.

When Moxon published *The Masque of Anarchy*, the *Athenaeum* again gloried in Shelley's rising fame. The writer could not refrain from recalling that only eleven years before the *Literary Gazette* had spoken sneeringly of "Adonais." Now the poet is honored, but still "England

[66] *Athenaeum*, July 16, 1831, pp. 456-457.

knows but too little of the poetry of Percy Bysshe Shelley.
. . . With all his faults, Shelley was one of the very noblest
of our latter poets." One of his chief defects as a poet was
his desire "to shadow forth his own peculiar beliefs and
notions in his characters and narratives: this has occasioned
a certain obscurity and mysticism, which few people will
take the trouble to unriddle." In discussing *The Masque
of Anarchy,* the reviewer recognized that "Shelley was too
much of a poet to be a good politician."[67]

Allan Cunningham's comment was a specimen of the
average criticism of the time. Shelley was "one of the most
inspired and unfortunate of modern poets."

As a poet . . . he is in nearly all things too shadowy and
mystical: his 'Prometheus Unbound,' for instance, is a magnificent riddle. His 'Cenci,' however, comes from nature; and some
of his smaller poems have a concise beauty and an antique grace
about them such as have seldom appeared since the time of
Milton.[68]

The reviewers under Maurice and Sterling seldom wrote
of Keats with the same warmth as they did of Shelley,
though they considered him a poet of promise victimized by
unfeeling party criticism. After Dilke became editor, he
and John Hamilton Reynolds inserted Keats propaganda
into frequent editorial notes and reviews of other poets,
since there was no opportunity to review a new edition of
Keats in the thirties, no publisher being willing to take the
risk of putting out a volume by a poet who had been so
much ridiculed and who had such a slender following.
Reynolds could not pass by the slighting references to Keats
in Moore's *Letters and Journals of Lord Byron:*

. . . the biographer has allowed all the ill-nature and sarcasm
against Keats to be perpetuated,—without regard to the feelings

---

[67] *Athenaeum,* Nov. 3, 1832, pp. 705-707.
[68] *Athenaeum,* Nov. 16, 1833, pp. 771-772.

of surviving relations and friends. The idle stuff of Keat's [*sic*] dying of the Quarterly Review is preserved carefully—although it is well known that consumption, and not criticism, destroyed him.[69]

In a footnote signed "Ed. Athen.," Dilke himself came to the defense of his friend when roused by a sentence of Medwin in the *Memoir of Shelley*. Speaking of the "Cockney School" of which Keats was the supposed representative, Medwin said that Shelley was "too Classical . . . to have fallen into the sickly affectation . . . of that perverse and limited school."[70] Dilke replied:

We go as far as Captain Medwin in admiration of Shelley; but as far as Shelley . . . in admiration of Keats. Shelley was a worshipper of truth—Keats of beauty; Shelley had the greater power —Keats the finer imagination: both were single-hearted, sincere, admirable men. . . . Shelley and Keats . . . had the same hopes of the moral improvement of society—of the certain influence of knowledge—and of the ultimate triumph of truth . . . Keats had naturally much less of . . . political philosophy; but he had neither less resolution, less hope of, or less goodwill towards man. . . . We . . . shall not . . . touch on the 'Endymion' further than to say, that Captain Medwin cannot produce anything in the 'Revolt of Islam' superior to the Hymn to Pan; nor in the English language, anything written by any poet at the same age with which it may not stand in honourable comparison.[71]

Cunningham gave a kindly though brief notice to Keats in his series of articles on "British Literature of the Last Fifty Years." "Of John Keats," he wrote, "no memoir has been written—which is mentioned to the reproach of good friends and gifted ones, who survive him."[72] When he was under twenty, Keats "published a singular poem called 'Endymion,' which his admirers describe as filled with noble

[69] *Athenaeum*, Jan. 1, 1831, pp. 5-6.
[70] *Athenaeum*, Aug. 4, 1832, p. 503. [71] *Ibid.*, n.
[72] Probably a hint to Dilke and Reynolds.

fancies, and dreamy and delightful. His 'Hyperion' and other works are less mystical; but they have all more or less of the obscure and the dark, save a remarkably fine fragment, called "The Eve of St. Agnes.' "[73]

Coleridge continued to be spoken of with respect and even a great deal of admiration by Dilke's reviewers, though the worship of his distilled German philosophy ceased after Maurice and Sterling left the *Athenaeum*. Of the other older writers, Southey, Moore, Campbell, and Rogers usually got their meed of praise, whenever it was not a question of transcendental powers and superhuman visions. Among the mortals they ranked high until some impertinent critic tried to "degrade Wordsworth under the feet of Campbell, and Rogers, and Moore, and a host of other elegant small wits."[74]

Hunt and Hazlitt were given sympathetic attention as writers of merit who had been únfairly attacked by *Blackwood's* and the *Quarterly,* and Lamb, even before he became a contributor to the *Athenaeum,* found an able champion in that magazine when he was subjected to sneering and contemptuous criticism in *Blackwood's* and the *Literary Gazette*.[75] Godwin had been a favorite of Dilke in his early manhood and had helped to shape the radical ideas which he held with more consistency as well as more flexibility than his mentor through a long life; but that did not prevent the recognition by the *Athenaeum* of the falling off of

[73] *Athenaeum*, Nov. 16, 1833, p. 772.

[74] Review of Shelley's *Adonais* (Cambridge edition), *Athenaeum*, Sept. 2, 1829, p. 544.

[75] See the review of *Album Verses, Athenaeum*, July 17, 1830, pp. 435-436. The reviewer said: "Mr. Lamb was never, in our judgment, a very powerful, though always a pleasant writer. . . . But at whatever we might estimate Mr. Lamb, he is certainly not a man to write anything valueless and contemptible." Later accounts of Lamb in the *Athenaeum* were generally more laudatory. See, for example, "Recollections of Charles Lamb" by Barry Cornwall, *Athenaeum*, Jan. 24, and Feb. 7, 1835 (pp. 71-73, 107-110); and the review of Lamb's *Letters*, June 10 and July 8, 1837, (pp. 414-416, 492-494).

Godwin's powers, especially when he turned his hand to the writing of a three-volume novel for Colburn and Bentley.[76]

Of the living playwrights of the older generation, Joanna Baillie was by far the favorite. The reviewer was pleased and surprised by the publication of some new dramas by her in 1836. He had become content with lesser songsters in her absence, but now he was glad to find that the new dramas "exhibit all the genius of her earlier works: they have the same moral grandeur of conception, the same massive vigour of thought, and the same felicity of language." He reluctantly bade farewell "to one who, with many faults, is, without question, the greatest of all living poetesses."[77] And as late as 1841 a reviewer of her *Fugitive Verses* could say:

> The literary career of Joanna Baillie is almost without parallel ... the flattery of the coteries has never tarnished the freshness of her inspirations. . . . Out of the fulness of a true heart her works have been written, rather than from any vast or precious store of book-learning.[78]

The *Athenaeum* did not disdain the popular writers, even though it might class them as lesser luminaries. Its preference was for those who had a "universal appeal," provided that appeal was to the "higher nature" and tended towards "improvement." In practice, though this critical principle made room for almost anything, the best of the *Athenaeum* circle of critics were guided by native good taste

[76] See p. 31. See also the review of *Cloudesley, a Tale, Athenaeum*, March 20, 1830, pp. 162-164.   [77] *Athenaeum*, Jan. 2, 1836, pp. 4-5.
[78] *Athenaeum*, Jan. 23, 1841, p. 69. It is interesting to note that the critic added: "The ballads which this volume contains are not Miss Baillie's happiest efforts. Strange to say, in spite of all her old world simplicity, and her fine musical ear, she has been far exceeded in this class of composition by her younger contemporaries: We need but name Mary Howitt, Alfred Tennyson, and Miss Barrett." Miss Barrett herself shared the *Athenaeum* enthusiasm for Joanna Baillie. In a letter to Chorley on Jan. 3, 1845, thanking him for a review of her own poems, she added that in her opinion Joanna Baillie was the first real poetess of England. (*Letters of Elizabeth Barrett Browning*, I, 229.)

formed from a wide knowledge of the literature of past and present, and a natural bias, within the limits of the period, for works governed by the intellect.

It is difficult enough to generalize from the evidence here gathered concerning the attitude of the *Athenaeum* toward the older writers among its contemporaries. After the statement has been made that it favored the romantic writers whose creeds could be harmonized with the most common wishful desire of the period—"improvement," moral and social, through the infinite power of the mind fed from intuitive sources—there come to mind immediately numerous and important exceptions. Some of the *Athenaeum* reviewers attacked the philosophical foundations of Romanticism itself, and even preferred sceptics such as Gibbon and Hume to Wordsworth. These critics kept the balance of the magazine's opinion on the side of intellectual rather than merely moral or sentimental judgments.[79]

But still it is impossible to read much of the criticism in the magazine without coming to the conclusion that the broad base of its point of view was what has already been defined as the essence of Victorian Romanticism—the desire for a satisfying interpretation of or adjustment to actual life by means of intuitive wisdom. In this the *Athenaeum* was both a reflector of the mood of the time and a leader of the most important force in Victorian literature.

THE YOUNGER GENERATION

The survey already made of the criticism in the *Athenaeum* may facilitate somewhat the understanding of its estimate of younger contemporaries and rising writers, though it would be foolish to try to explain every judgment

[79] Even some of the defenders of romanticism had a fondness for the intellectual qualities of the Age of Reason. Allan Cunningham, in the midst of a defense of the romantic revolt against classical artificiality and restraint, could say: "The 'Decline and Fall of the Roman Empire' is, without doubt, the most noble history ever produced." (*Athenaeum*, Oct. 26, 1833, p. 714.)

in terms of a simple formula. The individual temperament, personality, and bias of the reviewer furnish the most immediate explanation of any critique, but from a distance it is also possible at times to observe influences which justify generalizations concerning the dominant preoccupations of a period.

It will soon become evident that the majority of the younger writers who have now taken the top place in the literary history of the Victorian period were not always those most highly regarded by the *Athenaeum*. Does this then confirm Lounsbury's opinion that contemporary criticism is utterly worthless? Before attempting to answer that question, let us trace the reputations of a few outstanding Victorian writers—outstanding according to later judgments— who began their work in the period of Dilke's editorship. This sampling of the *Athenaeum* criticism may be more illuminating than an attempt to get a complete panorama of its literary evaluations.

Tennyson

It is impossible to to give here more than the briefest outline of the critical reception of Tennyson in the periodicals of the thirties and forties. Fortunately Professor Lounsbury has made a minute study of it in all its phases and has drawn some conclusions which it may be useful to examine before we come to the criticism of the poetry of Tennyson in the *Athenaeum*.[80]

The *Poems, Chiefly Lyrical* (1830) had been puffed by Tennyson's friends, especially through the efforts of the "Apostles." Extravagant praise in *The Westminster* and *The Englishman's Magazine* (the latter by Arthur Hallam) had aroused the mirth and wrath of Christopher North who, though he gave generous and warm praise to Tennyson's

[80] See Lounsbury's *The Life and Times of Tennyson*. Lounsbury finished his study only to 1850.

promising genius,[81] warned against the dangers of a young poet becoming the "Pet of a Coterie."[82] North humorously maintained that the article by Hallam had killed the *Englishman's Magazine:* "The Essay 'On the Genius of Alfred Tennyson,' awoke a general guffaw, and it expired in convulsions."[83]

The ridicule of the critics became fastened upon the poet, and when the 1832 volume appeared (December, 1832—dated 1833), the general critical reception was hostile, even the most friendly reviews shying away from enthusiasm. Many critics agreed that the poems in this volume were inferior to those of 1830, and this judgment, together with the stock accusation of affectation, was echoed repeatedly through the ten years' silence.

Tennyson had had the bad taste to include in the volume the lines to Christopher North which aroused the ire of

[81] There were two notices of Tennyson in the *Noctes.* In the first, Feb., 1832, p. 277, North said: "I have good hopes of Alfred Tennyson. But the Cockneys are doing what they may to spoil him. . . . I should be sorry for it—for though his wings are far from being full-fledged, they promise now well in the pinions—and I should not be surprised to see him yet a sky-soarer. His 'Golden Days of good Haroun Alraschid' are extremely beautiful. . . . He has a fine ear for melody and harmony too—and rare and rich glimpses of imagination. He has—*genius.*" The interlocutor replied: "Affectations." "Too many," North agreed. "But I admire Alfred—and hope—nay trust—that one day he will prove himself a poet." A writer less sensitive than Tennyson could not have taken offense at such criticism.

[82] This was in the second criticism in *Blackwood's,* May, 1832, pp. 721-741, wherein North returned to a more detailed examination of the poems. Though he made merry sport of the critics and of what he considered the silly poems, the second half of the article was devoted to praise of Tennyson. He quoted a number of poems in laudatory terms, and in the end he almost apologized for the depreciation of the first part: ". . . we may have exaggerated Mr. Tennyson's not unfrequent silliness . . . but we feel assured that in the second part we have not exaggerated his strength—that we have done no more than justice to his fine faculties . . . that Alfred Tennyson is a poet." This was the article which wrankled in the poet's mind and which elicited the lines to Christopher North.

[83] *Ibid.* Quoted by Lounsbury, *op. cit.,* p. 233. North said the review in the *Westminster* was "the purest mere matter of moonshine ever mouthed by an idiot-lunatic, slavering in the palsied dotage of the extremest superannuation ever inflicted on a being, long ago, perhaps, in some slight respects and in low degrees human."

Wilson, who, however, passed over the task of flaying Tennyson to the *Quarterly*.[84] The reviewer (Croker) started with a mock apology for the earlier review of Keats in the *Quarterly* (April, 1818—also by Croker), pretending that Keats was then (1833) everywhere read and widely known. He lamented ironically the inability which had been displayed in the *Quarterly* to foresee the unbounded popularity which Keats was to have. The review continued in the strain of mock praise of Tennyson which was altogether scathing. Lounsbury says: "There was not the slightest effort made to give any real conception of the nature of the work under examination. . . . The least valuable pieces were largely selected for extended comment . . . while some of it is witty, it is dishonest throughout and at times little more than vulgarly vituperative."[85]

This article had a profound influence on the magazine criticism of Tennyson until after the appearance of the 1842 volumes; in fact, it was remembered by critics until the publication of *In Memoriam* silenced all detractors. "There is little danger of our underrating the effect Lockhart's [*sic*] article had in confirming and intensifying the tone of depreciatory criticism which had begun to show itself in many of the minor periodicals of the time."[86] Lounsbury adds: "It became the fashion to speak disparagingly of the poet

[84] This famous "literary attack," (*Quarterly*, April, 1833, pp. 81-96) long ascribed to Lockhart, has now been shown conclusively to have been written by Croker. See letter to the *Times Literary Supplement* by H. J. C. Grierson, April 24, 1937, p. 308. Grierson quotes an unpublished letter from Lockhart to Croker, Jan. 23, 1833: "I have read the revised article on Tennyson and think you have most completely effected your purpose, and that as shortly as it could have been done. It is wonderful that such folly should pass for poetry with anybody."

[85] *Op. cit.*, p. 320.

[86] *Ibid.*, p. 324. See also the *Memoir* by Tennyson's son, I, 208. Aubrey de Vere had written a review of *The Princess* for the *Edinburgh* (Oct., 1849), in which he called Tennyson a "great poet." The editor struck out "great" and substituted "true." "He considered that the public would not tolerate so strong an eulogium."

whenever it was thought worth while to speak of him at all."[87]

Tennyson's extreme sensitivity to criticism more than either his grief at the death of Hallam or his resolve to make his poems perfect caused the ten years' silence.[88] His recognition was retarded by his failure to publish again, but his reputation grew in the interim by the enthusiasm of friends of the Cambridge group and others, who had copied and circulated his poems in manuscript before the 1842 volumes were published.

In the meantime, the accusation of "affectation," given currency by *Blackwood's,* continued to be passed along by critics. Two other charges were also common in the criticism of the time: he was obscure, and he failed to show profound reflectiveness. Lounsbury concludes that "no man ever owed less than he to the aid of favorable criticism."[89] The reviewers followed grumblingly the popular taste instead of guiding it. Critical appreciation of the 1842 volumes was hesitant and lagging. "Never was the critical fraternity more at a loss as to what they should say, or rather what it was safe for them to say."[90]

The *Edinburgh* didn't review the 1842 poems until April, 1843. The article was by Spedding and was "as enthusiastic as it was allowed to be."[91] Macvey Napier consented to his reviewing the poems on condition that he would not make an "undue" estimate or forecast. Napier toned down a few words.

---

[87] *Ibid.,* p. 327.

[88] See Lounsbury, *op. cit.,* pp. 334-335: "No one can understand Tennyson's conduct throughout his whole career who does not recognize his abnormal sensitiveness to criticism. . . . This sensitiveness was more than morbid; it partook almost of the nature of actual disease. . . . Even in the height of his fame the sting of the puniest literary insect gave him as much pain as the applause of the loftiest intellect gave him pleasure." See also the *Memoir* by his son, II, 120. Tennyson said: "I remember all the malignant things said against me, but little of the praise."   [89] *Op. cit.,* p. 306.

[90] *Ibid.,* p. 418.   [91] *Ibid.,* p. 436.

It was still good sport to attack Tennyson on the old lines until the end of the forties. Bulwer, in the second part of *The New Timon* (early in 1846), wrote:

> Let School-Miss Alfred vent her chaste delight
> On 'darling little rooms so warm and bright.'[92]

Only after *In Memoriam* had won him the Laureateship was his fame secure. By the time the first of the *Idylls* appeared (1859) the main chorus of criticism was on his side. A. H. Clough wrote, July 18, 1859: "The reception of the 'Idylls of the King' will I hope satisfy all Farringford. . . . I have heard no words of dispraise." And the Duke of Argyll proclaimed two days later: "The applause of the 'Idylls' goes on crescendo, and so far as I can hear without exception. Detractors are silenced."[93]

The first mention of Tennyson in the *Athenaeum* was a laudatory review of his prize poem *Timbuctoo*. It was undoubtedly written by one of the "Apostles," who were already pushing Tennyson as their poet rather on the basis of his seeming to accept their beliefs than on the evidence of anything he had yet written.

> We have accustomed ourselves to think . . . that Poetry was likely to perish among us for a considerable period after the great generation of poets which is now passing away. The age seems determined to contradict us, and that in the most decided manner, for it has put forth poetry by a young man, and that where we should least expect it, namely, in a prize-poem . . . we have never before seen one of them which indicated really first-rate poetical genius, and which would have done honour to any man that ever wrote. Such, we do not hesitate to affirm, is the little work before us.[94]

---

[92] Tennyson's sensitivity was pricked again and he replied in "The New Timon and the Poets," *Punch*, Feb. 28, 1846. He was soon ashamed of this (which he later said Forster and not he had sent to *Punch*) and in the next number there appeared his poem on "Literary Squabbles."

[93] *Memoir*, by his son, I, 450. [94] *Athenaeum*, July 22, 1829, p. 456.

After extracting a few lines, the reviewer concludes: "How many men have lived for a century who could equal this?"[95]

For some reason, perhaps because Dilke, just then launching his anti-puffery campaign, shied away from a writer whose friends were everywhere puffing him and urging favorable reviews in all quarters, the *Athenæum* did not notice the 1830 volume. But on October 27, 1832, it announced: "Alfred Tennyson [has forthcoming] a second series of poems."[96] And it was prompt in reviewing the poems when they appeared. The review began and ended with laudation unspoiled by condescension, but expressed regret for the poet's "love of singularity," his delight in being fanciful to the verge . . . of unintelligibility," and his spoiling the poetry of "unstudied enthusiasm" by artificialities of word or phrase.

Mr. Tennyson is unquestionably a poet of fancy, feeling, and imagination; gifted with a deep sense of the beautiful, and endowed with a spirit 'finely touched,' and often to 'fine issues.' Where he suffers his thoughts to follow the natural current of his feelings, instead of sending them painfully out in search of metaphysical subtleties, and ingenious refinements, they lead him invariably into regions breathing the legitimate and undeniable air of poetry.[97]

The reviewer expressed his admiration for "The Miller's Daughter" and "New Year's Eve," both of which he quoted, and for "Mariana in the South." He was willing to turn "The Hesperides" over to Christopher North immediately, and he didn't care for "The Palace of Art." Tennyson might have saved himself "the trouble (however small)" of writing such verses as "O Darling Room," but there is compensation in "The Death of the Old Year," which the reviewer quoted as he did also a part of "Œnone."

[95] *Ibid.* See *ante*, p. 105.   [96] P. 699.
[97] *Athenaeum*, Dec. 1, 1832, pp. 770-772.

There is fine dream-like poetry in the 'Lotus Eaters'—and the lines 'To J. S.' [Sterling] are full of sweet and quiet beauty. But the poem of poems in this volume, is 'Œnone'; wild—fanciful—chaste—and touching. . . .

In reverence and respect for his genius, we have not hesitated to point out the errors of the poet—his beauties will speak for themselves.[98]

This was not unreasonable praise, nor was it unjust criticism. When the *Athenaeum* referred to Tennyson again it was to strike a balance between the excesses of the *Westminster* and the *Quarterly:*

. . . the article on Tennyson in the *Quarterly* is strangely provocative of comment. No sane man imagines that Tennyson is the Homer which the *Westminster* affected to believe; but he has much fine poetry about him; and if we are to give the name of poets only to those whose works are illustrated by Turner and Calcott, then Wordsworth is no poet, neither is Wilson.[99]

Allan Cunningham struck the cautious though generous average note again in his *Biographical and Critical History* wherein he gave Tennyson a short paragraph:

Alfred Tennyson has a happy fancy; his originality of thought is sometimes deformed by oddity of language; and his subject has not unfrequently to bear the weight of sentiments which spring not naturally from it. He has lyrical ease and vigour, and is looked upon by sundry critics as the chief living hope of the Muse.[100]

[98] *Ibid.*   [99] April 13, 1833, p. 234.
[100] *Athenaeum*, Nov. 16, 1833, p. 772. Lounsbury's comment shows that he was riding his thesis concerning the neglect and abuse of Tennyson by the critics a little hard: "The criticism it [Cunningham's series] contains is usually of the most commonplace character. To us now, the work, however, is interesting for the cautious way in which it dealt with Tennyson, its careful repetition of the current critical cant about his language and expression, but above all for the acknowledgment it makes of the existence of a band of men who had more insight than their contemporaries." (*Op. cit.*, p. 343.)

This was the tone of the few random references to Tennyson in the *Athenaeum* before 1842. The critics were never contemptuous and they always expressed admiration for the "beauties" of his style and hope or confidence in his genius.

Unfortunately the *Poems* of 1842 fell into the hands of Henry Chorley, whose criticism was not the best or most representative that the *Athenaeum* might then have offered. The review was cautious and hypercritical and justifies most of Lounsbury's accusations of Chorley and some of his scorn of the magazine for its fear of "destroying its own reputation for discriminating sobriety of judgment."[101] Chorley started out by expressing regret "at certain changes, clippings, omissions, and additions" in the first volume. "Grant that the expressions retrenched, the stanzas struck out, were but conceits, (which is anything but the case,) they were still part and parcel of the whole. . . . 'Fusty Christopher' and the 'Darling Room' have vanished; but we would rather have retained the pertness of the one, and the puerility of the other, than miss, as we do, the 'Deserted House,' one of the most simply impressive of its author's minor poems."[102] The reviewer had also to "dissent from those who praise our poet as having emancipated himself from the crotchets which distinguished his earlier efforts . . . his new offerings supply as many as those he has expunged." But, he conceded, "the new volume is so thickly studded with evidences of manly force and exquisite tenderness—with feelings so true, and fancies so felicitous, clothed in a music often peculiar in its flow, but never cloying—as to substantiate Mr. Tennyson's claim to a high place among modern poets."[103]

---

[101] Lounsbury, *op. cit.*, p. 422. When Tennyson was appointed Laureate in 1850, Chorley, disgruntled at the refusal of the Ministry to listen to his pleas for the candidacy of Elizabeth Barrett, wrote that the Prime Minister "has a trick of looking for his favourites down the back stairs." (*Athenaeum*, Nov. 23, 1850, p. 1218.)

[102] *Athenaeum*, Aug. 6, 1842, p. 700.   [103] *Ibid.*

He avoided quoting "Locksley Hall" and "Godiva" only because they had already been made common property by the reviewers.[104] "As a specimen of power, we might refer to 'St. Simeon Stylites,' but we prefer taking our extracts from the 'Vision of Sin.' " Other poems which he chose for quotation were: "The Sleeping Beauty," "The Sleeping Palace," "The Arrival," "The Revival," "The Departure," and "The Talking Oak." And he ended with an eulogium, which, considering the general opinion of Tennyson at the time, must have seemed generous enough to contemporaries: "Mr. Tennyson in these new poems asserts his claim to be crowned as chief of the modern *minnesingers*. There have been few love-verses comparable to his since Coleridge's 'Genevieve.' "[105]

Reverberations of the growing feeling that Tennyson was a true prophet of the new times echoed through the pages of the *Athenaeum* frequently in the forties, showing that its critics sensed his significance as an interpreter of contemporary ideals. A clear indication of the gradual transference of allegiance from Wordsworth to Tennyson is to be seen in a series of letters on "Modern Poetry" which ran in successive numbers from March to June, 1844. "Beta" complained that modern poets "are incapable of moving the passions; they have no command over the sympathies of humanity." He bemoaned "the silly simplicities, the cold philosophy, and shadowy nothings, of the present day. . . . Our present poets, with Wordsworth at their head, may be considered as the emasculated school of Poetry, cold and

---

[104] The volumes were published in the spring, and it was Aug. 6 before they were reviewed in the *Athenaeum*. Lounsbury, who complained that Chorley was "careful to maintain a proper decorum by not expressing any wild enthusiasm," felt that the phrase "to a high place among modern poets," was too mild. That, he said bitterly, "was the result reached by this thoughtful critic after three months of time and apparently of some moments of reflection." (*Op. cit.*, p. 423.)

[105] *Athenaeum*, Aug. 6, 1842, p. 702.

unimpassioned." Is there one living poet, he asks, who has the appeal of Scott and Byron?[106]

"Sigma," who perhaps voiced the opinions of the *Athenaeum* editors, replied: "What but human emotion is it that glows and thrills through such poems as the 'Locksley Hall,' the 'Two Voices,' the 'May Queen,' the 'Ulysses,' and the 'Vision of Sin,' of Tennyson. . . ?" "Beta" has complained that the present poets do not represent the age because they are not passionate, but isn't it a truism "that the present age is eminently cautious and reflective?" The poets don't have to represent the whistling of a locomotive to reflect the life of their own times. "But we may require them to express in their pages the earnestness, the manly courage, the cheerful faith and hope, which all triumphs over material obstacles, and all generous struggles with social injustice, ought to awaken in their minds." Then the writer quotes from "Locksley Hall," "For I dipped into the future . . ." ending with the lines "Better fifty years of Europe . . ." "When did ever poet more eloquently express the hopes and efforts of his age than Tennyson, in these gorgeous and heart-stirring lines?"[107]

"Beta" came back with further praise for Byron and disparagement of Wordsworth, whose influence "has been the little warmth from which have sprung gnats and sparrows, not eagles. . . . 'The child is father of the man,' and the men, *consequently,* are all children." The great poets "serve the cause of progression, simply by exciting the feelings."[108]

"Sigma" next took issue with the statement that the object of poetry is to "excite the passions." He preferred to "check and counteract the encroaching tendencies of *passive* emotion . . . by making . . . [readers] think!" He called upon the "Poets of England" to follow their own true genius

[106] *Athenaeum*, March 23, 1844, pp. 270-271.
[107] *Athenaeum*, April 6, 1844, pp. 318-319.
[108] *Athenaeum*, April 20, 1844, pp. 357-358.

and employ it "for enlightening with it, and guiding with it, through the misty wilderness of doubt and error and prejudice and ignorance, the benighted souls of men." With them it rests "to prove that Thought is not incompatible with Feeling." He ends with praise for Beta's call upon the poets to turn their attention to the "wants, and tendencies, and efforts of practical life."[109] Finally "Theta" summed up the arguments, agreeing with both "Beta" and "Sigma" on the merits of Tennyson, in whom he saw "an earnest and truthful spirit." "The middle course, the true way of transmutation, or rather new creation, upon the basis of life's realities, is hard to follow; but this alone can lead to true excellence."[110]

And this is precisely what the most forward-looking critics had begun to expect from Tennyson. The first disappointment came with *The Princess,* wherein the poet attempted to grapple at close quarters with contemporary problems.[111] J. Westland Marston, a somewhat more robust critic than Chorley, reviewed the volume for the *Athenaeum.* As usual the reviewer found much to admire in individual passages, but "while we could recognize the whole if tendered as a pledge of genius, we cannot accept it as a due consummation of that faculty."

We find in these pages little which denotes advance. . . . No wholesome severity has discarded former puerilities. . . . Our analysis of the poem will have sufficiently exhibited the discordant nature of its elements. . . . With the power which Mr. Tennyson has here evinced for the familiar and the ideal regarded separately, it is much to be deplored that by their unskilful combination he has produced simply—the grotesque.[112]

[109] *Athenaeum,* April 27, 1844, pp. 381-383.
[110] *Athenaeum,* June 8, 1844, pp. 525-526.
[111] See Routh, *op. cit.,* p. 89. Those who had counted so greatly on Tennyson's "Mission" began to be disappointed, and not yet daring to find fault with him as a prophet, ascribed his weakness to technical shortcomings.
[112] *Athenaeum,* Jan. 1, 1848, pp. 6-8.

Marston's admiration for *In Memoriam* was sufficiently unreserved, but he was not swept off his feet to the extent that he could not criticise some details and so save the reputation of the *Athenaeum* for "sobriety of judgment."

So elemental are most of these outpourings, that the mere intellect scarcely furnishes any clue to their beauty and their reality. We recognize their power less by any mental estimate than by their vibration on the deepest and most mysterious chords of the heart. . . .

Thoughts in themselves subtle, peculiarly require sensuous utterance for their apprehension; but the language which the poet employs in these cases is sometimes almost as abstract as the idea which it involves. We could have wished, too, that the hopeful moral of the book had been wrought out with a more interdependent connexion. With Mr. Tennyson the argument for trust in the future seems often to rest chiefly on the mental disposition to trust.[113]

T. K. Hervey, in reviewing the "Ode on the Death of the Duke of Wellington," excused the poet for its weakness on the ground that it was a hurried composition and a "pièce d'occasion."[114] Hepworth Dixon tried to understand the Voice in "Maud," and concluded that Tennyson tells us that we are rotting with Peace. And he agrees that "something of high sound and sacred authority may be urged in support of such a fable. . . . We are abdicating our intellectual thrones. Great books are no longer written: great passions no longer stir us."

This volume is not worthy of its author. Not a few lines . . . are singularly harsh, broken and unmusical. . . . We rank Mr. Tenny-

---

[113] *Athenaeum*, June 15, 1850, pp. 629-630.

[114] *Athenaeum*, Nov. 20, 1852, p. 1263. Hervey, in his critical judgments of poetry, was likely to be governed partly by his exalted sense of what he himself might accomplish in that field and partly by the older *Athenaeum* habit of measuring all contemporary poetry of high pretensions against a model, supposedly ideal, but subconsciously built upon the past.

son's muse so high that we unwillingly receive from her any song which is less than perfect.[115]

The *Athenaeum* joined in the general chorus of unqualified panegyrics of the first of the *Idylls* in 1859. The review was the joint work of Dr. John Doran and Blackburne. They wrote in a glow of admiration, but found that criticism "is but dull music after such minstrelsy as we find here," and could do no better than to paraphrase a line in "Elaine": "A diamond is a diamond—and this one especially of the finest water."[116]

Dixon went off at a moralizing tangent with *Enoch Arden:* "Are the young ladies of a coming age to be trained in a complaisant belief that it is rather a poetical incident than a dark and shameful misery to have two husbands living at one time? If not, why all this prostitution of art? Even when it is an accident, bigamy is an offence. To veil this offence under romantic lights and poetical idioms, may be to lessen the shame and dull the horror in feeble minds."[117] But the Pre-Raphaelite, F. G. Stephens, in reviewing the illustrated edition, saw "the intrinsic value of the idyl as a work of ineffable Art" standing "among English literary treasures."[118]

By 1872, when *Gareth and Lynette* appeared, the *Athe-*

[115] Aug. 4, 1855, pp. 893-895. See again p. 277, footnote 111. Dixon apparently was puzzled by "Maud" as most of the critics were, but so firmly had the tradition been established that Tennyson was the great teacher and prophet of his age that he was afraid to face squarely the fact that the poet "had lost his hold on modern life." (See Routh, *Towards the Twentieth Century*, p. 90.)

[116] July 16, 1859, II, pp. 73-76.

[117] *Athenaeum*, Aug. 13, 1864, II, pp. 201-202.

[118] *Athenaeum*, Dec. 23, 1865, II, p. 894. The Pre-Raphaelites helped to turn the interest in Tennyson from the moral and didactic to the aesthetic qualities of his work. Routh says: "As soon as Tennyson's younger readers awoke to the responsibilities and disillusionments of their age, they were bound to conclude that the author of *In Memoriam* was behind the times." (*Towards the Twentieth Century*, p. 88.) So Tennyson came to be admired as a melodist, a painter of word pictures, an artist rather than a prophet. After 1860 criticism of his poems more frequently concerns their artistry than their ideas.

naeum had caught its breath again, and besides had turned several corners which revealed a different perspective upon the work of Tennyson as well as of others of its contemporaries.[119] Joseph Knight pointed out that, though "Mr. Tennyson's work, as it stands, is full of loveliness," the weakest thing is the conception of the subject, in which there is more of the poet than of the original.

Arthur stands . . . a shadowy abstraction among living, breathing, and acting men. . . . The simple force of the knightly character shown in the original legends is sacrificed to the whimsical endeavor, admitted by Mr. Tennyson in his dedication, to present an idealized Prince Albert thrown back into premediaeval times. . . . By taking away from Arthur that lighter quality which is abundantly exemplified in the opening scenes of his history, Mr. Tennyson has rendered his character and position wholly false.[120]

Knight adds that Arthur's acquiescence in the love affair of Launcelot and Guinevere is enough to reduce him from an eagle to a "tame, villatic fowl."

In the eighties and nineties Theodore Watts took command of the poetry criticism in the *Athenaeum*. His enthusiasm for Tennyson was not hesitant, but its grounds were other than those of the critics of the earlier "Period of Hope." His view of *Tiresias, and Other Poems* is typical:

In temper throughout, and often in rhythm, Lord Tennyson's 'Tiresias' must be placed in the front rank of his work. . . . In that artistic economy of which Sophocles and Dante are the great masters among the poets of the world, Lord Tennyson has, ever since 1842 at least, taken a high, if not the highest, place among English poets, and this notwithstanding a long struggle with euphuistic tendencies. . . . Altogether the volume is laden with every kind of poetic wealth.[121]

[119] With the change of editorship from Dixon to Norman MacColl, a new spirit is manifest in the *Athenaeum,* the spirit of late Victorian liberalism.

[120] *Athenaeum*, Oct. 26, 1872, II, pp. 521-524.

[121] Dec. 26, 1885, II, pp. 831-834.

He found *Locksley Hall Sixty Years After* the "outcome of a polemical rather than of a purely artistic impulse." He commented on the pessimism of the poem as an indication of the attempt of Tennyson to catch the new mood of the times. The poem reveals that "the fifth decade of the Victorian era . . . does not realize all the fervid hopes of the first."[122]

In his obituary notice of Tennyson in the *Athenaeum* Watts said that the charm of the poet lay in his "great veracity of soul," but "above all things . . . [he] was a great forthright English gentleman." He had great simplicity of nature—he couldn't realize what a transcendent position he held, and always felt himself "a poet at struggle more or less with the Wilsons and the Crokers." No one "since Shakespeare's time," Watts concluded, "has met with anything like Tennyson's success in effecting a reconciliation between popular and artistic sympathy with poetry in England."[123]

Finally, in reviewing the posthumous "Death of Œnone," Watts poured out a warmth of praise which might have pleased Tennyson's earlier champions had they not perceived a singular lack of reference to their poet's prophetic "vision." The period which produced Tennyson, Browning, Rossetti, Morris, Arnold, and Swinburne, he said, need not fear to be compared with that which produced Coleridge, Keats, Shelley, and Wordsworth. "As far as we know, the modern world furnishes no parallel to the unbroken continuity of power running over a period of sixty years, such as is shown in this volume."[124] The new poet is accepted, but on terms which might have surprised if not chagrined the critics of the thirties.

It is not difficult to see how completely the history of Tennyson's literary reputation can be traced in the *Athe-*

[122] Jan. 1, 1887, I, pp. 31-33.   [123] Oct. 8, 1892, II, pp. 482-483.
[124] *Athenaeum*, Nov. 19, 1892, II, pp. 695-697.

naeum, nor is it less clear how well its opinions of the most typical Victorian poet reveal the character of the magazine itself as a leader and a reflector of the culture of the time.

Browning

Although Browning encouraged the tradition that the critics had always been against him, it cannot be rightly said of his work as of Tennyson's that criticism lagged behind popular approval. At least, before the publication of *Sordello* had given him a reputation for obscurity, he had little reason to complain that he was without friendly reviewers.[125] If we start with *Paracelsus,* which is not unfair, since it was the first volume published under Browning's name, and since he repudiated *Pauline* after reading Mill's unpublished criticism,[126] we may say that the tone and the expectations of critics were both very favorable. Lounsbury says that in every other respect, except sale, *Paracelsus* "was the most unqualified of successes. It gave its author at once a recognized position in the world of letters."[127] The reviews were not all wildly enthusiastic, but they were not vituperative or contemptuous. Browning was not the butt of ridicule as Tennyson had been, and all the major reviews treated him with respect. Forster's article in the *Examiner* is credited by Browning and his biographers with an astounding influence in stemming a tide of hostile criticism, but the author in later years was inclined to exaggerate the extent of the hostility to his early work.[128]

[125] For an account of the reviews of *Pauline* see Thomas R. Lounsbury, *The Early Literary Career of Robert Browning,* pp. 8-18. See also Wm. C. DeVane, *A Browning Handbook,* pp. 12-13, 42-44. Browning had sent a flattering letter to W. J. Fox, editor of *The Monthly Repository* announcing the coming appearance of *Pauline.* The attempt to get a favorable review was successful, for Fox wrote (*Monthly Repository,* April, 1833): "We felt certain of Tennyson before we saw the book [1832 volume] by a few verses which had struggled into a newspaper; we are not the less certain of the author of 'Pauline.' "

[126] See DeVane, *op. cit.,* pp. 12-13.

[127] *Early Literary Career of Robert Browning,* p. 29.

[128] Browning wrote to Elizabeth Barrett in 1845 that *Paracelsus* had been a

Forster was eulogistic enough, but his criticism did not arouse other critics to protest as in the case of Tennyson. He began: "Since the publication of 'Philip van Artevelde,' we have met with no such evidence of poetical genius and of general intellectual power as are contained in this volume." He conceded that some passages were tedious and some obscure, but he predicted for the author "a brilliant career, if he continues true to the present promise of his genius."[129]

Fox gave him a hearty eulogium in the *Monthly Repository*. Leigh Hunt devoted nine columns of his *Journal* to extracts and a criticism which was altogether favorable though he added a warning against peculiarities of style which might degenerate into a slovenly mannerism. *Fraser's* in March, 1836, had "a long, elaborate, and cordial review of 'Paracelsus.'" Its superiority to *Philip van Artevelde* was "somewhat aggressively proclaimed."[130] In the same month Forster had a twenty-page article in the *New Monthly* on "Evidence of a New Genius for Dramatic Poetry": "Without the slightest hesitation we name Mr. Robert Browning at once with Shelley, Coleridge, Wordsworth. He has entitled himself to a place among the acknowledged poets of the age."[131]

failure. "Out of a long string of notices which his publisher received, each one vied with its predecessor in expressing disgust at his 'rubbish,' until something of a change was effected by the article in *The Examiner*." (See *ibid.*, pp. 31-32.) Lounsbury found nothing to justify Browning's assertions.

[129] *Examiner*, Sept. 6, 1835. See Lounsbury, *Early Career of Robert Browning*, pp. 36-37.

[130] *Fraser's*, March, 1836, pp. 362-375. Henry Taylor's poem was the touchstone of greatness in contemporary poetry for at least ten years after its publication in 1834. Lounsbury, however, says: "No volume of verse—not even excepting 'Philip van Artevelde'—was published during the fourth decade of the nineteenth century which created a profounder impression than did 'Paracelsus' upon that body of men who are indeed limited in number, but whose verdict is the verdict which posterity never undertakes to set aside." (*Early Career of Robert Browning*, p. 44.) Lounsbury amusingly neglects to consider the verdict of posterity on *Philip van Artevelde*, whose author was esteemed as the chief hope of literature by the same or an equally serious and notable group.

[131] *New Monthly*, March, 1836, p. 289.

The "high-wrought anticipation" created by this early praise, according to Lounsbury, accounted for the retrogression and neglect that followed. He found a tone of regret in the criticism of *Strafford*. The critics desired to see the play successful, because of the general admiration of *Paracelsus*. But *Sordello* gave a blow to Browning's reputation from which it recovered even more slowly than did Tennyson's after Croker's review. The *Spectator* was the first to notice the poem: "What this poem may be in its extent we are unable to say, for we *cannot* read it." The reviewer saw in it nothing but "digression, affectation, obscurity."[132] Two weeks later the *Atlas,* which had praised *Paracelsus,* said *Sordello* was worse than *Strafford*.[133] The *Literary Gazette* and the *Examiner* did not review *Sordello*. It was too much even for the friendly Forster.[134]

Lounsbury declared that the appearance of *Sordello* caused a prejudice against Browning which was not dispelled for more than a third of a century. It put a formidable obstacle in the way of appreciation of the works just following, particularly the lyrics of the *Bells and Pomegranates* series which might on their own merit have had a better reception. Lounsbury says that though there was nothing obscure in *Pippa Passes,* the first of the series, its reception was mostly cool. The general public, even the educated public, continued to ignore or to be indifferent to all the "Bells." The reception of *Dramatic Lyrics* was nowhere enthusiastic. And of the *Dramatic Romances* there "was even more than lack of appreciation; there was sometimes

---

[132] *Spectator*, March 14, 1840, p. 257.   [133] *Atlas*, March 28, 1840, p. 203.
[134] The following year Forster made some amends by praising *Pippa Passes* warmly and apologizing for *Sordello* (*Examiner*, Oct. 2, 1841). But he aimed a few shots at the latter poem in his very favorable review of *Dramatic Lyrics*. (*Examiner*, Nov. 26, 1842, pp. 756-757.) And his dubious praise of *Colombe's Birthday* ended with a statement which caused a complete though temporary rift between him and Browning: "As far as he has gone, we abominate his tastes as much as we respect his genius." (*Examiner*, June 22, 1844, p. 389.) See De-Vane, *op. cit.*, p. 135.

positive condemnation."[135]   The praise was always accompanied with qualifications. The public refused to read. Browning's reputation was overshadowed by that of his wife.[136]

Dramatis Personae (1864) was the first of Browning's books which sold well. The tone of criticism became cordial and the book soon went into a second edition. Browning's reputation and popularity were finally established with the publication of *The Ring and the Book*. The critics found plenty of things to carp about, such as the sordidness of the theme and the method of presenting the story, but the great reviews "gave the poet unstinted praise."[137] Most reviewers considered Browning "perverse and wayward" in his psychological studies such as *Hohenstiel-Schwangau, Fifine at the Fair, Red Cotton Night-Cap Country, The Inn Album,* and *Aristophanes' Apology,* but his popularity continued to increase, if not to the extent of Tennyson's, at least with the "thinking" public. That he was not then considered an esoteric poet is indicated by the fact that in the seventies the Chicago Railway Company "began to publish his works, part by part, as an appendix to their periodical time-tables, of which 10,000 copies circulated monthly."[138]

The Browning Society, founded in 1881 by Dr. Furnivall and Miss Hickey, did a good deal to extend the fame of Browning though not always with the result of encouraging a right appreciation of his poetry apart from the "meaning" which they insisted upon reading into it. The Society's canonization of Browning naturally helped to bring on a

[135] Lounsbury, *op. cit.,* p. 160.

[136] Edgar Allan Poe in 1844 rated Elizabeth Barrett higher than any living poet except Tennyson. (See Lounsbury, *op. cit.,* pp. 161-162.) See also Chorley's view of Mrs. Browning in 1850, *ante,* p. 274, n. 101.

[137] See DeVane, *op. cit.,* p. 305.

[138] D. C. Somervell, *The Reputation of Robert Browning,* "Essays and Studies by Members of the English Association," XV, 126.

reaction, which, however, did not come in time to affect his reputation before his death.

The first *Athenaeum* review of Browning was a cordial and encouraging notice of *Pauline* by Allan Cunningham.[139]

There is not a little true poetry in this very little book: here and there we have a touch of the mysterious, which we cannot admire; and now and then a want of true melody, which we can forgive; with perhaps more abruptness than what is necessary: all that, however, is as a grain of sand in a cup of pure water, compared to the nature, and passion, and fancy of the poem. . . . We hope the author's next strains will be more cheerful, and as original as these.[140]

The critic failed to see the deeper implications of the poem as a piece of self-revelation. But his failure was no greater than that of the rest of the critics and the public who were then so eager to welcome anything which seemed to promise, in its sound if not in its articulation, something more transcendent than individual experience. It is a little unfair to look back now and say with the superiority of our later knowledge that the critics were blind to the significance of *Pauline* because they failed to see as clearly as Mill the "intense and morbid self-consciousness" of its author.

Paracelsus was noticed only in a short paragraph in the miscellanies of "Our Library Table." Nothing can be said for the perspicacity of the critic, except perhaps his observation of the influence of Shelley on Browning.

There is talent in this dramatic poem, (in which is attempted a picture of the mind of this celebrated character, but it is dreamy and obscure. Writers would do well to remember, (by way of

---

[139] See Edmund Gosse, *Robert Browning: Personalia*, p. 32: "But to the world at large *Pauline* was a sealed book, by nobody, and the reviewers simply ignored it. One very creditable exception was the *Athenaeum*, then in its infancy, which dedicated several columns to a kindly, if not very profound, analysis, and to copious quotations. Mr. Browning discovered long afterward that this notice was written by Allan Cunningham."   [140] April 6, 1833, p. 216.

example,) that though it is not difficult to imitate the mysticism and vagueness of Shelley, we love him and have taken him to our hearts as a poet, not *because* of these characteristics—but *in spite* of them.[141]

Nor had the *Athenaeum* changed its opinion after the *Examiner* and other magazines began to speak of Browning as "among the acknowledged poets of the age." It expressed its scepticism in a note in the "Weekly Gossip" of March 5, 1836: "It is not our purpose here to examine how far the dramatic poem ('Paracelsus') which forms the subject of an elaborate article in the *New Monthly,* and another in *Fraser,* deserves the high praise here bestowed on it."[142]

The *Athenaeum* review still rankled in Browning's mind ten years later when he wrote to Elizabeth Barrett that this "was a most flattering sample of what the 'craft' had in store for me."[143] It even made him forget or minimize in retrospect the flattering attention given to *Paracelsus* in other magazines.

After Macready's first night performance of "Strafford," the drama critic of the *Athenaeum* (possibly George Darley) wished the author many "happy *returns*" of a full house.

. . . but we do not think that 'Strafford' has interest enough about it, either of plot or dialogue, to give it more than a temporary existence . . . the speeches generally contain so many broken sentences, that they become quite unintelligible; indeed . . . we at last discovered that the best way of obtaining an impression of what was going on was, to take care not to follow the speaker too closely, but to hear the opening of a sentence, and supply the remainder by imagination.[144]

Sordello was not reviewed in the *Athenaeum* until three months after it was published. One may be tempted to

[141] *Athenaeum,* Aug. 22, 1835, p. 640.
[142] P. 178.   [143] Quoted in DeVane, *op. cit.,* p. 53.
[144] *Athenaeum,* May 6, 1837, p. 331.

suppose that it took the critic, T. K. Hervey, that long to read the book. At any rate Lounsbury says that this was "seemingly the only contemporary notice of the work in which a serious attempt was made to study it as a whole."[145] Hervey begins:

If it were Mr. Browning's desire to withdraw himself from the inquest of criticism, he could scarcely have effected that purpose better than by the impenetrable veil, both of manner and language, in which he has contrived to wrap up whatever truths or beauties this volume may contain.[146]

There are two difficult tasks which the reader must undertake, he says: one, to master the syntax in order to understand what is said; the other, to fathom the oracles of the author's thought. "The song of the bard falls dull and muffled on the ear, as from a fog." Only for a moment does a breath of purer air filter through.

It is, nevertheless, these occasional outbreaks of light, giving assurance of a spiritual presence, that win the reader onward,— tempted, as he is again and again, to throw down the book in despair . . . but the author who chooses deliberately to put 'his light under a bushel' of affectations, must not be surprised if men refuse the labour of searching it out, and leave him to the peaceful enjoyment of that obscurity which he has courted.[147]

The reviewer makes an honest effort to bring up a few pearls of the philosophic thought, but he finds most of them "when examined, to be very commonplace truths," though they are "surrounded by an array of language which makes them look provokingly oracular."

If we understand Mr. Browning's philosophic purpose, it is to paint the contest between the spiritual aspirations of an ardent nature and the worldly influences by which it is opposed; the

---

[145] *Early Career of Robert Browning*, p. 84.
[146] *Athenaeum*, May 30, 1840, pp. 431-432.
[147] *Ibid.*

disappointment which an enthusiastic heart, nursed, amid natural influences, into dreams of perfectability, experiences in its attempts to impress its own character upon surrounding objects, and confer, by the act of its own will, those boons upon its fellow men, which are the slow and gradual gift of the ages. If this be the object of the writer, his meaning is wrapped up in a very needless and absurd profusion of words.[148]

After pointing out a few examples of "pregnant thought, and quaint poetry, and significant illustration, that lure the reader over the rough ground of the general page," Hervey concludes:

Having placed the author in this favourable and intelligible point of view before the public, we will leave him there, with a final word of advice. Let his Muse be ever so eccentric in her flights, so long as she remains within sight she will find admirers even of her eccentricities; but if she would be appreciated by understandings of this earth, she must keep somewhere or other on this side of the clouds.[149]

For the next twenty years the *Athenaeum* continued to scold Browning, lamenting that he should "persist in thinking it necessary for a poet to adopt the tricks of a conjuror,"[150] at the same time that it did not fail to recognize the "lofty spirit" and the "master hand." Hervey's review of *Pippa Passes* is typical.

We have taken uncommon pains to understand Browning, he says, because of his "disposition to think." "Our faith in him . . . is not yet extinct,—but our patience *is*." His themes are nearly as obscure as ever—though we get a glimpse occasionally of "meanings which it might have been well worth his while to put into English."[151]

The critic then points out the "beauties" including the famous "All's right with the world" song, and he finds the

---

[148] *Ibid.*
[149] *Ibid.*
[150] Dec. 11, 1841, p. 952.
[151] *Ibid.*

idea of the whole drama "remarkably beautiful, and well
worth working out in language suited to its own simple
and healthy moral." One scene (just before the wife of the
miser and her paramour murder the husband) "is written
with such power of passion and of painting (with a volup-
tuousness of colour and incident, however, which Mr. Browning may find it convenient to subdue, for an English public)
as marks a master hand."[152]

In like manner the reviewer of *King Victor and King
Charles*[153] expressed regret "at the extent to which Mr.
Browning allows his manner to interpose between his own
fine conceptions and the public," for "we have faith in [him]
. . . and trust to see him realize a higher destiny than that
of the thousand and one claimants to the laurel crown."[154]
Hervey did not cease to protest, even when he encountered
such fine things as the *Dramatic Lyrics*. "That it is Mr.
Browning's pleasure to be enigmatical, may now, we suppose, be considered as an accepted condition of his literary
dealings with the public." But we wish it were not so. The
dramatic pieces are misnamed, he adds, since they are for
the most part lyrical.[155]

Chorley, more cordial in his first reviews, soon adopted

[152] *Ibid*. See Lounsbury, *Early Career of Robert Browning*, p. 97, for comment on this review. See also H. Allingham and E. B. Williams, *Letters to
William Allingham*, pp. 41-42.

[153] According to the marked file this review was by "Hemans," possibly a
son of Felicia Hemans.

[154] *Athenaeum*, April 30, 1842, pp. 376-377.

[155] *Athenaeum*, April 22, 1843, pp. 385-386. This was the review which
caused Elizabeth Barrett to write that "the 'Athenaeum' . . . made me quite cross
and misanthropical last week." (See *Letters of Elizabeth Barrett Browning*, I,
133.) Miss Barrett's irritation with the *Athenaeum* was probably increased by the
fact that *A Blot in the 'Scutcheon* had been handled cavalierly in that publication
a few weeks earlier. DeVane says: "Of all the reviews, that in the *Athenaeum*,
for Feb. 18, 1843, was the most severe." (*Op. cit.*, pp. 130-131.) DeVane adds:
"This review still rankled in Browning's mind forty years later." The *Athenaeum* critic called it "a very puzzling and unpleasant piece of business. The
plot is plain enough, but the acts and feelings of the characters are inscrutable
and abhorrent, and the language is as strange as their proceedings."

Hervey's attitude and as late as 1855 he was still harping on the same tune. He allowed "fertility of invention" to Browning in *Colombe's Birthday* and *Dramatic Romances and Lyrics*. And he recognized the power of character analysis in the former.

. . . a feeble-handed writer [would have] hesitated to show the play of light and shade in the character of his heroine; but Mr. Browning has done it, and skillfully, so that we continue to love and trust in Colombe; and none the less because she vacillates. . . .

So ends this drama: beautiful in the lofty and chivalrous spirit it illustrates, in the noble lesson it teaches, and in the rich and poetical eloquence of its language, in which Mr. Browning has advanced many steps nearer to simplicity, without his fancy, or feeling, or stores of imagery showing a trace of impoverishment.[156]

Chorley's admiration did not cease, even when he found that Browning had not heeded his gentle admonitions. "Though his manner changes less than might be wished . . . there are few of his contemporaries who embrace so wide a field of subjects; be they of thought or description, or passion, or character. Sometimes *baroque,* Mr. Browning is never ignoble. . . . His aims are truth and freedom. His art is sometimes consummate."[157]

J. Westland Marston, though he was a friend of Browning, was disturbed by the shocking oddities of the treatment of a serious subject in *Christmas-Eve and Easter-Day*. "The form of doggrel . . . is not that in which the mysteries of faith, doubt, and eternity can be consistently treated." The critic feared that "it is only a 'wanton mood' that ever leads Mr. Browning to follow after the coarse and grotesque," for he is capable of creating "new images of beauty."[158]

[156] *Athenaeum*, Oct. 19, 1844, pp. 944-945. Though not marked in the editorial file, this review was probably by Chorley. The phrasing and the point of view both suggest his hand.

[157] *Athenaeum*, Jan. 17, 1846, pp. 58-59.

[158] *Athenaeum*, April 6, 1850, pp. 370-371.

Chorley again was too thoroughly wedded to his pre-
conceived notions of a dignified and noble style and too
much grieved by Browning's failure to give up his audacities
of language to appreciate the full merit of *Men and Women.*
Who will not grieve over energy wasted and power misspent,—
over fancies chaste and noble, so overhung by the 'seven veils' of
obscurity that we can oftentimes be only sure that fancies
exist? . . .

We had hoped that 'Men and Women' would enable us to
register progress in the poet's mind (always rich to overflowing)
and in the artist's hand (always able to draw whatever its owner
pleased). The riches and the ability are there, but the employment and the expression of them seem to us, on the whole, more
perverse, personal, and incomplete than they were formerly.[159]

Gerald Massey had more enthusiasm for Browning's
"predilection for doing things which no other writer has
done, or could have done." His review of *Dramatis Personae*
took a step in advance of the usual *Athenaeum* position with
relation to Browning's peculiarities of manner. He could
praise "Caliban" as well as "Prospice"; the former would
have delighted Shakespeare, he says—"Only a great dramatic
poet could have written this poem."

. . . with all faults admitted and all hindrances acknowledged,
Mr. Browning is one of our very few living poets, and this book
is a richer gift than we shall often receive at the hands of poetry
in our time.[160]

The most fulsome and unreserved praise of Browning in
the *Athenaeum* was written by Robert Buchanan, who reviewed *The Ring and the Book* for that journal. He began

---

[159] *Athenaeum,* Nov. 17, 1855, pp. 1327-1328. See DeVane's comment on
this review, *op. cit.,* p. 190.

[160] *Athenaeum,* June 4, 1864, I, pp. 765-767. See DeVane, *op. cit.,* p. 251:
"From the almost unmitigated censure of 1855, of which the *Athenaeum* criticism
—with its description of *Men and Women* as 'energy wasted and powers misspent'—is the worst representative, the tone had become almost entirely cordial."

the review of Volume I somewhat cautiously, but, after calling attention to a few of Browning's characteristic faults and mannerisms (many of which could now be looked upon indulgently as a part of his genius), he relaxed and enjoyed. "The rest must be only wonder and notes of admiration. . . . Whatever else may be said of Mr. Browning . . . it will be admitted on all hands that nowhere in any literature can be found a man and a work more fascinating in their way."[161]

After Volumes II, III, and IV appeared, he let down all critical reserve:

At last, the *opus magnum* of our generation lies before the world . . . and we are left in doubt which to admire most, the supremely precious gold of the material or the wondrous beauty of the workmanship. The fascination of the work is still so strong upon us, our eyes are still so spell-bound by the immortal features of Pompilia (which shine through the troubled mists of the story with almost insufferable beauty), that we feel it difficult to write calmly and without exaggeration; yet we must record at once our conviction, not merely that 'The Ring and the Book' is beyond all parallel the supremest poetical achievement of our time, but that it is the most precious and profound spiritual treasure that England has produced since the days of Shakespeare. Its intellectual greatness is as nothing compared with its transcendent spiritual teaching. . . . Once and for ever must critics dismiss the old stale charge that Browning is a mere intellectual giant, difficult of comprehension, hard of assimilation.[162]

Though the *Athenaeum* accepted Browning henceforth as the outstanding poet of his time, its critics were never again so completely overawed by him. Williams, who wrote the reviews of Browning from 1871 to 1876, thought that *Balaustion's Adventure* added nothing to the fame of the poet and that he had read much of his own meaning into

[161] Dec. 26, 1868, II, pp. 875-876.   [162] March 20, 1869, I, pp. 399-400.

the "Alcestis" of Euripides.[163]   He predicted a greater popularity for *Prince Hohenstiel-Schwangau* because the ideas
float upon the surface rather than lie buried in conundrums
as in *Sordello*. "There is always in Mr. Browning . . . a
habit of straining to mean more than he says, until his verse
becomes, like Hercules in Atlas's place, bow-legged with its
crushing burden."[164]

Fifine at the Fair at first appeared to the reviewer to be a
riddle almost equal to *Sordello,* but an analysis showed it
to contain one of Browning's recurrent ideas: the face is but
the soul's mask, but it is well to admire the mask too. It
has now become the fashion to read Browning, the critic
said, but he becomes "day by day less of the poet and more
of the philosopher."[165]

MacColl pronounced *Red Cotton Night-Cap Country*
"more comprehensible to the general public . . . than . . .
some of his earlier works."[166]   Williams found *Aristophanes'
Apology* "as puzzling, as full of subtleties and ironies, as
capricious, and as iridescent as his 'Sordello.' "[167]   But in
The Inn Album he saw nothing obscure or involved and
thought it the finest character portrayal since Shakespeare.[168]
In his review of *Pacchiarotto* he summed up Browning's
strength and weaknesses, maintaining that the poet had al-

---

[163] Aug. 12, 1871, II, pp. 199-200. DeVane says that *Balaustion's Adventure*
was the most popular of all Browning's works.

[164] Dec. 23, 1871, II, pp. 827-828.

[165] June 8, 1872, I, pp. 711-712. See DeVane, *op. cit.,* p. 327: "The poem
was especially misunderstood by the critics, and Browning's reputation for per-
versity, which for a while had given indications of being lived down, grew again
to great proportions."

[166] *Athenaeum*, May 10, 1873, I, pp. 593-594.

[167] *Athenaeum*, April 17, 1875, I, pp. 513-514. Most other reviews made less
of the poem than did the *Athenaeum*. See DeVane, *op. cit.,* p. 339.

[168] *Athenaeum*, Nov. 27, 1875, II, pp. 701-702. DeVane says: "The poet
must have read with mixed feelings the praise of the volume in the *Athenaeum*
. . . for the reviewer was inclined to rank *The Inn Album* higher than *The Ring
and the Book* and to couple it with *Pippa Passes* as among the poet's best work."
(*Op. cit.,* p. 347.)

ways been an etcher, making sketches upon which the reader must build with his imagination. Some of the enigmatical longer pieces were failures, he said, while the smaller ones might be read by anyone with pleasure. Browning should realize, he added, that he has brewed a drink in his poetry that is stiff for most readers—he should accept that and not quarrel with his critics.[169]

The Hon. John Leicester Warren had much praise for Browning's translation of *The Agamemnon of Aeschylus*, which, he said, came nearer to the original than most other translations, verse or prose, partly because Browning is not afraid of the vulgarity of Aeschylus, and "is almost the only one of our poets who is thoroughly at home in this perplexing borderland of beauty and deformity."[170]

From 1878 on Theodore Watts was the regular reviewer of Browning's works for the *Athenaeum*. His criticism was generally more cordial and at the same time more keenly analytical of Browning's qualities than that of previous reviewers.[171] *La Saisiaz* elicited the warmest appreciation for Browning's powers as a poet. "No poet since Burns—none, perhaps, since Shakespeare—has known and felt so deeply as Mr. Browning the pathos of human life."[172] The poem, however, is ratiocinative rather than lyric; his thesis is that he "believes in soul—is very sure of God." But "what god" does he believe in? His argument boils down to Pantheism

---

[169] *Athenaeum*, July 22, 1876, II, pp. 101-102.

[170] *Athenaeum*, Oct. 27, 1877, II, pp. 525-527.

[171] The closeness of Watts to the Pre-Raphaelites may have predisposed him to a greater aesthetic appreciation of Browning's innovations than that of the average critic. The Pre-Raphaelites had early formed an attachment for Browning's most obscure poems. Rossetti had copied out the whole of *Pauline* from a copy in the British Museum, guessing it to be Browning's, and he had forced *Sordello* on the Brotherhood about 1850, "reading fifty pages at a sitting to his friends," thus anticipating the Browning Society worshippers by more than thirty years. "Swinburne knew *Sordello* from beginning to end when he was nineteen, and got 'ploughed for Smalls' at Oxford because he preferred the poem to Euclid." (DeVane, *op. cit.*, p. 81.)

[172] *Athenaeum*, May 25, 1878, I, pp. 661-664.

—all that is not Browning is God. The poem is a protest against the scientific materialism of the day, but, Watts says, there is probably no more materialism now than formerly, though it may be more voluble. Nevertheless the poem as a whole is full of "beautiful thoughts, beautifully expressed. . . . Mr. Browning has lost none of his marvelous vigour of intellect, and there are passages here and there which can compare with his very best work."[173]

In the *Dramatic Idyls* Watts saw a falling off of Browning's power to retain the "unknowing poetic mood" which Tennyson had kept. He had "almost every poetic gift, . . ." but he was "hampered, for a time at least, by the modern vice of knowingness."[174] The critic made a penetrating study of Browning's characteristics in his notice of the second series of *Dramatic Idyls*. Browning doesn't do well with an anecdote because he has "that irresistible impulse to 'tease' a subject into a sermon. . . ." He "enjoys nothing that is not under lock and key"; he must probe into the inner secrets of motive. Often he forces the rhythm of the thought against the rhythm of the metre, Watts observed. This is natural for Browning, he said, because of his passion for the grotesque. His quest is not for beauty, but for "the wonderful, the profound, the mysterious." He has "produced a new thing in English Literature."[175]

What an earlier generation of critics had frowned upon as bad taste, Watts credited to Browning's robust individuality. In a leader on *Jocoseria* he said: "Mr. Browning, for originality in temper, in style, in movement, is the most striking figure in our poetic literature, not even excepting

[173] *Ibid.*

[174] *Athenaeum*, May 10, 1879, I, pp. 593-595. DeVane says the volume was well received and widely reviewed and that one of the most penetrating reviews was that by Watts. (*Op. cit.*, p. 385.)

[175] *Athenaeum*, July 10, 1880, II, pp. 39-41. According to DeVane, most critics saw a subsidence of inspiration but couldn't account for it. Watts in the *Athenaeum* "gave what was perhaps the fairest judgment." (*Op. cit.*, p. 399.)

Donne or Burns." This volume doesn't indicate any decline in "his dazzling and unique powers."[176]

The *Athenaeum* critic felt a "hollow ring" in Browning's optimism in *Ferishtah's Fancies,* but still there was no decadence in his "intellectual strength and subtlety."[177] In Watts's final judgment Browning came just below the highest rank of poets. The greatest poetry, he said in reviewing the *Parleyings,* has spoken with a great simplicity—but there is a place too for idiosyncrasy. "Never in English literature . . . has the poetry of idiosyncrasy spoken with so powerful a voice."[178]

Joseph Jacobs, who wrote the obituary notice of Browning for the *Athenaeum,* expressed much the same idea. "One by one the *Dii majores* are leaving us: Carlyle, George Eliot, Matthew Arnold; and now Robert Browning, a greater name than all these, has passed into silence." Browning displayed gigantic powers, he said—even in his failures. But, the critic concluded, there is in his work an oversubtlety of intellect which is not the property of the greatest poet whose force is in simplicity.[179]

With this much of a summary of Browning's critical reception in the *Athenaeum* before us, it is impossible to say that, first and last, he was unfairly treated, or that the magazine was not generally ahead of the current opinion of his work.[180] As for the comparative neglect or lack of appreciation of Browning in the middle years, the *Athenaeum* critics certainly made a more determined effort to find meaning and extract the essence of value from his poems

[176] *Athenaeum,* March 24, 1883, I, pp. 367-368.

[177] Dec. 6, 1884, II, pp. 725-727. DeVane says again: "Of all the reviews, that in the *Athenaeum* . . . was the fullest and most capable." (*Op. cit.,* p. 427.)

[178] Feb. 19, 1887, I, pp. 247-249.

[179] Dec. 21, 1889, II, pp. 858-860. Watts added his tribute to Browning in the review of *Asolando,* published on the day of the poet's death.

[180] It was perhaps a recognition on the part of the poet of his later appreciation in the *Athenaeum* that he sent to that periodical his verse "To Edward Fitzgerald," a few months before his death. (July 13, 1889, II, p. 64.)

than did most of the reviewers at the time—a phenomenon sufficiently indicative of critical tolerance in those whose gaze was fixed on a star that promised to lead to a prophet rather than to a perverse trifler with "Bells and Pomegranates."

Dickens

The reputation of Dickens rose rapidly after Sam Weller appeared in the fourth number of Pickwick.[181] But the mere fact that he was acclaimed as a popular writer of fiction militated against his immediate acceptance by the serious critics of the *Athenaeum*. The prejudice against the novel as a literary form still persisted in the thirties. Exceptions were made for the historical novels of Scott and a few contemporary novels with a purpose or a moral such as R. P. Ward's *De Vere;* and admiration was occasionally expressed for some fictional works of the eighteenth century which were hallowed by time, though the critics could not fail to recognize the immoral tendencies of many of them.

The attitude of the *Athenaeum* was complicated by its contempt for the novels of fashion which were still coming from the presses of the puffing publishers when Dickens began to write. The "Newgate novel," of which Bulwer's *Paul Clifford* and Ainsworth's *Rookwood* are representative

---

[181] It is interesting to note that the *Literary Gazette* gave the first critical appreciation of Sam Weller and helped to boost the sales of *Pickwick*. (See Walter Dexter and J. W. T. Ley, *The Origin of Pickwick*, pp. 80-81.) Forster says of the reception of the book: "For its kind, its extent, and the absence of everything unreal or factitious in the causes that contributed to it, it is unexampled in literature . . . after four or five parts had appeared, without newspaper notice or puffing. . . . [Dexter and Ley show that this was not strictly true—the earlier numbers had been noticed, though not in the major reviews; and it had good advertising, including a half page in the *Athenaeum*] it sprang into a popularity that each part carried higher and higher, until people at this time talked of nothing else, tradesmen recommended their goods by using its name, and its sale, outstripping at a bound that of all the most famous books of the century, had reached to an almost fabulous number. Of part one, the binder prepared four hundred, and of part fifteen, his order was for more than forty thousand." (Forster, John, *The Life of Charles Dickens*, I, 129.)

examples, did not increase respect for the genre.[182]   Apostles of the new enlightenment distrusted the novel, not only as the literature of escape, of mere amusement, but often as a real menace because of its inculcation of wrong ideals, its catering to the lowest instincts.

The reviewer of "Mr. Colburn's List" in 1828, deploring the fact that it contained seventy-four volumes of novels and only four of poetry, said that "when, from a conviction that the highest state of mental consciousness is the highest state of happiness, we wish to prolong and increase that vigour— we take up a poem. When, on the contrary, we find the strife and tumult of the faculties painful . . . we court imbecility and inanition in the pages of a novel."

But the novel, in its simple uncompounded essence, is essentially antipathetic to poetry. It is the object of the one to exalt manners over characteristics, accidents over essentials, circumstances over man; it is the object of the other to describe what is accidental as the shrine and incorporation of what is universal, essential principles as exhibiting themselves in the varieties of changing phenomena, and the *free will* of man as victorious over sense and matter . . . as in the education of our own minds, few books can be of less use, or more prejudicial, than Novels, so there are very few indeed which can tend so much to call forth and discipline all the capacities of those minds as Poems.[183]

Though under Dilke there was a growing tendency to give the novel its due when it showed itself worthy of consideration, it was not until the social novel of the forties and fifties had demonstrated its possibilities as a practical agent in the enlightenment, that the novel as a literary form came to be accepted without condescension. At least it was felt

---

[182] Though more humanitarian in purpose than most of the type, *Oliver Twist* was generally thought of as belonging to this class of novels of criminal and "low life." That was the general view at least until the middle of the century. See Henry Mayhew, *London Labour and the London Poor*, "Narrative of a Burglar," p. 347.

[183] *Athenaeum*, Sept. 17, 1828, pp. 735-736.

by the critics who had waited in vain for the great epic poem (that the new romanticism should have produced) that here was something concrete, though of a lower order, which was worthy of praise. As early as 1833, Scargill defended the possibilities of the novel as a medium for setting forth philosophical truth.

Novel writing has been considered by many as a low pursuit, exceedingly unintellectual and unphilosophical; and a writer of a great big book of travels, half lies and nine-tenths nonsense, has the arrogance to look down with contempt upon a mere novel writer; but where has a traveller half the exercise for skill and philosophy that a novel writer has? . . . he must love his species well, in order to enter *con amore* into their interests and pursuits, and yet he must be alive to all their faults and imperfections, in order to delineate their characters truly.[184]

But these were the words of a far-sighted critic. The prejudice lingered even when not openly avowed. The majority of Dilke's reviewers felt apologetic when constrained to admire a work of fiction.[185]

For this and other reasons Dickens won his way to favor more slowly in the *Athenaeum* than he did in other magazines; even the quarterlies had more unqualified praise for his early work. The latter, however, soon became suspicious of his social criticism and the tables were turned, for the *Athenaeum* took a more kindly interest in him when it perceived that his writing tended to something more than mere amusement.[186]   It barely noticed the *Sketches by Boz* when

[184] *Athenaeum*, Nov. 9, 1833, pp. 752-753.

[185] This was not true of Lady Morgan who did a goodly number of fiction reviews. She said boldly in her notice of *Timon, but not of Athens*, a light novel published by Saunders and Otley: "The one legitimate end of novel writing is amusement; and if, in the conduct of a story, matter of edification arises, it should be regarded merely as a god-send: for, whenever the secondary purpose of instruction is designedly run after, the effort inevitably is made at the expense of the amusement." (*Athenaeum*, June 13, 1840, p. 469.)

[186] The *Quarterly* in 1839 praised the artistic skill of Dickens but didn't like the subject matter or the implications of *Oliver Twist*, which was "directed against

they appeared in book form in 1836. Two sentences in "Our Library Table" granted that these papers contained "scenes and characters sketched with admirable truth; but a suspicion crossed our minds during the perusal, whether the subjects were always worthy of the artistic skill and power of the writer. . . ."[187]

But by the end of the year the fame of Dickens had spread sufficiently to warrant a leader on the first nine numbers of *The Posthumous Papers of the Pickwick Club.* The critic did not view Dickens as quite an original genius, but still thought the *Papers* would "tickle the palates of many of the particular, as well as of many of the deeply voracious."

> The Pickwick Papers, in fact, are made up of two pounds of Smollett, three ounces of Sterne, a handful of Hook, a dash of grammatical Pierce Egan—incidents at pleasure, served with an original *sauce piquante.*[188]

"Let it not be thought that we dislike Boz," the reviewer hastened to add, "we like him, at fit moments, intensely." The author has the knack of pressing it upon you "though the article he offers is strong, and to many offensive." It is the narrative "of one who tries, in a *treble* style, to 'chronicle small beer.'" But some of the characters are "admirably hit off." After quoting seven and a half columns, the reviewer concludes: "We have spoken of Boz honestly, if plainly; but we earnestly hope and trust nothing we have said will tend to *refine* him."[189]

---

the poor-law and workhouse system, and in our opinion with much unfairness. The abuses which he ridicules are not only exaggerated, but in nineteen cases out of twenty do not at all exist." (*Quarterly Review,* June, 1839, pp. 83-102.)

[187] *Athenaeum*, February 20, 1836, p. 145.

[188] *Athenaeum*, Dec. 3, 1836, pp. 841-843.

[189] *Ibid.* Compare with this the cordiality of the *Edinburgh Review* (Oct., 1838, pp. 41-53): "We think him a very original writer—well entitled to his popularity . . . and the truest and most spirited delineator of English life, amongst the middle and lower classes, since the days of Smollett and Fielding." But the *Quarterly* was much more severe than the *Athenaeum:* "His 'gentle and genteel

The *Athenaeum* presented *Nicholas Nickleby* as "caricatures from life" and "incidents . . . from those of every day occurrence—the humour minute and *wordy* . . . ," and the whole refurbished from *Pickwick Papers,* "refreshed, renovated, re-beavered, and, in short, made to look almost 'as good as new.' "[190] It passed over *Oliver Twist* with a page of quotations, since "nine-tenths of this story have already appeared in *Bentley's Miscellany*."[191]

The first cordial notice was Thomas Hood's review of *Master Humphrey's Clock.* He complained of the clumsiness and complication of the construction of the story, but he accepted both "Little Nelly" and Quilp as characters quite conceivable in the world that Dickens pictured.

. . . we do not know where we have met, in fiction, with a more striking and picturesque combination of images than is presented by the simple, childish figure of Little Nelly . . . we should say that she thinks, speaks, and acts, in a style beyond her years, if we did not know how poverty and misfortune are apt to make advances of worldly knowledge to the young at a most ruinous discount—a painful sacrifice of the very capital of childhood.[192]

Quilp "is one of the most highly-wrought characters of the work." Before deciding that no such creature could exist, it would be well to visit his haunts. "It has been said that one-half of the world does not know how the other half lives; an ignorance, by the way, which Boz has essentially helped to enlighten."[193]

Hood saw a special significance in the new view of "low life" which Dickens presented:

Above all, in distributing the virtues, he bestows a full proportion of them amongst a class of our fellow creatures, who are favoured

---

folks' are unendurable." He is "practically a co-operator with those whose aim is to degrade the national mind." (*Quarterly*, June, 1839, pp. 83-102.)

[190] March 31, 1838, pp. 227-229.   [191] Nov. 17, 1838, pp. 824-825.
[192] Nov. 7, 1840, pp. 887-888.   [193] *Ibid.*

in Life's Grand State Lotteries, with nothing but the declared blanks. . . . The poor are his especial clients. He delights to show Worth in low places.[194]

It was perhaps appropriate for the poet who was shortly to write "The Song of the Shirt" to recommend Dickens "to the Million" on these grounds. He had kind words again for the "amiable tone and moral tendency" of *Barnaby Rudge,* which was "better built than any of its predecessors," but he chided Dickens for picturing the "godfather of Riots, Lord George Gordon" as weak rather than wicked. There is a fine moral lesson for the "whole race of cruelty mongers" in the justice that comes to the hangman.[195]

The *Athenaeum* accepted the *American Notes* without critical comment, contenting itself with extracts such as the description of Niagara which it praised as "fine writing." It predicted that the protest against the personalities of the American press would probably be more offensive to the Americans than any other charge brought against them by travellers.[196]

Leeds, viewing Pecksniff from the standpoint of an architect, found that Boz had undertaken more than he could handle in *Martin Chuzzlewit.* "There is more of caricature than of character about him, for he is a mere pompous hypocrite, who so overacts his part that he could scarcely impose upon anyone. . . . But Mr. Dickens has opened to himself an opportunity of doing much more than amuse— of exposing the mal-practices which take place at architectural competitions."[197]

The Christmas stories were generally received in the

[194] *Ibid.*   [195] Jan. 22, 1842, pp. 77-79.
[196] Oct. 22, 1842, pp. 899-902; Oct. 29, 1842, pp. 927-929. The *Athenaeum* had not hesitated to take other English critics of America severely to task; but Dickens was not so unfair as Mrs. Trollope in his view of American manners and institutions.
[197] *Athenaeum,* March 4, 1843, pp. 209-210. (This was a review of the first two numbers of the novel which appeared in monthly parts.)

holiday spirit of good feeling when all harsh criticism is laid aside. *A Christmas Carol* was a story "to make the reader laugh and cry—open his hands, and open his heart to charity even towards the uncharitable,—wrought up with a thousand minute and tender touches of the true 'Boz' workmanship."[198] Each one was better than the last. *The Chimes* was "genial and spirit-stirring; and there is not much to call for critical objection in the story."[199] *The Cricket on the Hearth* "rises to a tone of sentiment that, in its elevation, must command the sympathy of the wisest and the best."[200]

But in the reviews of other books of Dickens at this period the eulogy was not unqualified. Chorley looked upon *Martin Chuzzlewit* as the story of Scrooge told more diffusely—but the reformation of Chuzzlewit is not convincing and is unworthy to be employed "by a person so sound at heart as Mr. Dickens." The "events and vicissitudes *reel* rather than march to a conclusion." There is no real hero or heroine, but the author riots among his minor characters. As for Mrs. Gamp, "there are not many things of their kind so living in fiction as this nightmare." But there is no improvement in the serious dialogue of Dickens who is too fond of "propagating good sentiments in the form of harangues. . . . His style, too, continues more freakish and affected, on occasions, than a writer who has a European reputation should permit."[201]

This is the usual tone of the *Athenaeum* criticism of Dickens in the forties: his heart is in the right place, but he takes liberties with form and style. The same basic criticism

[198] *Athenaeum*, Dec. 23, 1843, pp. 1127-1128. This review was by Chorley, who already counted Dickens among his acquaintances, though the friendship did not become intimate until 1854.

[199] *Athenaeum*, Dec. 21, 1844, pp. 1165-1166. Chorley probably also wrote this review.

[200] *Athenaeum*, Dec. 20, 1845, pp. 1219-1221. Reviewed by Heraud.

[201] *Athenaeum*, July 20, 1844, pp. 665-666. Reviewed by Chorley. (See J. W. T. Ley, *The Dickens Circle*, p. 285.)

was made of Browning, and we shall see it repeated for most of the other outstanding Victorian writers. There was, however, also an occasional voice raised against the over-strained sentiment in Dickens. In the series of letters on "Modern Poetry" already mentioned[202] "Sigma" replied to "Beta's" paean to that "glorious Dickens" who "exalts and purifies as much as Shakespeare":

Far be it from me to underrate the power and genius of this truly great writer; but I cannot observe without sorrow, and without a feeling very much like disgust, the unhealthy stimulants by which alone he can now satisfy the craving for excitement which his unnatural diet of spices has nourished in his readers.[203]

But Marston sang the praises of two of the Christmas stories in the familiar key: "The noblest feature of our current literature is its reverence for the affections. . . . To few living writers are we more indebted than to Mr. Dickens for lessons in the Philosophy of the Heart."[204] It was as a humanitarian moralist that Dickens was finally accepted, and not as a caricaturist of "low life." "Of all truths the power of human suffering to educate human sympathy is one of the most salutary and consoling. . . . These . . . are the lessons which Mr. Dickens has here sought to inculcate."[205]

Hervey was somewhat puzzled by the first number of *David Copperfield*. He thought Miss Betsey was "drawn in pure waste," for she disappeared from the story, and, as it seemed, not to appear again.[206] Chorley, however, though he took exception to the looseness of the plot and the melo-dramatic stage effect of some incidents such as the storm

[202] See *ante*, pp. 275-277.

[203] *Athenaeum*, April 27, 1844, pp. 381-383.

[204] *Athenaeum*, Dec. 26, 1846, pp. 1319-1321. This is a review of *The Battle of Life; a Love Story*.

[205] Dec. 23, 1848, pp. 1291-1293. Review of *The Haunted Man and the Ghost's Bargain*.

[206] *Athenaeum*, May 5, 1849, pp. 455-457.

wherein perished lover and seducer, had generous applause for the finished work:

In no previous fiction has he shown so much gentleness of touch and delicacy of tone,—such abstinence from trick in what may be called the level part of the narrative,—so large an amount of refined and poetical yet simple knowledge of humanity. The Chronicler himself is one of the best heroes ever sketched or wrought out by Mr. Dickens.[207]

But the flimsiness of the plot is "sought to be disguised by afterthoughts." There are "strained incidents and forced scenes." Uriah Heep melts away like a bad genie in a fairy tale. And what is the purpose of Betsey Trotwood's phantom husband and of Rosa Dartle? "Mr. Dickens must announce his devices with less pomp, and arrange them in less artificially imposing forms. . . ." Then the reviewer enumerates the characters and scenes which stand out. The Micawbers and Mrs. Gummidge justify his "high admiration of this best work of a genial and powerful writer."[208]

Chorley also reviewed *Bleak House*. "There is progress in art to be praised in this book,—and there is progress in exaggeration to be deprecated." Dickens has gone too far in his caricature of living people who must be recognizable to his contemporaries.[209] But in his "own particular walk" (creation of Dickensian characters), he has "rarely if ever, been happier than in 'Bleak House.' "[210]

Chorley did not get a chance to review Dickens again

---

[207] *Athenaeum*, May 23, 1850, pp. 1209-1211.

[208] *Ibid.*

[209] This is, of course, a reference to the caricature of Leigh Hunt as Mr. Skimpole. See *Athenaeum*, Dec. 24, 1859, II, p. 855, concerning a note of Dickens denying that he had Leigh Hunt in mind when he pictured Harold Skimpole's disagreeable characteristics, but only when he painted his admirable qualities.

[210] *Athenaeum*, Sept. 17, 1853, pp. 1087-1088. Hervey had reviewed the first number of the serial publication, *Athenaeum*, March 6, 1852, pp. 270-271, as usual confining himself mainly to quotation of extracts.

until *Great Expectations* came out in 1861.[211] In the meantime, Hepworth Dixon, editor of the *Athenaeum* after 1853, did not neglect him, though he exhibited a strange preference for *Little Dorrit* and was offended by passages in *Hard Times* that were "coarse, violent, and awkward."[212]

Mr. Dickens has obtained the ear of his country more completely than any other man; and, on the whole, he uses his glorious privilege for the noblest ends.[213]

During the time of the serial publication of *Little Dorrit* "we have heard that it was cloudy, diffuse, uninteresting— that it was false in Art, exaggerated as to character, and the like." But the critic did not find it so.

. . . looking at the story as a contribution to literature—weighing it as we should weigh 'Tom Jones' or 'The Bride of Lammermoor,' we have found it neither false nor weak . . . we know of no other author in our time who could have produced 'Little Dorrit.' . . . What an invention is the Circumlocution Office! . . . We see . . . no decrease of power, no closing of eyes, no slackening of pulse.[214]

It will, of course, meet with opposition from "all who are interested in the maintenance of humbug and circumlocution." But the reviewer was glad to hear that the circulation of Dickens's last book had exceeded that of any other of his works.

Chorley's accumulated warmth of feeling for Dickens

[211] It is possible that Chorley's growing intimacy with Dickens made him reluctant to criticise the latter's work, or it may be that Dixon, knowing of it, preferred to do the reviews himself. Chorley's biographer says: "During the last few years of Dickens's life they were in constant correspondence; and there was probably no other man of letters, with the exception of Mr. Forster, to whom his confidence was so entirely given." (Chorley, *Autobiography,* II, 228.) Still another explanation is possible. Chorley had complained that Hervey, as editor, had taken the choice books himself to review; perhaps Dixon did the same.

[212] *Athenaeum,* Aug. 12, 1854, p. 992.

[213] *Athenaeum,* Dec. 1, 1855, pp. 1393-1395.

[214] *Athenaeum,* June 6, 1857, pp. 722-724.

burst forth in his review of *Great Expectations*.[215] He doubted if the library of English fiction contained a romance comparable to it. In it "familiar and tame scenery is wrought up so as to exceed in picturesqueness the Apennine landscape of a Radcliffe, or the deep-sea storms of a Fenimore Cooper," and it displayed "such variety of humour, such deep and tender knowledge of the secrets of a yearning human heart, as belong to a novel of the highest order."[216] All the rest was a glowing rapture unqualified by any of the usual *Athenaeum* balancing of "beauties and blemishes."

Our Mutual Friend gave Chorley another opportunity to show his unbounded admiration. "A new novel by the greatest novelist living is not to be dismissed with a few jaunty phrases of rapture, or of qualification." Time and success have not made the author careless. Still, in some instances "truth and nature" are strained for the sake of the plot, but "the author of 'Pickwick' never reveled among richer whimsies than are to be found in the comic parts of this tale." In this novel there is enjoyment for all tastes. ". . . if, among his tales, we rank the highest 'David Copperfield,' which includes, so to say, neither plot nor surprise,— 'Our Mutual Friend' must be signalized for an accumulation of fine, exact, characteristic detail."[217]

It is not surprising to find Chorley in his obituary notice of Dickens referring to the "amazing vitality" of "one of

[215] Chorley could not but be generous. Dickens wrote him on Feb. 3, 1860, assuring him that Chorley's own novel *Roccabella* was "a very remarkable book indeed," and he added the best Victorian compliment: ". . . my girls would testify to you, if there were need, that I cried over it heartily." (Chorley, *op. cit.*, II, 161.)

[216] *Athenaeum*, July 13, 1861, II, pp. 43-45.

[217] Oct. 28, 1865, II, pp. 569-570. Dickens wrote to Chorley the day the review was published: "I have seen the 'Athenaeum,' and most heartily and earnestly thank you. Trust me, there is nothing I could have wished away, and all that I read there affects and delights me. I feel so generous an appreciation and sympathy so very strongly, that if I were to try to write more, I should blur the words by seeing them dimly." (Chorley, *op. cit.*, II, 230.)

the greatest and most beneficent men of genius England has produced since the days of Shakespeare."[218] But there was more than the personal friendship of Chorley to account for the gradual change from qualified praise to almost uncritical partiality towards Dickens in the *Athenaeum*. It was characteristic of that journal, as of the culture which it so accurately mirrored, that an original or eccentric genius could win his way to its esteem by the strength of a sentimental humanism rather than, almost in spite of, any force of artistry or ideas. And no eccentric talent was ever more completely and honestly given over to the expression of an advancing cultural norm than that of Dickens.

Thackeray

Although Thackeray was fundamentally no less a man of his age than Dickens, a number of circumstances combined to delay his recognition by the critical world and the reading public. It is probable that he began contributing satirical sketches to *Fraser's* even before Dickens published his "Boz" papers,[219] but he was still comparatively little known ten years after *Pickwick* had made Dickens famous. Macvey Napier, editor of the *Edinburgh Review*, wrote on April 1, 1845, to Abraham Hayward:

Will you tell me, confidentially of course, whether you know anything of a Mr. Thackeray, about whom Longman has written me, thinking he would be a good hand for light articles? He says (Longman) that this Mr. Thackeray is one of the best writers in *Punch*. One requires to be very much on one's guard in engaging with mere strangers. In a journal like the *Edinbro'* it is always of importance to keep up in respect of names.[220]

When Thackeray did contribute an article to the *Edinburgh* later in the same year, his name meant so little that

[218] June 18, 1870, I, pp. 804-805.
[219] See M. M. H. Thrall, *Rebellious Fraser's*, Chap. III.
[220] Quoted, Herman Merivale and Frank T. Marzials, *Life of W. M. Thackeray*, p. 128.

Napier had no hesitation in cutting and mutilating the manuscript without consulting the author.[221]   After the first monthly number of *Vanity Fair* had appeared (January, 1847), Thackeray was so little assured of critical support that he called on his friends to give him a "push at the present minute."[222]   A year later a review was published in the *Edinburgh,* written by his friend Abraham Hayward. Thackeray's biographer says: "The article is on the whole appreciative, though here and there it seems as if the reviewer had been afraid that his enthusiasm was too great."[223] The reviewer's attitude was defensive.

. . . at this moment the rising generation are supplied with the best part of their mental aliment by writers whose names are a dead letter to the mass, and among the most remarkable of these is Michael Angelo Titmarsh, alias William Makepeace Thackeray.[224]

But he added rather daringly, " 'Vanity Fair' is assured of immortality as ninety-nine hundredths of modern novels are sure of annihilation."[225]

Thackeray had somewhat retarded his own recognition by writing for so many years under a variety of pseudonyms. "When it became known that the author of 'Jeames's Diary' and of 'The Snobs of England' was one and the same person, . . . [he] was regarded as a person of considerable importance in literary circles, and began to taste the sweets of success."[226]   But even so it was the success of a clever young writer for *Fraser's* and *Punch,* and not that of a literary genius who was to be taken quite seriously.

[221] *Selections from the Correspondence of Macvey Napier,* by his son, Macvey Napier, p. 499.
[222] Merivale and Marzials, *op. cit.,* pp. 136-137.
[223] Lewis Melville [pseud.], *William Makepeace Thackeray,* p. 239.
[224] *Edinburgh Review,* Jan., 1848, p. 26.
[225] See Merivale and Marzials, *op. cit.,* p. 140.
[226] Melville, *op. cit.,* p. 229.

The *Irish Sketch-Book* (1843), the first work to which Thackeray put his name, was mildly successful, the first edition of one thousand copies having sold out, and a second being called for in 1845.[227] But it only continued to strengthen his reputation as an amusing writer without a serious purpose.

It is true that a few men saw a promise of something deeper in his early work. Sterling had written to his mother after seeing *The Great Hoggarty Diamond* that he thought the author a true genius. "What is there better in Fielding or Goldsmith?"[228] But no critic would have ventured such a view in print until after the success of *Vanity Fair*.

Of the reception of that book Melville says: "The first numbers failed to attract attention, and the question of stopping the publication was actually mooted. Fortunately, later in the year, the sale increased by leaps and bounds."[229] Some have attributed the change in the public attitude to the favorable review in the *Edinburgh,* and others to the eulogistic dedication to Thackeray in the second edition of *Jane Eyre,* while Thackeray himself, perhaps presumptuously, "thought the publication of his Christmas book 'Mrs. Perkins's Ball' had much to do with it.' "[230]

But even that success did not mean that Thackeray was generally accepted by the arbiters of serious literature. Another obstacle now presented itself and a most difficult one for a writer of a novel without a hero to overcome in the eyes of Victorian critics.

It was after the publication of 'Vanity Fair' that the charge of cynicism first suggested by 'The Second Funeral of Napoleon' was seriously, and for so many years persistently, brought against Thackeray, though it was left for Edmund Yates eleven years later to declare that the novelist 'wrote himself "cynic"—for it pays.'[231]

[227] *Ibid.,* pp. 146-148. [228] *Ibid.,* p. 185.
[229] *Ibid.,* p. 236. [230] *Ibid.* [231] *Ibid.,* pp. 239-240.

This was the undertone of criticism of his work thence-forth. Though Thackeray argued (in his essay on Swift in the *English Humourists* and elsewhere) that he was a lay preacher with a scorn only for "untruth, pretension, im-posture" and a "tenderness for the weak, the poor, the oppressed, the unhappy," and though he leaned further and further towards sentimentalism, his efforts to counteract the charge of cynicism were mostly futile.

His characters were not sufficiently idealized to suit the times. Charlotte Brontë thought he was "unjust to women —quite unjust."[232] Harriet Martineau said that "the first drawback in his books, as in his manners, is the impression conveyed by both that he can never have known a good and sensible woman."[233] Frederic Harrison found a dearth of "generous and fine natures" in his novels.[234] Ruskin said in *Fors Clavigera* that "Thackeray settled like a meat-fly on whatever one had got for dinner, and made one sick of it."[235] This was not the universal opinion, but it was a common one, and was not infrequently the dominant tone of con-temporary reviews of his books in periodicals even after his fame as a writer was established.

Since it was not the usual practice of the *Athenaeum* to review works which appeared serially in other periodicals, *The Paris Sketch-Book* by Mr. Titmarsh was the first of Thackeray's productions to be noticed by it. The review, possibly by Lady Morgan, who was then the *Athenaeum* authority on French manners, politics, and history, was cor-dial enough, though slightly condescending. "Mr. Titmarsh understands his Paris well . . . the Paris of theatres, courts of justice . . . , of the students ruling the Pays Latin. . . ." But for the world of fashion he is "too free and easy," and "for the world of philosophizers, a trifle, we think, too

[232] *Ibid.*, p. 247.
[233] *Ibid.*   [234] *Ibid.*
[235] *The Works of John Ruskin*, XXVII, 562.

jocose and familiar." He is most at home "when writing down the little history of his maid-of-all work, Beatrice Merger, whose story is as simple, honest, and touching, as if Goldsmith or Charles Lamb had told it." The critic recommends Mr. Titmarsh to travel again and the public to read "his clever, humorous, and, best of all, unborrowed speculations on men and manners in Paris.[236]

A short quotation without critical comment was given from *The Second Funeral of Napoleon* in "Our Library Table,"[237] and in the same column a few months later there was brief mention of the *Comic Tales and Sketches*.[238]

Though Lady Morgan was inclined to be hypercritical of books on Ireland not written by herself, she let Titmarsh's *Irish Sketch-Book* by as "pleasant,—coarse now and again, but honest and kindly on the whole; above all, free from hypocrisy." Still, Titmarsh was not free from prejudice. "A close observer, and often a shrewd reasoner, he is still somewhat decided in his party views; and he does not possess that enlarged and grasping philosophy which is necessary to the perfect understanding of the 'case of Ireland.' "[239]

The *Journey from Cornhill to Grand Cairo* got two notices. The first one observed that "the purpose of the writer is attained if the reader be amused. We think he will be."[240] The second, after quoting generously, concluded: "All this is amusing enough, and we doubt not that the worthy Michael has honestly recorded his own feelings; but after all, though he may pride himself on being honest and 'impartial,' is he not a little 'stony-hearted'?"[241]

The genial Chorley was pleasant enough towards *Mrs. Perkins's Ball* wherein "we have a bit of sentiment; a bit

---

[236] July 25, 1840, pp. 589-590.
[237] Jan. 16, 1841, pp. 52-53.   [238] May 15, 1841, p. 385.
[239] *Athenaeum*, May 13, 1843, pp. 455-457.
[240] Jan. 24, 1846, pp. 89-91.
[241] Jan. 31, 1846, pp. 118-120. Here is already a foretaste of accusations which were common enough after the publication of *Vanity Fair*.

of philosophy— and *two* of vulgarity" in the scenes of middle-class life "done to a turn."[242] But his reckoning of the first seven numbers of *Vanity Fair* was between admiration for Thackeray's handling of the general harlequinade and fatherly advice to the author to avoid presenting disagreeable characters. But the worst tempered of critics could not chastise severely "a writer so good-humoured as this new Preacher."

Nevertheless, we are in truth bound to observe that these are rather 'Pen and Pencil Sketches' of 'mean persons' than of 'English Society.' Mr. Thackeray announces his novel 'as without a hero,'—and therefore a somewhat selfish Osborne and a dull simple Dobbin, and a fool called Captain Crawley, are perhaps men as worshipful as we had any right to expect.[243]

As for the women he has been somewhat too niggardly. Amelia is at best a secondary figure, "the power of the tale lying in the nature and performances of Becky Sharpe. As a piece of character we rate this lady very highly. . . . It was probably Mr. Thackeray's design to exhibit the sins of Society in such a creature as their inevitable result." Repulsive though she is, we feel a sort of pity for her and "a strange trouble while we contemplate Humanity without a heart."

Should 'Vanity Fair' fail to take a fast and permanent hold of the public, it will be the fault of the preference on the author's part for the unpleasing . . . and not because he fails in force of portraiture and in probability of dialogue.[244]

At present we shall "content our consciences with warning Mr. Thackeray to beware of banter," while we "await with more than ordinary curiosity for the 'reckoning' of 'Vanity

[242] *Athenaeum*, Dec. 19, 1846, pp. 1290-1291.
[243] *Athenaeum*, July 24, 1847, pp. 785-786.
[244] *Ibid.*

Fair.' "[245]   This attack, in its general asininity, marks a low point in the *Athenaeum* criticism of contemporaries; yet it is perhaps no worse than the bulk of judgments of Thackeray in periodicals at this time.

When the book as a whole was published it was given to George Henry Lewes to review.[246]   His more analytical and penetrating eye revealed the peculiar qualities of Thackeray in a manner which later criticism has seldom improved upon.   He did not hesitate to proclaim *Vanity Fair* "one of the most remarkable works of modern fiction."   Heretofore Thackeray has been an amusing sketcher and a light contributor to periodicals, but his reputation is now established. "The strength which lay within him he has here put forth for the first time."   But there are still traces of his old fault —"a sort of indifference to the serious claims of literature, a cavalier impertinence of manner as if he were playing with his subject."

The style of 'Vanity Fair' is winning, easy, masculine, felicitous, and humorous. Its pleasant pages are nowhere distorted by rant. The author indulges in no sentimentalities—inflicts no fine writing on his readers. Trusting to the force of truth and humour, he is the *quietest* of contemporary writers,—a merit worth noting in a literary age which has a tendency to mistake spasm for force. The book has abundant faults of its own . . . but they are not the faults most current in our literature. The writer is

[245] *Ibid.* If we are to accept the judgment of some contemporary as well as some later critics, Chorley is not to be blamed too much for not seeing the full significance of the story in the first few numbers. Melville says that "the simplest and most probable explanation of the rise in circulation of the shilling numbers is that the book increases in interest as it goes on." (*Op. cit.,* p. 236.) This was Edward Fitzgerald's view, but Mrs. Carlyle commented after reading the first number: "Very good indeed, beats Dickens out of the world." And Carlyle said that Thackeray "would cut up into a dozen Dickenses." (D. A. Wilson, *Carlyle,* IV, 126.)

[246] Lewes had just begun to review for the *Athenaeum.* Why the book was taken away from Chorley and given to him it is impossible to say. Perhaps the editor, in view of Thackeray's success, wanted a stronger review than could be expected from the wishy-washy, sentimental Chorley.

quite free from theatricality. No glare from the footlights is thrown upon human nature, exaggerating and distorting it.[247]

He is free too from "a purpose." "Unfettered by political or social theories, his views of men and classes are not cramped."

It is one of Thackeray's peculiar excellencies that he almost always ridicules *ab intra*. An absurdity is stated by him in the quietest and gravest manner, as if he were himself a believer in it like others, and—enforced by such means of self-accumulation as leave it to unmitigated contempt. His irony of this kind is perfect,—but it is a weapon which he uses far too exclusively. . . . Mr. Thackeray grows serious and pathetic at times—but almost as if he were ashamed of it, like a man caught in tears at the theatre. It is one weakness of the satirist that he is commonly afraid of the ridicule of others![248]

Many of Thackeray's deficiencies spring from the fact that he is a satirist rather than an artist, Lewes says. He has not kept proportion—he runs on "recording the suggestions of the moment." He is deficient too in passion, but we feel that he is "painting after Nature: and this conviction it is which makes his work so delightful." The satirical tendency accounts for the "prodigality of vice and folly to be found in his pages."

The character of Becky is amongst the finest creations of modern fiction. . . . With great art, she is made rather selfish than wicked. . . . Profound immorality is made to seem consistent with unfailing good humor. . . . It is very strange that the reader has a sort of liking for her in spite of his better knowledge. . . . The charm of the work *pervades* it—and is not gathered up into separate 'bits.' Knowledge of life, good humoured satire, penetration into motive, power of characterization, and great truthfulness are qualities in fiction as rare as they are admirable; and no work that has been published for many years past can claim these qualities so largely as 'Vanity Fair.' "[249]

[247] *Athenaeum*, Aug. 12, 1848, pp. 794-797.
[248] *Ibid*.   [249] *Ibid*.

Hervey took up the first number of *Pendennis* warily and would make no guess as to what it would be in finished form, at the same time taking the opportunity to excuse the *Athenaeum* for its failure to recognize the genius of Thackeray in the first numbers of *Vanity Fair*, "which turns out ultimately to be perhaps the most remarkable book of fiction that late years have produced." In that book he "contrived also to escape the foresight of the critics. . . . So poor were the beginnings of the tale, that the subsequent numbers ran a great chance of being thrown aside on the faith of the early ones. . . . But the present work begins well."[250]

In *The History of Samuel Titmarsh and the Great Hoggarty Diamond*, republished from the periodicals in 1849, Chorley, employing his after sight, saw evidence of the developing power which had produced *Vanity Fair*. He expressed a wish, however, that "since he has 'made a clean breast' of 'Vanity Fair' he would favour us in future with revelations and characters of a more agreeable quality." He is too fond of "accumulating revelations of folly, frivolity and false pretense."[251]

Chorley returned to lecturing Thackeray in his review of the completed *Pendennis*.

His authorship seems in some danger of becoming a performance on one string: an execution of a long *fantasia*, with several variations, but all in the same key and all on the same theme of 'Humbug everywhere.' . . . Thus, as critics who would fain be of use, we must to the utmost urge our objections to such a monotonous crusade against an enemy whose existence every one admits,—to such a ruthless insistence on the blemishes, incompleteness, and disappointments which canker every human good and happiness. . . .

There seems to us great need that an alarm should be rung pretty loudly in the ears of one of our most shrewd, vigorous, accom-

[250] *Athenaeum*, Nov. 4, 1848, pp. 1099-1101.
[251] *Athenaeum*, Feb. 10, 1849, pp. 137-138.

plished, and kindly writers,—bidding him beware of his own tendencies lest they become organic defects.[252]

For once Chorley made a shrewd hit: "The observer who is always watching the follies and pretensions of the second table . . . lies open to the charge, not of despising such 'conventionalisms,' but of being tormented by an irritating sense of their authority." While he protested against the principle of making dismal effects everywhere, he could not but "do honour to the power and acuteness of the painter." There is one character, Major Pendennis, who is surpassed only by Becky, but even here Thackeray has "outraged average nature"—Major Pendennis would not have stooped to secure the Clavering seat and the Begum fortune. As for the story, the ending is helter skelter and the relief provided for the Begum "is Minerva Press every grain of it."[253]

Marston thought Thackeray's *English Humourists* lacking in humor though filled with his usual "sallies of liveliness" or "zest of pungent satire." His purpose seems to have been "to select a few points in the career of his hero, and to deduce from them a series of moral reflections." But still the lecturer sustained his reputation as a writer of pure and graphic English. His characterization of Swift was "epigrammatic, lucid, and picturesque."[254]

In reviewing *Henry Esmond* D. Owen Maddyn harped again on the continuation of the theme of *Vanity Fair*.

Vanitas Vanitatum is still the text on which Mr. Thackeray everywhere moralizes . . . much of it [*Esmond*] reads like a

[252] Dec. 7, 1850, pp. 1273-1275.

[253] *Ibid*. (The Minerva Press, founded in 1790 by William Lane, came to be a synonym for popular literature appealing to the lowest taste.)

[254] *Athenaeum*, May 24, 1851, p. 551. The *English Humourists* lectures were reviewed again after they were published, by Chorley, who said that Thackeray was handicapped in presenting these eighteenth-century men by his audience of both sexes—he had to ignore and camouflage too much. The result was "a pleasant song . . . rather than a literary essay of any deep authority or value." (*Athenaeum*, June 18, 1853, pp. 732-733; see also second notice, June 25, pp. 762-764.)

monologue in the author's peculiar manner on the hollowness of the world as seen in Queen Anne's time . . . his pathos is now sweeter, less jarred against by angry sarcasm, but perhaps scarcely so powerful. . . . Beatrix is but another Becky. . . . Of the wits of the period Steele fares best, and is the most lifelike figure. The attempts at portraying Swift and Bolingbroke are decided failures. . . . As an historical novel this cannot be accepted.[255]

The story must be read "for its romantic though improbable plot, its spirited grouping, and its many thrilling utterances of the anguish of the human heart." But the ending is "painfully disappointing," when the affections of Esmond are abruptly transferred from the daughter to the mother.[256]

We must add, that the display of literary art is too strong in every chapter of these volumes. There is too much of the retrospective wisdom of the nineteenth century—and too frequent an interposing of the writer as a sentimental moralist in his own peculiar way,—not to disturb the . . . narrative . . . as in 'Vanity Fair,' there is often a curious and not quite satisfactory conjunction of the sarcastic and the sentimental,—as if a cynic were resolving to chastise with his satire, and relenting into tears.[257]

But the reviewer ended with extracts which he praised for their "lyrical sweetness and poetical pathos."

Hervey was cautious again in heralding the first number of *The Newcomes,* but awaited with confidence the coming enjoyment.[258] Chorley, on taking up the completed work

[255] *Athenaeum,* Nov. 6, 1852, pp. 1199-1201. Charlotte Brontë thought *Esmond* was "too much history—too little story." (Melville, *op. cit.,* p. 339.)

[256] The thinness of this episode and of the character of the mother was detected by many Victorian critics, particularly women. Mrs. Jameson wrote: "The virtuous woman, *par excellence,* who 'never sins and never forgives'; who never resents, nor relents, nor repents; the mother who is the rival of her daughter; the mother who for years is the *confidante* of a man's delirious passion for her own child, and then consoles him by marrying him herself! O Mr. Thackeray, this will never do!" (Quoted in Melville, *op. cit.,* p. 247.) George Eliot, perhaps with the same thing in mind, said that it was "a most uncomfortable book." (*Ibid.,* p. 339.)

[257] *Athenaeum,* Nov. 6, 1852, pp. 1199-1201.

[258] *Athenaeum,* Oct. 1, 1853, p. 1158.

found that it "furnishes little new matter for the critic." There is a sameness in his "one view of life and manners."

We are arrested by some brilliant piece of writing—by some ingenious mosaic where cynicism is imbedded in the midst of pathos; and while we pause to admire, to discriminate lights from shades . . . the tale and all the cares and concernments of its actors vanish.[259]

The *Miscellanies* and the reprinted *Irish Sketch-Book* were reviewed by James Hannay,[260] who gave the most favorable account of Thackeray in the *Athenaeum* since Lewes's eulogium of *Vanity Fair*.

He is, we should say, one of the healthiest writers who has attained celebrity since the days of Scott and Byron [*sic!*]. . . . Agreeable, manly, colloquial English—the English of cultivated men, but still with as little bookishness about it as possible,— such is the clear atmosphere we breathe in reading him. Very sparing of imagery, perfectly free from conceits, rarely touching the deeper-toned chords of passion and sentiment—he is always at once a master of himself, and never takes his eye off his reader. He is so quiet and reasonable that he is apt to seem prosaic. Perhaps nobody awakens tears which surprise those who shed them so much. . . . Now a common fault in our later literature has been a want of balance. . . . But when Mr. Thackeray's genius attained maturity, the whole reading world could enjoy the change. . . . Here was one who talked in the style of the everyday world, —who could stir humour and passion without disturbing that equilibrium which the Englishman of our century loves to maintain.[261]

Dixon was generous enough with *The Virginians* and *The Four Georges*. The former had more preaching than any other of Thackeray's volumes, but most of these ser-

---

[259] *Athenaeum*, Aug. 4, 1855, pp. 895-896.

[260] Hannay, a journalist of some reputation and one of the founders of *Punch*, had met Thackeray in 1848. He had given a series of lectures on *Satire* and *Satirists* in 1853 (published 1854). Later he published *Studies on Thackeray* (1869).   [261] Oct. 3, 1857, pp. 1229-1231.

mons "are delightful for their insight and their satire. They stop the story, cries a cynic. Who cares?"[262] The people who, for moral reasons, refuse to read novels or see plays will relish "The Four Georges," the critic says, because they can get from it many things they would like to know about the wickedness of the great world without seeking it in improper places. The tone of the book is highly decorous. "To the staid British female whose reading has been narrow and selected, it will present many attractions. A little wickedness is very alluring when we have it in good company and served up by an eminent pen." It is "an airy, humorous, and brilliant picture of English life and manners."[263]

The severest judgment of Thackeray in the *Athenaeum* was the work of Geraldine Jewsbury, who reviewed *Lovel the Widower*. To her the story was a bitter ale and "we doubt whether the most cynical will not decline to gulp it down."

At every line . . . Mr. Thackeray brings out his little bottle of sulphuric acid: the result is hideous disfigurement, without any end gained or aimed at, beyond the coarse insolent laugh of fools, who feel that if all this be true to nature, they are as good as their betters;—or, rather, that everything is mean and bad, and that better is only a pretence . . . we every one of us revolt against being told and taught that there is nothing better than the worst part of ourselves—that the aspiration to be better than we are is only pretence and humbug.[264]

The instinct to hide our flaws "is not, as Mr. Thackeray broadly says, hypocrisy; it is a confession to ourselves that they ought not to exist." In this story "there is not one single touch to kindle in the reader a spark of generosity or kindly feeling; not one word to awaken or to stimulate a noble thought." The reader will "feel conscious of having

[262] *Athenaeum*, Oct. 23, 1858, II, pp. 515-516.
[263] *Athenaeum*, Nov. 30, 1861, II, pp. 718-720.
[264] Dec. 7, 1861, II, p. 758.

suffered a moral deterioration, from the intense ingrained vulgarity of spirit which pervades and shapes the whole story."[265]

So the *Athenaeum,* with all its variable opinion, went true to form on the whole. Indulgent but not enthusiastic over Thackeray when he was considered a mere entertainer, it finally recognized his power but never quite forgave him for failing to shape his art to the prevailing pattern of Victorian purposiveness based on the romantic dogma of the goodness of man in a state of nature and the infinite power of the human mind to progress.

Carlyle

To write a brief summary of the history of Carlyle's reputation among contemporary critics is a difficult and a rather dangerous task. So extensive and so varied were the references to him in his own day, and so searching has been the later study of his influence upon contemporaries, that every generalization must be guarded and qualified. A rough outline, however, may be useful as a background against which to place the *Athenaeum* reviews of his work.[266]

Before the publication of *The French Revolution* in 1837 Carlyle was known to only a few, mostly the literary circle he had met in London and Edinburgh, as the translator of German works and a defender and interpreter of German philosophy and literature in the periodicals. His own overscrupulous fear of puffery,[267] and his determina-

[265] *Ibid.*

[266] I have been aided somewhat in making this summary by David Alec Wilson's monumental life of Carlyle, but much more by the succinct résumés and interpretations of the critical reactions to Carlyle's works in Emery Neff's *Carlyle,* to which I have referred at every turn.

[267] Carlyle saw his name in the *Athenaeum* office window in the Strand the day before publication and wrote in his journal that he "hurried on with downcast eyes, as if I had seen myself in the Pillory. Dilke asked me for a scrap of writing with my *name:* I could not quite clearly see my way through the business —for he had twice or thrice been civil to me. I gave him *Faust's Curse,* which hung printed there. Incline now to believe that I did wrong; at least imprudently.

tion to remain anonymous were in part responsible for his not being better known, for his essays on the Germans were generally appreciated, at least by a select group who had an interest in the subject, and he was considered a writer of promise and of poetic though somewhat eccentric style.

Sartor Resartus, when it appeared serially in *Fraser's* was more neglected than reviled by critics, and it was not very widely known to be by the author of the articles on German literature. *The French Revolution* brought Carlyle's name definitely and almost sensationally before the public, though critical approval did not go beyond those favorable to the new view of the Revolution which was just then gaining ground with the growth of "Reform" and the liberal spirit. Conservative journals refused to touch it. The *Quarterly Review* did not notice Carlyle until 1840. Mill had written what Carlyle called a "courageous article" for the *London and Westminster.*[268] Thackeray wrote an appreciative review for the *Times.*[269] The *Literary Gazette* mistakenly thought the author was a staunch conservative because of his mistrust of the mob which had taken things into its own hands during the Revolution.[270] The *Edinburgh* and the *Quarterly,* when they reviewed the book belatedly in 1840, were both hostile.[271] Among those critics who didn't like

Why yield even a hair's-breadth to Puffing? Abhor it, utterly divorce it, and kick it to the Devil! This little adventure, however, *hat nichts zu bedeuten.*" (Wilson, *Carlyle,* II, 267.)

[268] See Wilson, *op. cit.,* II, 416-417. Carlyle told Mill that the review "said openly of my poor Book what I durst not myself dream of it, but should have liked to dream, had I dared." This friendly review "accelerated" the success of the history, as Mill boasted in his *Autobiography* (1873, p. 217). Wilson says: [Mill] "leaves modern critics little to say but ditto. Surely it was a great feat to write a criticism in which there is nothing out of date after eighty years except perhaps the 'Mr.' "

[269] Thackeray's review was favorable except that he was uneasy about the style which might affront "admirers of Addisonian English." (See Emery Neff, *op. cit.,* p. 180.) [270] See Neff, *op. cit.,* p. 178.

[271] *Ibid.,* p. 180, and Wilson, *op. cit.,* III, 112-113. The critic in the *Edinburgh* was an Oxford man, Herman Merivale, a professor of Political Economy. Carlyle wrote to Thomas Ballantyne, the Anti-Corn Law Lancashire editor (Aug.

his ideas much of the abuse turned upon his "bastard English" and the Germanisms of his style.[272]

Carlyle's lectures on *German Literature* and on *Heroes and Hero Worship* did more to increase his popularity than any books he had so far written, and by 1840 it was no longer safe to ignore him. He was beginning to have a following among the younger men, particularly those who believed, and they were not few, that German mysticism could be made useful in the aid of progress and practical reform.

Chartism and *Past and Present* stirred up variously those who were concerned with the "Condition-of-England question." The *Quarterly* expressed her Tory approval of his dislike of the materialistic radicalism of the eighteenth century, but disapproved of his remedy for the evils which he pointed out. The *Edinburgh* objected to his proposals for a paternalistic government, whiggishly preferring a "vast and powerful class interested in the maintenance of order."[273] *Blackwood's* professed not to take Carlyle seriously.[274] But in less conservative circles he was appreciated, and was much talked about everywhere. By October, 1843, "The reviews and newspapers were still full of *Past and Present*."[275] Though variously interpreted, it was a success, "a literary sensation."[276] Its championing of the poor, its broad generalizations, its high seriousness and seeming piety of language, gave it a hearing among all classes, but particularly the middle-class reformers and humanitarians, and religious people fired with a new zeal for social service. The *North British Review* (Evangelical) spoke with approval of

---

10, 1840): "My critic in the *Quarterly* is Sewell, a leading Puseyite. I do not like the Puseyites so ill as you do, I rather like them well. . . . My reviewer in the *Edinburgh* seemed to me of a much more detestable school than these poor Quarterlies. He writes down this doctrine, that *'hunger'* is perennial, irremediable among the lower classes of men."   [272] See Neff, *op. cit.*, p. 180.
 [273] See Neff, *op. cit.*, p. 192.   [274] *Ibid.*, p. 206.
 [275] Wilson, *op. cit.*, p. 240.   [276] Neff, *op. cit.*, p. 199.

Carlyle's influence in 1846: "While other authors may be, in a looser sense, more popular, and more rapidly and eagerly read, we doubt if there is any one, whose works have gone more deeply to the springs of character and action, especially throughout the middle classes."[277] He was welcomed by the Catholics of the *Dublin Review* and by the socially conscious Broad Church Anglicans like Maurice and Kingsley.

Carlyle himself, as well as his wife and his publisher, was surprised at the success of *Cromwell*.[278] Its wide popularity was due to the belief of the Dissenters and Evangelicals that Carlyle was on their side.[279] Although he estranged the Catholics and some democrats like Mill by this book, his popularity grew. Humanitarians were offended still more by his defense of negro slavery in the *Latter Day Pamphlets*.[280] But all the critics could join in praising the *Life of Sterling,* partly because of the greater simplicity and straightforwardness of the style. Henceforth his reputation grew by accretion, and when *Frederick* appeared, William Allingham wrote to the Brownings: "In fact, the critics are simply huzzaing after him . . . the scoffers have disappeared."[281]

Carlyle was early and favorably mentioned in the *Athenaeum* in a leader on "The Foreign Reviews" in the first number of 1829. The Coleridgeans who then edited the journal were eager for the dissemination of knowledge of German literature and gave frequent attention to transla-

[277] Quoted in *ibid.,* p. 207.

[278] Wilson, *op. cit.,* p. 297. Wilson says elsewhere: "Mrs. Carlyle thought the English 'a singular people' to give the *Letters and Speeches* 'such a cordial reception,' while comparatively indifferent to 'a book so interesting as *Past and Present.'* " (*Ibid.,* p. 315.)   [279] Neff., *op. cit.,* p. 211.

[280] Carlyle wrote in his Journal, Feb. 7, 1850: "No. 1 [of the *Latter-Day Pamphlets*] came out a week ago; yields me a most confused response. Little save *abuse* hitherto, and the sale reported to be vigorous. . . . Among other very poor attacks on it was one in *Fraser* from John Mill." (Quoted in Wilson, *op. cit.,* IV, 249.) W. E. Forster wrote of the *Pamphlets:* "They have had an immense reading, but probably less effect than almost any of his writings." (*Ibid.,* p. 295.)   [281] Wilson, *op. cit.,* V, 326.

tions and periodical articles upon it. The first and best of these magazines, the *Athenaeum* critic thought, was the *Foreign Quarterly Review*.[282] But " 'The Foreign Review' has greater vivacity than its contemporary."[283]

The most lively, persevering, and able writer in this Review, is the translator of Wilhelm Meister, if we are not mistaken in attributing to that gentleman two articles, on Goethe, one on the life of Heyne; and one in the last Number, 'On German Playwrights.' The most obvious peculiarity in these articles, is their quaint and lively style, a style which, though it sometimes degenerates into what an intolerant critic might call affectation, seems on the whole, a very appropriate expression of the enthusiastic spirit of the writer, and possesses the power which more regular styles often do not possess, of communicating that spirit to the reader. But there are much greater merits than this doubtful one in Mr. Carlyle's articles. Putting his opinions out of the question (and though the colouring of these may be foreign, they are painted, as far as we can judge, upon a ground of good old English feeling), his articles contain unquestionably the most lively, and the most accurate picture of different phases of the German mind that has ever been presented to our countrymen.[284]

In July of the same year, in another notice of *The Foreign Review,* honorable mention was made of the essay on "Novalis," "which is evidently, we think, by the distinguished translator of 'Wilhelm Meister.' "[285]

Dilke and his reviewing circle continued to give much consideration to foreign literature, though they were un-

[282] Carlyle contributed to it after the demise of the *Foreign Review* in 1830. It was started in 1827 by the German publishers Treutel, Wurtz, Treutel, Jr., and Richter.

[283] Carlyle's "chief employer during the early years at Craigenputtock was the *Foreign Review,* published by the London importing booksellers Black, Young and Young to arouse an interest in their wares of Continental literature." (Neff, *op. cit.,* p. 101.) He contributed to every number but two during its short existence (1828-1830).

[284] *Athenaeum,* Jan. 7, 1829, p. 1. The *Athenaeum* was not mistaken in attributing to him the articles mentioned. [285] July 22, 1829, p. 456.

doubtedly as a whole less favorable to the Germans than had been Maurice's coterie. It is not altogether strange that no notice should have been taken of *Sartor Resartus* when it appeared in serial form in *Fraser's* in 1833-34. During his stay in London in 1831-32, Carlyle had met Dilke, had been kindly disposed towards him, and had even yielded to his request for something with his name attached for the *Athenaeum*.[286] Dilke, moreover, had seen the manuscript of *Sartor* while Carlyle was seeking a publisher for it.[287] What he thought of it we do not know, but he had absorbed in his youth enough of the eighteenth-century radical and rationalist ideas not to be carried away by the extremes of transcendentalism. He was trying to establish the reputation of a literary journal which aimed at intellectual balance and which hoped to live down the bias towards religious mysticism of its early editors. Mere personal kindness might have prompted the ignoring of so wild an effusion, which, appearing in a periodical, the *Athenaeum* was not obliged by its own policy to review.

After the first two installments of *Sartor* had been published, Allan Cunningham, a Scottish townsman of Carlyle, gave a single sentence to him in his "Biographical and Critical History of the Literature of the Last Fifty Years," but did not refer to the work then running in *Fraser's*.

Thomas Carlyle has added the German feeling of Criticism to that of his native land: his articles, amid much that is odd and startling, abound with flashes of natural fire, and show a spirit searching, profound, and philosophic.[288]

During all the months that *Sartor Resartus* was coming out Carlyle's name was not mentioned in the *Athenaeum*, though it was the regular custom to give brief comment on outstanding articles in other magazines through the "Weekly

[286] See *ante*, p. 322, n. 267.   [287] Wilson, *op. cit.*, II, 253.
[288] *Athenaeum*, Dec. 28, 1833, p. 893.

Gossip" column. The last of the series appeared in August, 1834, and still through the rest of the year the silence was maintained. But in the first number of 1835 the editors, speaking of *Fraser's* in the "Weekly Gossip," proclaimed: "Mr. Carlyle, (for there is no mistaking his cast of thought and expression,) [gives us] a most eloquent page upon the late Edward Irving."[289]

A single sentence of "Gossip" (December 12, 1835, p. 931) gave a favorable report of the American edition of *Sartor*. Commenting on the *North American Review* for October, the writer says: "Mr. Carlyle appears to be in the highway to Fame in America; his 'Sartor Resartus' having been collected and reprinted from *Fraser's Magazine;* it is here commented upon with many and deserved good words."

On March 25, 1837, the *Athenaeum* announced pleasantly: "We have heard that Mr. Carlyle is about to deliver a course of lectures on German Literature." But two months later came its blasting review of the *French Revolution*.

This review, which was without much doubt written by Lady Morgan,[290] has long been considered the acme of

[289] Jan. 3, 1835, p. 15.
[290] The internal and external evidence point conclusively enough to Lady Morgan. She was a close friend of Dilke and shared his views of practical reform. From 1833 to 1843 she was a regular *Athenaeum* contributor and reviewer of important books, particularly works on French history, politics, and manners. In 1834 she reviewed Henry Lytton Bulwer's *France, Social, Literary, and Political,* giving a passing tribute to her own book *France in 1829-30.* In 1840 she reviewed de Tocqueville's *Democracy in America* (Henry Reeve's translation) and volumes III and IV of Michelet's *Histoire de France.* The following year she wrote a critique of David W. Jobson's *History of the French Revolution Till the Death of Robespierre.* She was noted for her vanity which would never let her give quite whole-hearted praise to any work on France, Ireland, or Italy except her own. She was fond of foreign phrases which she repeated frequently in her reviews as in her books. In the notice of Bulwer's book she wrote: "If the *crambe repetita, et decies repetita, et centies repetita,* of Fashionable Novels, Methodist Tracts, and Diffusion Treatises, are tolerated and bought, there is no reason why there should not be a repetition of ideas about France, though all these things are well known now that Lady Morgan's book and the daily papers have brought the knowledge of that country down to date." In reviewing *Chartism*

stupidity among the contemporary judgments of Carlyle.[291]
The writer misinterpreted much of Carlyle's meaning and
failed to appreciate the literary excellence of the book because of its departure from the conventions of straightforward English style—a fault attributed to the vagaries of
German thought.

The extravagance of the purist objection to the supposed
affectations of language and style has, however, caused some
later critics to overlook the fact that the review contained a
few shrewd thrusts at the fundamental philosophy of the
work such as have frequently been reiterated since, though
usually in a less heated manner. It voiced the "common
sense" liberal-radical point of view which had its roots in
the eighteenth century rather than in the new German
philosophy; it had little patience with the attack on scepticism and lack of faith, and still less with the mistrust of
the democratic ideal.

"Originality of thought," the critic began, "is unquestionably the best excuse for writing a book; originality of
style is a rare and a refreshing merit; but it is paying rather
dear for one's whistle, to qualify for obtaining it in the
university of Bedlam. Originality, without justness of

---

she used the phrase again: ". . . these nostrums . . . [are] in truth, the very
crambe repetita of pamphlets, journals, and parliamentary speeches." And the
favorite phrase occurred in the review of the *French Revolution:* "There is,
moreover, in . . . [these volumes] the deadly *crambe repetita* of referring the
faults and the failures of the Revolution to the speculative opinions, or 'Philosophism' as the author calls it, of the eighteenth century." The general pertness of
phrase and liveliness of style as well as the ideas make a close parallel with the
reviews indicated as Lady Morgan's in the marked file.

[291] It is included in *Notorious Literary Attacks,* edited by Albert Mordell. It
is possible that Carlyle had this review in mind, but confused it with some
notice of *Sartor Resartus* in another periodical when he told Sir C. Gavan Duffy
in 1849 (*Conversations with Carlyle,* p. 90) that the "Bookseller's Taster" in the
Appendix to *Sartor* was genuine: "It was the verdict of one of Murray's critics;
Lockhart was believed to be the man. His opinion was altogether more favourable . . . than the writers of the *Athenaeum* and the like of them pronounced
on the book when it was at last published as a whole."

thought, is but novelty of error; and originality of style, without sound taste and discretion, is sheer affectation." We do not advocate a permanent Augustan Age, the critic says. "Language is a natural fluent; and to arrest its course is as undesirable as it is difficult." But there comes "an epoch of transition in which all monstrous and misshapen things are produced in the unguided search for an unknown and unimagined beauty." That is the present state of the literature of Germany and of *la jeune France,* the critic adds.

. . . but when an English writer is found to adopt the crudities and extravagancies of these nascent schools of thought, and to copy their mannerisms without rhyme, reason, taste, or selection, we can only set it down to an imperfection of intellect, to an incapacity for feeling, truth, and beauty, or to a hopeless determination to be singular, at any cost or sacrifice.

The applicability of these remarks to the History of the French Revolution now before us, will be understood by such of our readers as are familiar with Mr. Carlyle's contributions to our periodical literature. But it is one thing to put forth a few pages of quaintness, neologism, and a whimsical coxcombry; and another, to carry such questionable qualities through three long volumes of misplaced persiflage and flippant pseudo-philosophy . . . we must take occasion to protest against all and sundry attempts to engraft the idiom of Germany into the king's English, or to transfuse the vague verbiage and affected sentimentality of a sect of Germans into our simple and intelligible philosophy.[292]

What need have we anyhow for a new history of the French Revolution, the writer continued.[293] "We have looked carefully through these volumes; and, their peculiarity of style and the looseness of their reasoning apart, we have not found a fact in them that is not better told in Mignet, and twenty other unpretending historians." The

[292] *Athenaeum,* May 20, 1837, pp. 353-355.
[293] Compare with the statement concerning Bulwer's book in the review mentioned previously. See p. 328, n. 290.

author refers the faults and failures of the Revolution, the critic says, to the "philosophism" (scepticism) of the eighteenth century. "Now, faith and scepticism had nothing directly to do with, the affair; it was want, and misery, and oppression in the lower classes, utter corruption and incapacity in the higher, that made the revolt."[294]

The author is not without ability to see some truths clearly, the critic allowed, but he is inconsistent.

Thus while he attributes evils innumerable to infidelity and philosophism, and openly preaches passive obedience, religious and political, he does not the less wisely sum up the material causes of the revolt, . . . and of the multiplied errors committed both "within and without the walls of Troy." So, too, as to style, there are passages of great power, and occasionally of splendid, though impure eloquence.[295]

The reviewer quoted passages full of capitalized abstractions giving evidence of "downright jargon and no-meaning." But sometimes a dramatic description, "with all its mannerisms, its affected present tense, and its absurdities, is lively and pregnant." And in the author's remarks on the Girondins "there is much truth buried in mere jargon." So Mr. Carlyle goes on until he arrives at a "vague, unsatisfactory, childish 'most lame and impotent conclusion.'" And after quoting it, the critic asks, triumphantly: "Readers, have we made out our case?"[296]

Lady Morgan was still impatient with what she considered Carlyle's mannerisms and jargon when she reviewed *Chartism* in 1840, but her irritation was even greater with his propensity for uttering half-truths, with the disparity between his ability to catch "glimpses of important realities," and his "elaborate missing of the mark" when it came to suggestions for practical reform. We are told that some-

[294] *Athenaeum,* May 20, 1837, pp. 353-355.
[295] *Ibid.*   [296] *Ibid.*

thing should be done, but are offered nothing definite except education and emigration, nostrums which are not new, "being, in truth, the very *crambe repetita* of pamphlets, journals, and parliamentary speeches." Nor are we told how to find the "summities" of the nation who are to bring peaceful reform. "On arriving at the end of such a volume it is impossible not to exclaim—'In the name of the prophet—figs.' "

Still, with all these formidable drawbacks we are far from thinking the work wholly deficient in pith or utility. If Mr. Carlyle be not a cogent logician, his thoughts are sufficiently suggestive. Like Hotspur, he apprehends a world of figures. Through the rolling vapours of his Platonic atmosphere, he catches glimpses of important realities; and if he fails to grapple with them effectually, and to bring out their conclusions legitimately and clearly, he still reflects their images with sufficient vigor and freshness of colouring, to arouse other persons to think of them to a better purpose.[297]

The chapter on laissez faire "is pregnant with thick-coming suggestions." But there is a deep fallacy, the reviewer says, in his argument for aristocracy.

He teaches that the one thing needful is, that the aristocracy of the land (meaning, we suppose, its true aristocracy, that of virtue and of intelligence) should combine to guide and govern the working classes, who are incapable of guiding and governing themselves; and he appears to consider all debates on franchises, and the machinery of government, as little better than lost labour. . . . But the whole experience of the world unites in proving that exclusive aristocracies will always govern for exclusive interests. . . . If the uneducated are forever to be excluded from voting for members of parliament, we are in a vicious circle. . . . The educated are the few, and the few will take care to exclude the many in perpetuity. The masses must have a share in government, even in order that their intellectual necessities may be pro-

[297] Jan. 11, 1840, pp. 27-29.

vided for. Vicarious government has been tried for six thousand years, and been found wanting. The theory of self-government is not therefore to be fillipped off with a sarcasm or a sneer.[298]

Such a bold championing of popular government was not very different from its later defense by men like Mill and Sir Charles Dilke. Lady Morgan summed up Carlyle's conclusions, which were too much hidden under "an accumulation of words," and suggested finally that the work was worth reading by all who were honestly interested in the condition of England and able to think for themselves.

The impatience of the practical reformer is evident again in her review of *Past and Present* three years later. "It is the besetting sin of Mr. Carlyle to imagine himself in advance of his age, when he is only disguising its most familiar thoughts under a quaint phraseology, which obscures their import and drift." *Chartism* added nothing to the knowledge of the public; the same is true of this book which repeats the ideas of the earlier one.

There is a like repudiation of statistics, political economy, of all investigations tending to appreciate and define; a like substitution of picture writing for analysis; a like affection for metaphysical generalities; a like intense and challenging opening, followed by the same lame and impotent conclusion.

Coinciding, for the most part, with Mr. Carlyle, in his view of the political and economic position and prospects of the country, we are not often directly opposed to his detached opinions, as far as he succeeds in giving them intelligible utterance; yet we contend that in his hands they lead to nothing. . . .

It is therefore with pain and vexation we witness our premises turned to no better conclusion; and find ourselves compelled to censure defects in a writer, whose aim is the same as our own, and of whose mind, in despite of all its oddities and whims, we must still think with respect.[299]

[298] *Ibid.*   [299] May 13, 1843, pp. 453-454.

Whatever its opinion might be, the *Athenaeum* could no longer ignore Carlyle. Lady Morgan returned to a second notice, giving specimens of his "plain truths" and his "partial truths," and concluding that he was too impractical in his demand for reform of each individual. Mankind is the product of its antecedents, she said. What we need is step by step of practical reform.[300]

Oliver Cromwell's Letters and Speeches fell to Abraham Heraud, a disciple and imitator of Carlyle.[301] His review of the first edition ran into three long notices in successive numbers, and the verdict was almost wholly favorable, though he could not refrain from making some comment on the "perverse eccentricities of the author's style." It is "a worthy and manly book," which attempts to furnish evidence to justify his "hero-worship" of Cromwell. But Carlyle concludes that we must not finally rest our faith *in* Cromwell, but look *beyond* him, Heraud adds—we must not rest in the Past, for "The Future is possible." The reviewer observes approvingly that the author believes there is human progress, social as well as individual. Heraud praised Carlyle's work in editing. The manner in which he set the letters against the background of events "now makes them lustrous with meaning," and "popularly readable as dramatic presentations of a character able and worthy to sway the destinies of an empire." There is one fault, however, which stands in the way of dramatic truth, Heraud continues—a want of antagonism. We see Cromwell but no one else. Carlyle sums up contemptuously the speeches of parliament leaders, and gives Cromwell's in detail. The documentary evidence is therefore "one-sided and *ex parte*."[301a] In the final notice Heraud summed up the qualities of the book and expressed the opinion that "Mr. Carlyle has, in these two elaborate volumes, with all their faults of bad taste and

[300] May 20, 1843, pp. 480-481.   [301] See *ante*, pp. 214-215.
[301a] *Athenaeum*, Dec. 6, 1845, pp. 1165-1167.

exaggerated diction, raised a monument to public merit which cannot fail to insure to it perpetual and grateful remembrance, and prevent the memory of his hero from being again maligned in general history."[302]

Hepworth Dixon, who reviewed all but one of the *Latter Day Pamphlets* for the *Athenaeum,* saw, in most matters of practical reform, eye to eye with his friend Lady Morgan. It is not surprising that he handled the *Pamphlets* rather roughly. In the first one he observed "several pages of the old 'cant about cant'; and some scores of lusty warnings to all the tribes of *shams* to get themselves removed out of the way—done decently to death, and so an end." And there are the familiar capitalized abstractions such as "the Immortal Gods" and "the Immensities." "Of a truth, this style begins to lose its power of conjuration."

Dixon, like Lady Morgan, accepted the challenge of Carlyle's attack on democracy.

We all desire to see the wisest in the seat of power. The only real question is—how is the wisest to get into that seat? Two modes have been commonly resorted to:—Scrambling and Election. In the first method, the strong, the crafty, and the unscrupulous have usually won the seat. The other plan, in which the people quietly choose out the man they most approve, Mr. Carlyle denounces as absurd. How are the ignoble to choose the noble? He is evidently in favour of the first, thinking that thereby the true King will find his place. . . . He confesses that the true King is not a man to *seek* power. How, then, is he to come by it in a scramble? . . .

We cannot deal seriously—and are almost ashamed to deal at all—with a book like this.[303]

[302] Dec. 20, 1845, pp. 1218-1219. The second notice, Dec. 13, 1845, pp. 1193-1195, consisted mostly of a summary of Cromwell's life and character as given by Carlyle. See also the review of the Supplement to the First Edition, *Athenaeum,* June 20, 1846, pp. 623-624.

[303] *Athenaeum,* Feb. 2, 1850, pp. 126-127.

It was to be expected that Hervey, who had led the fight in the *Athenaeum* during the forties for prison reform, should have read with righteous indignation the pamphlet on *Model Prisons*.

> Mr. Carlyle has exhibited a larger dose, we hope, than the digestion of his disciples can master. . . . Model prisons and schools for the criminal are to him an abomination. 'Pity for the scoundrel species' raises his bile, and occasions him to call very bad names. His soul yearns after the condemned tread-wheel, and he has great faith in the management of prisoners by half starvation. He will have no moral hospitals—no attempts at redeeming the sinner. The 'woman taken in adultery' he would 'stone to death.'[304]

After quoting a few sentences, the critic concludes: "Surely all this is little better than raving."

Dixon read Carlyle a lecture on popular preferences in reviewing *Hudson's Statue*. He denied that "either the morals or the History of a nation can be read in the absolute sense which Mr. Carlyle affirms by the monuments erected in its market-places." Neither in the selection of the hero nor in the "sculptured ugliness" have the people any voice. If the author would take the matter to the people for once, "the result might be, that Cromwell would obtain a statue and Mr. Carlyle abandon one of his dogmas."[305] As a prophet of progress Dixon was thankful for the ending of the series of *Latter-Day Pamphlets*. If it were possible to answer Carlyle seriously, the reviewer might point out that bad as the world is now, it was worse before. "The true golden age is in the future."[306]

Though he had a small opinion of Sterling, "a recently deceased dreamer of dreams and inditer of failures!" Dixon

[304] *Athenaeum*, March 2, 1850, pp. 227-228.
[305] *Athenaeum*, July 6, 1850, pp. 704-705.
[306] *Athenaeum*, Aug. 24, 1850, pp. 894-895.

could not withhold his admiration for Carlyle's unaffected biography.

Since the 'Life of Schiller,' which this performance often calls to mind, we remember nothing from the author's pen so free from rant, eccentricity, and extravagance. His earnestness makes his manner at times simple, beautiful and pathetic. . . . Our old opinion that Mr. Carlyle's turgid style was the growth of an affectation, is confirmed by the very simplicity of his new volume . . . so far as it contains . . . [his] commentary on men and things as they exist around us in the present world of letters—a world so calm compared with that stormy arena in which his voice is usually heard—it has many merits, and will be likely to find an eager and a gratified audience.[307]

It was as a painter and a colorist of history rather than a profound man of ideas that the *Athenaeum* praised Carlyle for his work on *Frederick*. But mingled with the plaudits were a few gibes yet at his "outlandish speech." Of volumes I and II Blackburn said:

The great feature of this history is its political and judicial tone, —the light which it sheds on courts, kings, governments, religions —on Austrian, Prussian, and English intrigues . . . but our experience of two-thirds of the first volume is, that it is an historical world, 'whose margin fades for ever and forever', as we read.[308]

With even more enthusiasm for the narrative which "rushes grandly and swiftly on," St. John was troubled too by "the old Carlyle mannerism."

. . . there are moralizings grotesquely phrased, scatterings of a quaint sort of gipsy idiom invented by the historian for his own use, extravaganzas of invective, and complications of epithets enough to bewilder a Chinese; but the story, in the main, is superbly told, and contains so much life, is marked by so much

[307] *Athenaeum,* Oct. 18, 1851, pp. 1088-1090.
[308] Sept. 18, 1858, II, pp. 351-354. Second notice, Sept. 25, 1858, II, pp. 388-390.

emphasis, and flows on so abundantly and brilliantly, that there is a fascination even in the bubbles and the fantastic drift which are swept along with it, and follow its exulting course.[309]

Dr. John Doran was content to let Carlyle have his way, though not without protest against the peculiarities of the style, when the result was such a work as the picturesque history of Frederick, the last three volumes of which he reviewed. "His research, his judgment, his peculiar powers, his comprehensiveness, his grandeur and his 'burlesque' of history were never more conspicuous than in this portion of the work." But the final verdict was that "Mr. Carlyle's hero-worship approaches a little to fanaticism when he deals with Frederick."[310]

The *Athenaeum* view of Carlyle under the new liberal regime of MacColl was expressed by Edmund Gosse, who wrote a leader on the *Early Kings of Norway* and the *Portraits of John Knox*. One may wonder, he said, what caused Carlyle to "scrutinize with such loving care the more or less brutal deeds of hard-headed Norwegian monarchs of eight centuries ago." The answer is "that they gave to the most determined opponent of modern liberalism a splendid opportunity of depicting a state of things when the many were ruled by one, and when brain and muscle combined in the person of a single man of men were enough to awe a rude population into order." It is not surprising then to find the book "a fantastic, but ingenious and eloquent defence of the tyranny, healthy in that age, but, most unprophetic souls will think, unsuited to our own, which was in the long run the ruin, though at first the glory of Norway."[311]

[309] Review of Vol. III, *Athenaeum*, May 3, 1862, I, pp. 585-588. This is probably Horace St. John, son of the explorer and miscellaneous writer J. A. St. John. He reviewed foreign works for the *Athenaeum* for a number of years after the death of John Chorley.

[310] Vol. IV, *Athenaeum*, March 12, 1864, I, pp. 369-371. Vols. V and VI, March 25, 1865, I, pp. 413-414.   [311] April 10, 1875, I, pp. 481-482.

The obituary notice by H. R. Fox-Bourne was a keen analysis of Carlyle's character and position in the history of thought and literature. "Whatever his immediate topic, one central thought ran through all his life and prompted all his work." He was a "transcendental Puritan."

Carlyle's isolation was savage in appearance rather than in reality, and even his isolation itself was only half real. . . . He could not stand apart from the world which he loved while he thought that he was hating it. . . . Defiance and Reverence were the two forces, working against one another, yet with a common purpose, in Carlyle's mind and inspiring all his work. . . . His style, even when most extravagant, was not an affectation, but a reality. He wrote in eccentric ways only because he thought in eccentric ways; and his greatest eccentricities can be traced directly from the central idea of life and duty. . . .[312] In picturesque writing when at his best he is almost without a rival. . . .

Of science, both physical and metaphysical, he was never tired of speaking contemptuously . . . his own notion that knowledge is an inspiration, not a thing that can be acquired, not only led him into errors, but has encouraged men less wise to lose themselves in mazes from which he himself managed to escape.[313]

If the total picture of Carlyle in the *Athenaeum* was not a very favorable one, the reason was that the most readily understandable purport of his writing went counter to the main stream of Victorian culture. That magazine expressed the average intellectual reactions of a period which desired above all else, not to repudiate science and material progress, but to make them the legitimate heirs of the older roman-

[312] The idea that Carlyle's style was natural to him was not often granted by periodical critics. Later T. H. Huxley wrote: "If he is chargeable with affectation at all (and I do not think he is) it is rather when he writes the classical English. . . . As anyone who ever heard Carlyle talk knows, the style natural to him was that of *The Diamond Necklace*." ("Professor Tyndall," by T. H. Huxley, *Nineteenth Century*, Jan., 1894, p. 4.) Carlyle had once dreamed that he wrote the "approved commonplace style," but the knack was wanting. (Wilson, *op. cit.*, IV, 95.)

[313] *Athenaeum*, Feb. 12, 1881, I, pp. 232-235.

ticism. The stylistic and linguistic conservatism of the *Athenaeum* made it the less sympathetic to a writer who took such liberties with "classical English."

Ruskin

Ruskin was seldom mildly received by the critics. He was greeted either with enthusiasm or with ridicule, bitterness, abuse. There was perhaps more of the latter than of the former in the periodical criticism of the first volume of *Modern Painters*. Ruskin's biographer says that "while the book contained something that promised to suit every kind of reader, every one found something to shock him."[314] The critics, however, were not mainly recruited from the professors of art and the connoisseurs—from those who had a lingering fondness for the "grand style" and "the ideal" as propounded in the famous *Discourses* of Sir Joshua Reynolds.[315]

But still the critics lagged behind the popular taste,[316] which Ruskin, when he was better understood, particularly after he was known to be the defender of nature and realism against the formalism and classical restraint of the older schools, led and guided more than any other man of his

[314] W. G. Collingwood, *The Life and Work of John Ruskin*, I, 133.

[315] The differences between eighteenth- and nineteenth-century criticism of art are admirably set forth in the introductory chapters of Henry Ladd's *The Victorian Morality of Art*.

[316] Ladd says (*op. cit.*, p. 40): ". . . by 1840 criticism was out of line with the facts of popular taste." Critics of the established reviews "led arduous lives trying to apply established principles to new poetry, fiction, architecture and painting. The dissemination of an interest in nature illustration clashed with the principles of the grand style; archaeology upset the historical prejudices of the academies; publishers, assured of the rapid growth of the reading public, encouraged unknown authors. There were a large number of people ready to listen to any message that could sanction the successful progress of new enterprise and reinterpret the cultural hopes of a new age." The literary turn to nature, Ladd continues, explains more than half of Ruskin's early popularity. "The serious, almost religious regard for landscape which swept over England and America before 1850 was by no means the superimposed preference of an aristocratic society; it was indigenous to a new industrial, pious and ambitious bourgeoisie." (*Op. cit.*, p. 49.)

day. When the second edition, which in itself indicated a rapidly growing popularity, came out in 1844, Sydney Smith mentioned it in public, in the presence of "distinguished literary characters," as a work of "transcendent talent, presenting the most original views in the most elegant and powerful language, which would work a complete revolution in the world of taste."[317]   Ruskin himself said later: "The press notices of my second volume had been either cautious or complimentary—none, to the best of my memory, contemptuous."[318]

Henceforth his reputation increased rapidly with the public if not with the connoisseurs, who, when they wrote for the popular journals, were constrained at least to praise his eloquence and his colorful style while deprecating his theories.   What his work meant to a great many earnest Victorians who were not professional art critics is perhaps best expressed by Charlotte Brontë in a letter to Ruskin's publishers just before she had seen the *Seven Lamps*.

Hitherto I have only had instinct to guide me in judging of art; I feel now as if I had been walking blindfold—this book [*Modern Painters*] seems to give me new eyes. . . .

I like the author's style much; there is both energy and beauty in it. I like himself, too, because he is such a hearty admirer. He does not give half-measure of praise or veneration. He eulogizes, he reverences, with his whole soul.[319]

The *Seven Lamps of Architecture* was one of Ruskin's most widely read books, for it possessed just the right combination of piety of tone and affirmation and certainty in the expression of tenets that justified the tastes of those who wished to see "soul" rather than "senses" in the faithful

---

[317] Collingwood, *op. cit.*, I, 151.

[318] *The Works of John Ruskin*, Vol. XXXV (*Praeterita*), p. 421.   Ruskin had either forgotten or ignored the review in the *Athenaeum*.

[319] Quoted, Collingwood, *op. cit.*, I, 162-163.

representation of natural objects.[320]   The critics, except the
intransigent professionals, followed in the wake of the popular acclaim.   Ruskin's father wrote: "In *British Quarterly,*
under Aesthetics of Gothic architecture, they take four
works, you first. . . . As a critic they almost rank you with
Goethe and Coleridge, and in style with Jeremy Taylor."[321]
"Reviews in the daily and weekly press were prompt and
numerous, and for the most part long and complimentary.
The monthly and quarterly magazines were equally appreciative of the book."[322]

The Stones of Venice made Ruskin the acknowledged
leader of the change in taste which critics could no longer
ignore.   "Some of his reviewers mixed something of bitter;
but with the majority the praise was undiluted."[323]   "The
Times, which had not hitherto noticed any of Ruskin's
books, and which indeed in those days allotted very little
space to literature, now gave marked and unusual prominence to *The Stones of Venice.* Two long reviews were
devoted to the second volume, and another of yet greater
length to the third."[324]   Ruskin thought the last "incom-
parably the best critique I ever had."[325]

[320] See Ladd, *op. cit.,* pp. 58-59: "The early theories tend over and over
again to throw Ruskin's emphasis on the side of objective truth instead of subjective inspiration in art, though it is obvious that there were other forces pulling
him in an opposite direction. Fact or material substance, rather than ideal essence,
is his characteristic standard. Seeing true is for him the *sine qua non* of fine
art." Ladd continues: "The most dramatic thing about the growth of Ruskin's
theory is the ever recurring emphasis now on the ideal, now on the realistic aspect
of artistic truth." But "he was clearly an idealist at heart." (*Ibid.,* pp. 71-72.) "Yet
he continued to pile emotional preferences on top of his doctrine of truth. . . .
Qualifications of his first principle are to be explained by the fact that Ruskin
was psychologically incapable of looking at all natural truths as they are seen
today represented in literature and painting. He could not face literally the implications of unrestricted naturalism. He wanted to keep his faith in 'characteristic
truth' unconditional; but he is crippled not only by his temperament, but by the
prevailing views of the period." (*Ibid.,* pp. 77-78.)
[321] E. T. Cook, *The Life of John Ruskin,* I, p. 235.
[322] *Ibid.*   [323] *Ibid.,* p. 295.
[324] *Ibid.,* p. 299.   [325] *Ibid.*

The last volume of *Modern Painters* brought forth a "chorus of congratulation." But the tide turned with the serial publication of *Unto This Last* in the *Cornhill Magazine* in 1860. The criticism became acrimonious and bitter. The critic of art had attacked the current theories of political economy at a time when a chastened utilitarianism, with the thorn of materialism extracted, had all but won its way among the adherents of progress. The *Literary Gazette* found the new work "one of the most melancholy spectacles, intellectually speaking, that we have ever witnessed."[326] The *Saturday Review* couldn't find enough epithets of opprobium—"eruptions of windy hysterics," "absolute nonsense," "utter imbecility," "intolerable twaddle." The author was "a perfect paragon of blubbering," his "whines and snivels" were contemptible; the world was not going to be "preached to death by a mad governess."[327] This was representative of much of the criticism, in both magazines and newspapers, not only of *Unto This Last,* but also of *Munera Pulveris,* which Froude was bold enough to publish in *Fraser's* in 1863, and of most of his writings on political economy. Eventually he had his following, but it was not mainly among writers for the critical journals.

The comparatively innocuous *Sesame and Lilies* and the penetratingly satiric *Crown of Wild Olive* brought him a popularity which was reflected in the somewhat greater indulgence of criticism from 1870 onwards. The deference which the English, according to Mr. Maugham,[328] pay to simple longevity, may sufficiently account for the critical leniency towards the eccentricities of Ruskin's later years. The subject of Ruskin's reception in the *Athenaeum* in-

[326] Cook, *op. cit.,* II, 6.   [327] *Ibid.*

[328] See Somerset Maugham, *Cakes and Ale,* pp. 141-143. Of course, Ruskin's authority as an art critic and exponent of the then generally accepted Victorian moral interpretation of art gained him the respect of many who detested or ridiculed or merely excused his social and economic views.

volves so many complexities—the personal predilections of its art critics, the artistic tastes of the time, and finally its social, political and economic points of view—that it properly should be discussed under another heading than that of the literary criticism of contemporaries. But an examination of the reviews of his books in its pages may help to round out the conception of its character as a literary journal reflecting a seemingly varied but ultimately consistent stream of opinion. The seriousness with which the *Athenaeum* regarded its task as guardian and director of the tastes, literary and artistic, of the middle class, together with its policy of having experts and connoisseurs to do the reviewing in specialized fields, particularly art and science, militated against a favorable reception of Ruskin's early work in that journal.

George Darley, who was foreign correspondent and art critic for the *Athenaeum* from 1834 until his death in 1846, was least likely of anyone on the staff to welcome the heresies of *Modern Painters* against the traditions of the "grand style" and the "ideal" as they were in his eyes rightly to be seen in the *Discourses* of Reynolds, whom he had defended against Hazlitt's attack in 1838.[329] In his opposition to Reynolds, Hazlitt anticipated Ruskin in some degree, opposing "his romantic 'gusto' to the classical 'restraint.' "[330] Starting from the belief that the Elgin Marbles "have every appearance of absolute *facsimiles* or casts taken from nature" and are excellent because of their direct or immediate imitation of natural details, Hazlitt boldly undertook to refute the reigning dogma of Reynolds that "the grand style in

[329] See the reviews of "Painting and the Fine Arts," by B. R. Haydon and W. Hazlitt, *Athenaeum*, July 14, 21, 28, 1838, pp. 482-484, 510-512, 526-528. Though these reviews are in one of the unmarked volumes in the editorial files, Abbott, Darley's biographer, has identified them from information supplied by Miss Evelyn Darley.

[330] C. Colleer Abbott, *The Life and Letters of George Darley*, p. 161.

art, and the most perfect imitation of Nature, consists in avoiding the details and peculiarities of particular objects."[331]

Darley showed that Hazlitt "misinterpreted Reynolds and gave an erroneous view of the *Discourses.*"[332] The low state of English art Darley believed to be due partly to the unintelligent middle-class patronage and partly to lack of proper education on the part of artists, who were deficient in design, neglect of which was Sir Joshua's great defect. But "let English painters be assured they cannot find anywhere, in the same compass, a solider 'globe of precepts' on their art, than Reynolds's treatise, nor an emptier bubble than Hazlitt's."[333]

Darley had a high regard for the art criticism of Lessing, Goethe, and Tieck, particularly for the *Laocoön,* in which "the purest, loftiest principles of art are sought out and set forth."[334] Darley's biographer says: "Broadly speaking, the qualities that he desires in art are spiritual, not realistic. By revealing the virtues of the old masters to his countrymen he wishes to startle a Philistine generation out of a stubbornly complacent regard for such realistic painters as Teniers and Gerard Dou. . . . It was his distinction to rediscover, before Ruskin and the Pre-Raphaelites, the painters of the early Italian schools."[335]

Basically, perhaps, Darley did not differ so much from Ruskin in principles as in temperament, training, and literary approach. But the severest criticism sometimes comes from disciples of the same school when they think one of their number has perverted or badly presented their doctrine. Darley (like Ruskin) "distrusts the scientific tendency of

[331] *Ibid.,* p. 160.
[332] *Ibid.,* p. 162. In this brief summary of Darley's general point of view as an art critic I have paraphrased and used freely the information in Abbott's seventh chapter.   [333] *Ibid.,* p. 163.
[334] *Ibid.* The quotation is from a review, written by Darley, of W. Ross's translation of the *Laocoön, Athenaeum,* Oct. 8, 1836, pp. 713-715.
[335] Abbott, *op. cit.,* p. 164.

the age, and scourges its Philistine materialism. He believes in a hierarchy of schools and painters and subjects, emphasizing the supreme importance of spiritual values in a picture, attempting to reach the soul behind it. Thence springs his enthusiasm for the early masters, and that dangerous subjective habit, shared by Ruskin, of 'reading into' a picture abstract qualities. There is little difference, in the main, between his idea of the aim, scope, and value of art, and Ruskin's. Either of them might have written, 'painting or art, generally, as such, . . . is nothing but a noble and expressive language, invaluable as the vehicle of thoughts, but by itself nothing.' "[336]

But while Darley used some of the moral phraseology of the time, he had not the Evangelical background of Ruskin; his "high seriousness" was Greek rather than Hebraic, in Matthew Arnold's sense. "He holds that the education of public taste lies, as it has always lain, with a body of apostles whom he calls 'amateurs,' the 'Athenian people in the Republic of Art.' "[337] The fault of the age was not lack of faith but lack of proportion which must be the guide to taste. "Middle-class taste admired crudity and colour, and from its patronage resulted trivialities and 'low' subjects."[338]

At first glance it may seem that Darley's contempt for middle-class preferences went counter to the main current of *Athenaeum* criticism, but his desire to educate that class and refine its tastes was in the full tradition of the journal. This will be seen in his reviews of Ruskin.

The *Athenaeum* attitude towards Turner had already been expressed in a way little to Ruskin's liking in a review of the Royal Academy Exhibition in May, 1842.[339] In fact

[336] *Ibid.*, p. 190. [337] *Ibid.*, p. 171.

[338] *Ibid.*, p. 167. It must be remembered that Turner's appeal to Ruskin as well as to untutored admirers was based largely on the vividness of his colors, which were defended in *Modern Painters* as being more "natural" than the dull or subdued tones of Claude and other landscapists.

[339] May 7 and 14, 1842, pp. 409, 433. Abbott says it is unlikely that Darley

it is possible that this review was the immediate cause for the writing of *Modern Painters*. Cook says: "The . . . impulse was the same as in the case of the Essay of 1836;[340] for at Geneva a review of the Royal Academy's Exhibition of 1842, ridiculing Turner's pictures of the year, reached him. He had seen the pictures before leaving England and had admired them. . . . The review was probably that in the *Literary Gazette* or the *Athenaeum,* both of which papers W. H. Harrison was in the habit of sending to Ruskin or his father."[341]

The *Athenaeum* critic found two of the five pictures exhibited by Turner "among the loveliest, because least exaggerated . . . which this magician . . . has recently given us," and he nearly went into rhapsodies over them (*The Dogana, Venice,* and the *Campo Santo*).[342] But the other three he ridiculed with a lashing tongue. "This gentleman has on former occasions chosen to paint with cream, or chocolate, yolk of egg, or currant jelly,—here he uses his

wrote this review of the Academy Exhibition. The reviewer is not indicated in the marked file, but in the number following (May 21, 1842, pp. 455-458) Hervey is given as the author of the Royal Academy article. "Darley, rarely, if ever, wrote notes on the Royal Academy, or indeed, on any exhibitions of contemporary pictures." (Abbott, *op. cit.,* p. 188.)   But on the other hand, "The writing often resembles Darley's, and he later refers to part of the review in such a way as to suggest that he agreed with it." (*Ibid.,* p. 189, n.)   Darley expressed himself as strongly concerning sensational use of color in speaking of "the painter who bedaubs his canvas like the cheek of a demirep, and makes his picture a salad of anemones and butterfly-wings to please the sensual taste of a luxurious people." (*Ibid.,* p. 168.)   But the final evidence given by Abbott is a reference which the reviewer of the Academy notes made in a footnote to a portrait by Kaulbach which "might be seen at Munich in that artist's studio last autumn. A finer modern portrait does not exist." Abbott adds: "Darley was not in Munich at that time." (*Ibid.,* p. 189, n.)

[340] An article in *Blackwood's,* in 1836, criticising Turner greatly incensed Ruskin, then 17, and he wrote a reply which he sent to Turner. It wasn't published, but the painter sent it on to the purchaser of his *Juliet.* It is interesting to note that *Blackwood's* and the *Athenaeum* were the most severe in their criticism of Ruskin, but *Blackwood's* was less fair and more relentless. It made the fifth volume of *Modern Painters* the occasion for a personal attack on the author, whereas by that time (1860) the *Anthenaeum* had become much more favorable.

[341] Cook, *op. cit.,* I, 127.   [342] May 7, 1842, p. 409.

whole array of kitchen stuff. . . . We cannot . . . believe in
any future revolution, which shall bring the world round to
the opinion of the worshipper, if worshipper such frenzies
still possess."[343]

Ruskin, roused by these gibes at his favorite, went on to
Chamouni, hoping to write a reply in a pamphlet. But the
pamphlet grew into a book (the first volume of *Modern
Painters*) which was published the following year and reviewed in the *Athenaeum* in February, 1844. Darley thought
the volume important enough to deserve two notices, though
it had "too much parade of logic and too little real power.
Yet it is a clever book—neither less nor more. It exhibits
what may recommend it to many readers, some characteristics of Hazlitt's style—boldness and brilliancy, bigotry
amidst liberality, and great acuteness amid still greater
blindness." In criticism the author is a very freshman;
"sanguine and self-confident, he would cut the Gordian knot
with a bulrush. . . ." Full of professional prejudices, and
pet systems, his chief concern seems to be, not to show that
the moderns surpass the ancients, but that the ancients are
"all but *utterly contemptible.*" On the other hand, he pictures Turner as "supreme Art personified, the God of Landscape-painting incarnate!" His praise of that artist is "just
not blasphemous because it is crackbrained." He is like "a
Whirling Dervish, who at the end of his well-sustained reel
falls, with a higher jump and a shriller shriek, into a fit."[344]

If the author had not been so eager for overstatement
he might have made out a case, Darley thought.

. . . it has always been our opinion, that but few *landscapes* by
the ancient masters deserve to rank among first-rate productions
of art . . . even Claude's performances have often left little deeper

---

[343] May 14, 1842, p. 433. For an account of earlier criticism of Turner in the
Athenaeum, see *ante*, pp. 174, 180.

[344] Feb. 3, 1844, pp. 105-107. Abbott is authority for the statement that
Darley wrote this review which occurs in a volume unmarked in the editorial file.

impressions upon us than so many glass-windows. . . . Had our author been content to reduce popular reverence on this subject within just bounds, we should have approved his efforts, but when he pronounces Claude, Salvator, and Poussin 'contemptible,' . . . it only proves his language stronger than his judgment.[345]

In the second notice Darley pointed to the specious persuasiveness of the argument as evidence that the author could if he changed sides cry down Turner and praise Claude with equal eloquence. The Oxford Graduate declares that "the most erratic genius among all Modern Painters exhibits in his works a consolidated fund of perfections without the shadow of a single fault! Monomania could scarce go much farther. . . . Nevertheless, as we said at first, the book before us contains a great deal of cleverness and a good deal of truth, even amidst its manifold inconsistencies."[346]

And then the critic glanced at the artistic principles of the author.

We apprehend the Oxford Graduate, despite his enormous apparatus of axioms, postulates, lemmas, categories, divisions, and subdivisions, has omitted the true principles of landscape-painting. . . . He seems to think landscapes should be, throughout their details, little facsimiles of real objects, and that no other merit surpasses minute faithfulness. . . . He professes, indeed, a noble disdain of servile imitation in art, but half his book is a ding-dong against the Ancient Masters on its sole account.[347]

Darley concluded, as did so many other critics after him, that the author's forte was fine writing rather than sound reasoning, and he quoted the passage beginning: "It had been wild weather when I left Rome, and all across the Campagna. . . ."

In the preface to the second edition of the book pub-

[345] *Ibid.*
[346] Feb. 10, 1844, pp. 132-133. [347] *Ibid.*

lished in 1844 Ruskin took some space to defend the principle of faithfulness to nature against Darley's criticism.[348]

It is just as impossible to generalize granite and slate as it is to generalize a man and a cow. . . . If there were a creature in the foreground of a picture of which he could not decide whether it were a pony or a pig, the *Athenaeum* critic would perhaps affirm it to be a generalization of pony and pig, and consequently a high example of 'harmonious union and simple effect.' But *I* should call it simple bad drawing. . . . I repeat then, generalization . . . is the act of a vulgar, incapable and unthinking mind.[349]

Although Darley regretted the extravagance of language resulting from Ruskin's unbalanced enthusiasms and prejudices, he found more merit on the whole in the second volume of *Modern Painters.* "We never excepted against our author's 'controversial tone,' but against the *tone* of that tone. . . . It is neither Mr. Graduate's mill-hammer, nor his sulphuric acid we object to, but his brickbat and his kennel-water. . . . Our professor of pious veneration for genius, bawls out 'the *corrupted* Raffael.' . . . How does he reconcile such eructations of idle wind, such levities and rashnesses . . . with the lecture he reads 'this present age of ours . . . its mean and shallow love of jest and jeer'[?]"

[348] In the same preface Ruskin replied to the criticism of *Blackwood's.* Cook says (*op. cit.,* I, 150): "Ruskin, as he read such attacks, was eager for the fray. His father, on the other hand, was distressed by them, and like a cautious and prudent man of business, was doubtful of the expediency of controversy. At an early period he tried to screen his son from the sight of adverse criticisms; now the parts were reversed. 'We had seen the *Athenaeum* before' writes Ruskin to W. H. Harrison. 'I do not forward it to my father, simply because the later he is in seeing it, the less time he will have to fret himself about what is to come *next* week. . . . I believe you know pretty well how much *I* care for such matters.' He cared for them only as blows to be returned."

[349] Quoted, Abbott, *op. cit.,* p. 195. Darley had written: "We disapprove of the 'natural style' in painting, not because we dislike Nature, but because we adore her; she is so far above any imitation of her, that the very best disappoints us and dissatisfies. Ancient landscapists took a broader, deeper, higher view of their art: they neglected particular traits, and gave only general features: thus they attained mass, and force, harmonious union, and simple effect, the elements of grandeur and beauty." (*Athenaeum,* Feb. 10, 1844, pp. 132-133.)

As for rashness, the Graduate "seems a very Hotspur, beyond self and all extrinsic control. . . . He begins his book . . . with a contrite avowal of over-hastiness, and he ends it with a recantation of his former creed about Mr. Turner's infallible paintership:—yet from first paragraph almost to last he plunges headlong through a new series of frying-pans and fires." His side-sight is no better than his foresight— he fails to see collateral facts. This leads to inconsistencies and nonsensical statements. He declares, for example, that we can see beauty in all of God's doing, but the one-sidedness of flatfish is *disagreeable.*

And still—and still—nothwithstanding what we have said, and left unsaid, about the faults and follies committed almost every page, almost every paragraph—the book before us deserves perusal, deserves praise. Never did we see such acuteness and confusedness of mind—such power and impotence—such trains of error and of truest deduction—such pure taste and perverted judgment—such high and low feeling for Art—we must add, such an elevated and vulgarian spirit of criticism—evinced in any treatise pretending to legislate upon Aesthetics. . . .

In conclusion, let us recommend to those of our readers who love a little intellectual agitation, this very perturbative volume. Its bewildered and bewildering eloquence is at worst like a mountain-squall upon a stagnant lake, which though it tosses up weeds from the surface and slime from the bottom, gives insight into the depths, and causes a multitudinous sparkle over the waves beneath its changeful wing . . . our long critique proves we part with Mr. Oxford Graduate unwillingly.[350]

Digby Wyatt tried to take the professional architect's point of view in criticising the *Seven Lamps,* but he scarcely got to the core of Ruskin's meaning. It is "a book of the moment; almost the sole merit of which consists in its general idea of endeavoring to supply a want the true character of which can be estimated only after an exact apprehension

[350] *Athenaeum,* July 25, 1846, pp. 765-767.

of the present condition of the study which it seeks to illuminate . . . of a truth, it must be confessed that the performance has by no means equalled the profession."

The author is clever and brilliant, "but his 'lamps' shine most brightly when they illuminate any other subject than Architecture. On Nature and her laws—Man and his affections, his responsibilities and his short-comings—Mr. Ruskin is uniformly luminous:—but on points of architecture his prejudices are so strong, his affinities so wire-drawn, his antipathies so unsupported by even common sense, that we have stared equally at the conclusion at which he has in many cases arrived and at the extraordinary mental processes by which he appears to have reached them."

Still, the reviewer could admire the beautiful passages in "The Lamp of Power" and wonder that, in spite of exaggerated statements and lack of "tranquil utterance," from a little distance "the author's picture should be so correct, and its relative parts should fall so satisfactorily into their places." He found "The Lamp of Obedience" on the whole the brightest, "inasmuch as it is more abstract and less architectural than most of the others." The book gave him "some violent, yet withal pleasant, exercise." But "this kind of mental shaking would prove rather strong medicine for weak minds."[351]

The professional architect's narrowly superior view was taken again in the criticism by Leeds of the first volume of *The Stones of Venice.*

His censures are so widely flung about, his denunciations are so dogmatic and curt, his doctrine is so directly counter to all the teachings and practices of our own time, and so subversive of nearly all hitherto received authority, that those who are otherwise at variance with each other will make common cause against Mr. Ruskin . . . the dogmatism has an extravagance about it which is much too amusing to be dangerous.[352]

[351] *Athenaeum*, Sept. 1, 1849, pp. 889-890.
[352] March 22, 1851, pp. 330-331.

The critic objected to the facetiousness of comparing the base of York column to a huge 'sausage' and to Ruskin's "capricious and arbitrary innovations in architectural language," but he conceded that some "really wholesome advice and sound as well as ingenious remarks . . . may be discovered scattered up and down throughout a stratum of transcendental conceits and fantastical phraseology."

The second and third volumes fell to Chorley, who had neither the technical knowledge of Wyatt and Leeds nor the thorough background in artistic theory of Darley to aid him in judging a work which was too "fanciful and capricious" to be worthy of his heartiest approval. But he so cautiously balanced his epithets that even the author, used to harsher treatment from that quarter, was surprised at the mildness of the criticism. Writing to his father (August 1, 1853), Ruskin said: "I was surprised by the *Athenaeum,* which I think is intended for a most favourable review; nay, I think it is their idea of eulogium."[353]

Chorley found in the second volume a bewildering "intermixture of paradox and vagary with much that is deep in thought, acute in distinction, and eloquent in language. . . . As a rhapsody it is charming,—though as a piece of reasonable teaching, it is anything rather than impeccable."[354] He was still in a mood to protest against the "self-contradiction, paradox, and false principles" exhibited in the third volume, though he despaired of reforming Ruskin, upon whom he already saw the influence of another non-conformist: ". . . arrogance and inconsistency like his, co-existent with bright and peculiar genius, are at the present epoch epidemic. They have elsewhere found utterance, in the historical works and philanthropic essays of Mr. Carlyle."[355]

---

[353] Cook, *op. cit.,* I, 299.
[354] *Athenaeum,* July 23, 1853, pp. 879-881.
[355] *Athenaeum,* Oct. 22, 1853, pp. 1249-1250.

George Walter Thornbury, art critic for the *Athenaeum* in the fifties, came to somewhat closer grips with Ruskin's theories, though he had even less tolerance than Chorley for the eccentricities and prejudices of genius. Like Chorley, he could not write about Ruskin without balancing the budget of paradoxes in his character and works: "Cleverness and absurdity—deep insight in one direction, stone blindness in every other—vigour and weakness—power of explanation and unfairness of statement—are found on every page . . ." of the *Lectures on Architecture and Painting*.[356] Thornbury had little use for the Gothic revival and the idealization of the Middle Ages. As for the medieval workman, he was "bigotted, cruel, and superstitious." In a second notice the reviewer says Ruskin "commences his apotheosis of Turner by erecting a pile of dead painters' coffins on which to rear up his statue," and he ridicules Ruskin's statement that all great painters of the past painted their "own present world plainly and truly." The same writer who idealizes the Middle Ages and concludes that modern Art is not great because it builds to no god, the critic points out with some relish, still insists that this godless age has produced the greatest painter of all time, Turner, whom he also idealizes beyond recognition.[357]

Ruskin's work on Giotto should have been better than it was, Thornbury thought, for if there is anything upon which he is fitted to write, "both from natural gifts and the acquisitions of education, it is the Life of Giotto and the works of early Italian Art. The thirteenth century, Florence,

[356] *Athenaeum*, May 20, 1854, pp. 611-612.

[357] *Athenaeum*, May 27, 1854, pp. 650-652. Thornbury had an admiration for Turner, too, though a more moderate one. Of his *Life of J. M. W. Turner* Charles Kent says in his *D. N. B.* article on Thornbury: "He wrote the whole of it under the watchful observation of Mr. Ruskin; and, as Thornbury himself remarked to the present writer, it was 'very much like working bareheaded under a tropical sun!'" It is interesting to speculate as to whether Ruskin had any knowledge of the authorship of the reviews of his own work in the *Athenaeum*.

Dante, Christian symbolism and Gothic Art are all involved in the favourite subject of one of the deepest, most poetical, and perhaps most crotchety thinkers on Art England has ever known." But he is contemptuous of history and ignores any associative reading. "It is a peculiar feature of Mr. Ruskin's mind that he no sooner strikes out a theory than he lays it down as a 'finality' dogma; and he no sooner conceives a poetical analogy than he tries to petrify it into a logical axiom." The confession that he had never seen Giotto's finest works at Assisi and Naples, "nor *carefully studied even those at Florence*" was to Thornbury's mind nothing less than "literary suicide."[358]

The third volume of *Modern Painters* indicated the steps taken by the writer in ten years, but the steps were not upward, according to Chorley. The book is "amusing to read, though hard to believe in,—a curious mixture of eloquence, impertinence, poetry, prose run wild, of indifferent English and felicitous descriptions: a book of dogmatism, a book of rhapsody, a book of criticism,—a book by which, were its canons taken seriously, every fault could be defended, every contradiction reconciled, every monstrosity received as a model. . . . We cannot close this volume without regretting such waste of power, knowledge, and fancy. Mr. Ruskin has eloquence and taste enough to interest the best audience of his age:—and he chooses to throw away the choicest gifts of nature on paradox."[359] Chorley was agreeably surprised to find Ruskin "by comparison so moderate in his paces" in the fourth volume, but there was still evident an "utter disdain of self-consistency."[360]

The Harbours of England, having more of poetic description than of theory or dogmatic statement, was the first of Ruskin's books to receive an unqualified warmth of praise

[358] *Athenaeum,* Dec. 2, 1854, pp. 1453-1454.
[359] *Athenaeum,* Jan. 26, 1856, pp. 97-99.
[360] May 10, 1856, pp. 578-580.

in the *Athenaeum*. Thornbury was quite carried away by Ruskin's rhetoric.

Since Byron's 'Address to the Ocean,' a more beautiful poem on the sea has not been written than Mr. Ruskin's preliminary chapter. It is a prose poem worthy of a nation at whose throne the seas, like captive monsters, are chained and bound. . . . After this book has been mastered and got by heart—as it will be—the waves that lap and wash our cliffs . . . will speak to Englishmen in a fuller and more articulate voice. . . . Mr. Ruskin, with his earnest, meditative wisdom, teaches us to see in the exhausted theme of poets and painters a beauty as yet untouched and a mystery as insolvable as eternity.[361]

But the epithets still flowed stingingly from Thornbury's pen when he reviewed the art criticism of Ruskin. *Notes on the Turner Gallery* he took up with impatience. "Most men have a rock on which they split. . . . Mr. Ruskin's rock is on the lee shore of Crotchet Island, two degrees from Jesuits' Corner. He grows more and more super-subtle, sophistical, fantastic, more fond of small and intricate threads of allegory."[362] It was Ruskin's style rather than his theories which elicited praise when the critic considered the letters on *The Elements of Drawing*. "As a writer Mr. Ruskin makes a perceptible advance. His words are now so exact and so luminous that they fall like lightning to destroy or illumine. He has a wonderful eye for analogies."[363]

Thornbury's final view of Ruskin was summed up in the review of *The Two Paths*, five lectures "by the Don Quixote of heretical Art."

Nothing is now more obvious to us than that Mr. Ruskin, though ingenious, femininely subtle, learned, and laborious, is not strong, massive, and simple enough in intellect ever to become a real Justinian, or even a Blackstone of English Art. He is

[361] July 26, 1856, pp. 921-923.
[362] *Athenaeum*, Jan. 24, 1857, pp. 108-109.
[363] July 11, 1857, pp. 879-881.

too crotchety, too petulant, too intricate and entangled in mind. . . .

Mr. Ruskin is really nothing but an architectural poet. . . .

If all charm of poetry and description were discharged from . . . [his] writings, and they had to depend merely upon their logic, they would not keep out of the dust-hole a week.[364]

Frederick George Stephens, friend of Rossetti and Holman Hunt, reviewed Ruskin with more sympathy though not without critical reserve. His first notice of the last volume of *Modern Painters* was devoted to strictures on the inconsistencies of Ruskin's demand for minute detail.[365] But in the second notice he complimented the author on having "risen out of his habit of delight in the ascetic forms of Early Italian Art," and having acquired "a great admiration for the robuster schools." Stephens was pleased with the fine studies of Dürer and Rosa, but he thought Ruskin berated needlessly the Dutch painters who had no moral purpose.

Our duty is to report that . . . [the work as a whole] is well, admirably, and nobly done . . . taken in the mass these five volumes contain the most valuable contributions to art-literature the language can show. Unstable, crotchety, passionate, too intense at times to be just, still they contain worlds of thought, imagination, and knowledge such as no other art-writer can educe. A strong and earnest purpose runs through them all, given to the highest ends.[366]

The art criticism of Ruskin, henceforth given to Stephens for review, continued to be favorably noticed in the *Athenaeum*. *The Lectures on Art* at Oxford were reviewed with unusual cordiality.

With his eloquence, his brilliant thoughts, his vivid style of discussion, and his attractive manner, he seems to us precisely the

[364] May 28, 1858, I, pp. 703-704.
[365] *Athenaeum,* June 23, 1860, I, pp. 850-852.
[366] June 30, 1860, I, pp. 878-880.

man to undertake the duties of such a post. . . . Mr. Ruskin seems to live in order to enunciate his sentiments about the dignity, the all-saving nobility of Art.[367]

Ruskin's social and economic criticism was treated more sympathetically in the *Athenaeum* than in most other periodicals of the time. Of course, its self-conscious avoidance of political controversy in its character of an unbiased journal of belles lettres made its reviewers a little wary and cautious in discussing the political implications of his work. William Moy Thomas refused to take the author seriously when he "put off his singing-robes" to talk of *The Political Economy of Art.* He preferred to pick out for quotation some "noble passages" which "may turn the laugh at Mr. Ruskin's speculations on wealth and government into gratitude and delight."[368]

As it did with *Sartor Resartus,* the *Athenaeum* could avoid embarrassment by ignoring *Unto This Last* and *Munera Pulveris* which were first published in periodicals. Hepworth Dixon, who read Ruskin with delight and differed from him with regret, exhibited the usual *Athenaeum* caution in reviewing *The Crown of Wild Olive.* "His purpose is to teach the nations how to live: an ungrateful task at the very best, and one for which, in Mr. Ruskin's case, the world is particularly ungrateful."[369] What do we care about the political science of a man who can paint such beautiful word pictures? Dixon asks. This was a familiar note in the criticism of Ruskin in the sixties; admirers of his colorful prose and his art criticism apologized for his social critique or passed it off lightly.

Time and Tide had a more sympathetic critic in Augustus De Morgan, who saw in it a "searching inquiry into the abuses of trade and manufacture," though he thought the

[367] July 23, 1870, II, pp. 120-121.
[368] *Athenaeum,* Dec. 26, 1857, pp. 1615-1617.
[369] June 2, 1866, I, pp. 734-735.

remedy too "peculiar and extreme." Too much efficacy "is ascribed to institutions which after all can only be the result of national character, and must inevitably be always a degree behind the highest intellect of the nation."[370]

W. E. Henley reviewed *Arrows of the Chase* and paid the author the tribute which was representative of the *Athenaeum* criticism under MacColl.

At his worst Mr. Ruskin is a better writer than most men; at his best he is incomparable. He has a magnificent vocabulary, a perfect and unerring sense of expression, a wonderful instinct of rhythm. . . . [He] is not only great as a writer, but great as an intelligence and a man. . . . His influence, direct and indirect, may very possibly have been for evil rather than for good; but in intention, and his premises being granted, it has been unimpeachable.[371]

Taken as a whole, the *Athenaeum* reception of Ruskin followed the general pattern of its criticism of Carlyle. Despairing of the prophet, whose strange clothes were shocking, but recognizing the power of the writer, the critics, with something of a sigh for the divorce of Literature and Life, whose dual existence they had tried to make both proper and agreeable throughout the Period of Hope, turned at last to an aesthetic evaluation which was all that was left to the disillusioned later Victorians.

Mill

An examination of the causes of the exceptionally favorable criticism of the works of John Stuart Mill in the *Athenaeum* may throw further interesting light on the character of that journal and its relationship to the period that produced it. Mill was not a writer to inspire enthusiasm among those with strong leanings towards the transcendental optimism of the current philosophy. These looked upon him

[370] *Athenaeum*, April 25, 1868, I, pp. 586-587.
[371] Dec. 18, 1880, II, pp. 807-809.

as a cold "logic-chopper," guided by no warmth of feeling springing from the heart, the true intuitive well of inspiration, but by a barren, reasoned, materialistic utilitarianism. That was the view of the Coleridgeans who conducted the magazine during its first two years.[372] But a change took place as soon as Dilke had full control.

There is nothing more illuminating with respect to the fundamental attitude of the *Athenaeum* in matters of philosophy and ideas than a right understanding of the sources of the enthusiasm expressed by W. Cooke Taylor for Mill's *System of Logic*. First of all, it must be kept in mind that Mill's better informed contemporaries were aware that a change had come over him in the years that he had been engaged in writing the *Logic* (1830-42). Working himself out of a mental crisis by deliberately cultivating his imagination and human sympathies through contact with creative literature, he was known or thought to have departed from the inflexible system of his father and Jeremy Bentham. He humanized his own teachings by "visualizing his conclusions in the lives of the people around him,"[373] and he continued throughout his life to have an interest in imaginative literature which could blend the emotions and the intellect. He was one of the first to appreciate Tennyson, and he gave generous praise to Carlyle, different though they were in their fundamental views.[374]

Moreover, Mill had come under the influence of Comte, whose Positive Philosophy seemed to open up a wide field for intellectual speculation on a practical plane. "Instead

---

[372] E.g., see "The Utilitarian Set," *Athenaeum,* Oct. 1, 1828, pp. 777-778; see also comment on the *Westminster Review, Athenaeum,* July 15, 1829, p. 440.

[373] Routh, *Towards the Twentieth Century,* p. 237.

[374] For an extended study of the strange friendship between Carlyle and Mill, see Emery Neff, *Carlyle and Mill.* Mill probably saw before Carlyle was fully aware of it the distance that separated them. Mill's reticence prevented many of his contemporaries from realizing the thorough-going radicalism of his mind, particularly in matters of religion.

of trying to understand facts, it was now proved to be more desirable to study their effects."[375] According to one interpretation, Mill used logic "to review the possibilities of human power, to demonstrate how a rigorous and unimaginative process is to lead to the betterment of the human race; how an imperfect knowledge of facts, but perfect handling of their relationships, will enable us to think out the best way to govern, to distribute wealth, to lead moral lives, and to cultivate self-assurance."[376]

The book kept the reader aware that the human mind can conquer a new world, not by metaphysical abstractions but by the application of logic to current problems. Routh says: "It demonstrated that his thoughts were tending towards the analysis of nineteenth-century civilization, and that in such a task hard-headed reason would be the motive-power. Yet within these limits, imagination accompanies his inductions and enables him to allow for the human factor, to detect the misfits, inadequacies, and privations of the systems which society was elaborating. Already his voice was being raised against the institutionalizing of man."[377]

Among those who wished as strongly as did the more intelligent critics of the *Athenaeum* circle for a justification of the reason as an instrument of progress such doctrine could not but have been pleasing. It mattered little that the ultimate implications of Mill's logic might carry the germs of destruction of the romantic premises upon which they were still building. The influence of a thinker in any period can be measured only in terms of what he is believed to believe, and enthusiasm for his work does not necessarily comprehend an understanding of his views, except in so far as they may be a useful support to wishful thinking.

The appeal which Mill had for the critics of this circle must have been increased by the quiet enthusiasm of his

[375] Routh, *op. cit.*, p. 238.
[376] *Ibid.*   [377] *Ibid.*

style. Routh states the case succinctly: "He writes as if he had tidings of great joy to bring, almost a new religion such as one associates with the Victorian exponents of art and literature. No poet or humanist could labor more zealously to reform and enlighten our conduct. Educated opinion was ready to acclaim such idealism, so people respected his aims and his admirably lucid style. But when they began to ask whither his arguments led them, the majority found only the negation of what they most valued. His promised land was to be reached by destroying the time-honoured and reliable approaches in which their fathers had learnt to trust."[378]

Some of the *Athenaeum* reviewers were "tough-minded" enough to follow Mill even when they understood fully where his path led, but it is possible that Taylor, judging from his other contributions to the paper,[379] would have drawn back had he comprehended the ultimate reaches of Mill's philosophical radicalism. For the moment, at any rate, he was carried away by the clarity and comprehensiveness of the book. Mill's "systematic analysis and arrangement of the principles of inductive reasoning," he says, will secure for him high rank among the masters of modern science. The "Treatise on Fallacies . . . has given to . . . [this] form of reasoning, a consistency and completeness which it had never before attained."

Mill's Sixth Book deals with the application of Logic to the Moral Sciences. Taylor said that "on these points, his views are expressed with great force and clearness, and his illustrations exhibit a grasp of intellect and a range of information, such as M. Comte has alone rivalled amongst modern writers . . . we cannot take leave of Mr. Mill, without expressing our gratification at meeting, in this age of

[378] *Ibid.*, p. 233.   [379] See *ante*, pp. 193-198.

plagiarism, a work of original thought, deserving to take rank with the immortal works of Locke and Bacon."[380]

The highest compliment that Newmarsh could pay to Mill's *Principles of Political Economy* was that it was founded upon, but completed and corrected, the work of Adam Smith and Malthus.

It appears to us to be one of the most valuable merits of these volumes that Mr. Mill is not a teacher who displays any sympathy with over-drawn partialities. . . . There can be no hazard in predicting that it is precisely to this rare attribute of philosophical equilibrium that the ultimate and, we cannot doubt, great success of this work will be chiefly attributable . . . Mr. Mill has attempted to write a book which shall stand in the same relation to the Political Economy of the nineteenth as the work of Smith to the Political Economy of the eighteenth century. We think he has succeeded.[381]

Newmarsh observed with satisfaction that "Mr. Mill founds his hopes on the advancement of the species in morality and knowledge much more than on their participation in a happier lot from some extraordinary improvement in the resources which enable mankind to live easily."

On Liberty was reviewed by the liberal-spirited mathematician Augustus De Morgan, who could follow Mill without strain to any point of the intellectual compass. He accepted the fundamental tenets of the book without question and turned to admire the ease and grace with which the author could propound what from another might be too shocking to win an audience. "Of the style and the matter, we need only say that it is John Mill all over." Mill holds, the critic says, that the "sole end for which mankind are

[380] *Athenaeum*, Dec. 16, 1843, pp. 1101-1102.

[381] *Athenaeum*, May 27, 1848, pp. 525-527. The second notice, June 3, 1848, pp. 554-557, takes up details of Mill's practical proposals, agreeing with most of them, including the Wakefield plan of colonization—selling the land and using the proceeds to send laboring families to the colonies—establishing *petite culture*, and making the cotters peasant proprietors in Ireland.

warranted, individually or collectively, in interfering with the liberty of action of any of their number, is *self-protection*." De Morgan anticipated the convenient interpretation which would be made of that rule. Everyone will agree with this *in principle,* he said. But those "who still think that the honour of God is to be upheld, meaning that their own religious opinions are to be enforced by the State, also maintain that such upholding is necessary to the protection of society." Still the rule is not therefore useless, "because it is a true principle . . . and will do all that is wanted when properly used." Mill is preëminent, De Morgan concludes, for calm discussion of controversial matters. "He is always in good humour with the bodies and souls of those whose opinions he condemns."[382]

Though generally favorable to Mill's doctrines, William Moy Thomas saw difficulties in the attempt to dilute democracy by giving plural votes to the more intelligent, as advocated in *Considerations on Representative Government.* The reviewer observed that Mill's chief difference with Bentham was his distrust of majorities which override the interests of minorities. "Beside Mr. Mill's Essay the treatises of Bentham, of James Mill or of Mr. Baily, and the systems practically at work in the world, appear altogether rude and empirical." But, Thomas says, realizing the necessity of popular power in good government, Mill has hedged it about with so many restrictions and qualifications that one wonders how it is to work.

To sympathize with minorities is natural to the philosophic mind. The philosopher, or at least the discoverer of new truths, is almost always in a minority, and he cannot help an occasional glance of envy at the short and easy methods by which inferior men are able to impose their views upon others. . . . Although we look with doubt upon any project for bringing about the ac-

[382] *Athenaeum,* Feb. 26, 1859, I, pp. 281-282.

ceptance of the views of an enlightened minority by a political machinery, it is some consolation to observe that our best minds already wield a power compared with which even the proposed system of sextuple votes for the wise must be trifling in its results . . . we do not think it too much to hope that Mr. Mill will live to see all that is good and true in this volume find acceptance, even with that majority whom he so much distrusts.[383]

Thomas reviewed the essay on *Utilitarianism* together with a 350-page book written to refute Mill. The author of the latter volume accused Mill of not defining happiness, but Thomas says he has grappled with the definition with great boldness. "This, indeed, apart from the lucid and beautiful style of his exposure of the popular misconceptions of the Benthamite doctrine, constitutes the chief value of Mr. Mill's book as a contribution to ethical philosophy." One service which Mill has rendered, he says, is to show how small a difference there is between the "moral sense," of Whewell and others, and Bentham's utilitarianism.[384]

Mill's *Examination of Sir William Hamilton's Philosophy* left De Morgan "in a chaos of agreements and disagreements." Hamilton has wide knowledge, but it is not balanced. "Mr. Mill, on the other hand, with a fully distributed fund of deep information, is well versed in the mathematics and physics, which Hamilton never mastered sufficiently to talk about without exciting a smile." But De Morgan did not discuss the significance of Mill's attack upon the intuitionists in that volume.[385]

Dixon shared something of Sir Charles Dilke's admiration for Mill, though he had not the intellectual stamina to follow him as far as did the grandson of the old editor.[386]

[383] *Athenaeum*, April 20, 1861, I, pp. 521-522.
[384] April 30, 1864, I, pp. 607-608.
[385] *Athenaeum*, May 27, 1865, II, pp. 709-711.
[386] C. W. Dilke III was one of the most able and intelligent of Mill's followers. Knowledge of Dilke's respect for Mill may have colored Dixon's reviews and made them more sympathetic than they might otherwise have been. One

In *England and Ireland,* Dixon said, "Mr. Mill speaks out his thoughts with a boldness and clearness that will take away some people's appetites for many a day. He uses the plainest terms to express the plainest things. He proposes measures which are described by himself as revolutionary, and he expresses his strong conviction that what is needed as a cure for the evils under which Ireland groans is a revolution."[387]

If Dixon failed to accept the whole of Mill's argument in *The Subjection of Women,* he was not behind many of the most enlightened men of his day. And yet he presented Mill's point of view with seriousness and sympathy and not with ridicule. According to Dixon, Lady Morgan first raised the cry for female rights into a literary question in *Woman and Her Master* (1840), and Talfourd carried the first remedial measure through Parliament in the third year of Victoria, when the courts first recognized some part of a mother's right in her own children.

In Mr. Mill's hands, the question takes a wider range than was ever imagined by the Irish wit and the English poet. Mr. Mill asks for political equality, where they would have been content with legal justice. He extends into public life an argument which they had confined to private life.[388]

It is common opinion that masculine domination is a law of nature, Dixon says, since it seems to prevail universally, among savage and civilized. "A challenge to try the cause afresh is, therefore, certain to provoke the anger of thoughtless men." Few women will "smile upon their knight. . . . All happy women are conservative in spirit." The trouble is, according to Dixon, that Mill doesn't separate

modern critic has said that the fall of Dilke (who was put out of politics in 1885 by a divorce scandal) "left Liberalism without a brain." (G. M. Young, *Victorian England,* p. 174.)

[387] *Athenaeum,* Feb. 22, 1868, I, pp. 279-281.
[388] *Athenaeum,* June 19, 1869, I, pp. 819-820.

the question of Equity from that of Equality. "The day for Equity has come; the day for Equality has not come." Not even Kansas, the critic adds, perhaps the most forward state on earth, has given suffrage to women, though it has given the vote to Negroes and Shawnees; and even the most liberal party in England is afraid of female suffrage. "In claiming a full share of public power for women, Mr. Mill is preparing for us the greatest revolution ever yet effected on this planet." Many "prudent men" would shrink from such a change who would "lend a ready hand in removing the domestic grievance."[389]

The obituary notice of Mill by Rennie attempted to sum up his significance as a thinker, and gave him large credit for working out the thoughts of Hume, particularly in logic.

Few are the students or thinkers in Europe or America whom the intelligence of the death of John Stuart Mill has not shocked as the tidings of the death of a master. Not a physicist, logician, metaphysician, moralist, or scientific historian, is there of this generation who will not respectfully, at least, if not also gratefully, acknowledge indebtedness to his writings.[390]

If Mill's own system is incomplete because he has not resolved the problem of the origin of knowledge which divides the schools of Idealism and Materialism, Rennie says, we at least owe him a debt of gratitude for pointing out so clearly (to use Mill's own words) "the difficulties of metaphysics that lie at the root of all science; that these difficulties can only be quieted by being resolved; and that, until they are resolved, positively if possible, but at any rate negatively, we are never assured that any human knowledge, even physical, stands on solid foundations."

He not only further developed that Utilitarian theory of morals which we owe, in modern times, to Hume, but developed it with that open sense, candour, and largeness of view, of which the

[389] *Ibid.*   [390] May 17, 1873, I, pp. 629-630.

presence in Hume, and the absence in most of his and Bentham's disciples, is so conspicuous.[391]

Norman MacColl reviewed Mill's character in a notice of the posthumous *Autobiography*. Mill, he said, had followed his father in believing that character is formed by circumstances and is not innate. He himself is an illustration of his theory and its opposite, MacColl pointed out: his early years were moulded by his education, but later his own nature came to the front in a manner that would have been distasteful to his father if he had lived. "It was not so much that reasoning had convinced him of the weaknesses of his earlier philosophy, as that one of the most sensitive, nervous, and poetic of temperaments had worked its way through a mass of prejudices implanted in the physically weak pupil by the strong, energetic, and rigid father."[392] He was more human and lovable in his later years, MacColl added.[393] His judgment concerning his own writing and speeches is remarkably just, the critic concluded, though he probably overemphasized the influence for good exerted over him by his wife.

Henderson, the reviewer of *Nature, the Utility of Religion, and Theism*, saw it as "the record of one more pure-minded and true-hearted man to whom the reconciliation of thought and feeling, by the attainment of convictions regarding the satisfying reality of the objects that minister to both, was never realized."[394]

[391] *Ibid.*

[392] *Athenaeum*, Oct. 25, 1873, II, pp. 521-522.

[393] This accords with the view of Rennie, who said that a false impression would be gained of Mill "if he is thought of only as the dry logician and political economist. In him, a tender and passionate heart was united with a splendid intellect." (Obituary notice before mentioned.)

[394] *Athenaeum*, Oct. 31, 1874, II, pp. 572-574.

Epilogue

It is something more than an accident that of the seven major figures in Victorian literature whose careers may be said to have begun in the period of Dilke's editorship of the *Athenaeum,* between 1830 and 1846, Mill was the only one to escape censure in that journal, either early or late, for wasting powers undeniably of the first order. Tennyson and Browning, in the view of the greater number of the *Athenaeum* critics, were poets who should have been prophets. Dickens and Thackeray were novelists who, at least in their earlier work, spent their talents in mere entertainment. Carlyle and Ruskin, earnest enough in their aims, were too eccentric in their manner of writing or too transcendental in their programs of social reform or artistic theory.

With due allowance for all notable exceptions to these judgments arising from the multiple complexities of individual prejudice and circumstance, none of these writers seems to have satisfied wholly the ideal expectations of the *Athenaeum* critics. The uniform cordiality towards Mill, though exceeded in warmth and rhetoric in some of the later reviews of Tennyson, Browning, and Dickens, may be interpreted as an indication of the longing for intellectual balance to control the emotional drives of early and middle

Victorian life. This longing gives the most distinguishable unity of tone to the criticism in the *Athenaeum,* even when the attainment of such a balance may be frustrated in the individual critic by limited capacities or the strong prejudices of the romantic past.

The sort of balance aimed at by the critics of the *Athenaeum* circle was analyzed rather acutely by Mill himself in the middle of the century: "In the present age the writers of reputation and influence are those who take something from both sides of the great controversies, and make out that neither extreme is right, nor wholly wrong. By some persons, and on some questions, this is done in the way of mere compromise; in some cases, again, by a deeper doctrine underlying both the contrary opinions; but done it is, in one way or the other, by all who gain access to the mind of the present age: and none but those who do it, or seem to do it, are now listened to." This change is explained and partly justified, Mill said, "by the superficiality, and real one-sidedness, of the bolder thinkers who preceded. But if I mistake not, the time is now come, or coming, for a change the reverse way."[1]

Though Mill was speaking in general terms he might have been thinking of the *Athenaeum* reviewers. But it must always be remembered that the point of emphasis in the journal was in a state of constant if gradual change. The earlier transcendentalists gave place to the more "reasoning" romanticists of Dilke's first years, and they in turn yielded gradually to the radical and scientific-minded critics of the best days of MacColl's editorship. The *Athenaeum* represented a vastly different view after 1870 from that of the thirties, but it continued to reflect in much the same way the

[1] *The Letters of John Stuart Mill,* ed. Hugh S. R. Elliot, II, 360-361. (The quotation is from an entry in Mill's diary of Jan. 18, 1854.) A few weeks later Mill had another note on the compromise of English writers, who "pare away and qualify" all their statements. (*Ibid.,* p. 378.)

prevailing average intelligent Victorian thought. A study of the difference is a study of the change in the Victorian scene. The figure of the mirror is still the most satisfactory to describe the periodical in all its phases.

It cannot but strike a reader familiar with the critical literature of the past twenty years that essentially he has been reading of controversies and points of view which sound strangely modern. Change a few conventional or pious or sentimental phrases of the past to their equivalents of today, and the critiques might fit any of several modern periodicals. If we but knew it, we are fighting over again on a slightly different ground some of the battles which many of the *Athenaeum* critics engaged in with skill and daring, and the thought may sober our laughter at the quaintness and self-absorbed seriousness of our Victorian ancestors. On the whole, its critics were not slower than we are in recognizing new genius, though they often wishfully ascribed that genius to the workings of transcendental powers in which we have ceased to believe or have found other names to describe. They were as quick as we to perceive artistic power, and they justified their admiration in terms as acceptable to the times as the scientific, historical, or psychological criticisms have been to a later period.

Bibliography

MANUSCRIPTS

The Dilke Papers. British Museum, Department of Manuscripts.
Add. 43,910-43,913.
Letters from Sir C. W. Dilke to Hepworth Dixon. British Museum, Department of Manuscripts. Add. 38,794.

PERIODICALS

The Athenaeum [especially the marked file in the office of the *New Statesman and Nation*, London].
The Atlas.
Blackwood's Edinburgh Magazine.
The Bookman (London).
The Court Journal.
The Edinburgh Review.
The Examiner.
The Fortnightly Review.
Fraser's Magazine.
The Literary Gazette.
The London Magazine.
The Metropolitan Magazine.
The Nation and Athenaeum.
The New Monthly Magazine.
The New Statesman and Nation.
Notes and Queries.
The Quarterly Review.

The Times Literary Supplement.
The Westminster Review.

GENERAL WORKS OF REFERENCE

British Museum Catalogue.
Dictionary of Anonymous and Pseudonymous English Literature.
Dictionary of National Biography.

BOOKS PRINCIPALLY CONSULTED OR REFERRED TO IN THE
TEXT AND NOTES

Abbott, C. Colleer. See under Darley, George.
Alden, Raymond, M., ed. *Critical Essays of the Early Nineteenth Century.* New York, 1921.
ALLINGHAM, WILLIAM. Allingham, H. and Williams, E. Baumer, eds. *Letters to William Allingham.* London and N. Y., 1911.
Astin, Marjorie. See under Mitford, Mary Russell.
AUSTIN, SARAH. Ross, Janet Ann. *Three Generations of English Women. Memoirs and Correspondence of Susannah Taylor, Sarah Austin, and Lady Duff Gordon.* London, 1893.
Babbage, Charles. *On the Economy of Machinery and Manufactures.* London, 1832.
Bain, Alexander. See under Mill, John Stuart.
BANIM, JOHN. Murray, Patrick J. *The Life of John Banim.* New York, 1869.
BLACKWOOD, WILLIAM. Oliphant, Mrs. Margaret. *Annals of a Publishing House: William Blackwood and his Sons.* 2 vols. New York, 1897-98.
Blunden, Edmund. *Leigh Hunt's "Examiner" Examined.* London, 1928.
────── See also under Keats, John and under Lamb, Charles.
Bourne, H. R. Fox. *English Newspapers: Chapters in the History of Journalism.* 2 vols. London, 1887.
Brookfield, F. M. *The Cambridge Apostles.* London, 1906.
BROWNING, ELIZABETH BARRETT. Kenyon, Frederic G., ed. *The Letters of Elizabeth Barrett Browning.* 2 vols. London, 1897.
BROWNING, ROBERT. *The Letters of Robert Browning and Elizabeth Barrett Barrett.* 2 vols. New York and London, 1899.

—— DeVane, William, C. *A Browning Handbook*. New York, 1935.

—— Gosse, Edmund. *Robert Browning: Personalia*. Boston and New York, 1890.

—— Lounsbury, Thomas R. *The Early Literary Career of Robert Browning*. New York, 1911.

—— Somervell, D. C. "The Reputation of Robert Browning" in *Essays and Studies by Members of the English Association*. Vol. XV. Oxford, 1929.

BUCKINGHAM, JAMES SILK. Turner, Ralph E. *James Silk Buckingham*. London, 1934.

Bulwer-Lytton, Edward (first baron). *Paul Clifford (The Works of Bulwer Lytton*. Knebworth Edition. Vol. 22).

BUTLER, SAMUEL. Jones, Henry Festing. *Samuel Butler: A Memoir*. 2 vols. London, 1919.

CAMPBELL, THOMAS. Beattie, William, ed. *Life and Letters of Thomas Campbell*. 3 vols. London, 1849.

—— Redding, Cyrus. *Literary Reminiscences and Memoirs of Thomas Campbell*. 2 vols. London, 1860.

CARLYLE, THOMAS. Duffy, Sir C. Gavan. *Conversations with Carlyle*. New York, 1892.

—— Neff, Emery. *Carlyle*. New York, 1932.

—— Neff, Emery. *Carlyle and Mill*. New York, 1926.

—— Wilson, David Alec. *Carlyle*. 6 vols. [various sub-titles]. London, 1923-34.

—— See also under Sterling, John.

CARY, HENRY FRANCIS. King, R. W. *The Translator of Dante: The Life, Work, and Friendships of Henry Francis Cary*. London, 1925.

Chateaubriand, François René, Viscount de. *Mélanges Littéraires*. (*Œuvres Complètes*. Nouvelle Edition. Tome VI. Paris, n.d.)

CHORLEY, HENRY FOTHERGILL. *Autobiography, Memoir and Letters*. Compiled by Henry G. Hewlett. 2 vols. London, 1873.

—— *Thirty Years' Musical Recollections*. Edited with an Introduction by Ernest Newman. London, 1926.

Collingwood, W. G. See under Ruskin, John.

Collins, A. S. *The Profession of Letters.* London, 1928.

Cook, E. T. See under Ruskin, John.

Cruse, Amy. *The Victorians and their Books.* London, 1935.

CUNNINGHAM, ALLAN. Hogg, Reverend David. *Life of Allan Cunningham.* Dumfries, 1875.

Curwen, Henry. *A History of Booksellers, the Old and the New.* London, [1873].

DARLEY, GEORGE. *Complete Poetical Works of George Darley.* With an Introduction by Ramsay Colles. London, 1906.

—— Abbott, C. Colleer. *Life and Letters of George Darley.* London, 1928.

DeVane, William C. See under Browning, Robert.

Dexter, Walter. See under Dickens, Charles.

DICKENS, CHARLES. Dexter, Walter and Ley, J. W. T. *The Origin of Pickwick.* London, 1936.

—— Forster, John. *The Life of Charles Dickens.* 3 vols. Philadelphia, 1872-74.

—— Lehmann, R. C. *Charles Dickens as Editor.* London, 1912.

—— Ley, J. W. T. *The Dickens Circle.* London, 1918.

DILKE, CHARLES WENTWORTH. *The Papers of a Critic.* Selected from the Writings of the Late C. W. Dilke with a Biographical Sketch by his Grandson, Sir Charles Wentworth Dilke, bart. 2 vols. London, 1875.

DILKE, SIR CHARLES WENTWORTH [2nd Bart.]. Gwynn, Stephen L. *The Life of the Rt. Hon. Sir Charles W. Dilke.* 2 vols. London, 1916. [Completed and edited by Gertrude M. Tuckwell.]

Douglas, James. See under Watts-Dunton, Theodore.

Everett, Edwin M. *The Party of Humanity: the Fortnightly Review and its Contributors, 1865-74.* Chapel Hill (N. C.), 1939.

Fairchild, Hoxie Neale. *The Romantic Quest.* New York, 1931.

Forster, John. See under Dickens, Charles.

FRANCIS, JOHN. *John Francis, Publisher of the Athenaeum: A Literary Chronicle of Half a Century.* Compiled by John C. Francis, with an Introductory Note by H. R. Fox Bourne. 2 vols. London, 1888.

Gosse, Edmund. See under Browning, Robert.

Graham, Walter. *English Literary Periodicals.* New York, 1930.

—— *Tory Criticism in the "Quarterly Review."* New York, 1921.

Gunnell, Doris. See under Stendhal.

Gwynn, Stephen L. See under Dilke, Sir Charles W.

HOOD, THOMAS. *Memorials of Thomas Hood.* Collected, arranged, and edited by his daughter. With a preface and notes by his son. 2 vols. London, 1860.

—— Jerrold, Walter. *Thomas Hood: His Life and Times.* London, 1907.

Hake, Thomas. See under Watts-Dunton, Theodore.

Hirst, F. W. See under Morley, John.

Hooker, Kenneth Ward. See under Hugo, Victor.

Hogg, Reverend David. See under Cunningham, Allan.

HOPE, BERESFORD. Law, Henry William and Irene. *The Book of the Beresford Hopes.* London, 1925.

HOWITT, MARY. *Autobiography.* Edited by her daughter, Margaret Howitt. 2 vols. Boston and New York, 1889.

HUGO, VICTOR. Hooker, Kenneth Ward. *The Fortunes of Victor Hugo in England.* New York, 1938.

HUNT, LEIGH. Blunden, Edmund. *Leigh Hunt and his Circle.* New York, 1930.

JERDAN, WILLIAM. *The Autobiography of William Jerdan.* 4 vols. London, 1853.

Jones, Henry Festing. See under Butler, Samuel.

Jerrold, Walter. See under Hood, Thomas.

Judd, John W. *The Coming of Evolution.* Cambridge, 1910.

KEATS, JOHN. Blunden, Edmund. *Keats's Publisher: A Memoir of John Taylor (1781-1864)* London, 1936.

—— *The Letters of John Keats.* M. Buxton Forman, ed. 2 vols. London, 1931.

—— Lowell, Amy. *John Keats.* 2 vols. Boston and New York, 1925.

King, R. W. See under Cary, Henry Francis.

Knight, Charles. *Passages of a Working Life.* 3 vols. London, 1864-65.

Ladd, Henry. See under Ruskin, John.

LAMB, CHARLES. Blunden, Edmund. *Charles Lamb and his Contemporaries*. Clark Lectures. Cambridge, 1933.

—— Lucas, E. V., ed. *The Letters of Charles Lamb*. 3 vols. New Haven, 1935.

—— Lucas, E. V. *The Life of Charles Lamb*. 2 vols. New York and London, 1905.

Lang, Andrew. See under Lockhart, John Gibson.

Law, Henry William. See under Hope, Beresford.

Lehmann, R. C. See under Dickens, Charles.

L'Estrange, A. G. See under Mitford, Mary Russell.

Ley, J. W. T. See under Dickens, Charles.

LOCKHART, JOHN GIBSON. Lang, Andrew. *The Life and Letters of John Gibson Lockhart*. 2 vols. London, 1897.

Lounsbury, Thomas R. See under Browning, Robert, and under Tennyson, Alfred.

Lowell, Amy. See under Keats, John.

Lucas, E. V. See under Lamb, Charles.

MARTINEAU, HARRIETT. *Harriet Martineau's Autobiography*. With Memorials, edited by Maria Weston Chapman. Boston, 1877.

Masson, David. *Memories of London in the Forties*. Edinburgh and London, 1908.

MAURICE, FREDERICK DENISON. *The Life of Frederick Denison Maurice,* edited by his son, Frederick Maurice. 2 vols. New York, 1884.

—— Rice, Jessie Folsom. *The Influence of Frederick Dennison* [sic] *Maurice on Tennyson*. [Unpublished Master's Dissertation, University of Chicago, 1913—typed copy in New York Public Library.]

Mayhew, Henry. *London Labour and the London Poor*. London, 1861.

Merriam, Harold G. See under Moxon, Edward.

Merivale, Herman. See under Thackeray, William Makepeace.

MILL, JOHN STUART. *Autobiography*. (Columbia University Press edition). New York, 1924.

—— Bain, Alexander. *John Stuart Mill, a Criticism with Personal Recollections*. London, 1882.

—— *The Letters of John Stuart Mill.* Edited with an Introduction by Hugh S. R. Elliot. 2 vols. London, 1910.

—— Neff, Emery. *Carlyle and Mill.* New York, 1926.

MITFORD, MARY RUSSELL. Astin, Marjorie. *Mary Russell Mitford. Her Circle and Her Books.* London, 1930.

—— L'Estrange, A. G. *The Life and Letters of Mary Russell Mitford.* 3 vols. London, 1870.

Mordell, Albert, ed. *Notorious Literary Attacks.* New York, 1926.

MORGAN, SYDNEY [OWENSON] LADY. *Passages from my Autobiography.* New York, 1859.

—— Stevenson, Lionel. *The Wild Irish Girl: the Life of Sydney Owenson, Lady Morgan.* London, 1936.

MORLEY, JOHN. Hirst, F. W. *Early Life and Letters of John Morley.* London, 1927.

MOXON, EDWARD. Merriam, Harold G. *Edward Moxon, Publisher of Poets.* New York, 1939.

Mumby, Frank A. *Publishing and Bookselling.* London, 1930.

Murray, Patrick J. See under Banim, John.

NAPIER, MACVEY. *Selections from the Correspondence of the Late Macvey Napier,* edited by his son, Macvey Napier. London, 1879.

Neff, Emery. See under Carlyle, Thomas, and under Mill, John Stuart.

Nesbitt, George L. *Benthamite Reviewing: Twelve Years of the Westminster Review, 1824-1836.* New York, 1934.

Nicolson, Harold. See under Tennyson, Alfred.

Oliphant, Mrs. Margaret. See under Blackwood, William.

POPE, ALEXANDER. Sherburn, George. *The Early Career of Alexander Pope.* London, 1934.

Redding, Cyrus. *Fifty Years' Recollections, Literary and Personal.* 3 vols. London, 1858.

—— See also under Campbell, Thomas.

REYNOLDS, JOHN HAMILTON. *Poetry and Prose.* Edited with an Introduction by George L. Marsh. London, 1928.

Rice, Jessie Folsom. See under Maurice, Frederick Denison.

Rosa, Matthew. *The Silver Fork School.* New York, 1936.

Ross, Janet Ann. See under Austin, Sarah.

Routh, H. V. *Money, Morals and Manners as Revealed in Modern Literature*. London, 1935.

—— *Towards the Twentieth Century*. New York, 1937.

RUSKIN, JOHN. *The Works of John Ruskin*. Library Edition. London, 1907.

—— Collingwood, W. G. *The Life and Work of John Ruskin*. 2 vols. Boston and New York, 1893.

—— Cook, E. T. *The Life of John Ruskin*. 2 vols. London, 1911.

—— Ladd, Henry. *The Victorian Morality of Art: an Analysis of Ruskin's Esthetic*. New York, 1932.

—— Wilenski, R. H. *John Ruskin: an Introduction to Further Study of his Life and Work*. New York, 1933.

Sherburn, George. See under Pope, Alexander.

Shorter, Clement King. *Victorian Literature: Sixty Years of Books and Bookmen*. London, 1897.

Somervell, D. C. See under Browning, Robert.

Steeves, Harrison Ross. *Learned Societies and English Literary Scholarship*. New York, 1913.

STENDHAL [Beyle, Henri]. Gunnell, Doris. *Stendhal et l'Angleterre*. Paris, 1908.

STERLING, JOHN. *Essays and Tales*. Collected and edited with a memoir of his life by J. C. Hare. 2 vols. London, 1848.

—— Carlyle, Thomas. *The Life of John Sterling*. (World's Classics, Oxford Press). London, 1907.

Stevenson, Lionel. See under Morgan, Sydney.

TENNYSON, ALFRED. Lounsbury, Thomas R. *The Life and Times of Tennyson*. New Haven, 1915.

—— Nicolson, Harold. *Tennyson: Aspects of his Life Character and Poetry*. Boston and New York, 1930.

—— [See Rice, Jessie Folsom, under Maurice, Frederick Denison].

—— Tennyson, Hallam. *Alfred Lord Tennyson, A Memoir, by his Son*. 2 vols. London, 1897.

THACKERAY, WILLIAM MAKEPEACE. Melville, Lewis [pseud.]. *William Makepeace Thackeray*. New York, 1928.

—— Merivale, Herman and Marzials, Frank T. *The Life of W. M. Thackeray*. London, 1891.

Thomas, William Beach. *The Story of the Spectator*. London, 1928.

Thrall, Miriam M. H. *Rebellious Fraser's*. New York, 1934.

TICKNOR, GEORGE. *A History of Spanish Literature*. 3 vols. (Third American edition, corrected and enlarged). Boston, 1864.

—— *Life, Letters, and Journals of George Ticknor*. Edited by George S. Hillard, assisted by Mrs. Ticknor and her eldest daughter. 2 vols. Boston, 1876.

TRENCH, RICHARD CHENEVIX. *Letters and Memorials*. Edited by Miss M. Trench. 2 vols. London, 1888.

Turner, Ralph E. See under Buckingham, James Silk.

WATTS-DUNTON, THEODORE. Douglas, James. *Theodore Watts-Dunton: Poet, Novelist, Critic*. London, 1904.

—— Hake, Thomas and Compton-Rickett, Arthur. *The Life and Letters of Theodore Watts-Dunton*. 2 vols. London, 1916.

Wilenski, R. H. See under Ruskin, John.

Wilson, David Alec. See under Carlyle, Thomas.

Young, G. M., ed. *Early Victorian England*. 2 vols. London, 1934.

Young, G. M. *Victorian England: Portrait of an Age*. London, 1936.

Index